William Smart, Eugen von Böhm-Bawerk

Capital and Interest

critical history of economical theory

William Smart, Eugen von Böhm-Bawerk

Capital and Interest
critical history of economical theory

ISBN/EAN: 9783337238650

Printed in Europe, USA, Canada, Australia, Japan

Cover: Foto ©Suzi / pixelio.de

More available books at **www.hansebooks.com**

A CRITICAL
HISTORY OF ECONOMICAL THEORY

BY

EUGEN V. BÖHM-BAWERK

PROFESSOR OF POLITICAL ECONOMY IN THE UNIVERSITY OF INNSBRUCK

TRANSLATED WITH A PREFACE AND ANALYSIS

BY

WILLIAM SMART, M.A.

LECTURER ON POLITICAL ECONOMY IN QUEEN MARGARET COLLEGE
GLASGOW

London
MACMILLAN AND CO.
AND NEW YORK
1890

TRANSLATOR'S PREFACE

My only reasons for writing a preface to a work so exhaustive, and in itself so lucid, as Professor Böhm-Bawerk's *Kapital und Kapitalzins*, are that I think it may be advisable to put the problem with which it deals in a way more familiar to English readers, and to show that the various theories stated and criticised in it are based on interpretations implicitly given by practical men to common phenomena.

First, to state the problem. A manufacturer who starts business with a capital of £20,000 takes stock at the end of a year, and finds that he is richer by £2000—that is to say, if he sold plant, stock, and debts at a fair valuation, he would obtain for them £22,000. The increment of £2000 he will probably call his "profit." If asked to explain what is the origin of profit in general, and of this amount of profit in particular, and, further, why this profit should fall to him, his first answer will probably be that the goods he manufactures meet a want felt by a certain section of the public, and that, to obtain the goods, buyers are willing to pay a price high enough to allow him, over the whole field of his production for one year, to obtain the profit of £2000.

This, however, immediately suggests the question why a public which, as a rule, is not willing to pay more than it can help for anything, should pay prices such as allow of this profit. The manufacturer's answer probably would be, that it would not be worth his while to put forth his energies in manufacturing for less than this amount of profit, as he could, with at least equal safety and without personal exertion, obtain, say £1000 by lending his capital to any ordinary productive undertaking.

In this answer two statements are involved: first, that of the £2000 one part is wage for personal exertion, and, second, that the remainder is the "usual return to capital" without personal exertion. Thus is drawn a rough dividing line between what is usually called "undertaker's profit" and interest. Interest seems to be defined as that annual return to capital which may be obtained, as a rule, without personal exertion. Accepting this answer we should expect to find the phenomenon of interest most easily studied in the case of a Limited Liability Company, where the personal exertion of the shareholders is limited to choosing the investment, subscribing the capital, and receiving the dividends. The portion of total "profit" obtained by the private employer or undertaker, as such, is here eliminated; or, rather, it is made definite and measurable in being divided among the managing director, the ordinary directors, and the secretary, who are paid a fixed fee, salary, or, accurately and simply, a wage.

A careful consideration of the balance sheet of any such company will guard us against a common misunderstanding. Such a balance sheet will generally show two funds—a Depreciation Fund and an Insurance Fund. The former, sometimes called Sinking, Wear and Tear, Repairs, or Replacement of Capital Fund, secures that fixed capital, or its value, is replaced in the proportion in which it is worn out, and thus provides a guarantee that the value of the parent capital is not encroached upon, or inadvertently paid away in dividend. The latter, sometimes called Equalisation of Dividend Fund, is a provision for averaging the losses that are sure to occur over a series of years, and are really a portion of the current expenses. It is only after these funds are provided for that the dividend is paid over to the shareholders, and this accentuates two important facts: (1) that interest properly so called is something distinct from any portion of parent capital, and (2) that it is not accounted for by insurance against risks.

The question now is, Is such a dividend pure interest? Here we have to reckon with the familiar fact that limited companies, under similar conditions, pay the most various rates of dividend. If then we accept "dividend" as the equivalent of "interest" we shall have to conclude that varying rates of interest are obtainable on equal amounts of capital.[1] On looking closer, however, we find the dividing line again reasserting itself. If a sound industrial company is known to be paying a dividend higher than a certain definite percentage on its capital, the value of the stock, or parent capital, will rise to the point where dividend corresponds to an interest no greater than this definite percentage—*e.g.* the £100 stock of a great railway paying 5 per cent will rise to something like £125, at which price the 5 per cent dividend on the original capital shows a return of 4 per cent on the new value of the capital.

[1] This consideration of itself suggests the indefiniteness of what is usually called Undertaker's Profit. In the Limited Liability Company this "wage of intellect" is measured and paid, but the varying dividend shows that it by no means exhausts this "profit." The solution probably is that the attempt to assess undertaker's wage on any principle is hopeless in present circumstances. It is a "glorious risk," depending, among other things, on adroitness, foresight, opportunity, and exploitation of labour—four factors scarcely reducible to figures. But with this line of thought, interesting and important as it is, we have nothing to do here.

There is, in short, in every country, although varying from country to country, a certain annual return which can be obtained by capital with a minimum of risk, without personal exertion of the owner. Its level is usually determined by the market price of the national security. We count the $2\frac{3}{4}$ per cent interest of Consols an absolutely safe return, because the British Constitution is pledged for the annual payment of this amount of interest on its debt—on the capital borrowed by the nation from its members in past years. This we should probably consider the proper economic interest for capital invested in Great Britain. Any return above this level we should consider, either as due to the insecurity of the capital as invested (*i.e.* as a premium for insurance), or as that still vague quantity called "profit." Thus we should probably consider the 4 per cent of our railway stocks as consisting of, say $2\frac{3}{4}$ per cent for interest proper, and $1\frac{1}{4}$ per cent insurance or equalisation of dividend.

Now it is this interest proper, obtainable by the owner of capital without risk and without personal effort, that is the object of our problem.

In which of the many forms that interest takes can we best study its nature? It might seem that the $2\frac{3}{4}$ per cent of Consols was the most appropriate subject for examination, but a glance will show that this form of interest is secondary and derivative. The nation as a whole cannot pay interest on its debts unless the citizens as individuals produce the wealth wherewith this interest is paid, otherwise the nation will be paying away its capital. To study interest as expressed in the annual payments on the Consolidated National Debt would be to make the common mistake of explaining Natural Interest by Contract Interest, which is very much the same as explaining why people pay interest by showing that they do pay it. The phenomenon, then, must, primarily, be studied as it appears in some or other of the forms of production of wealth. Let us take the case of a manufacturing company.

The essential features here, as regards our problem, are that, over a year's time, the products manufactured are sold at a price which not only covers the value of raw materials, reimburses the various wages of manual and intellectual labour, and replaces the fixed capital as worn out, but leaves over that amount of value which is divided out among the capitalist shareholders as interest. In normal capitalist production, that is to say, not only is the value of capital consumed in the production process replaced, but a surplus of value appears. It has not always been perceived by economists that this surplus value is the essential phenomenon of what we call interest,—that interest on capital consists of this very surplus value and nothing else,—but whenever it is perceived the question almost suggests itself, What does this surplus value represent? Is it merely a surplus, or is it of the nature of a wage? In other words, is it something obtained either by chance or force, and corresponding to no service rendered by anybody or anything; or is it something connected with capital or the capitalist that, economically speaking, deserves a return or a wage?

A little consideration will show that the idea of a "mere surplus" is untenable. When a manufacturer engages his capital in production he, as it were, throws it into solution, and risks it all on the chance of the consuming public paying a certain price for the products into which his capital is transformed. If they will not pay any price at all the capital never reappears; even the labour, which bound up its fortunes with the materials and machinery of manufacture, loses its wage, or would do so except for the wage contract which pays labour in advance. If the consumers, again, will only pay a price *equal to* the value of the capital consumed, the various workers, including the employer proper, will get their wage, and the value of the capital itself will be unimpaired, but there will be no interest. It is only if the consumers are willing to pay a higher price that capital can get its interest.

The surplus then, which we call interest, appears primarily in the value or price of products—that is to say, interest is, in the first instance, paid over by the consumer of goods in the price of the products he buys.

Now it seems intelligible, although it is not really so intelligible as is usually assumed, that the public will always pay a price for products sufficient to reimburse the wages paid in producing them. The labourer, theoretically, is paid by what he makes—although this proposition requires more careful statement and limitation than can be given it here—and wages are supposed, *prima facie*, to represent an equivalent in value contributed to the product by the worker. But that the consuming world, over and above this wage, will pay a surplus which does not represent any equivalent value given to the product, is only conceivable on the supposition that the public is unconscious that it is paying such a surplus. This supposition, however, is incredible in a community where most of the consumers are also producers. To lose as consumer what one gains as producer is a game of Beggar my Neighbour which would scarcely commend itself to business men.

The surplus then may be assumed to represent something contributed by capital to the value of products. This view is supported by the common consciousness of practical men, who certainly believe that capital plays a distinct and beneficent rôle in production.

If, now, we appeal to the common consciousness to say what it is that capital does, or forbears to do, that it should receive interest, we shall probably get two answers. One will be that the owner of capital contributes a valuable element to production; the other, that he abstains from using his wealth in his own immediate consumption. On one or other of these grounds, the capitalist is said to deserve a remuneration, and this remuneration is obtained by him in the shape of interest.

Now it might possibly be the case that both answers point to elements indispensable in the explanation of interest, but a slight consideration will show that the two answers are very different from one another. The one is positive—that capital does something; the other negative—that the capitalist abstains from doing something. In the one case interest is a payment for a tool; in the other, a recompense for a sacrifice. In the one case the capitalist is paid because the capital he lends produces, or helps to produce, new wealth; in the other he is paid because he abstains from diminishing wealth already produced.

It will become evident as we go on that, on these two answers, which spring to the lips of any business man asked to account for interest, are based the most important of the theories criticised in the present book. The first answer is the basis of the Productivity theories and of the Use theories; the second is the basis of the Abstinence theory.

The argument of the Productivity theory may be put thus. Human labour, employing itself on the materials given free by nature, and making use of no powers beyond the natural forces which manifest themselves alike in the labourer and in his environment, can always produce a certain amount of wealth. But when wealth is put into the active forms of capital—of which machinery may be taken as instance and type—and capital becomes intermediary between man and his environment of nature, the result is that the production of wealth is indefinitely increased. The difference between the results of labour unassisted and labour assisted by capital is, therefore, due to capital, and its owner is paid for this service by interest.

The simpler forms of this theory (where capital is credited with a direct power of creating value, or where surplus of products is tacitly assumed to be the same thing as surplus of value) our author has called the Naïve theory. The more complex formulations of it —where, for instance, emphasis is laid on the displacement of labour by capital, and interest is assumed to be the value formerly obtained as wage, or where prominence is given to the work of natural powers which, though in themselves gratuitous, are made available only in the forms of capitalist production—he has called the Indirect theories.

How slight a claim this explanation has to the dignity of a scientific theory appears in its practical definition of interest as the whole return to capitalist production which is not accounted for by labour. Yet the statement just given is elaborate and logical in comparison with that of many of the economists who profess the Productivity theory. Their usual treatment of the interest problem is to co-ordinate capital with the other factors of production, land and labour, and assume that interest is the payment for the services of capital, as wage is for the services of labour, give ample illustration of the triumphs of capitalist production, and pass on to discuss the rise and fall of its rate.

If, however, we demand an answer to what we have formulated as the true problem of interest, we shall make the discovery that the Productivity theory has not even put that problem before itself. The amount of truth in the theory is that capital is a most powerful factor in the production of wealth, and that capital, accordingly, is highly valued. But to say that capital is "productive" does not explain interest, for capital would still be productive although it produced no interest; *e.g.* if it increased the supply of commodities the value of which fell in inverse ratio, or if its products were, both as regards quantity and value, greater than the products of unassisted labour. The theory, that is to say, explains why the manufacturer has to pay a high price for raw materials, for the factory buildings, and for the machinery—the concrete forms of capital generally. It does not explain why he is able to sell the manufactured commodity, which is simply these materials and machines transformed by labour into products, at a higher price than the capital expended. It may explain why a machine doing the work of two labourers is valued at £100, but it does not explain why capital of the value of £100 *now* should rise to the value of £105 twelve months *hence*; in other words, why capital employed in production regularly increases to a value greater than itself.

It must be admitted that there is something very plausible in this theory, particularly in apparently simple illustrations of it. A poor widow owns a chest of tools valued at £50. An unemployed carpenter borrows them. The fifty shillings interest he pays seems almost an inadequate return for the added productiveness given to his labour over the year. Is not the interest made possible by the qualities of the tools? The facts here are as stated: without production there would be no interest. So without land there would be no turnips, but the existence of land is scarcely the sufficient cause of the turnips. Suppose the widow *sold* the chest of tools to another carpenter for £50. His labour also would be rendered productive, and in the same degree, but he would pay no interest. Or suppose she sold the tools for £50, but did not get payment for a year; the reason she would give for asking fifty shillings extra would be, not that the tools were productive, but that the payment was deferred. The important circumstance forgotten in this theory is that the productiveness of concrete capital is already discounted in its price. The chest of tools would be of no value but for the natural forces embodied in them or made available by them. To ascribe interest to the productive power of capital is to make a double charge for natural forces—in the price and in the interest. Meanwhile we may note one significant circumstance in all these transactions,—that the emergence of interest is dependent on a certain lapse of time between the borrowing and the paying.

It cannot be too often reiterated that the theory which explains interest must explain *surplus value*—not a surplus of products which may obtain value and may not; not a surplus of value over the amount of value produced by labour unassisted by capital; but a surplus of value in the product of capital over the value of the capital consumed in producing it. The insufficiency of the present theory to meet these requirements may be shown in another way. It is often assumed that, if a labouring man during his week's work consumes the value of, say 20s. in food, tools, etc., and during that week turns 20s. worth of raw material into finished commodities, these commodities, together, will sell in the market for something *over* 40s. But the ordinary life of many a peasant proprietor who lives by continual toil, and never "gets out of the bit,"—that is, never does more than reproduce his bare living—might show that the assumption is not universally valid, and that labour by no means always produces more value than it consumes. But the plausibility of the Productivity theory is the parallelism it assumes between labour and capital—the suggestion that interest is wage for capital's work. If, however, the emergence of surplus value in the case of simple labour needs explanation, much more does it in the case of capitalist production. What is a product or commodity but raw material plus labour? Labour and capital co-operate in making it, and the individual form and share of each is lost in the joint product. But, of the two, labour is the living factor, and if surplus value does emerge in capitalist production as a regularly recurring phenomenon, it is more likely that it comes from the living agent than from the dead tool. Thus the Productivity theory ends in suggesting that other and hostile theory according to which surplus value comes from labour, and is only snatched away by capital.

But the fact is that, in all this, we have an entire misconception of the origin of value. Value cannot come from production.[1] Neither capital nor labour can produce it. What labour does is to produce a quantity of commodities, and what capital co-operating with labour usually does is to increase that quantity. These commodities, under certain known conditions, will usually possess value, though their value is little proportioned to their amount;

[1] See the striking passage on pp. 134, 135.

indeed, is often in inverse ratio. But the value does not arise in the production, nor is it proportional to the efforts and sacrifices of that production. The causal relation runs exactly the opposite way. To put it in terms of Menger's law, the means of production do not account for nor measure the value of products ; on the contrary, the value of products determines and measures the value of means of production. Value only arises in the relation between human wants and human satisfactions, and, if men do not "value" commodities when made, all the labour and capital expended in the making cannot confer on them the value of the smallest coin. But if neither capital nor labour can create value, how can it be maintained that capital employed in production not only reproduces its own value, but produces a value greater than itself?

I confess I find some difficulty in stating the economic argument of what our author has called the Use theory of interest, and I am almost inclined to think that he has done too much honour to some economists in ascribing to them this theory, or, indeed, any definite theory at all.

It is of course a familiar expression of everyday life that interest is the price paid for the "use of capital," but most writers seem to have accepted this formula without translating it. If the formula, however, is considered to contain a scientific description of interest, we must take the word "use" in something like its ordinary signification, and consider the "use of capital" as something distinct from the capital itself which affords the use. The loan then will be a transfer and sale of this "use," and it becomes intelligible how, at the end of the loan period, the capital lent is returned undeteriorated in value; it was not the capital that was lent, but the use of the capital. To put it in terms of Bastiat's classical illustration: James, who lends a plane to William, demands at the year's end a new plane in place of the one worn out, and asks in addition a plank, on the ostensible ground that over a year William had the advantage, the use of the plane.

If, however, we look carefully into this illustration, we shall see that William not only had the use of the plane but the plane itself, as appears from the fact that the plane was worn out during the year. Here then the using of the plane is the same thing as the consumption of the plane ; payment for a year's "use" is payment for the whole capital value of the plane. Yet the payment demanded at the year's end is not the capital value of the plane, the sum lent, but also a surplus, a plank, under the name of interest. To put it another way. If William on the 1st of January had bought the plane outright from James, he would have paid him on that date a value equivalent, say, to a precisely similar plane ; he would have had the "use" of the plane over 365 days ; and by 31st December the plane onsumed. As things are, he pays nothing on 1st the use of the plane over the year; by 31st e is consumed; and next day he has to pay over ely similar plane plus a plank. The essential the two transactions is that, on 1st January the is another similar plane; on the 31st December plank.

ests a very different source of interest, viz. that it he difference of time between the two payments. heory, as put in this illustration, has only to be now that it involves a confusion of thought as 'use." It is not difficult to find the origin of the fallacy of the theory may be most easily shown arisen in too exclusively studying the loan under called Hire—that is, where a durable good is lent t the year's end, deteriorated indeed but not lend out a horse and cart, a tool, a house, we are at the interest paid us is a price for the "use" of get the goods themselves back in a year's time, ated in value, but visibly the same goods; and is would fall into the common error of supposing he equivalent of the wear and tear, *i.e.* a portion ital. This is rendered more plausible by the s of capital are made in money; we unconsciously r notes we receive to be the same gold or notes e take the case of coals, or grain, or perishable nd ask how it is possible to conceive of these use and being returned to us substantially the s wear and tear, we must perceive that interest, st, cannot be a payment for the "use" of goods, ption of them, for the goods themselves. Are we that durable goods admit of an independent use ident value, and that perishable goods do not? ot be the price of the "use" of capital, as interest tal, whether durable or perishable.

fact, affords a striking instance of how our science lf for our unscientific treatment of it. It was e that Adam Smith put its first great treatise in orm that "the wayfaring men, though fools, might The result, in a good many cases, has been ng economists to keep their work at the same nd attractiveness, and this was more easily effected he great social and industrial problems than by o scientific method. In no other way can I ct that, a hundred years after the appearance *ms*, the great American and German economists should be devoting so much of their time to elementary and neglected conceptions. One of these neglected conceptions is that of the "Use of goods," and one of the most important contributions to economic theory is the section devoted by Dr. Böhm-Bawerk to that subject. Briefly it amounts to this, that all material "goods," the objects of economical attention as distinct from mere "things," are economic only in virtue of their use, real or imaginary. Every good is nothing but the sum of its uses, and the value of a good is the value of all the uses contained in it. If a good, such as gunpowder, can only serve its purpose or afford its use all at one time, we employ the word "consumption" for the act by which the good gives forth its use. If, on the contrary, it is so constituted that its life-work extends over a period of time, then each individual use diminishes the sum of uses which constitutes the essential nature of the good. But Consumption is only a single exhaustive use, and Use is only a prolonged consumption.

This at once enables us to estimate the Use theory of interest. The "use of capital" is not something apart from the *using* of the goods which constitute the capital; it is their consumption, fast or slow as the case may be; and a payment for the use of capital is nothing but a payment for the consumption of capital. The true nature of the loan transaction is, not that in it we get the use of capital and return it deteriorated, but that we get the capital itself, consume it, and *pay for* it by a new sum of value which somehow includes interest. If, however, we admit this, we are landed in the old problem once more—how do goods, when used as capital in production, increase in value to a sum greater than their own original value? and the Use theory ends in raising all the difficulties of the Productivity theories.

We have seen that the previous theories were founded on some positive work supposed to be done by capital. The Abstinence theory, on the other hand, is founded on the negative part played by the capitalist. Wealth once produced can be used either in immediate consumption—that is, for the purposes to which, in the last resort, all wealth is intended; or it can be used as capital—that is, to produce more wealth, and so increase the possibilities of future consumption. The owner of wealth who devotes it to this latter purpose deserves a compensation for his abstinence from using it in the former, and interest is this compensation. It must be carefully noted that the abstinence here spoken of is not abstinence from personal employment of capital in production—that would simply throw us back on the previous question, viz. how the owner could make interest (as distinct from wage) by the use of his capital—but abstinence from immediate consumption in the many forms of personal enjoyment or gratification.

At the back of this theory of interest is that theory of value ich makes it depend upon costs of production. Senior, the first and ncipal apostle of the Abstinence theory, saw very clearly that the lusion of interest or profit among costs was an abuse of language. e word "Cost" implies sacrifice, not surplus. But in production, it seemed to him, there was another sacrifice besides the prominent ɜ of labour, that of abstinence, and interest in his view was the npensation for this sacrifice.

It must be confessed that to those who are in the habit of king upon all work as sacrifice, and all wage as compensation, ɜre is something a little ridiculous in the statement of this theory. e "abstinence" of a rich man from what he probably cannot ısume, the capitalist's "compensation" for allowing others to ɜserve his wealth from moth and rust by using it, the millionaire's ıcrifice" measured by his £100,000 a year—these are the familiar apons of those who consider the evils of interest aggravated by claim. Yet if we ask whether the amount of capital in the rld would have been what it is if it had not been for the bstinence" of those who had the command over wealth, to umulate or dissipate it, we can see that such jibes are more tching than convincing. The strength of the Abstinence theory that the facts it rests on really give the explanation how capital nes into being in primitive conditions and in new countries. The t efforts to accumulate capital must be attended by sacrifice; a nporary sacrifice, of course, to secure a permanent gain, but, in first instance at least, a material sacrifice. It is with the ginnings of national capital as it is with the beginnings of lividual capital; there is need of foresight, effort, perhaps even tailment in necessaries.

But to account for the origin of *capital* by abstinence from ısumptive use is one thing; to account for *interest* is another. all production labour sacrifices life, and capital sacrifices nediate enjoyment. It seems natural to say that one part of the duct pays wage and another pays interest, as compensation for respective sacrifices. But labour is not paid because it makes ıcrifice, but because it makes products which obtain value from nan wants; and capital does not deserve to be paid because it ke sacrifices—which is a matter of no concern to any one but capitalist—but because of some useful effect produced by its operation. Thus we come back to the old question, What vice does capital render that the abstinence which preserves and ımulates it should get a perpetual payment? And if, as we saw, luctivity cannot account for interest, no more can abstinence.

Dr. Böhm-Bawerk's chief criticism, however, is directed to a more lamental mistake in Senior's famous theory. Senior included inence among the costs of production as a second and independent sacrifice. In a singularly subtle analysis Böhm-Bawer shows that abstinence is not an independent sacrifice but a alternative one. The analysis may be more easily understood fro the following concrete example. An owner of capital embarks it i a productive undertaking. In doing so he decides to undergo th sacrifice of labour (in personally employing his capital), and tha labour is made productive and remunerative by the aid of th capital. If, in calculating the remuneration due him, he claims on sum as wage for labour, and another as reward for abstaining fron the immediate enjoyment of his own wealth, he really makes th double calculation familiarly known as eating one's cake and having it. His labour would not have yielded the profitable result which returns him the (undertaker's) wage without the assistance of the capital; he cannot charge for the sacrifice of his wealth as wealth and for the sacrifice of his wealth as capital. The truth is that, in this case, the one sacrifice of labour admits of being estimated in two ways: one by the cost to vital force; the other and more common, by the greater satisfaction which would have been got from the immediate use of capital as wealth at an earlier period of time.

In view of the unsatisfactoriness of the answers hitherto given to our problem it is easy to see how another answer would arise. The power wielded by the owners of wealth in the present day needs no statement. It is not only that "every gate is barred with gold," but that, year by year, the burden of the past is becoming heavier on the present. Wealth passes down from father to son like a gathering snowball, at the same time as industry gets massed into larger and larger organisations, and the guidance and spirit of industry is taken more and more out of the hands of the worker and given to the capitalist. Of two men, in other respects equal, the one who has wealth is able not only to preserve the value of his wealth intact, but to enjoy an annual income without risk or trouble, and, providing that he lives well within his income, can add steadily to the sum of his wealth. The other has to work hard for all he gets; time does nothing for him. If he saves it is at a sacrifice; yet only in this sacrifice is there any chance of his rising out of the dull round which repeats each day the labour of the last—that is, only as he becomes an owner of capital. Thus, in course of time there appears a favoured class who are able not only to live without working, but to direct, control, and even limit the labour of the majority.

Now if, when the onus of justifying its existence is thrown upon capital, economic theory can only account for this income without risk and without work by pointing to the "productive power" of capital, or to the "sacrifice of the capitalist," it is easy to see how another theory should make its appearance, asserting that interest is nothing else than a forced contribution from helpless or ignorant people; a tribute, not a tax. Rodbertus's picture of the working man as the lineal descendant of the slave—"hunger a good substitute for the lash"; Lassalle's mockery of the Rothschilds as the chief "abstainers" in Europe; Marx's bitter dialectic on the degradation of labour, are all based on generous sympathy with the helpless condition of the working classes under capitalist industry, and many shut their eyes to the weakness of Socialist economics in view of the strength of Socialist ethics.

The Exploitation theory then makes interest a concealed contribution; not a contribution, however, from the consumers, but from the workers. Interest is not a pure surplus obtained by combination of capitalists. It does represent a sacrifice made in production, but not a sacrifice of the capitalists. It is the unpaid sacrifice of labour. It has its origin in the fact that labour can create more than its own value. A labourer allowed free access to land, as in a new country, can produce enough to support himself and the average family, and have besides a surplus over. Translate the free labourer into a wage earner under capitalism, pay him the wage which is just sufficient to support himself and his family, and here also it is the case that he can produce more than his wage. Suppose the labourer to create the value of his wage, say 3s. in six hours' work, then, if the capitalist can get the worker to work longer than six hours for the same wage, he may pocket the extra value in the name of profit or interest. Here the modern conditions of industry favour the capitalist. The working day of ten to twelve hours is a sort of divine institution to the ignorant labourer. As the product does not pass into his own hand, he has no means of knowing what the real value of his day's work is. The only lower limit to his wage is that sum which will just keep himself and his family alive, although, practically, there is a lower limit when the wife and children become the breadwinners and the capitalist gets the labour of five for the wage of one. On the other hand, the increase of wealth over population gradually displaces labour, and allows the same amount of work to be done by fewer hands; this brings into existence "reserve" to the industrial army, always competing with those left n work, and forcing down wages. Thus the worker, unprotected, ets simply the reproduced value of a portion of his labour; the est goes to capital, and is falsely, if conscientiously, ascribed to the fficiency of capital.

I feel that it would be impertinence in me to say anything here hat would anticipate the complete and masterly criticism brought gainst this theory in Book VI. The crushing confutation of the abour Value theory is work that will not require to be done twice n economic science, and the vindication of interest as a price for an conomic service or good suggested by the very nature of things "which may be modified but cannot be prevented") will necessitate reconsideration by the Socialist party of their official economic basis.

But it would be easy to misunderstand the precise incidence of this criticism, and perhaps it is well to point out what it does and what it does not affect.

It proves with absolute finality that the Exploitation theory gives no explanation of interest proper. But this is far from saying that Exploitation may not explain a very large amount of that further return to the joint operation of capital and labour which is vaguely called "profit." We saw that the value paid by a Limited Liability Company as dividend, or the return to capital which a private owner generally calls his profit, consists of two parts: of interest proper and of undertaker's profit. The latter, rightly considered, is a wage for work, for intellectual guidance, organisation, keen vision, all the qualities that make a good business man. There are two ways in which this wage may be obtained: to use a Socialist phrase, by exploiting nature and by exploiting man. To the first category belongs all work of which the farmer's is the natural type: that which visibly produces its own wages, whether by directly adding to the amount and quality of human wealth, or preserving that already produced, or changing it into higher forms, or making it available to wider circles. In this category A's gain is B's gain. To the second category belong those perfectly fair modes of business activity where one uses his intelligence, tact, taste, sharpness, etc., to get ahead of his fellows, and "take the trade" from them. Here A's gain is B's loss, but the community share in A's gain, and even B shares in it, by being better served as a consumer. But to this category also belong those numerous forms of occupation which involve taking advantage of poor men's wants and necessities to snatch a profit, and one of those forms is the underpaying of labour.

Any one who has realised the difficulty of the wages question will understand that this underpaying may be quite unintentional. Capitalists, no less than labourers, are under the domination of the capitalist system, and, under the steady pressure of competition, it is difficult for an employer to be just, not to say generous. His prices are regulated not by his own cost of production, but by the costs of production in the richest and best appointed establishments of his rivals; and yet his workers' wages have to be regulated by an equation between these prices, and the wages of labour in similar trades and in the near vicinity. In fact the difficulties of determining a "just" wage are so great that the temptation is overwhelming to ascertain what labour is worth by the easy way of ascertaining what labour will take, and if fifty women are at the gate offering their services for a half of what fifty men are earning, who is to determine what a "fair wage" is?

It should then be at once and frankly confessed that the Socialis contention may afford an explanation of a great proportion of what is vaguely known as "undertaker's profit." To go farther however, and extend this explanation to *all* return to capitalist production which is not definitely wage, is economic shortsightedness, that brings its own revenge.

Böhm-Bawerk's refutation of the Exploitation theory is not a refutation of Socialism, but of a certain false economical doctrine hitherto assumed by the great Socialist economists as negative basis for that social, industrial, and political reconstitution of things which is Socialism. Morality and practical statesmanship may determine that, in the interests of the community, purely economic laws be subordinated to moral and political laws; or, to put it more accurately, that economic laws, which would assert themselves under "perfect competition," be limited by a social system which substitutes co-operation for competition. That is to say, the work of capital in production may be quite definitely marked out, and its proper relation to the value it accompanies be exactly determined, and yet the distribution of its results may be taken from private owners and given over to the corporate owning of the state. But while the advantage accruing from the use of capital would here be regulated by a mechanical system, interest would remain, economically, exactly as Böhm-Bawerk has stated it.

As to Dr. Böhm-Bawerk's own theory of interest I do not feel at liberty to anticipate, or put in short compass, the contents of the second volume now published, *Die Positive Theorie des Kapitals.* The reader will find the essence of it in pp. 257-259 of the present work.

It might be advisable, however, to put his theory into concrete terms. According to it, when we lend capital, whether it be to the nation or to individuals, the interest we get is the difference in popular estimation and valuation between a present and a future good. If we lend to direct production, the reason we get interest is not that our capital is capable of reproducing itself and more. The explanation of this reproduction is to be found in the work of those who employ the capital, both manual and intellectual workers. We get interest simply because we prefer a remote to a present result. It is not that by waiting we get *more* than we give; what we get at the year's end is no more than the equivalent value of what we lent a year before. Capital plus interest on 31st December is the full equivalent of capital alone on 1st January preceding. Interest then is in some sense what Aquinas called it, a price asked for time. Not that any one can get the monopoly of time, and not that time itself has any magic power of producing value, but that the preference by the capitalist of a future good to a present one enables the worker to realise his labour in undertakings that save labour and increase wealth. But as capital takes no active rôle in production, but is simply material on which and tools by which labour works, the reward for working falls to the worker, manual and intellectual; the reward for waiting, to the capitalist only. Economically speaking, as wage is a fair bargain with labour, because labour can produce its own wage, so is interest a fair bargain with the capitalist, because in waiting the capitalist merely puts into figures the universal estimate made by men between present and future goods, and the capitalist is as blameless of robbery as the labourer.

Dr. Böhm-Bawerk's theory of Interest, then, is an expansion of an idea thrown out by Jevons but not applied. "The single and all-important function of capital," said Jevons, "is to enable the labourer to await the result of any long-lasting work—to put an interval between the beginning and the end of an enterprise." Capital, in other words, provides an indispensable condition of *fruitful* labour in affording the labourer time to employ lengthy methods of production.

If we view the possession of riches as, essentially, a command over the labour of others, we might say that interest is a premium paid to those who do not present their claims on society in the present. The essence of interest, in short, is Discount.

In concluding, I should like to say with Dr. James Bonar[1]—that, while it would be bold to affirm that Professor Böhm-Bawerk has said the last word on the theory of Interest, his book must be regarded as one with which all subsequent writers will have to reckon.

My thanks are due to Professor Edward Caird, of Glasgow University, at whose instance this translation was undertaken, for many valuable suggestions, and, not less, for the stimulus afforded by hope of his approval; to my former student Miss Christian Brown, of Paisley, whose assistance in minute and laborious revision of the English rendering has been simply invaluable; and not least, to Professor Böhm-Bawerk himself, who has most patiently answered all questions as to niceties of meaning, and to whose criticism all the proofs—and this preface itself—were submitted.

The time I have given to this work may excuse my suggesting that a valuable service might be rendered to the science, and a valuable training in economics given, if clubs were organised, under qualified professors, to translate, adapt, and publish works which are now indispensable to the economic student.

[1] *Quarterly Journal of Economics*, April 1889.

GLASGOW, *April* 1890.

ANALYTICAL TABLE OF CONTENTS

INTRODUCTION

The Problem of Interest

BOOK I

The Development of the Problem

CHAPTER I

THE OPPOSITION TO INTEREST IN CLASSICAL AND MEDIÆVAL TIMES

CHAPTER II

THE DEFENCE OF INTEREST FROM THE SIXTEENTH TILL THE EIGHTEENTH CENTURY

CHAPTER III

TURGOT'S FRUCTIFICATION THEORY

CHAPTER IV

ADAM SMITH AND THE DEVELOPMENT OF THE PROBLEM

CHAPTER V

THE COLOURLESS THEORIES

BOOK II

The Productivity Theories

CHAPTER I

THE PRODUCTIVE POWER OF CAPITAL

CHAPTER II

THE NAÏVE PRODUCTIVITY THEORIES

CHAPTER III

THE INDIRECT PRODUCTIVITY THEORIES

BOOK III

The Use Theories

CHAPTER I

THE USE OF CAPITAL

CHAPTER II

HISTORICAL STATEMENT

CHAPTER III

PLAN OF CRITICISM

CHAPTER IV

THE USE OF CAPITAL ACCORDING TO THE SAY-HERMANN SCHOOL

CHAPTER V

THE TRUE CONCEPTION OF THE USE OF GOODS

CHAPTER VI

CRITICISM OF THE SAY-HERMANN CONCEPTION

CHAPTER VII

THE INDEPENDENT USE: AN UNPROVED ASSUMPTION

CHAPTER VIII

THE INDEPENDENT USE: ITS UNTENABLE CONCLUSIONS

CHAPTER IX

THE INDEPENDENT USE: ITS ORIGIN IN LEGAL FICTION

CHAPTER X

MENGER'S CONCEPTION OF USE

CHAPTER XI

FINAL INSUFFICIENCY OF THE USE THEORY

BOOK IV

The Abstinence Theory

CHAPTER I

SENIOR'S STATEMENT OF THE THEORY

CHAPTER II

CRITICISM OF SENIOR

CHAPTER III

BASTIAT'S STATEMENT

BOOK V

The Labour Theories

THESE THEORIES AGREE IN EXPLAINING INTEREST AS WAGE OF THE CAPITALIST'S LABOUR

The English Group

The French Group

The German Group

BOOK VI

The Exploitation Theory

CHAPTER I

HISTORICAL SURVEY

CHAPTER II

RODBERTUS

CHAPTER III

MARX

BOOK VII

Minor Systems

CHAPTER I

THE ECLECTICS

CHAPTER II

THE LATER FRUCTIFICATION THEORY

Conclusion

INTRODUCTION

THE PROBLEM OF INTEREST

It is generally possible for any one who owns capital to obtain from it a permanent net income, called Interest.[1]

This income is distinguished by certain notable characteristics. It owes its existence to no personal activity of the capitalist, and flows in to him even where he has not moved a finger in its making. Consequently it seems in a peculiar sense to spring from capital, or, to use a very old metaphor, to be begotten of it. It may be obtained from any capital, no matter what be the kind of goods of which the capital consists: from goods that are barren as well as from those that are naturally fruitful; from perishable as well as from durable goods; from goods that can be replaced and from goods that cannot be replaced; from money as well as from commodities. And, finally, it flows in to the capitalist without ever exhausting the capital from which it comes, and therefore without any necessary limit to its continuance. It is, if one may use such an expression about mundane things, capable of an everlasting life.

Thus it is that the phenomenon of interest, as a whole, presents the remarkable picture of a lifeless thing producing an everlasting and inexhaustible supply of goods. And this

[1] Many German economists use the word *Kapitalrente* as well as *Kapitalzins*. Sanders defines *Rente* as "Einkünfte die man als Nutzung von Grundstücken, Kapitalien, und Rechten bezieht." So Littré gives *Rente* as "Revenu annuel." The word occurs in Chaucer as equivalent of income :—

"For catel (chattels) hadden they ynough and rent."—*Canterbury Tales*, Prologue, l. 375. In English we still retain the word Rent instead of interest in a few cases outside of its special application to land.—W. S.

remarkable phenomenon appears in economic life with such perfect regularity that the very conception of capital has not infrequently been based on it.[1]

Whence and why does the capitalist, without personally exerting himself, obtain this endless flow of wealth?

These words contain the theoretical problem of interest. When the actual facts of the relation between interest and capital, with all its essential characteristics, are described and fully explained, that problem will be solved. But the explanation must be complete both in compass and in depth. In compass, inasmuch as all forms and varieties of interest must be explained. In depth, inasmuch as the explanation must be carried without a break to the very limits of economical research: in other words, to those final, simple, and acknowledged facts with which economical explanation ends; those facts which economics rests on, but does not profess to prove; facts the explanation of which falls to the related sciences, particularly to psychology and natural science.

From the theoretical problem of interest must be carefully distinguished the social and political problem. The theoretical problem asks why there *is* interest on capital. The social and political problem asks whether there *should be* interest on capital—whether it is just, fair, useful, good,—and whether it should be retained, modified, or abolished. While the theoretical problem deals exclusively with the causes of interest, the social and political problem deals principally with its effects. And while the theoretical problem is only concerned about the true, the social and political problem devotes its attention first and foremost to the practical and the expedient.

As distinct as the nature of the two problems is the character of the arguments that are used by each of them, and the strictness with which the arguments are used. In the one case the argument is concerned with truth or falsehood, while in the other it is concerned for the most part with expediency. To the question as to the causes of interest there can be only one answer, and its truth every one must recognise if the laws of thought are correctly applied. But whether

[1] Thus Hermann in his *Staatswirthschaftliche Untersuchungen*, p. 211, defines capital as "Vermögen, das seine Nutzung, wie ein immer neues Gut, fortdauernd dem Bedürfniss darbietet, ohne an seinem Tauschwerth abzunehmen."

interest is just, fair, and useful or not, necessarily remains to a great extent a matter of opinion. The most cogent argumentation on this point, though it may convince many who thought otherwise, will never convert all. Suppose, for instance, that by the soundest of reasoning it was shown to be probable that the abolition of interest would be immediately followed by a decline in the material welfare of the race, that argument will have no weight with the man who measures by a standard of his own, and counts material welfare a thing of no great importance—perhaps for the reason that earthly life is but a short moment in comparison with eternity, and because the material wealth that interest ministers to will rather hinder than help man in attaining his eternal destiny.

Prudence urgently demands that the two problems which are so fundamentally distinct should be kept sharply apart in scientific investigation. It cannot be denied that they stand in close relation with each other. Indeed it appears to me that there is no better way of coming to a correct decision on the question whether interest be a good thing, than by getting a proper knowledge of the causes which give rise to it. But we must remember that this connection only entitles us to bring together the results; it does not justify us in confusing the investigations.

Confusing these investigations will, in fact, endanger the correct solution of either problem, and that on several grounds. In the social and political question there naturally come into play all sorts of wishes, inclinations, and passions. If both problems are attempted at the same time, these will find entrance only too easily into the theoretical part of the inquiry, and there, in virtue of the real importance they have in their proper place, weigh down one of the scales—perhaps that very one which would have remained the lighter if nothing but grounds of reason had been put in the balance. What one wishes to believe, says an old and true proverb, that one easily believes. And if our judgment on the theoretical interest problem is perverted, it will naturally react and prejudice our judgment on the practical and political question.

Considerations like these show that there is constant danger that an unjustifiable use may be made of arguments in themselves justifiable. The man who confuses the two problems, or perhaps mistakes the one for the other, and, looking at the matter in this way, forms one opinion upon both, will be apt to confuse the two groups of arguments also, and allow each of them an influence on his total judgment. He will let his judgment as to the causes of the phenomenon of interest be guided, to some extent, by principles of expediency—which is wholly and entirely bad; and he will let his judgment as to the advantages of interest as an institution be, to some extent, directly guided by purely theoretical considerations—which, at least, may be bad. In the case, *e.g.* where the two problems are mixed up, it might easily happen that one who sees that the existence of interest is attended by an increased return in the national production, will be disposed to agree with a theory which finds the cause of interest in a productive power of capital. Or it may happen that one comes to the theoretical conclusion that interest has its origin in the exploitation of the labourer, made possible by the relations of competition between labour and capital; and on that account he may, without more ado, condemn the institution of interest, and advocate its abolition. The one is as illogical as the other. Whether the existence of interest be attended by results that are useful or harmful to the economical production of a people, has absolutely nothing to do with the question why interest exists; and our knowledge of the source from which interest springs, in itself gives us no ground whatever for deciding whether interest should be retained or abolished. Whatever be the source from which interest comes—even if that source be a trifle muddy—we have no right to decide for its abolition unless on the ground that the real interests of the people would be advanced thereby.

In economical treatment this separation of the two distinct problems, which prudence suggests, has been neglected by many writers. But although this neglect has been the source of many errors, misunderstandings, and prejudices, we can scarcely complain of it, since it is the practical problem of interest that has brought the theoretical problem and its scientific treatment to the front. Through the merging of the two problems into one, it is true, the theoretical problem has of necessity been worked at under circumstances which were not favourable for the discovery of truth. But without this merging very many able writers would not have worked at it at all. It is all the more important that we profit in the future by such experiences of the past.

The intentionally limited task to which I intend to devote myself in the following pages is that of writing a critical history of the *theoretical* problem of interest. I shall endeavour to set down in their historical development the scientific efforts made to discover the nature and origin of interest, and to submit to critical examination the various views which have been taken of it. As to opinions whether interest is just, useful, and commendable, I shall only include them in my statement so far as that is indispensable for getting at the theoretical substance that they contain.

Notwithstanding this limitation of subject, there will be no lack of material for a critical history, either as regards the historical or as regards the critical part. A whole literature has been written on the subject of interest, and a literature which, in mere amount, is equalled by few of the departments of political economy, and by none in the variety of opinion it presents. Not one, nor two, nor three, but a round dozen of interest theories testify to the zeal with which economists have devoted themselves to the investigation of this remarkable problem.

Whether these exertions were quite as successful as they were zealous may with some reason be doubted. The fact is that, of the numerous views advanced as to the nature and origin of interest, no single one was able to obtain undivided assent. Each of them, as might be expected, had its circle of adherents, larger or smaller, who gave it the faith of full conviction. But each of them omitted considerations enough to prevent its being accepted as a completely satisfactory theory. Still even those theories which could only unite weak minorities on their side showed themselves tenacious enough to resist extinction. And thus the present position of the theory exhibits a motley collection of the most conflicting opinions, no one of them strong enough to conquer, and no one of them willing to admit defeat; the very number of them indicating to the impartial mind what a mass of error they must contain.

I venture to hope that the following pages may bring these scattered theories a little nearer to a point.

Before I can apply myself to my proper task I must come to an understanding with my readers as to some conceptions and distinctions which we shall have to make frequent use of in the sequel.

Of the many meanings which, in the unfortunate and incongruous terminology of our science, have been given to the word Capital, I shall confine myself, in the course of this critical inquiry, to that in which capital signifies a *complex of produced means of acquisition*—that is, a complex of goods that originate in a previous process of production, and are destined, not for immediate consumption, but to serve as means of acquiring further goods. Objects of immediate consumption, then, and land (as not produced) stand outside our conception of capital.

I shall only justify my preference for this definition meantime on two grounds of expediency. Firstly, by adopting it a certain harmony will be maintained, so far, at least, as terminology is concerned, with the majority of those writers whose views we shall have to state; and secondly, this limitation of the conception of capital defines also most correctly the limits of the problem with which we mean to deal. It does not fall within our province to go into the theory of land rent. We have only to give the theoretical explanation of that acquisition of wealth which is derived from different complexes of goods, exclusive of land. The more complete development of the conception of capital I reserve for a future occasion.[1]

Within this general conception of capital, further, there are two well-known shades of difference that require to be noted. There is the National conception of capital, which embraces the national means of economic acquisition, and only these; and there is the Individual conception of capital, which includes everything that is a means to economic acquisition in the hands of an individual—that is to say, those goods by means of which an individual obtains wealth for himself, no matter whether the goods are, from the point of view of the national economy,

[1] A promise now fulfilled by the publication of the *Positive Theorie des Kapitales*, Innsbruck, 1889.—W. S.

means of acquisition or means of enjoyment, goods for production or goods for consumption. Thus, *e.g.* the books of a circulating library will fall under the individual conception of capital, but not under the national conception. The national conception, if we except those few objects of immediate consumption lent at interest to other countries, includes merely the produced means of production belonging to a country. In what follows we shall chiefly be concerned with the national conception of capital, and shall, as a rule, keep this before us when the word capital by itself is used.

The income that flows from capital, sometimes called in German Rent of Capital, we shall simply call Interest.[1]

Interest makes its appearance in many different forms.

First of all, we must distinguish between Gross interest and Net interest. The expression gross interest covers a great many heterogeneous kinds of revenue, which only outwardly form a whole. It is the same thing as the gross return to the employment of capital; and this gross return usually includes, besides the true interest, such things as part replacement of the substance of capital expended, compensation for all sorts of current costs, outlay on repairs, premiums for risk, and so on. Thus the Hire or Rent which an owner receives for the letting of a house is a Gross interest; and if we wish to ascertain what we may call the true income of capital contained in it, we must deduct a certain proportion for the running costs of upkeep, and for the rebuilding of the house at such time as it falls into decay. Net interest, on the other hand, is just this true income of capital which appears after these heterogeneous elements are deducted from gross interest. It is the explanation of Net interest with which the theory of interest naturally has to do.

Next, a distinction must be drawn between Natural interest and Contract or Loan interest. In the hands of one who employs capital in production, the utility of his capital appears in the fact that the total product obtained by the assistance of the capital possesses, as a rule, a higher value than the total cost of the goods expended in the course of produc-

[1] *Kapitalzins.* The word "Interest" in English does not require any addition.—W. S.

tion. The excess of value constitutes the Profit of capital, or, as we shall call it, Natural interest.

The owner of capital, however, frequently prefers to give up the chance of obtaining this natural interest, and to hand over the temporary use of the capital to another man against a fixed compensation. This compensation bears different names in common speech. It is called Hire, and sometimes Rent (in German *Miethzins* and *Pachtzins*) when the capital handed over consists of durable or lasting goods. It is generally called Interest when the capital consists of perishable or fungible goods.[1] All these kinds of compensation, however, may be appropriately grouped under the name of Contract interest or Loan interest.

While, however, the conception of Loan interest is exceedingly simple, that of Natural interest requires more close definition.

It may with reason appear questionable if the entire profit realised by an undertaker from a process of production should be put to the account of his capital.[2] Undoubtedly it should not be so where the undertaker has at the same time occupied the position of a worker in his own undertaking. Here there is no doubt that one part of the "profit" is simply the undertaker's wage for the work he has done. But even where he does not personally take part in the carrying out of the production, he yet contributes a certain amount of personal trouble in the shape of intellectual superintendence—say, in planning the business, or, at the least, in the act of will by which he devotes his means of production to a definite undertaking. The question now is whether,

[1] "Es heisst Mieth-oder Pachtzins, wenn das überlassene Kapital aus dauerbaren Gütern bestand. Es heisst Zinsen oder Interessen, wenn das Kapital aus verbrauchlichen oder vertretbaren Gütern bestand." I have translated the passage to suit our English usage of the words. The adjective "vertretbar" (for which the legal "fungible" is the only equivalent) indicates that the thing lent is not itself given back, but another of the same kind. Grain and money are the typical fungibles.—W. S.

[2] I think it advisable to translate *Unternehmer* and *Unternehmung* throughout by Undertaker and Undertaking. Rowland Hill, when he adapted Greensleaves to a psalm, said he did not see why the devil should have all the good tunes. Neither, in my opinion, should our science any longer deny itself these useful words, introduced by Adam Smith himself, simply because they are usually confined with us to one special branch of industry.—W. S.

in view of this, we should not distinguish two quotas in the total sum of profit realised by the undertaking; one quota to be considered as result of the capital contributed, a second quota to be considered as result of the undertaker's exertion.

On this point opinions are divided. Most economists draw some such distinction. From the total profit obtained by the productive undertaking they regard one part as profit of capital, another as undertaker's profit. Of course it cannot be determined with mathematical exactitude, in each individual case, how much has been contributed to the making of the total profit by the objective factor, the capital, and how much by the personal factor, the undertaker's activity. Nevertheless we borrow a scale from outside, and divide off the two shares arithmetically. We find what in other circumstances a capital of definite amount generally yields. That is shown most simply by the usual rate of interest obtainable for a perfectly safe loan of capital. Then, of the total profit from the undertaking, that amount which would be enough to pay the usual rate of interest on the capital invested in it, is put down to capital, while the remainder is put to the account of the undertaker's activity as the profit of undertaking. For instance, if an undertaking in which a capital of £100,000 is invested yields an annual profit of £9000, and if the customary rate of interest is 5 per cent, then £5000 will be considered as profit on capital, and the remaining £4000 as undertaker's profit.

On the other hand, there are many, especially among the younger economists, who hold that such a division is inadmissible, and that the so-called undertaker's profit is homogeneous with the profit on capital.[1]

This discussion forms the subject of an independent problem of no little difficulty—the problem of Undertaker's Profit. The difficulties, however, which surround our special subject, the problem of interest, are so considerable that I do not feel it my duty to add to them by taking up another. I purposely refrain then from entering on any investigation, or giving any decision as to the problem of undertaker's profit. I shall only treat that as interest which

[1] On the whole question see Pierstorff, *Die Lehre vom Unternehmergewinn* Berlin, 1875.

everybody recognises to be interest—that is to say, the whole of contract interest,[1] and, of the "natural" profit of undertaking only so much as represents the rate of interest usually obtainable for capital employed in undertaking. The question whether the so-called undertaker's profit is a profit on capital or not I purposely leave open. Happily the circumstances are such that I can do so without prejudice to our investigation; for at the worst it is just those phenomena which we all recognise as interest that constitute the great majority, and contain the characteristic substance of the general interest problem. Thus we can investigate with certainty into the nature and origin of the phenomenon of interest without requiring to decide beforehand on the exact boundary-line between the two profits.

I need scarcely say that, in these scanty remarks, I do not suppose myself to have given an exhaustive, or even a perfectly correct statement of the principles of the theory of capital. All that I have attempted to do is to lay down as briefly as possible a useful and certain terminology, on the basis of which we may have a common understanding in the critical and historical part of this work.

[1] Of course only so far as it is *net* interest.

BOOK I

THE DEVELOPMENT OF THE PROBLEM

CHAPTER I

THE OPPOSITION TO INTEREST IN CLASSICAL AND MEDIÆVAL TIMES

It has often been remarked that not only does our knowledge of interesting subjects gradually develop, but also our curiosity regarding these subjects. It is very rarely indeed that, when a phenomenon first attracts attention, it is seen in its full extent, with all its constituent and peculiar details, and is then made the subject of one comprehensive inquiry. Much more frequently is it the case that attention is first attracted by some particularly striking instance, and it is only gradually that the less striking phenomena come to be recognised as belonging to the same group, and are included in the compass of the growing problem.

This has been the case with the phenomenon of interest. It first became the object of question only in the form of Loan interest, and for full two thousand years the nature of loan interest had been discussed and theorised on, before any one thought it necessary to put the other question which first gave the problem of interest its complete and proper range—the question of the why and whence of Natural interest.

It is quite intelligible why this should be so. What specially challenges attention about interest is that it has its source and spring, not in labour, but, as it were, in some bounteous mother-wealth. In loan interest, and specially in loan interest derived from sums of money that are by nature barren, this characteristic is so peculiarly noticeable that it must excite question even where no close attention has been given it. Natural interest, on the other hand, if not obtained through the labour, is certainly obtained under co-operation with the labour of the capitalist-undertaker; and to superficial consideration labour and co-operation with labour are too easily confounded, or, at any rate, not kept sufficiently distinct. Thus we fail to recognise that there is in natural interest, as well as in loan interest, the strange element of acquisition of wealth without labour. Before this could be recognised, and thus before the interest problem could attain its proper compass, it was necessary that capital itself, and its employment in economic life, should take a much wider development, and that there should be some beginning of systematic investigation into the sources of this income. And this investigation could not be one that was content to point out the obvious and striking forms of the phenomenon, but one that would cast light on its more homely forms. But these conditions were only fulfilled some thousands of years after men had first expressed their wonder at loan interest "born of barren money."

The history of the interest problem, therefore, begins with a very long period in which loan interest, or usury, alone is the subject of investigation. This period begins deep in ancient times, and reaches down to the eighteenth century of our era. It is occupied with the contention of two opposing doctrines: the elder of the two is hostile to interest; the later defends it. The course of the quarrel belongs to the history of civilisation; it is deeply interesting in itself, and has besides had an influence of the deepest importance on the practical development of economic and legal life, of which we may see many traces even in our own day. But as regards the development of the theoretical interest problem, the whole period, notwithstanding its length, and notwithstanding the great number of writers who flourished during it, is rather barren. Men were fighting, as we shall see, not for the centre of the problem, but for an outpost of it which, from a theoretical standpoint, was of comparatively subordinate importance. Theory was too much the bond servant of practice. People were concerned less to investigate the nature of loan interest for its own sake than to find in theory something that would help them to an opinion on the good or evil of interest, and would give that opinion a firm root in religious, moral, or economical grounds. Since, moreover, the most active time of the controversy coincided with the active time of scholasticism, it may be guessed that the knowledge of the nature of the subject by no means ran parallel with the number of the arguments and counter-arguments that were urged.

I shall therefore not waste many words in describing these earliest phases in the development of our problem, and this all the more readily that there are already several treatises, and some of them excellent ones, relating to that period. In them the reader will find much more detail than need be introduced for our purpose, or would even be appropriate here.[1] We begin, then, with some account of the hostility to loan interest.

Roscher has well remarked that on the lower stages of economical development there regularly appears a lively dislike to the taking of interest. Credit has still little place in production. Almost all loans are loans for consumption, and are, as a rule, loans to people in distress. The creditor is usually rich, the debtor poor; and the former appears in the hateful light of a man who squeezes something from the little of the poor, in the shape of interest, to add it to his own superfluous wealth. It is not to be wondered at, then, that both the ancient world and the Christian Middle Ages were exceedingly unfavourable to usury; for the ancient world, in spite of some few economical flights, had never developed very much of a credit system, and the Middle Ages, after the decay of the Roman culture, found themselves, in industry as in so

[1] From the abundant literature that treats of interest and usury in ancient times, may be specially mentioned the following:—

Böhmer, *Jus Ecclesiasticum Protestantium*, Halle, 1736, vol. v. tit. 19.

Rizy, *Ueber Zinstaxen und Wuchergesetze*, Vienna, 1859.

Wiskemann, *Darstellung der in Deutschland zur Zeit der Reformation herrschenden national-ökonomischen Ansichten* (Prize Essays of the Fürstliche Jablonowski'sche Gesellschaft, vol. x. Leipzig, 1861).

Laspeyres, *Geschichte der volkwirthschaftlichen Ansichten der Niederländer* (vol. xi. of same Prize Essays, Leipzig, 1863).

Neumann, *Geschichte des Wuchers in Deutschland*, Halle, 1865.

Funk, *Zins und Wucher*, Tübingen, 1868.

Knies, *Der Kredit*, part i., Berlin, 1876, p. 328, etc.

Above all, the works of Endemann on the canon doctrine of economics, *Die national-ökonomischen Grundsätze der kanonistischen Lehre*, Jena, 1863, and his *Studien in der romanisch-kanonistischen Wirthschafts-und Rechtslehre*, vol. i. Berlin, 1874; vol. ii. 1883.

many other things, thrown back to the circumstances of primitive times.

In both periods this dislike has left documentary record.

The hostile expressions of the ancient world are not few in number, but they are of trifling importance as regards development of theory. They consist partly of a number of legislative acts forbidding the taking of interest,—some of them reaching back to a very early date,[1]—partly of more or less incidental utterances of philosophic or philosophising writers.

The legal prohibitions of interest may, of course, be taken as evidence of a strong and widespread conviction of the evils connected with its practice. But it can scarcely be said that they were founded on any distinct theory; at any rate no such theory has been handed down to us. The philosophic writers, again—like Plato, Aristotle, the two Catos, Cicero, Seneca, Plautus, and others—usually touch on the subject too cursorily to give any foundation in theory for their unfavourable judgment. Moreover, the context often makes it doubtful whether they object to interest as such, or only to an excess of it; and, in the former case, whether their objection is on the ground of a peculiar blot inherent in interest itself, or only because it usually favours the riches they despise.[2]

[1] *E.g.* the prohibition of interest by the Mosaic Code, which, however, only forbade lending at interest between Jews, not lending by Jews to strangers, Exodus xxii. 25 ; Leviticus xxv. 35-37 ; Deuteronomy xxiii. 19, 20. In Rome, after the Twelve Tables had permitted an Unciarum Foenus, the taking of interest between Roman citizens was entirely forbidden by the Lex Genucia, B.C. 322. Later, by the Lex Sempronia and the Lex Gabinia, the prohibition was extended to Socii and to those doing business with provincials. See also Knies, *Der Kredit*, part i. p. 328, etc., and the writers quoted there.

[2] I may append some of the passages oftenest referred to. Plato in the *Laws*, p. 742, says: "No one shall deposit money with another whom he does not trust as a friend, nor shall he lend money upon interest." Aristotle, *Nichomachean Ethics*, iv. § 1 : "Such are all they who ply illiberal trades ; as those, for instance, who keep houses of ill-fame, and all persons of that class ; and usurers who lend out small sums at exorbitant rates: for all these take from improper sources, and take more than they ought." Cicero, *De Officiis*, ii. at end : "Ex quo genere comparationis illud est Catonis senis : a quo cum quaereretur, quid maxime in re familiari expediret, respondit, bene pascere. Quid secundum? Satis bene pascere. Quid tertium? Male pascere. Quid quartum? Arare. . . . Et, cum ille, qui quaesierat, dixisset, quid foenerari? Tum Cato, quid hominem, inquit, occidere?" Cato, *De Re Rustica:* "Majores nostri sic habuerunt et ita in legibus posuerunt, furem dupli condemnare, foeneratorem quadrupli. Quanto pejorem civem existimarunt foeneratorem quam furem, hinc licet

One passage in ancient literature has, in my opinion, a direct value for the history of theory, inasmuch as it allows us to infer what really was the opinion of its author on the economic nature of interest; that is, the often quoted passage in the first book of Aristotle's *Politics.* He there says: "Of the two sorts of money-making one, as I have just said, is a part of household management, the other is retail trade: the former necessary and honourable, the latter a kind of exchange which is justly censured; for it is unnatural, and a mode by which men gain from one another. The most hated sort, and with the greatest reason, is usury, which makes a gain out of money itself, and not from the natural use of it. For money was intended to be used in exchange, but not to increase at interest. And this term Usury (τόκος), which means the birth of money from money, is applied to the breeding of money, because the offspring resembles the parent. Wherefore of all modes of making money this is the most unnatural" (Jowett's *Translation*, p. 19).

What this positively amounts to may be summed up thus: money is by nature incapable of bearing fruit; the lender's gain therefore cannot come from the peculiar power of the money; it can only come from a defrauding of the borrower (ἐπ' ἀλλήλων ἐστίν). Interest is therefore a gain got by abuse and injustice.

That the writers of old pagan times did not go more deeply into the question admits of a very simple explanation. The question was no longer a practical one. In course of time the authority of the state had become reconciled to the taking of interest. In Attica interest had for long been free from legal restriction. The universal empire of Rome, without formally rescinding those severe laws which entirely forbade the taking of interest, had first condoned, then formally sanctioned it by the institution of legal rates.[1] The fact was that

existimari." Plautus, *Mostellaria*, Act iii. scene 1: "Videturne obsecro hercle idoneus, Danista qui sit? genus quod improbissimum est. . . . Nullum edepol hodie genus est hominum tetrius, nec minus bono cum jure quam Danisticum." Seneca, *De Beneficiis*, vii. 10: "Quid enim ista sunt, quid foenus et calendarium et usura, nisi humanae cupiditatis extra naturam quaesita nomina? . . . quid sunt istae tabellae, quid computationes, et venale tempus et sanguinolentae centesimae? voluntaria mala ex constitutione nostra pendentia, in quibus nihil est, quod subici oculis, quod teneri manu possit, inanis avaritiae somnia."

[1] See also Knies, *Der Kredit*, i. p. 330, etc.

economical relations had become too complicated to find sufficient scope under a system naturally so limited as that of gratuitous credit. Merchants and practical men were, without exception, steadily on the side of interest. In such circumstances, to write in favour of it was superfluous, to write against it was hopeless; and it is a most significant indication of this state of matters that almost the only quarter in which interest was still censured—and that in a resigned kind of way—was in the works of the philosophical writers.

The writers of the Christian Middle Ages had more occasion to treat the subject thoroughly.

The dark days which preceded and followed the break up of the Roman Empire had brought a reaction in economical matters, which, in its turn, had the natural result of strengthening the old hostile feeling against interest. The peculiar spirit of Christianity worked in the same direction. The exploitation of poor debtors by rich creditors must have appeared in a peculiarly hateful light to one whose religion taught him to look upon gentleness and charity as among the greatest virtues, and to think little of the goods of this world. But what had most influence was that, in the sacred writings of the New Testament, were found certain passages which, as usually interpreted, seemed to contain a direct divine prohibition of the taking of interest. This was particularly true of the famous passage in Luke: "Lend, hoping for nothing again."[1] The powerful support which the spirit of the time, already hostile to interest, thus found in the express utterance of divine authority, gave it the power once more to draw legislation to its side. The Christian Church lent its arm. Step by step it managed to introduce the prohibition into legislation. First the taking of interest was forbidden by the Church, and to the clergy only. Then it was forbidden the laity also, but still the prohibition only came from the Church. At last even the temporal legislation succumbed to the Church's influence, and gave its severe statutes the sanction of Roman law.[2]

[1] Luke vi. 35. On the true sense of this passage see Knies as before, p. 333, etc.

[2] On the spread of the prohibition of interest see Endemann, *Nationalökonomische Grundsätze*, p. 8, etc.; *Studien in der romanisch-kanonistischen Wirthschafts-und Rechtslehre*, p. 10, etc.

For fifteen hundred years this turn of affairs gave abundant support to those writers who were hostile to interest. The old pagan philosophers could fling their denunciations on the world without much proving, because they were neither inclined nor able to give them practical effect. As a "Platonic" utterance of the idealists their criticism had not sufficient weight in the world of practice to be either seriously opposed or seriously defended. But now the matter had again become practical. Once the Word of God was made victorious on earth, a hostility immediately showed itself, against which the righteousness of the new laws had to be defended. This task naturally fell to the theological and legal literature of the Church, and thus began a literary movement on the subject of loan interest which accompanied the canonist prohibition from its earliest rise far into the eighteenth century.

About the twelfth century of our era is observable a noteworthy departure in the character of this literature. Before that century the controversy is mainly confined to the theologians, and even the way in which it is treated is essentially theological. To prove the unrighteousness of loan interest appeal is made to God and His revelation, to passages of Holy Writ, to the commandments concerning charity, righteousness, and so on; only rarely, and then in the most general terms, to legal and economical considerations. It is the fathers of the Church who express themselves most thoroughly on the subject, although even their treatment can scarcely be called thorough.[1]

After the twelfth century, however, the discussion is conducted on a gradually broadening economic basis. To proofs from Revelation are added appeals to the authority of revered fathers of the Church, to canonists and philosophers—even pagan philosophers,—to old and new laws, to deductions from the *jus divinum*, the *jus humanum*, and—what is particularly important for us as touching the economic side of the matter—to deductions from the *jus naturale*. And now the lawyers begin to take a more active part in the movement alongside the theologians—first the canon lawyers and then the legists.

The very ample and careful attention which these writers gave to the subject is chiefly due to the fact that the prohi-

[1] See below.

bition of interest pressed more hardly as time went on, and required to be more strongly defended against the reaction of the trade it oppressed. The prohibition had originally been imposed in economical circumstances of such a nature that it was easily borne. Moreover, during its first hundred years the prohibition had so little command of external force, that where practical life felt itself hampered by the restraint it could disregard it without much danger. But later, as industry and commerce grew, their increasing necessity for credit must have made the hampering effects of the prohibition increasingly vexatious. At the same time the prohibition became more felt as it extended to wider circles, and as its transgression was punished more severely. Thus it was inevitable that its collisions with the economical world should become much more numerous and much more serious. Its most natural ally, public opinion, which had originally given it the fullest support, began to withdraw from it. There was urgent need of assistance from theory, and this assistance was readily obtained from the growing science.[1]

Of the two phases of the canonist writings on this subject, the first is almost without value for the history of theory. Its theologising and moralising do little more than simply express abhorrence of the taking of interest and appeal to authorities.[2]

Of greater importance is the second phase, although neither as regards the number of its writers nor the very

[1] See Endemann, *Studien*, pp. 11-13, 15, etc.

[2] To give the reader some idea of the tone which the fathers of the Church adopted in dealing with the subject I append some of their most quoted passages. Lactantius, book vi. *Divin. Inst.* chap. xviii. says of a just man: "Pecuniae, si quam crediderit, non accipiet usuram: ut et beneficium sit incolume quod succurat necessitati, et abstineat se prorsus alieno in hoc enim genere officii debet suo esse contentus, quam oporteat alias ne proprio quidem parcere, ut bonum faciat. Plus autem accipere, quam dederit, injustum est. Quod qui facit, insidiatur quodam modo, ut ex alterius necessitate praedetur." Ambrosius, *De Bono Mortis*, chap. xii.: "Si quis usuram acciperit, rapinam facit, vita non vivit." The same *De Tobia*, chap. iii.: "Talia sunt vestra, divites! beneficia. Minus datis, et plus exigitis. Talis humanitas, ut spolietis etiam dum subvenitis. Foecundus vobis etiam pauper est ad quaestum. Usurarius est egenus, cogentibus nobis, habet quod reddat: quod impendat non habet." So also chap. xiv.: "Ideo audiant quid lex dicat: Neque usuram, inquit, escarum accipies, neque omnium rerum." Chrysostom on Matthew xvii. Homily 56: "Noli mihi dicere, quaeso, quid gaudet et gratiam habet, quod sibi foenore pecuniam collocas: id enim crudelitate tua coactus fecit." Augustine on Psalm

imposing array of arguments they introduced.[1] For what originally emanated from the few was soon slavishly repeated by the many, and the stock of arguments collected by the earlier writers soon passed to the later as an heirloom that was above argument. But the greater number of these arguments are merely appeals to authority, or they are of a moralising character, or they are of no force whatever. Only a comparatively small number of them—mostly deductions from the *jus naturale*—can lay claim to any theoretical interest. If, even of these arguments, many should appear to a reader of to-day little calculated to convince anybody, it should not be forgotten that at that time it was not their office to convince. What man had to believe already stood fixed and fast. The all-efficient ground of conviction was the Word of God, which, as they understood it, had condemned interest. The rational arguments which were found to agree with the divine prohibition were scarcely more than a kind of flying buttress, which could afford to be the slighter that it had not to carry the main burden of proof.[2]

I shall very shortly state those rational arguments that have an interest for us, and verify them by one or two quotations from such writers as have given them clear and practical expression.

First of all, we meet with Aristotle's argument of the barrenness of money; only that the theoretically important point of interest being a parasite on the produce of other people's industry, is more sharply brought out by the canonists. Thus Gonzalez Tellez[3]: "So then, as money breeds no money, it is contrary to nature to take anything beyond the sum lent, and it may with more propriety be said that it is taken from industry than from money, for money certainly does not breed, as Aristotle

cxxviii.: "Audent etiam foeneratores dicere, non habeo aliud unde vivam. Hoc mihi et latro diceret, deprehensus in fauce: hoc et effractor diceret . . . et leno . . . et maleficus." The same (quoted in the *Decret. Grat.* chap. i. Causa xiv. quaest. 3): "Si plus quam dedisti expectas accipere foeneratores, et in hoc improbandus, non laudandus."

[1] Molinaeus, in a work that appeared in 1546, mentions a writer who had shortly before collected no less than twenty-five arguments against interest (*Tract. Contract.* No. 528).

[2] See Endemann, *Grundsätze*, pp. 12, 18.

[3] *Commentaria perpetua in singulos textus quinque librorum Decretalium Gregorii IX.* v. chap. iii.; *De Usuris*, v. chap. xix. No. 7.

has related." And in still plainer terms Covarruvias[1]: "The fourth ground is that money brings forth no fruit from itself, nor gives birth to anything. On this account it is inadmissible and unfair to take anything over and above the lent sum for the use of the same, since this is not so much taken from money, which brings forth no fruit, as from the industry of another."

The consumption of money and of other kinds of lent goods furnished a second "natural right" argument. This is very clearly and fully put by Thomas Aquinas. He contends that there are certain things the use of which consists in the consumption of the articles themselves, such as grain and wine. On that account the use of these things cannot be separated from the articles themselves, and if the use be transferred to any one the article itself must necessarily be transferred with it. When an article of this sort then is lent the property in it will always be transferred. Now it would evidently be unjust if a man should sell wine, and yet separate therefrom the use of the wine. In so doing he would either sell the same article twice, or he would sell something which did not exist. Exactly in the same way is it unjust for a man to lend things of this sort at interest. Here also he asks two prices for one article; he asks for replacement of a similar article and he asks a price for the use of the article, which we call interest or usury. Now as the use of money lies in its consumption or in its spending, it is inadmissible in itself, on the same grounds, to ask a price for the use of money.[2] According to this reasoning interest appears as a price filched or extorted for a thing that does not really exist, the separate and independent "use" of consumable goods.

A similar conclusion is arrived at by a third argument that recurs over and over again in stereotyped form. The goods lent pass over into the property of the debtor. Therefore the use of the goods for which the lender is paid interest is the use of another person's goods, and from that the lender

[1] *Variorum Resolutionum*, iii. chap. i. No. 5.

[2] *Summa totius Theologiae*, ii. chap. ii. quaest. 78, art. 1. Similarly Covarruvias: "Accipere lucrum aliquod pro usu ipsius rei, et demum rem ipsam, iniquum est et prava commutatio, cum id quod non est pretio vendatur . . . aut enim creditor capit lucrum istud pro sorte, ergo bis capit ejus aestimationem, vel capit injustum sortis valorem. Si pro usu rei, is non potent seorsum a sorte aestimari, et sic bis sors ipsa venditur."

cannot draw a profit without injustice. Thus Gonzalez Tellez: "For the creditor who makes a profit out of a thing belonging to another person enriches himself at the hurt of another." And still more sharply Vaconius Vacuna[1]: "Therefore he who gets fruit from that money, whether it be pieces of money or anything else, gets it from a thing which does not belong to him, and it is accordingly all the same as if he were to steal it."

Lastly, in a very strange argument, first, I believe, incorporated by Thomas Aquinas in the canonists' *répertoire*, interest is looked upon as the hypocritical and underhand price asked for a good common to all—namely, time. The usurers who receive more, by the amount of their interest, than they have given, seek a pretext to make the prohibited business appear a fair one. This pretext is offered them by time. They would have time recognised as the equivalent for which they receive the surplus income formed by the interest. That this is their intention is evident from the fact that they raise or reduce their claim of interest according as the time for which a loan is given is long or short. But time is a common good that belongs to no one in particular, but is given to all equally by God. When, therefore, the usurer would charge a price for time, as though it were a good received from him, he defrauds his neighbour, to whom the time he sells already belongs as much as it does to him, the seller, and he defrauds God, for whose free gift he demands a price.[2]

To sum up. In the eyes of the canonists loan interest is simply an income which the lender draws by fraud or force from the resources of the borrower. The lender is paid in interest for fruits which barren money cannot bear. He sells a "use" which does not exist, or a use which already belongs to the borrower. And finally, he sells time, which belongs to the borrower just as much as it does to the lender and to all men. In short, regard it as we may, interest always appears as a parasitic profit, extorted or filched from the defrauded borrower.

This judgment was not applied to the interest that accrues from the lending of durable goods, such as houses, furniture,

[1] Lib. i. *Nov. Declar. Jus. Civ.* chap. xiv. quoted in Böhmer's *Jus Eccles. Prot.* Halle, 1736, p. 340.

[2] Thomas Aquinas, *De Usuris*, i. chap. iv.

etc. Just as little did it affect the natural profit acquired by personal exertions. That this natural profit might be an income distinct from that due to the undertaker for his labour, was but little noticed, especially at the beginning of the period; and, so far as it was noticed, little thought was given to it. At any rate the principle of this kind of profit was not challenged. Thus, *e.g.* the canonist Zabarella[1] deplores the existence of loan interest on this ground among others, that the agriculturists, looking for a "more certain" profit, would be tempted to put their money out at interest rather than employ it in production, and thus the food of the people would suffer,—a line of thought which evidently sees nothing objectionable in the investment of capital in agriculture, and the profit drawn from that. It was not even considered necessary that the owner of capital should employ it personally, if only he did not let the ownership of it out of his hands. Thus profit made from a sleeping partnership was, at least, not forbidden.[2] And the case where one entrusts another with a sum of money, but retains the ownership of it, is decided by the stern Thomas Aquinas in the words: that such an one may unhesitatingly appropriate the profit resulting from the sum of money. He need not want for a just title to it, "for he, as it were, receives the fruit of his own estate"—not, as the holy Thomas carefully adds, a fruit that springs directly from the coins, but a fruit that springs from those things that have been obtained in just exchange for the coins.[3]

Where, as not seldom occurs notwithstanding this, exception is taken to profit obtained by personal exertions, the exception is not so much to the profit as such, as to some concrete and objectionable manner of getting it: as, *e.g.* by business conducted in an avaricious or quite fraudulent way, or by forbidden traffic in money, and such like.

[1] Secundo (usura est prohibita) ex fame, nam laborantes rustici praedia colentes libentius ponerent pecuniam ad usuras, quam in laboratione, cum sit tutius lucrum, et sic non curarent homines seminare seu metere."—See Endemann, *National-ökonomische Grundsätze*, p. 20.

[2] Endemann, *Studien*, i. p. 361. [3] *De Usuris*, ii. chap. iv. qu. 1.

CHAPTER II

THE DEFENCE OF INTEREST FROM THE SIXTEENTH TILL THE EIGHTEENTH CENTURY

THE canon doctrine of interest had to all appearance reached its zenith sometime during the thirteenth century. Its principles held almost undisputed sway in legislation, temporal as well as spiritual. Pope Clement V, at the Council of Vienna in 1311, could go so far as to threaten with excommunication those secular magistrates who passed laws favourable to interest, or who did not repeal such laws, where already passed, within three months.[1] Nor were the laws inspired by the canon doctrine content with opposing interest in its naked and undisguised form; by the aid of much ingenious casuistry they had even taken measures to prosecute it under many of the disguises by which the prohibition had been evaded.[2] Finally, literature no less than legislation fell under the sway of the canon doctrine, and for centuries not a trace of opposition to the principle of the prohibition dared show itself.

There was only one opponent that the canon doctrine had never been entirely able to subdue, the economic practice of the people. In face of all the threatened penalties of earth and heaven, interest continued to be offered and taken; partly without disguise, partly under the manifold forms which the inventive spirit of the business classes had devised, and by which they slipped through the meshes of the prohibitionist laws in spite of all their casuistry. And the more flourishing the economical

[1] *Clem. c. un. de Usuris*, 5. 5.

[2] See Endemann, *Grundsätze*, pp. 9, 21.

condition of a country the stronger was the reaction of practice against the dominant theory.

In this battle victory remained with the more stubborn party, and that party was the one whose very existence was endangered by the prohibition.

One of its first results, not marked by much outward circumstance, but actually of great importance, was obtained even when the canon doctrine was still, to all appearance, at the height of its authority. Too weak to hazard open war against the principle of prohibition, the business world yet managed to prevent its strict and complete legal enforcement, and to establish a number of exceptions some direct and some indirect.

The following, among others, may be regarded as direct exceptions: the privileges of the Mons de Piété, the toleration of other kinds of banks, and the very extensive indulgence shown to the usury practices of the Jews—an indulgence which, here and there, was extended, at least by secular legislation, into a formal legal permission.[1]

Of indirect exceptions there were: the buying of annuities, the taking of land in mortgage for lent money, the use of bills of exchange, partnership arrangements, and above all, the possibility of getting compensation from the borrower in the shape of *interesse* on the deferred payment (*damnum emergens et lucrum cessans*). Independent of this, the lender had had a claim to compensation in the shape of *interesse*, but only in the case of a culpable neglect (technically called *mora*) on the part of the borrower to fulfil his contract obligations; and the existence and amount of the *interesse* had to be authenticated in each case. But now a step farther in this direction was taken, although under protest of the strict canonists, by the introduction of two contract clauses. Under one clause the borrower agreed beforehand that the lender should be released from the obligation of authenticating the borrower's *mora*; and under the other a definite rate of *interesse* was agreed on in advance. Practically it came to this, that the loan was given nominally without interest, but that the creditor

[1] The opinion very commonly held that the Jews were generally exempted from the Church's prohibition of interest is pronounced erroneous by the late and very complete work of Endemann (*Studien*, ii. p. 383, etc.)

actually received, under the name of *interesse*, a regular percentage for the whole period of the loan, the borrower by a fiction being put in *mora* for that period.[1]

Practical results like these had in the long run their effect on principles.

To the observer of men and things it must in time have become questionable whether the obstinate and always increasing resistance of practical life really had its root, as the canonists affirmed, only in human wickedness and hardness of heart. Those who took the trouble to go more deeply into the technicalities of business life must have seen that practice not only would not, but could not dispense with interest; that interest being the soul of credit, where credit exists to any considerable extent interest cannot be prevented; and that to suppress it would be to suppress nine-tenths of credit transactions. They must have seen, in a word, that, even in a half-developed system of economy, interest is an organic necessity. It was inevitable that the recognition of such facts that had for long been commonplaces among practical men, should in the end force its way into literary circles.

The effects which it there exerted were various.

One party remained unshaken in their theoretical conviction that loan interest was a parasitic profit, admitting of no defence before any strict tribunal; but they consented to a practical compromise with the imperfection of man, on which they laid the blame of its obstinate vitality. From the standpoint of an ideal order of society, interest could not be permitted, but men being so imperfect, it cannot conveniently be eradicated, and so it were better to allow it within certain limits. This was the view taken, among others, by several of the great reformers, *e.g.* as Zwingli,[2] by Luther in his later days (although earlier he had been a relentless enemy of usury),[3] and, with still greater reserve, by Melanchthon.[4]

It had naturally a great effect on public opinion, and indirectly also on the later development of law, that such

[1] Endemann, *Studien*, ii. pp. 243, 366.

[2] Wiskemann, *Darstellung der in Deutschland zur Zeit der Reformation herrschenden national-ökonomischen Ansichten* (Prize Essays of the Jablonowski'sche Society, vol. x. p. 71).

[3] Wiskemann, p. 54. Neumann, *Geschichte des Wuchers*, p. 480, etc.

[4] Wiskemann, p. 65.

influential men as these declared for tolerance in the matter. However, as they were guided in their conduct not by principles, but altogether by motives of expediency, their views have no deeper importance in the history of theory, and we need not pursue them farther.

Another party of thinking and observing men went farther. Convinced by experience of the necessity of loan interest, they began to re-examine the theoretical foundations of the prohibition, and finding that these would not bear investigation, they commenced to write in opposition to the canon doctrine, basing their opposition on principles. This movement becomes observable about the middle of the sixteenth century, gathers impetus and power in the course of the seventeenth, and towards its end obtains so distinct an ascendency that during the next hundred years it has only to do battle with a few isolated writers who still represent the canon doctrine. And towards the end of the eighteenth century if any one had professed to defend that doctrine with the old specific arguments, he would have been thought too eccentric to be taken seriously.

The first combatants of the new school were the reformer Calvin and the French jurist Dumoulin (Carolus Molinaeus).

Calvin has defined his attitude towards our question in a letter to his friend Oekolampadius.[1] In this letter he does not treat it comprehensively, but he is very decided. At the outset he rejects the usual authoritative foundation for the prohibition, and tries to show that, of the writings adduced in its support, some are to be understood in a different sense, and some have lost their validity through entire change of circumstances.[2]

The proof from authority being thus disposed of, Calvin turns to the rational arguments usually given for the prohibition. Its strongest argument, that of the barrenness of money (*pecunia non parit pecuniam*), he finds of "little weight." It is with money as it is with a house or a field. The roof and walls of a house cannot, properly speaking, beget money, but when the use of the house is exchanged for money a legitimate

[1] Ep. 383, in the collection of his letters and answers, Hanover, 1597.

[2] "Ac primum nullo testimonio Scripturae mihi constat usuras omnino damnatas esse. Illa enim Christi sententia quae maxime obvia et aperta haberi solet: Mutuum dato nihil inde sperantes, male huc detorta est. . . . Lex vero Mosis politica cum sit, non tenemur illa ultra quam aequitas ferat atque humanitas. Nostra conjunctio hodie per omnia non respondet. . . ."

money gain may be drawn from the house In the same way money can be made fruitful. When land is purchased for money, it is quite correct to think of the money as producing other sums of money in the shape of the yearly revenues from the land. Unemployed money is certainly barren, but the borrower does not let it lie unemployed. The borrower therefore is not defrauded in having to pay interest. He pays it *ex proventu*, out of the gain that he makes with the money.

But Calvin would have the whole question judged in a reasonable spirit, and he shows, by the following example, how the lender's claim of interest may, from this point of view, be well grounded.

A rich man who has plenty of landed property and general income, but little ready money, applies for a money loan to one who is not so wealthy, but happens to have a great command over ready money. The lender could with the money purchase land for himself, or he could request that the land bought with his money be hypothecated to him till the debt is wiped out. If, instead of doing so, he contents himself with the interest, the fruit of the money, how should this be blameworthy when the much harder bargain is regarded as fair? As Calvin vigorously expresses it, that were a childish game to play with God, "Et quid aliud est quam puerorum instar ludere cum Deo, cum de rebus ex verbis nudis, ac non ex eo quod inest in re ipsa judicatur."

He concludes then that the taking of interest cannot be universally condemned. But neither is it to be universally permitted, but only so far as it does not run counter to fairness and charity. In carrying out this principle he lays down a number of exceptions in which interest is not to be allowed. The most noteworthy of these are: that no interest should be asked from men who are in urgent need; that due consideration should be paid to the "poor brethren"; that the "welfare of the state" should be considered; and that the maximum rate of interest established by the laws should in no case be exceeded.

As Calvin is the first theologian, so Molinaeus is the first jurist to oppose the canon prohibition on theoretical grounds. Both writers agree in their principles, but the way in which they state them differs as widely as do their callings. Calvin goes shortly and directly at what to him is the heart of the matter, without troubling himself to refute secondary objections. Thus he gets his convictions more from impressions he receives than from logical argument. Molinaeus, on the other hand, is inexhaustible in distinctions and casuistry. He is indefatigable in pursuing his opponents in all their scholastic turnings and twistings, and takes the most elaborate pains to confute them formally and point by point. Moreover, although more cautious in expression than the impetuous Calvin, he is quite as frank, pithy, and straightforward.

The principal deliverance of Molinaeus on the subject is the *Tractatus Contractuum et Usurarum redituumque pecunia Constitutorum*,[1] published in 1546. The first part of it has a great resemblance, perhaps accidental, to Calvin's line of argument. After a few introductory definitions, he turns to the examination of the *jus divinum*, and finds that the relevant passages of Holy Writ are misinterpreted. They are not intended to forbid the taking of interest in general, but only such interest as violates the laws of charity and brotherly love. And then he also introduces the effective illustration used by Calvin of the rich man who purchases land with borrowed money.[2]

But further on the reasoning is much fuller than that of Calvin. He points out conclusively (No. 75) that in almost every loan there is an "*interesse*" of the creditor—some injury caused or some use foregone,—the compensation for which is just and economically necessary. This compensation is interest or *usura*, in the right and proper sense of the word. The laws of Justinian which allow interest, and only limit its amount, are consequently not to be considered unjust, but actually in the interest of the borrower, inasmuch as the payment of a moderate interest gives him the chance of making a greater profit (No. 76).

Later (No. 528) Molinaeus passes under review the chief arguments of the canonists against interest, and completely refutes them by a running commentary.

To the old objection of Thomas Aquinas, that the lender who takes interest either sells the same thing twice, or sells

[1] Previous to this, in the same year, was published the *Extricatio Labyrinthi de eo quod Interest*, in which the question of *interesse* was freely handled, but no definite side taken on the interest question.—See Endemann, *Studien*, i. p. 63.

[2] *Tractatus*, No. 10.

something that has no existence at all (*vide* p. 22), Molinaeus answers that the use of money is a thing independent of the capital sum, and consequently may be sold independently. We must not regard the first immediate spending of the money as its use: the use that follows—the use of those goods that a man has acquired by means of the loaned money, or has got command over—is also its use (Nos. 510, 530). If, further, it be maintained that, along with the money itself, its use also has passed over into the legal property of the borrower, and that he therefore is paying in interest for his own property, Molinaeus answers (No. 530) that one is quite justified in selling another man's property if it be a debt due him, and that this is exactly the case with loans: "Usus pecuniae mihi pure a te debitae est mihi pure a te debitus, ergo vel tibi vendere possum."

Finally, to the argument of the natural barrenness of money Molinaeus replies (No. 530) that the everyday experience of business life shows that the use of any considerable sum of money yields a service of no trifling importance, and that this service, even in legal language, is designated as the "fruit" of money. To argue that money of itself can bring forth no fruit is not to the point, for even land brings forth nothing of itself without expense, exertion, and human industry. And quite in the same way does money when assisted by human effort bring forth notable fruits. The rest of the polemic against the canonists has little theoretical interest.

On the basis of this comprehensive consideration of the subject, Molinaeus ends by formulating his thesis (No. 535): First of all, it is necessary and useful that a certain practice of taking interest be retained and permitted. The contrary opinion, that interest in itself is absolutely objectionable, is foolish, pernicious, and superstitious (*Stulta illa et non minus perniciosa quam superstitiosa opinio de usura de se absoluta mala*) (No. 534).

In these words Molinaeus sets himself in the most direct opposition to the Church's doctrine. To modify them in some degree—as a Catholic might be compelled to do from other considerations—he makes certain practical concessions, without, however, yielding anything in principle. The most important of these is that, on grounds of expediency, and on account of prevailing abuses, he acquiesces for the present in the Church's prohibition of interest pure and simple in the shape of undisguised usury, wishing to retain only the milder and more humane form of annuities,—which, however, he rightly looks on as a "true species of usury business."[1]

The deliverances of Calvin and Molinaeus remained for a long time quite by themselves, and the reason of this is easily understood. To pronounce that to be right which the Church, the law, and the learned world had condemned with one voice, and opposed with arguments drawn from all sources, required not only a rare independence of intellect, but a rare strength of character which did not shrink from suspicion and persecution. The fate of the leaders in this movement showed clearly enough that there was cause for fear. Not to mention Calvin, who, indeed, had given the Catholic world quite other causes of offence, Molinaeus had much to suffer; he himself was exiled, and his book, carefully and moderately as it was written, was put on the Index. Nevertheless the book made its way, was read, repeated, and published again and again, and so scattered a seed destined to bear fruit in the end.[2]

Passing over the immediate disciples of Calvin, who naturally agreed with the views of their master, there were few writers in the sixteenth century who ventured to argue in favour of interest on economical grounds. Among them may be specially mentioned the humanist Camerarius,[3] Bornitz,[4] and above all, Besold.

Besold argues fully and ably against the canon doctrine in the dissertations entitled *Questiones Aliquot de Usuris*, (1598), the work with which he began his very prolific career

[1] "Ea taxatio" (the fixing of a maximum rate which was attached to the principle of the permission of interest in Justinian's Code) "nunquam in se fuit iniqua. Sed ut tempore suo summa et absoluta, ita processu temporis propter abusum hominum nimis in quibusdam dissoluta et vaga inventa est, et omnino super foenore negociativo forma juris civilis incommoda et perniciosa debitoribus apparuit. Unde merito abrogata fuit, et alia tutior et commodior forma inventa, videlicet per abalienationem sortis, servata debitori libera facultate luendi. Et haec forma nova, ut mitior et civilior, ita minus habet de ratione foenoris, propter alienationem sortis, quam forma juris civilis. Est tamen foenus large sumptum, et vera species negociationis foenoratoriae. . . ." (No. 536)

[2] Endemann, *Studien*, i. p. 64, etc. Endemann, however, underrates the influence that Molinaeus had on the later development. See below.

[3] In his notes on Aristotle's *Politics*; see Roscher, *Geschichte der National-Oekonomik in Deutschland*, p. 54.

[4] Roscher, *ibid.* p. 188.

as a writer.[1] He finds the origin of interest in the institutions of trade and commerce, in which money ceases to be barren. And as every man must be allowed to pursue his own advantage, so far as that is possible without injury to others, natural justice is not opposed to the taking of interest. Like Molinaeus, whom he often quotes with approval, he adduces on its behalf the analogy between the loan against interest and the hire against payment. The loan at interest stands to the loan not at interest in the same relation as the hire against payment—which is perfectly allowable—to the Leihe, where no payment is required (*commodatum*). He points out very well that the height of loan interest must at all times correspond with the height of natural interest, the latter indeed being the ground and source of the former; and he maintains that, where, owing to the use of money, the current rate of profit is higher, a higher limit of loan interest should be allowed (p. 32). Finally, he is as little impressed by the passages in Holy Writ which have been interpreted as forbidding interest (p. 38, etc.) as by the arguments of the "philosophers,"—considering these arguments very weak if one looks at the matter from the proper standpoint (p. 32).

From this short abstract it will be seen that Besold is a frank and able follower of Molinaeus. From Molinaeus indeed, as the numerous quotations show, he has taken the better part of his doctrine.[2] But it would be difficult to find in his writings any advance on that author.[3]

This is still more true of the great English philosopher Bacon, who wrote on the subject almost contemporaneously with Besold. He is not misled by the old ideas of the "unnaturalness" of interest. He has enough intellectual

[1] Besold resumed the discussion later, in an enlarged and improved form, as he says, in another work, *Vitae et Mortis Consideratio Politica* (1623), in which it occupies the fifth chapter of the first book. I had only this latter work at my disposal, and the quotations in the text are taken from it.

[2] There is a long quotation even in the first chapter of the first book (p. 6). In the fifth chapter the quotations are numerous.

[3] I think Roscher (*Geschichte der National-Oekonomik*, p. 201) does Besold too much honour when, in comparing him with Salmasius and Hugo Grotius, he gives him the honourable position of a forerunner on whom Salmasius has scarcely improved, and to whom Grotius is even inferior. Instead of Besold, who drew at second hand, Roscher should have named Molinaeus. Besold is not more original than Salmasius, and certainly less adroit and ingenious.

freedom and apprehension of the needs of economic life to weigh impartially its advantages and disadvantages, and to pronounce interest an economical necessity. But nevertheless he gives it sufferance only on the ground of expediency. "Since of necessity men must give and take money on loan, and since they are so hard of heart (*sintque tam duro corde*) that they will not lend it otherwise, there is nothing for it but that interest should be permitted."[1]

In the course of the seventeenth century the new doctrine made great strides, particularly in the Netherlands. There the conditions were peculiarly favourable to its further development. During the political and religious troubles among which the young free state was born, men had learned to emancipate themselves from the shackles of a slavish following of authority. It happened too that the decaying theory of the fathers of the Church and of the scholastics nowhere came into sharper conflict with the needs of actual life than in the Netherlands, where a highly developed economy had created for itself a complete system of credit and banking; where, consequently, transactions involving interest were common and regular; and where, moreover, temporal legislation, yielding to the pressure of practice, had long allowed the taking of interest.[2] In such circumstances a theory which pronounced interest to be a godless defrauding of the debtor was unnatural, and its continuance for any length of time was an impossibility.

Hugo Grotius may be regarded as forerunner of the change.

His attitude towards our subject is peculiarly nondescript. On the one hand, he clearly recognises that it is not possible to base the prohibition theoretically in natural right, as the canonists had done. He sees no force in the argument of the barrenness of money, for "houses also, and other things barren by nature, the skill of man has made productive." To the argument that the use of money, consisting as it does in being spent, cannot be separated from money itself, and therefore cannot be paid for independently, he finds an apt rejoinder; and, speaking generally, the arguments which represent interest as contrary to natural right appear to him "not of a kind to compel

[1] *Sermones Fideles*, cap. xxxix. (1597)

[2] See Grotius, *De Jure Pacis ac Belli*, book ii. chap. xii. p. 22.

assent" (*non talia ut assensum extorqueant*). But, on the other hand, he considers the passages in Holy Writ forbidding interest to be undoubtedly binding. So that in his conclusions he remains—in principle at least—on the side of the canonists. Practically he does resile from the principle of prohibition by allowing and approving of many kinds of compensation for loss, for renunciation of profit, for lender's trouble and risk,—describing these as "of the nature of interest."[1]

Thus Grotius takes a hesitating middle course between the old and the new doctrine.[2]

Undecided views like these were speedily left behind. In a few years more others openly threw overboard not only the rational basis of the prohibition as he had done, but the prohibition itself. The decisive point was reached shortly before the year 1640. As if the barriers of long restraint had all been torn down in one day, a perfect flood of writings broke out in which interest was defended with the utmost vigour, and the flood did not fall till the principle of interest, in the Netherlands at least, had conquered. In this abundant literature the first place, both in time and rank, was taken by the celebrated Claudius Salmasius. Of his writings, which from 1638 followed each other at short intervals, the most important are: *De Usuris*, 1638; *De Modo Usurarum*, 1639; *De Foenore Trapezitico*, 1640. To these may be added some shorter controversial writings that appeared under the pseudonym of Alexius a Massalia: *Diatriba de Mutuo: mutuum non esse alienationem*, 1640.[3] These writings almost by

[1] *De Jure Pacis ac Belli*, book ii. cap. xii. pp. 20, 21.

[2] Thus it is not possible to regard Grotius as a pioneer of the new theory. This view, held among others by Neumann, *Geschichte des Wuchers in Deutschland*, p. 499, and by Laspeyres, *Geschichte*, pp. 10 and 257, is authoritatively corrected by Endemann, *Studien*, I. p. 66, etc.

[3] The list of writings in which our extremely prolific author expatiates on the subject of interest is by no means exhausted by the works mentioned in the text. There is, *e.g.* a *Disquisitio de Mutuo, qua probatur non esse alienationem*, of the year 1645, whose author signs with the initials S. D. B., a signature which points, as does the whole style of writing, to Salmasius (Dijonicus Burgundus). There is besides in the same year an anonymous writing, also undoubtedly traceable to Salmasius, *Confutatio Diatribae de Mutuo tribus disputationibus ventilatae, auctore et preside Jo. Jacobo Vissembachio*, etc. Those named in the text, however, were the first to break ground.

themselves determined the direction and substance of the theory of interest for more than a hundred years, and even in the doctrine of to-day, as we shall see, we may recognise many of their after-effects. His doctrine therefore deserves a thorough consideration.

The views of Salmasius on interest are put together most concisely and suggestively in the eighth chapter of his book *De Usuris.* He begins by giving his own theory. Interest is a payment for the use of sums of money lent. Lending belongs to that class of legal transactions in which the use of a thing is made over by its owner to another person. In the case where the article in question is not perishable, if the use that is transferred is not to be paid for, the legal transaction is a Commodatum: if it is to be paid for, the transaction is a Locatio or Conductio. In the case where the article in question is a perishable or a fungible thing, if the use is not to be paid for, it is a loan bearing no interest (*mutuum*): if to be paid for, it is a loan at interest (*focnus*). The interest-bearing loan accordingly stands to the loan which bears no interest in exactly the same relation as the Locatio to the Commodatum, and is just as legitimate as it.[1]

The only conceivable ground for judging differently about the allowableness of payment in the case of the Commodatum (where a non-perishable good, as a book or a slave, is lent) as compared with the Mutuum (where a fungible good, like corn or money, is lent) might be the different nature of the "use" in the two cases. In the circumstances of the latter—where a perishable or fungible good is transferred—the use consists in one complete consumption; and it might be objected that, in such a case the use of a thing could not be separated from the thing itself. But to this Salmasius answers: (1) Such an argument would lead as well to the condemning and abolition of the loan bearing no interest, inasmuch as it is impossible, in the case of a perishable thing, to transfer a "use," whose existence is denied,

[1] "Quae res facit ex commodato locatum, eadem praestat, ut pro mutuo sit foenus, nempe merces. Qui eam in commodato probant, cur in mutuo improbent, nescio, nec ullam hujus diversitatis rationem video. Locatio aedium, vestis animalis, servi, agri, operae, operis, licita erit; non erit foeneratio quae proprie locatio est pecuniae, tritici, hordei, vini, et aliarum hujusmodi specierum frugumque tam arentium quam humidarum?"

even if no interest is asked for it. (2) On the contrary, the perishableness of loaned goods constitutes another reason why the loan should be paid. For in the case of the hire (*locatio*) the lender can take back his property at any moment, because he remains the owner of it. In the case of the loan he cannot do so, because his property is destroyed in the consumption. Consequently the lender of money suffers delays, anxieties, and losses, and by reason of these the claim of the loan to payment is even more consistent with fairness than that of the Commodatum.

After thus stating his own position Salmasius devotes himself to refuting the arguments of his opponents point by point. As we read these refutations we begin to understand how Salmasius so brilliantly succeeded where Molinaeus a hundred years before had failed, in convincing his contemporaries. They are extremely effective pieces of writing, indeed gems of sparkling polemic. The materials for them were, of course, in great part provided by his predecessors, principally by Molinaeus;[1] but the happy manner in which Salmasius employs these materials, and the many pithy sallies with which he enriches them, places his polemic far above anything that had gone before.

It may not be unwelcome to some of my readers to have

[1] To prove the relation in which Salmasius stands to Molinaeus, it may not be superfluous, considering the explicit statement of Endemann (*Studien*, i. p. 65) that Salmasius does not quote Molinaeus, to establish the fact that such quotations do exist in considerable number. The list of authors appended to the works of Salmasius shows three quotations from Molinaeus for the book *De Usuris*, twelve for the *De Modo Usurarum*, and one for the *De Foenore Trapezitico*. These quotations are principally taken from Molinaeus's chief work on the subject, the *Contractus Contractuum et Usurarum*. One of them (*De Usuris*, p. 21) refers directly to a passage which stands in the middle of the most pertinent of his writings (*Tractatus*, No. 529. Nos. 528, etc., contain the statement and refutation of the arguments of the ancient philosophy and of the canonists against interest). There can, therefore, be no doubt that Salmasius accurately knew the writings of Molinaeus, and it is just as much beyond doubt—as indeed his substantial agreement would lead us to suspect—that he has drawn from them. In the *Confutatio Diatribae* mentioned above (p. 36) it is said in one place (p. 290) that Salmasius at the time when, under the pseudonym of Alexis a Massalia, he wrote the *Diatriba de Mutuo*, was not acquainted with the similar writings of Molinaeus in his *Tractatus de Usuris*. But this expression must only relate to his ignorance of those quite special passages in which Molinaeus denies the nature of the loan as an alienation, or else, if what I have said be true, it is simple incorrect.

a few complete examples of Salmasius's style. They will serve to give a more accurate idea of the spirit in which people were accustomed to deal with our problem in the seventeenth century, and far into the eighteenth, and to make the reader better acquainted with a writer whom nowadays many quote, but few read. I therefore give below in his own words one or two passages from the polemic.[1]

What follows has less bearing on the history of theory. First comes a long-winded, and, it must be confessed, for all its subtlety a very lame attempt to prove that in the loan there is no alienation of the thing lent—a subject to which also the whole *Diatriba de Mutuo* is devoted. Then follows the reply to some of the arguments based by the canonists on fairness and expediency; such as, that it is unfair to the borrower, who assumes the risk of the principal sum lent him, to burden

[1] Salmasius begins with the argument of the improper double claim for one commodity. His opponents had contended that whatever was taken over and above the principal sum lent could only be taken either for the use of a thing which was already consumed—that is for nothing at all—or for the principal sum itself, in which case the same thing was sold twice. To this replies Salmasius: "Quae ridicula sunt, et nullo negotio difflari possunt. Non enim pro sorte usura exigitur, sed pro usu sortis. Usus autem ille non est nihilum, nec pro nihilo datur. Quod haberet rationem, si alicui pecuniam mutuam darem, ea lege ut statim in flumen eam projiceret aut alio modo perderet sibi non profuturam. Sed qui pecuniam ab alio mutuam desiderat, ad necessarios sibi usus illam expetit. Aut enim aedes inde comparat, quas ipse habitet, ne in conducto diutius maneat, vel quas alii cum fructu et compendio locet: aut fundum ex ea pecunia emit salubri pretio, unde fructus et reditus magnos percipiat: aut servum, ex cujus operis locatis multum quaestus faciat: aut ut denique alias merces praestinet, quas vili emptas pluris vendat" (p. 195).

And after showing that one who lends money to an undertaking is not under any obligation to inquire whether it is usefully employed by the borrower, any more than the hirer of a house need make similar inquiry, he continues: "Hoc non est sortem bis vendere, nec pro nihilo aliquid percipere. An pro nihilo computandum, quod tu dum meis nummis uteris, sive ad ea quae tuae postulant necessitates, sive ad tua compendia, ego interim his careo cum meo interdum damno et jactura? Et cum mutuum non in sola sit pecunia numerata, sed etiam in aliis rebus quae pondere et mensura continentur, ut in frugibus humidis vel aridis, an, qui indigenti mutuum vinum aut triticum dederit, quod usurae nomine pro usu eorum consequetur, pro nihilo id capere existimabitur? Qui fruges meas in egestate sua consumpserit, quas care emere ad victum coactus esset, aut qui eas aliis care vendiderit, praeter ipsam mensuram quam accepit, si aliquid vice mercedis propter usum admensus fuerit, an id injustum habebitur?, Atqui poteram, si eas servassem, carius fortasse in foro vendere, et plus lucri ex illis venditis efficere, quam quantum possim percipere ex usuris quas mihi reddent" (p. 196, etc.) Particularly biting is his reply to the argument of the unfruitfulness of money: "Facilis responsio. Nihil non sterile est, quod tibi sterile esse volueris. Ut contra

him with interest in addition, and to make him hand over the fruit of the money to another who takes no risk; that usury would lead to the neglect of agriculture, commerce, and the other *bonae artes*, to the injury of the common weal, and so on. In replying to this latter argument Salmasius gets an opportunity of commending the use of competition. The more usurers there are the better; their emulation will press down the rate of interest. Then, from the ninth chapter onwards, with extraordinary display of force and erudition, with many passages full of striking eloquence, but, it must be said, with endless prolixity, comes the disproof of the argument that interest is "unnatural." Quite at the end (*De Usuris*, chap. xx.), the question is finally put whether interest, thus sanctioned by the *jus naturale*, also expresses the *jus divinum*, and this naturally is answered in the affirmative.

nihil non fructuosum, quod cultura exercere, ut fructum ferat, institueris. Nec de agrorum fertilitate regeram, qui non essent feraces nisi humana industria redderet tales. . . . Magis mirum de aëre, et hunc quaestuosum imperio factum. Qui ἀερικὸν imposuerunt vectigal singulis domibus Constantinopolitani imperatores, aërem sterilem esse pati non potuerunt. Sed haec minus cum foenore conveniunt. Nec mare hic sollicitandum, quod piscatoribus, urinatoribus, ac nautis ad quaestum patet, ceteris sterilitate occlusum est. Quid sterilius aegroto? Nec ferre se, nec movere interdum potest. Hunc tamen in redditu habet medicus. Una res est aegroto sterilior, nempe mortuus. . . . Hic tamen sterilis non est pollinctoribus, neque sardapilonibus, neque vespillonibus, neque fossariis. Immo nec praeficis olim, nec nunc sacerdotibus, qui eum ad sepulcrum cantando deducunt. Quae corpus alit corpore, etiamsi liberos non pariat, non tamen sibi infecunda est. Nec artem hic cogites; natura potius victum quaerit. Meretricem me dicere nemo non sentit. . . . De pecunia quod ajunt, nihil ex se producere natura, cur non idem de ceteris rebus, et frugibus omne genus, quae mutuo dantur, asserunt? Sed triticum duplici modo frugiferum est, et cum in terram jacitur, et cum in foenus locatur. Utrobique foenus est. Nam et terra id reddit cum foenore. Cur natura aedium, quas mercede pacta locavero, magis potest videri foecunda, quam nummorum quos foenore dedero? Si gratis eas commodavero, aeque ac si hos gratis mutuo dedero, tum steriles tam hi quam illae mihi evadent. Vis scire igitur, quae pecunia proprie sterilis sit dicenda, immo et dicta sit? Illa certe, quae foenore non erit occupata, quaeque nihil mihi pariet usuraram, quas et propterea Graeci τόκον nomine appellarunt" (p. 198). The third argument of his opponents, that the loan should not bear interest because the things lent are a property of the debtor, Salmasius finds "ridiculous": "At injustum est, ajunt, me tibi vendere quod tuum est, videlicet usum aeris tuae. Potens sane argumentum. Atqui non fit tuum, nisi hac lege, ut pro eo, quod accepisti utendum, certam mihi praestes mercedem, usurae nomine, absque qua frustra tuum id esse cuperes. Non igitur tibi, quod tuum est, vendo, sed, quod meum est, ea conditione ad te transfero, ut pro usu ejus, quamdiu te uti patiar, mihi, quod pactum inter nos est, persolvas."

These are the essential features of Salmasius's doctrine. Not only does it indicate an advance, but it long indicates the high-water mark of the advance. For more than a hundred years any development there was consisted in nothing more than the adoption of it in wider circles, the repetition of it with more or less skilful variations, and the adapting of its arguments to the fashion of the time. But there was no essential advance on Salmasius till the time of Smith and Turgot.

As the number of those who accepted the doctrine represented by Salmasius increased, so did the number of those who adhered to the canon doctrine diminish. This defection, as may be easily understood, went on more rapidly in the Reformation countries and in those speaking the German language, more slowly in countries purely Catholic and in those speaking the Romance tongues.

In the Netherlands, as I have already said, the works of Salmasius were almost immediately followed by a whole series of writings of similar tenor. As early as the year 1640 we meet with the works of Kloppenburg, Boxhorn, Maresius, Graswinckel.[1] A little later, about 1644, the *Tafelhalterstreit*[2] gave occasion to a fiery literary feud between the two parties, and in 1658 this practically ended in a victory for the supporters of interest. Within the next few years, among the ever-increasing adherents of the new theory, stands out prominently the renowned and influential lawyer Gerhard Noodt, who in his three books, *De Foenore et Usuris*, discusses the whole interest question very thoroughly, and with great knowledge of facts and literature.[3] After that there are fewer and fewer expressions of hostility to interest, especially from professional men; still they do occur occasionally up till the second half of the eighteenth century.[4]

In Germany, whose political economy during the seventeenth and even during the eighteenth century is not of much

[1] Laspeyres, p. 257. [2] Very fully described by Laspeyres, p. 258, etc.

[3] Noodt is very much quoted as an authority in the learned literature of the eighteenth century; *e.g.* by Böhmer, *Protest. Kirchenrecht*, vol. v. p. 19 *passim*. Barbeyrac, the editor of several editions of Hugo Grotius, says that, on the matter of interest, there is an "opus absolutissimum et plenissimum summi jurisconsulti et non minus judicio quam eruditione insinis, Clariss. Noodtii" (*De Jure Belli ac Pacis:* edition of Amsterdam, 1720, p. 384).

[4] Laspeyres, p. 269.

account, the Salmasian doctrine made its way slowly and unsensationally, gaining nothing in development. On German soil the power of practical life was very clearly shown. It was to its pressure that the revolution in opinion was due, theory meanwhile halting clumsily behind the reform in public opinion and legislation. Half a century before the first German lawyer, in the person of Besold, had given his approval to it, the taking of interest, or at least the claim to a fixed *interesse* arranged in advance (which practically came to the same thing), was allowed in much of the German local law;[1] and when in 1654 the German imperial legislation followed this example,[2] few theorists sided with Besold and Salmasius. So late as 1629 it was possible for one Adam Contzen to demand that lenders at interest should be punished by criminal law like thieves, and that all Jews should be hunted out of the country like *venenatae bestiae*.[3] Not till the end of the seventeenth century does the conviction of the legitimacy of interest become firmly established in theory. The secession of such prominent men as Pufendorf[4] and Leibnitz[5] to the new doctrine hastened its victory, and in the course of the eighteenth century it is at last gradually taken out of the region of controversy.

In this position we find it in the two great cameralists who flourish at the end of our period, Justi and Sonnenfels. Justi's *Staatswirthschaft*[6] does not contain a single line relating to the great question on which in former times so many bulky volumes had been written, certainly none that could be taken as a theory of interest. He tacitly assumes it as a fact requiring no explanation that interest is paid for a loan; and if in one or two short notes (vol. i. § 268) he speaks against usury, he understands by that—but still tacitly—only an excessive interest.

[1] Neumann, *Geschichte des Wuchers in Deutschland*, p. 546, mentions permissions by local law of contract interest about the years 1520-30. Endemann, it is true (*Studien*, ii. pp. 316 and 365, etc.) would interpret these permissions as applying only to stipulated *interesse*, which, theoretically at least, was different from interest proper (*usura*). In any case the taking of interest had thus practically received toleration from the state.

[2] In the last *Reichsabschied*. On the disputed interpretation of the passages referred to, see Neumann, p. 559, etc.

[3] Roscher, *Geschichte*, p. 205.

[4] *Ibid.* p. 312, etc.

[5] *Ibid.* p. 338, etc.

[6] Second edition, 1758.

Sonnenfels is not so silent on the subject as Justi. But even he, in the earlier editions of his *Handlungswissenschaft*[1] never once touches on the controversy as to the theoretic legitimacy of interest. In the fifth edition (published 1787) he refers to it, indeed, but in the kind of tone which one usually adopts towards a foregone conclusion. In a simple note on p. 496, he dismisses with a few decided words the prohibition of the canonists, ridicules their absurd way of writing, and finds it preposterous to forbid 6 per cent interest for money when 100 per cent can be got when money is changed into commodities.

Sonnenfels's contempt for the canon doctrine carries all the more weight that he has nothing good to say of interest in other respects. Influenced by Forbonnais he finds its origin in an interception of the circulation of money by the capitalists, out of whose hands it can only be attracted by a tribute in the shape of interest.[2] He ascribes to it many injurious effects; such as, that it makes commodities dear, reduces the profits of industry, and allows the owner of money to share in these profits.[3] Indeed in one place he speaks of the capitalists as the class of those "who do no work, and are nourished on the sweat of the working classes." [4]

But alongside of expressions like these we find the accepted Salmasian doctrine. In one place, quite in the spirit of Salmasius, Sonnenfels adduces as arguments for the capitalists' claim, the want of their money, their risk, and the uses they might have got by the purchase of things that produced fruit.[5] In another place he recognises that a lowering of the legal rate is not the best means to repress the evils of high interest.[6] At another time he finds that, since the above mentioned conditions that determine interest are variable, a fixed legal rate is generally unsuitable as being either superfluous or hurtful.[7]

The deep silence which Justi maintains, if considered along with the inconsistent eloquence expended by Sonnenfels, seems to me to be a very characteristic proof of two things; (1) that, when these men wrote, the Salmasian doctrine had

[1] Second edition, Vienna, 1771.
[2] *Ibid.* pp. 419, 425, etc.
[3] *Ibid.* p. 427.
[4] *Ibid.* p. 430.
[5] *Ibid.* p. 426, etc.
[6] *Ibid.* p. 432, etc.
[7] Fifth edition, p. 497.

already secured so firm a footing in Germany, that even writers who felt most hostile towards interest could not think of going back to the strict canonist standpoint, but (2) that up till now the acceptance of the Salmasian doctrine had not been accompanied by any kind of further development in it.

England appears to have been the country where the throwing off of the canon doctrine was attended with the least amount of literary excitement. Through the rapid rise of its commerce and industry, interest transactions had early entered into its economy, and its legislation had early given way to the wants of industrial life. Henry VIII had by 1545 removed the prohibition of interest, and replaced it by a simple legal rate. For a little, indeed, the prohibition was reimposed under Edward VI, but in 1571 it was once more taken off by Queen Elizabeth, and this time for ever.[1] Thus the theoretical question whether loan interest was justifiable or not was practically answered before there was any theoretic economic doctrine, and when an economic literature at last emerged, the prohibition, now removed, had but little interest for it. All the more strongly was its attention drawn to a new controverted question raised by the change in legislation—the question whether there should be a legal rate, and what should be the height of it.

These circumstances have left their stamp on the interest literature of England during the seventeenth and eighteenth centuries. We find numerous and eager discussions as to the height of interest, as to its advantages and disadvantages, and as to the advisability, or otherwise, of limiting it by law But they now touch only rarely, and then, as a rule, quite casually, on the question of its economic nature, of its origin, and of its legitimacy. One or two short proofs of this stage in the development of the problem will suffice.

Of Bacon, who flourished very shortly after the age of the prohibition, and had avowed himself, on very shallow practical grounds, in favour of interest, we have already spoken.[2] Some twenty years later, Sir Thomas Culpepper, himself a violent opponent of interest, does not venture to put forward the canon arguments under his own name, but characteristic-

[1] See Schanz, *Englische Handelspolitik*, Leipzig, 1881, vol. i. p. 552, etc.
[2] See above, p. 34.

ally passes over the subject with the remark that he leaves it to the theologians to prove the unlawfulness of interest, while he will limit himself to showing how much evil is done by it.[1] In doing so, however, he directs his attacks not so much against interest in general as against high interest.[2]

In the same way another writer, very unfavourably disposed towards interest, Josiah Child, will no longer meddle with the question of its lawfulness, but simply refers[3] the reader who wishes to go deeper into the matter to an older and apparently anonymous work, which appeared in 1634 under the title of "The English Usurer." Further, he frequently calls interest the "price of money,"—an expression which certainly betrays no deep insight into its nature; expresses his opinion in passing that through it the creditor enriches himself at the expense of the debtor; but all the same contents himself with pleading for the limitation of the legal rate, not for entire abolition.[4]

His opponent, again, North, who takes the side of interest, conceives of it quite in the manner of Salmasius, as a "rent for stock," similar to land-rent; but cannot say anything more, in explanation of either of them, than that owners hire out their superfluous land and capital to such as are in want of them.[5]

Only one writer of the seventeenth century forms any exception to this superficial treatment of the problem, the philosopher John Locke.

Locke has left a very remarkable tract on the origin of loan interest, entitled "Some Considerations of the Consequences of lowering the Interest and raising the Value of

[1] Tract against the high rate of usury, 1621.

[2] *E.g.* in "A Small Treatise against Usury," annexed to Child's *Discourses*, 1690, p. 229: "It is agreed by all the Divines that ever were, without exception of any; yea, and by the Usurers themselves, that biting Usury is unlawful: Now since it hath been proved that ten in the hundred doth bite the Landed men, doth bite the Poor, doth bite Trade, doth bite the King in his Customs, doth bite the Fruits of the Land, and most of all the Land itself: doth bite all works of Piety, of Vertue, and Glory to the State; no man can deny but ten in the hundred is absolutely unlawful, howsoever happily a lesser rate may be otherwise."

[3] In his introduction to *Brief Observations concerning Trade*, 1668.

[4] "New Discourse of Trade," 1690. See Roscher, p. 59, etc.

[5] Roscher, p. 89.

Money," 1691. He begins with a few propositions that remind one very much of the canonists' standpoint. "Money,"[1] he says, "is a barren thing, and produces nothing; but by compact transfers that profit, that was the reward of one man's labour, into another man's pocket." Nevertheless Locke finds that loan interest is justified. To prove this, and to bridge over his own paradox, he uses the complete analogy that, in his opinion, exists between loan interest and land-rent. The proximate cause of both is unequal distribution. One has more money than he uses, and another has less, and so the former finds a tenant for his money[2] for the very same reason as the landlord finds a tenant for his land, namely, that the one has too much land, while the other has too little.

But why does the borrower consent to pay interest for the money lent? Again, on the same ground as the tenant consents to pay rent for the use of land. For money—of course only through the industry of the borrower, as Locke expressly adds—is able when employed in trade to "produce" more than 6 per cent to the borrower, just in the same way as land, "through the labour of the tenant," is able to produce more fruit than the amount of its rent. If, then, the interest which the capitalist draws from the loan is to be looked on as the fruit of another man's labour, this is only true of it as it is true of rent. Indeed, it is not so true. For the payment of land-rent usually leaves the tenant a much smaller proportion of the fruit of his industry than the borrower of money can save, after paying the interest, out of the profit made with the money. And so Locke comes to the conclusion: "Borrowing money upon use is not only, by the necessity of affairs and the constitution of human society, unavoidable to some men; but to receive profit from the loan of money is as equitable and lawful as receiving rent for land, and more tolerable to the borrower, notwithstanding the opinion of some over-scrupulous men" (p. 37).

It will scarcely be maintained that this theory is particularly happy. There is too marked a contrast between its

[1] I quote from the collected edition of Locke's works, London, 1777, vol. ii. p. 24. "Some Considerations," p. 36.

[2] In other places (*e.g.* p. 4) Locke calls interest a price for the "hire of money."

starting-point and its conclusion. If it be true that loan interest transfers the hard-earned wage of the man who works into the pocket of another man who does nothing, and whose money besides is a "barren thing," it is absolutely inconsistent to say that loan interest is nevertheless "equitable and lawful." That there is undoubtedly an analogy between interest and the profit from land rent, was very likely to lead logically to a conclusion involving land rent in the same condemnation as interest. To this Locke's theory would have presented sufficient support, since he expressly declares rent also to be the fruit of another man's industry. But with Locke the legitimacy of rent appears to have been beyond question.

But, however unsatisfactory Locke's theory of interest may be, there is one circumstance at any rate that confers on it an important interest for us; in the background of it stands the proposition that human labour produces all wealth. In the present case Locke has not expressed the proposition so much as made use of it, and has not, indeed, made a very happy use of it. But in another place he has given it clear utterance where he says: "For it is labour indeed that put the difference of value on everything."[1] We shall soon see how great a place this proposition is to have in the later development of the interest problem.

A certain affinity to Locke's conception of loan interest is shown somewhat later by Sir James Steuart. "The interest," he writes, "they pay for the money borrowed is inconsiderable when compared with the value *created* (as it were) by the proper employment of *their time and talents.*" "If it be said that this is a vague assertion, supported by no proof, I answer, that *the value of a man's work* may be estimated *by the proportion between the manufacture* when brought to market *and the first matter.*"[2]

The words I have emphasised indicate that Steuart, like Locke, looks upon the whole increment of value got by production as the product of the borrower's labour, and on loan interest, therefore, as a fruit of that labour.

[1] *Of Civil Government*, vol. ii. chap. v. § 40. See also Roscher, p. 95, etc.

[2] *Inquiry into the Principles of Political Economy*, 1767, vol. ii. book iv. part i. chap. viii. p. 137.

If, however, both Locke and Steuart were quite uncertain as to the nature of that which we now call the borrower's natural profit, they were far from making any mistake about the fact that loan interest has its origin and its foundation in this profit. Thus Steuart in one place writes: "In proportion, therefore, to the advantages to be reaped from borrowed money, the borrowers offer more or less for the use of it."[1]

Generally speaking, in England the literature on the subject took great pains to discuss the connection between loan interest and profit. In doing so it certainly did not surpass the Salmasian doctrine in clearness as to principles, but it enriched it by extending its knowledge of details. The favourite inquiry was, whether a high loan interest is the cause or the effect of a high profit. Hume passes judgment on the controversy by saying that they are alternately cause and effect. "It is needless," he says, "to inquire which of these circumstances, to wit, *low interest or low profits*, is the cause and which the effect. They both arise from an extensive commerce, and mutually forward each other. No man will accept of low profits where he can have high interest; and no man will accept of low interest where he can have high profits."[2]

Of more value than this somewhat superficial opinion is another discovery associated with the name of Hume. It was he who first clearly distinguished the conception of money from that of capital, and showed that the height of the interest rate in a country does not depend on the amount of currency that the country possesses, but on the amount of its riches or stocks.[3] But it was not till a later period that this important discovery was applied to the investigation of the source of interest.

How strange in the meantime the once widespread doctrine of the canonists had become to the busy England of the eighteenth century may be seen by the manner in which Bentham could treat the subject, towards the end of that century, in his *Defence of Usury*, 1787. He no longer thinks of seriously attempting to justify the taking of interest. The

[1] *Inquiry into the Principles of Political Economy*, 1767, vol. ii. book iv. part i. chap. iv. p. 117.

[2] "Of Interest," *Essays*, part. ii. chap. iv.

[3] *Ibid. passim.*

arguments of the ancient writers and of the canonists are only mentioned to afford welcome matter for witty remarks, and Aristotle, as the discoverer of the argument of the sterility of money, is bantered in the words: "As fate would have it, that great philosopher, with all his industry and all his penetration, notwithstanding the great number of pieces of money that had passed through his hands (more perhaps than ever passed through the hands of philosopher before or since), and notwithstanding the enormous pains he had bestowed on the subject of generation, had never been able to discover in any piece of money any organs for generating any other such piece."

Italy stood immediately under the eye of the Roman Church. But Italy was the country in Europe that earliest attained a great position in trade and commerce; and on that account it was bound to be the first to find the pressure of the canon prohibition unbearable. The general attitude towards it may be explained by two considerations; that nowhere in Europe did the prohibition of interest remain in fact more inoperative, and that nowhere in Europe was it so late before the theorists ventured to oppose the Church's statute.

Everything that could be done to evade the formally valid prohibition was done; and it seems that these attempts were sufficiently successful for all the requirements of practical life. The most convenient forms of evasion were offered by the traffic in bills, which had its home in Italy, and by the stipulation of *interesse* for "indemnification." The temporal legislation offered ready and willing assistance to such evasion from a very early period by allowing the interest to be arranged beforehand, at a fixed rate of percentage on the capital lent. It only fixed a maximum which could not be exceeded.[1]

On the other hand, no Italian writer appears to have made any open theoretic attack on the canon doctrine before the eighteenth century. Galiani in 1750 mentions Salmasius as the first who had given a complete statement of the doctrine of interest from the new point of view; and, in Italian literature previous to that time, the only mention he can find of the subject is the quarrel which had flared up a little before between the Marchese Maffei and the preaching monk Fra

[1] See the historical works of Vasco, *L'Usura Libera* (Scrittori Classici Italiani Parte Moderna, vol. xxxiv. p. 182, etc.; particularly pp. 195, 198, etc., 210, etc.)

Daniello Concina.[1] Other prominent writers of the same period usually quote among their predecessors Salmasius as most important, and after him some other foreigners, as Locke, Hume, and Forbonnais; but the first name that occurs among native writers is the Marchese Maffei.[2] Here again, in Italy also, we find Salmasius accepted as the pioneer of the new views.

The tardy acceptance which his doctrine met in that country does not appear to have been attended by any special improvement on it. There is only one writer who can be excepted from this criticism, Galiani. But he deals with the question of the nature and legitimacy of loan interest in a way that is altogether peculiar.

If interest, he says,[3] really were what it is usually taken to be, a profit or an advantage which the lender makes with his money, then indeed it would be objectionable, for "whatever profit, be it great or small, that is yielded by naturally barren money, is objectionable; nor can any one call such a profit the fruit of exertion, when the one who puts forth the exertion is the one who takes the loan, not the one who gives it" (p. 244).

But interest is not a true profit at all; it is only a supplementing of that which is needed to equalise service and counter-service. Properly speaking, service and counter-service should be of equal value. Since value is the relation in which things stand to our needs, we should be quite mistaken were we to seek for such an equivalence in an equality of weight, or in number of pieces, or in external form. What is required is simply an equality of use. Now in this respect present and future sums of money of equal amount are not of equal value, just as in bill transactions equally large sums of money are not of equal value at different places. And just as the profit of exchange (*cambio*), notwithstanding that it seems to be an additional sum (*soprappiù*), is in truth an equalisation, which, when added sometimes to the money on the spot, sometimes to the foreign money, establishes the equality of real value between the two, so is loan interest nothing else than the equalisation of the difference there is

[1] Galiani, *Della Moneta* (Scritt. Class. Ital. Parte Moderna, vol. iv. p. 240, etc.)

[2] *Impiego del Danaro.* Unfortunately I have not seen the book.

[3] *Della Moneta*, book v. chap. i.

between the value of present and future sums of money (p. 243, etc.)

In this interesting idea Galiani has hit on a new method of justifying loan interest, and one which relieves him from a certain doubtful line of argument that his predecessors were obliged to take. Salmasius and his followers, to avoid the reproach of destroying the equality between service and counter-service, were obliged to attempt to prove that in perishable as well as in durable things, and even in articles actually consumed at the beginning of the loan period, there is an enduring use which may be separately transferred, and for which a separate remuneration, namely, interest, is rightly claimed. This line of reasoning, always somewhat fatal, was rendered superfluous by the aspect which Galiani now gave to the argument.

But unfortunately the inference which Galiani draws from this idea is very unsatisfactory. The reason that present sums of money are, as a rule, more valuable than future sums he finds exclusively in the different degree of their security. A claim to future payment of a sum of money is exposed to many dangers, and on that account is less valued than an equally large present sum. In so far as interest is paid to balance these dangers, it appears in the light of an insurance premium. Galiani gives this conception very strong expression by speaking in one place of the "so-called fruit of money" as a price of heart-beats (*prezzo del batticuore*), p. 247; and at another time he uses the very words that that thing which is called the fruit of money might be more properly called the price of insurance (p. 252). This was of course thoroughly to misunderstand the nature of loan interest.

The way in which later Italian authors of the eighteenth century treated the interest problem is less worthy of notice. Even the more prominent men among them, such as Genovesi[1] and Beccaria,[2] as also those who wrote monographs on the subject, like Vasco,[3] follow for the most part in the tracks of the Salmasian doctrine, now become traditional.

[1] *Lezioni di Economia Civile*, 1769 (Scritt. Class. Ital. Parte Moderna, vol. ix. part ii. chap. xiii.)

[2] *Elementi di Economia Pubblica*, written 1769-71; first printed, 1804, in the collection of the Scrittori, vols. xi. and xii., particularly part iv. chaps. vi. and vii.

[3] *L'Usura Libera*, vol. xxxiv. of above collection.

The most worthy of mention among those is Beccaria. He draws a sharp distinction between *interesse* and *usura*. The former is the immediate use of a thing, the latter is the use of a use (*l'utilità dell' utilità*). An immediate use (*interesse*) is rendered by all goods. The special *interesse* of money consists of the use which the goods represented by it may render, for money is the common measure and representative of the value of all other goods. Since, in particular, every sum of money represents, or may represent, a definite piece of land, it follows that the *interesse* of the money is represented by the annual return of that land. Consequently it varies with the amount of this return, and the average rate of money-interesse is equalised with the average return of land (p. 116).

In this analysis the word *interesse* evidently means the same thing as we should call natural profit, and in it accordingly we may find an attempt—although a primitive one—to explain the existence and amount of natural interest by the possibility of a purchase of land. As we shall see later, however, the same thought had already, some years before, received much fuller treatment from another writer.

In one place Beccaria also touches on the influence of time, first brought forward by Galiani, and speaks of the analogy between exchange interest, which is an *interesse* of place, and loan interest, which is an *interesse* of time (p. 122), but he passes over it much more cursorily.

Catholic France was all this time far behind, both in theory and practice. Its state legislation against interest enjoyed for centuries the reputation of being the severest in Europe. At a time when in other countries it had been agreed either to allow the taking of interest quite openly, or to allow it under the very transparent disguise of previously arranged *interesse*, Louis XIV thought fit to renew the existing prohibition, and to extend it in such a way that even interest for commercial debts was forbidden,[1] Lyons being the only market exempted. A century later, when in other countries the long obsolete prohibitions of interest were scoffed at in the tone of a Sonnenfels or a Bentham, they remained in force and in baneful activity among the tribunals of France. It was only in the

[1] Vasco, p. 209.

year 1789, when so many institutions that still breathed the spirit of the middle ages were cleared away, that this institution also was got rid of. By a law of 12th October 1789 the prohibition of interest was formally rescinded, and its place taken by a maximum rate of 5 per cent.

French theory, like French legislation, held most religiously by the strictest standpoint of the canon. How little success Molinaeus had in the middle of the sixteenth century we have already seen. At the end of that century a writer so enlightened in other respects as Johannes Bodinus finds the prohibition fully justified; praises the wisdom of those legislators who publish it; and considers it safest to destroy it root and branch (*usurarum non modo radices sed etiam fibras omnes amputare*).[1] In the seventeenth century, it is true, the French Salmasius wrote brilliantly on the side of interest, but that was outside of France. In the eighteenth century the number of writers who take this side increases. Law already contends for the entire freeing of interest transactions, even from the fixed rate.[2] Melon pronounces interest a social necessity that cannot be refused, and leaves it to the theologians to reconcile their moral scruples with this necessity.[3] Montesquieu declares that lending a man money without interest is indeed a very good action, but one that can only be a matter of religious consideration, and not of civil law.[4] But notwithstanding, there are always writers who oppose such ideas, and contend for the old strict doctrine.

Among these late champions of the canon two are particularly prominent: the highly esteemed jurist Pothier and the physiocrat Mirabeau.

Pothier succeeded in collecting the most tenable arguments from the chaotic *répertoire* of the canon, and working them up with great skill and acuteness into a doctrine in which they really became very effective. I have added below the characteristic passage which has already attracted the attention of several writers on our subject.[5]

[1] *De Republica*, second edition, 1591, v. ii. p. 799, etc.

[2] *E.g.* *IIde. Mémoire sur les Banques*; *Economistes Financiers du xviii. Siècle*, Edition Daire, Paris, 1851, p. 571.

[3] *Essai Politique sur le Commerce*, ebenda p. 742.

[4] *Esprit des Lois*, xxii.

[5] The passage has been quoted by Rizy; by Turgot, *Mémoire sur les Prêts*

He was seconded—with more zeal than success—by the author of the *Philosophie Rurale*, Mirabeau.[1] Mirabeau's lucubrations on interest are among the most confused that have ever been written on the subject. A fanatical opponent of loan interest, he is inexhaustible in his arguments against it. He argues, among other things, that loaned money has no legitimate claim on payment. For, first, money has no natural use, but only *represents*. "But to obtain a profit from this representative character is to seek in a glass for the figure it represents." It is no argument then for the owners of money to say that they must live from the produce of their money, for to this it may be answered that they could change the money into other goods, and live from the produce obtained by hiring out those goods! Lastly, there is not the same wear and tear in the case of money as there is in the case of houses, furniture, and such like, and for that reason

d'Argent, § 26; and also by Knies, *Kredit*, part i. p. 347. It runs thus: "It is a fair claim that the values given in the case of a contract which is not gratuitous should be equal on either side, and that no party should give more than he has received, or receive more than he has given. Everything, therefore, that the lender may demand from the borrower over and above the principal sum, he demands over and above what he has given; for, if he get repayment of the principal sum, he receives the exact equivalent of what he gave. For things that can be used without being destroyed a hire may certainly be demanded, because, this use being separable at any moment (in thought at least) from the things themselves, it can be priced; it has a price distinct from the thing. So that, if I have given a thing of this sort to any one for his use, I am able to demand the hire, which is the price of the use that I have allowed him in it beyond the restitution of the thing itself, the thing having never ceased to be my property.

"It is not the same, however, with those objects that are known to lawyers as fungible goods—things that are consumed in the using. For since, in the using, these are necessarily destroyed, it is impossible in regard to them to imagine a use of the thing as distinct from the thing itself, and as having a price distinct from the thing itself. From this it follows that one cannot make over to another the using of a thing without making over to him wholly and entirely the thing itself, and transferring to him the property in it. If I lend you a sum of money for your use under the condition of paying me back as much again, then you receive from me simply that sum of money, and nothing more. The use that you will make of this sum of money is included in the right of property that you acquire in this sum. There is nothing that you have received outside of the sum of money. I have given you this sum, and nothing but this sum. I can therefore ask you to give me back nothing more than this amount lent, without being unjust; for justice would have it that only that should be claimed which was given."

[1] Amsterdam, 1764.

there should not, properly speaking, be any charge made to cover wear and tear.[1]

Probably the reader will think these arguments weak enough. But Mirabeau, in his blind zeal, gets still deeper. He cannot help seeing that the debtor, by employing the money (*emploi*), may obtain means to pay interest for the capital borrowed. But even this he turns against interest. He argues from it that the borrower must always suffer injury, because it is impossible to establish an equality between interest and *emploi*. One does not know how much agriculture will yield to the borrowing agriculturist. Unforeseen accidents happen, and *on that account* the borrower will *always* lose![2] And more than this. In one place, from the very natural fact that any private person is more willing to take interest than to pay it, he deduces, in all seriousness, an argument to prove that the paying of interest must be hurtful to the borrower![3]

Fortified by reasoning like this, his condemnation of money interest is not lacking in vigour. "Take it all in all," he says,[4] "money interest ruins society by giving incomes into the hands of people who are neither owners of land nor producers, nor industrial workers, and these people can only be looked upon as hornets, who live by robbing the hoards of the bees of society."

But for all that Mirabeau cannot avoid admitting that interest may be justified in certain cases. Sorely against his inclination, therefore, he is compelled to break through the principle of the prohibition and make some exceptions, the selection of which is based on quite arbitrary and untenable distinctions.[5]

Seldom can there have been a more grateful task than was the refutation of this doctrine in the second half of the eighteenth century. Long ago smitten with internal decay—detested by some, despised by others—forced to lean on very pitiful scientific props—it had long outlived its life, and only raised its head in the present like some old ruin. The task was taken up by Turgot, and performed with ability as remarkable as its results were brilliant. His *Mémoire sur les Prêts*

[1] P. 269, etc.
[2] Pp. 257-262.
[3] P. 267.
[4] P. 284.
[5] See particularly pp. 276, 290, 292, 298, etc.

d'Argent[1] may be named as companion-piece to Salmasius's writings on Usury. It is true that the student of to-day will find in his reasoning some good arguments, and not a few bad ones. But, good and bad alike, they are given with so much *verve* and acuteness, with such rhetorical and dialectical skill, and with such striking play of fancy, that we can easily understand how the effect on his times was nothing less than triumphant.

As the charm of his work lies not so much in the ideas themselves,—which for the most part we have already discussed in the arguments of his predecessors,—as in the charming way in which they are put, it would only repay us to go thoroughly into the contents of the *Mémoire* if a great deal of it were reproduced in his own words, which space forbids. I content myself, therefore, with bringing out some of the more marked features of Turgot's treatment.

The weightiest justification of interest he finds in the right of property which the creditor has in his own money. In virtue of this he has an "inviolable" right to dispose of the money as he will, and to lay such conditions on its alienation and hire as seem to him good—*e.g.* the condition of interest being duly paid (§ 23, etc.) Evidently a crooked argument which might prove the legitimacy and inoffensiveness of a usurious interest of 100 per cent, just as well as the legitimacy of interest in general.

The argument based on the barrenness of money Turgot dismisses on the same grounds as those taken by his predecessors (§ 25).

He gives special attention to the reasoning of Pothier just mentioned. Pothier's thesis that, in justice, service and counter-service should be equal to each other, and that this is not the case in the loan, he answers by saying that objects which, freely and without fraud or force, are exchanged against each other always have, in a certain sense, equal value. To the fatal argument that, in the case of a perishable thing, it is not possible to conceive of any use separate from the thing itself, he answers by charging his opponents with legal hair-splitting and metaphysical abstraction, and brings forward the old and favourite analogy between the hiring of money and

[1] Written in 1769; published twenty years later, 1789. I quote from the collected edition of Turgot's work, Daire, Paris, 1844, vol. i. pp. 106-152.

the hiring of any durable thing like a diamond. "What!" he says, "that some one should be able to make me pay for the petty use that I make of a piece of furniture or a trinket, and that it should be a crime to charge me anything for the immense advantage that I get from the use of a sum of money for the same time; and all because the subtle intellect of a lawyer can separate in the one case the use of a thing from the thing itself, and in the other case cannot! It is really too ridiculous!" (p. 128).

But a moment later Turgot himself does not hesitate at metaphysical abstraction and legal hair-splitting. To refute the argument that the debtor becomes proprietor of the borrowed money, and that its use consequently belongs to him, he makes out a property in the value of the money, and distinguishes it from the property in the piece of metal; the latter of course passing over to the debtor, the former remaining behind with the creditor.

Very remarkable, finally, are some passages in which Turgot, following Galiani's example, emphasises the influence of time on the valuation of goods. In one place he draws the parallel already familiar to us between exchange and loans. Just as in exchange transactions we give less money in one place to receive a greater sum in another place, so in the loan we give less money at one point of time to receive more money at another point of time. The reason of both phenomena is, that the difference of time, like that of place, indicates a real difference in the value of money (§ 23). On another occasion he alludes to the notorious difference that exists between the value of a present sum and the value of a sum only obtainable at a future period (§ 27); and a little later he exclaims: "If these gentlemen suppose that a sum of 1000 francs and a promise of 1000 francs possess exactly the same value, they put forward a still more absurd supposition; for if these two things were of equal value, why should any one borrow at all?"

Unfortunately, however, Turgot has not followed out this pregnant idea. It is, I might say, thrown in with his other arguments, without having any organic connection with them; indeed, properly speaking, it stands in opposition to them. For if interest and the replacement of capital only make up *together* the equivalent of the capital that was lent, the interest is then a part equivalent of the principal sum. How then can it be a payment for a separate use of the principal sum, as Turgot has just taken so much trouble to prove?

We may look on Turgot's controversy with Pothier as the closing act of the three hundred years' war which jurisprudence and political economy had waged against the old canon doctrine of interest. After Turgot the doctrine disappeared from the sphere of political economy. Within the sphere of theology it dragged out a kind of life for some twenty years longer, till, finally, in our century this also ended. When the Roman Penitentiary pronounced the taking of interest to be allowable, even without any peculiar title, the Church itself had confirmed the defeat of its erstwhile doctrine.[1]

Pausing for a moment, let us look back critically over the period we have traversed. What are its results; what has science gained during it towards the elucidation of the interest problem?

The ancient and the canon writers had said, Loan interest is an unjust defrauding of the borrower by the lender, for money is barren, and there is no special "use" of money which the lender may justly sell for a separate remuneration. In opposition to this the new doctrine runs, Loan interest is just; for, first, money is *not* barren so long as, by proper employment, the lender might make a profit with it, and by lending it gives up the possibility of this profit in favour of the borrower; and, second, there *is* a use of capital that is separable from capital itself, and may be sold separately from it.

If we put aside in the meantime the latter more formal point—it will come up again later in another connection—the central idea of the new doctrine is the suggestion that capital produces fruits to him who employs it. After an immense expenditure of ingenuity, dialectic, polemic, and verbiage, at bottom it is the emergence of the same idea that Adam Smith in his wonderfully simple way expressed shortly

[1] Funk, *Zins und Wucher*, Tübingen, 1868, p. 116. On the reception that this liberal decision of Rome, 18th August 1830, met from a portion of the Frenc clergy, see Molinari, *Cours d'Economie Politique*, second edition, vol. i. p. 333.

afterwards in the words that contain his solution of the whole question whether interest is justifiable or not: "As something can everywhere be made by the use of money, something ought everywhere to be paid for the use of it."[1] Translated into our modern terminology, this idea would run, "There is loan interest because there is natural interest."

Thus the theory of Salmasius and his followers in substance amounts to explaining contract interest or loan interest from the existence of natural interest.

How much did the elucidation of the interest problem gain by this? That the gain was not inconsiderable is attested by the fact that the intellectual labour of centuries was needed to secure credence for the new doctrine, in the face of opposing impressions and prejudices. But just as certain is it that, when this explanation was given, much remained still to be done. The problem of loan interest was not solved; it was only shifted a stage farther back. To the question, Why does the lender get from his loaned capital a permanent income not due to work? the answer was given, Because he could have obtained it if he had employed the capital himself. But why could he have obtained this income himself? This last question obviously is the first to point to the true origin of interest; but, in the period of which we have been speaking, not only was this question not answered, it was not even put.

All attempts at explanation got the length of this fact, that the man who has a capital in his hand can make a profit with it. But here they halt. They accept this as a fact without in the least attempting to further explain it. Thus Molinaeus, with his proposition that money, assisted by human exertion, brings forth fruit, and with his appeal to everyday experience. Thus Salmasius himself, with his delightful badinage over the fruitfulness of money, where he simply appeals to the fact without explaining it. And thus too even the later and most advanced economists of the whole period; such men as Locke, Law, Hume, James Steuart, Justi, Sonnenfels. Now and then they advance extremely clear and thorough statements of how loan interest is bound to emerge from the possibility of making a profit, and in the amount of

[1] *Wealth of Nations*, book ii. chap. iv.

that profit must find the measure of its own amount.[1] But not one of them ever comes to the question as to the why and wherefore of that profit.[2]

What Salmasius and his time had done for the interest problem cannot be better illustrated than by comparing it with the problem of land-rent. Salmasius—of course under accessory circumstances that made it much more difficult—did for the interest problem what never required to be done for the land-rent problem, just because it was too self-evident; he proved that the hirer pays the rent he has agreed to pay because that which is hired produces it. But he failed to do for the interest problem—indeed, did not in the least try to do—the one thing that required scientific effort in the sphere of land-rent; he did not explain why that which bears a rent when hired out should bear a rent if it remain in the hands of its owner.

Thus everything that had been done in the period we have just been considering was, as it were, the driving back of an advanced post on the main army. The problem of loan interest is pursued till it falls in with the general problem of interest. But this general problem is neither mastered nor even attacked; at the end of the period the heart of the interest problem is as good as untouched.

All the same, the period was not quite barren of results as

[1] *E.g.* Sonnenfels, *Handlung*, fifth edition, pp. 488, 497; Steuart, book iv. part i. p. 24; Hume, as above, p. 60. See above, pp. 42, 47.

[2] Some historians of theory, who are at the same time adherents of the Productivity theory (which we have to examine later), such as Roscher, Funk, and Endemann, are fond of ascribing to the writers of this period "presentiments" of the "productivity of capital," even "insight" into it; and of claiming them as forerunners of that theory. I think this is a misunderstanding. These writers do speak of the "fruitfulness" of money, and of all sorts of other things, but this expression with them serves rather to name the fact that certain things bring forth a profit than to explain it. They simply call everything "fruitful" that yields a profit or a "fruit," and it does not occur to them to give any formal theoretical explanation of the origin of these profits. This is very plain from the writings of Salmasius on the subject. When Salmasius calls air, disease, death, prostitution, "fruitful" (see note to p. 39 above), it is evidently only a strong way of putting the fact that the state which lays taxes on the air, the physician, the gravedigger, the prostitute, all draw a profit from the things just named. But it is just as evident that Salmasius did not in the least seriously think of deriving the sexton's fee from a productive power that resides in death. And the fruitfulness of money, which Salmasius wished to illustrate by comparing it with these, is not to be taken any more seriously.

regards the solution of the chief problem; it at least prepared the way for future work by elevating natural interest, the real subject of the problem, out of confused and hesitating statements, and bringing it gradually to clear presentation. The fact that every one who works with a capital makes a profit had long been known. But it was a long time before any one clearly distinguished the nature of this profit, and there was a tendency to ascribe the whole of it to the undertaker's activity. Thus Locke himself looks on the interest which the borrower pays to the lender as the "fruit of another man's labour," and, while conceding that the borrowed money employed in business may produce fruit, expressly ascribes the possibility of this to the exertion of the borrower. Now when, in justifying interest, one was led to accent the influence of capital in the emergence of such profits, he was bound in the end to come to see clearly that a part of the undertaker's profit was a branch of income *sui generis*, not to be confounded with the produce of labour—was, in fact, a peculiar profit of capital. This insight, which is to be found quite clearly in germ in Molinaeus and Salmasius, comes out with perfect distinctness at the end of the period in the writings of Hume and others. But once attention was called to the phenomenon of natural interest, it was inevitable that, sooner or later, people should begin to ask about the causes of this phenomenon. And with this the history of the problem entered on a new epoch.

CHAPTER III

TURGOT'S FRUCTIFICATION THEORY

So far as my knowledge of economical literature goes, I am bound to consider Turgot as the first who tried to give a scientific explanation of Natural Interest on capital, and accordingly as the first economist who showed the full extent of the problem.

Before Turgot the times had been quite unfavourable to any scientific investigation into natural interest. It was only very recently that people had come to clear consciousness that in this they had to deal with an independent and peculiar branch of income. But besides—and this was of still greater moment—there had been no outward occasion to draw discussion to the nature of this income. The problem of loan interest had been worked at from very early times, because loan interest had been attacked from the field of practical life; and it was thus early attacked because there had been from the beginning a hostile tension between the interests of the parties concerned in the loan contract, the creditors and the debtors. It was quite different in this respect with natural interest. People had scarcely learned to distinguish it with certainty from the reward due to the employer's personal labour, and in any case they were still indifferent about it. The power of capital was yet insignificant. Between capital and labour, the two parties concerned in natural interest, scarcely any opposition had yet shown itself; at all events it had not developed into any sharp opposition of classes. So far, therefore, no one was hostile to this form of profit on capital, and consequently no one had any occasion from outside to defend it, or to make any thorough inquiry into its nature.

If, under such circumstances, there was any one to whom it occurred to do so, it could only be some systematic thinker with whom theorising was a necessity that took the place of the external impulse. But up till that time there had been no true systematiser of political economy.

The Physiocrats were the first to bring in a real system. For a long time, however, even they passed over our problem without consideration. Quesnay, the founder of the school, so little comprehends the nature of natural interest that he sees in it replacement costs—a kind of reserve fund, out of which the loss, in wearing out of capital and by unforeseen accidents, is to be defrayed—rather than a net income of the capitalist.[1]

Mercier de la Rivière,[2] more correctly, recognises that capital produces a net profit; but he only points out that there must be this profit on the capital that is employed in agriculture, if agriculture is not to be abandoned for other pursuits. He does not go on to ask why capital in general should yield interest. As little does Mirabeau, who, as we saw, has written a great deal on the subject of interest, and has written very badly.[3]

It was Turgot, then, the greatest of the physiocrats, who was also first among them to seek for a fuller explanation of the fact of natural interest. Even his way of treating the problem is modest and naïve enough: it is easy to see that it was not the fiery zeal in a great social problem that forced him to take up the pen, but only the need for clear consistency in his ideas—a need that would, if necessary, be content with an explanation of very moderate depth, provided only it found a plausible formula.

[1] "Les intérêts des avances de l'établissement des cultivateurs doivent donc être compris dans leur reprises annuelles. Ils servent à faire face à ces grands accidents et à l'entretien journalier des richesses d'exploitation, qui demandent à être réparés sans cesse" (*Analyse du Tableau Economique*, Edition Daire, p. 62). See also the more detailed statement that precedes the passage quoted.

[2] *L'Ordre Naturel*, Edition Daire, p. 459.

[3] On his attitude towards loan interest see above, p. 53. As regards natural interest, he approves of interest as regards capital invested in agriculture (*Philosophie Rurale*, p. 83, and then p. 295) without going any deeper in explanation; but he speaks of what is gained in commerce and industry in hesitating terms, looking on it rather as a fruit of activity, *de la profession*, than of capital (p. 278).

In the *Mémoire sur les Prêts d'Argent*, already known to us, Turgot simply deals with the question of loan interest. His more comprehensive interest theory is developed in his chief work, *Réflexions sur la Formation et la Distribution des Richesses*.[1] To be correct, it is not so much developed as contained in it; for Turgot does not put the question as to the origin of interest formally, nor is the consideration he devotes to it a very connected one. What we find is a number of separate paragraphs (§§ 57, 58, 59, 61, 63, 68, and 71), containing a series of observations, out of which we have to put together his theory on the origin of interest for ourselves.[2]

Seeing that this theory bases the entire interest of capital on the possibility always open to the owner of capital to find for it an ulterior fructification through the purchase of rent-bearing land, I propose to call it shortly the Fructification theory.

The argument is as follows. The possession of land guarantees the obtaining of a permanent income without labour, in the shape of land-rent. But since movable goods, independently of land, also permit of being used, and on that account obtain an independent value, we may compare the value of both classes of goods; we may price land in movable goods, and exchange it for them. The exchange price, as in the case of all goods, depends on the relation of supply and demand (§ 85). At any time it forms a multiple of the yearly income that may be drawn from the land, and it very often gets its designation from this circumstance. A piece of land, we say, is sold for twenty or thirty or forty years' purchase, if the price amounts to twenty or thirty or forty times the annual rent of the land. The amount of the multiple, again, depends on the relation of supply and demand; that is, whether more or fewer people wish to buy or sell land (§ 88).

[1] First published in 1776. I quote from Daire's collected edition of Turgot's works, Paris, 1844, vol. i.

[2] The outward want of form in Turgot's explanation of interest has led a usually exact investigator of his works to maintain that Turgot does not explain interest (Sivers, *Turgots Stellung*, etc., Hildebrand's *Jahrbücher*, vol. xxii. pp. 175, 183, etc.) This is a mistake. It is, however true, as we shall see, that his explanation does not go particularly deep.

In virtue of these circumstances every sum of money, and, generally speaking, every capital, is the equivalent of a piece of land yielding an income equal to a certain percentage on capital (§ 59).

Since in this way the owner of a capital, by buying land, is able to obtain from it a permanent yearly income, he will not be inclined to put his capital in an industrial (§ 61), agricultural (§ 63), or commercial (§ 68) undertaking, if he cannot —leaving out of account compensation for all ordinary kinds of costs and trouble—expect just as large a profit from his capital thus employed as he could obtain through the purchase of land. On that account capital, in all these branches of employment, must yield a profit.

Thus, then, is the economical necessity of natural interest on capital first explained. Loan interest is deduced from it simply in this way: the undertaker without capital finds himself willing, and economically too may find himself willing, to give up to him who trusts him with a capital a part of the profit which the capital brings in (§ 71). So in the end all forms of interest are explained as the necessary result of the circumstance, that any one who has a capital may exchange it for a piece of land bearing a rent.

It will be noticed that in this line of thought Turgot takes for his foundation a circumstance which had been appealed to for some centuries by the defenders of loan interest, from Calvin downward. But Turgot makes an essentially different and much more thorough-going use of this circumstance. His predecessors availed themselves of it occasionally, and by way of illustration. Turgot makes it the centre of his system. They did not see in it the sole ground of loan interest, but co-ordinated with it the possibility of making a profit from capital engaged in commerce, industry, etc. Turgot puts it by itself at the head of everything. Finally, they had only used it to explain loan interest. Turgot explains the entire phenomenon of interest by it. Thus was built up a new doctrine, although out of old materials,—the first general theory of interest.

As regards the scientific value of this theory, the fate which has befallen it is very significant. I cannot recollect ever reading a formal refutation of it: people have tacitly declared it unsatisfactory, and passed on to seek for other explanations. It seems too plausible to be refuted; too slight to base anything on. We leave it with the feeling that it has not got down to the last root of interest, even if we cannot give any very accurate account of why and where it fails.

To supply such an account seems to me at the present time by no means a work of superfluity. In doing so I shall not be merely fulfilling a formal duty which I imposed on myself when I undertook to write a *critical* history of theory. In pointing out where and how Turgot failed I hope to make perfectly clear what the heart of the problem is, and what it is that every earnest attempt at solution must reckon with, and thus to prepare the way for the profitable pursuit of our future task. The example of a very lively writer of our own day shows that we are not yet so far past Turgot's line of thought as we might perhaps think.[1]

Turgot's explanation of interest is unsatisfactory, because it is an explanation in a circle. The circle is only concealed by the fact that Turgot breaks off his explanation at that very point where the next step would inevitably have brought him back to the point from which he started.

The case stands thus. Turgot says: A definite capital must yield a definite interest, because it may buy a piece of land bearing a definite rent. To take a concrete example. A capital of £10,000 must yield £500 interest, because with £10,000 a man can buy a piece of land bearing a rent of £500.[2]

But the possibility of such a purchase is not in itself an ultimate fact, nor is it a fact that carries its explanation on its face. Thus we are forced to inquire further: Why can a person with a capital of £10,000 buy a rent-bearing piece of land in general and a piece of land bearing £500 rent in particular? Even Turgot feels that this question may be put, and must be put, for he attempts to give an answer to it. He appeals to the relation of demand and supply, as at any moment furnishing the ground for a definite relation of price between capital and land.[3]

But is this a full and satisfactory answer to our ques-

[1] See the chapter on Henry George's Later Fructification theory.

[2] Usually the rent of land is somewhat less than interest on the price paid. But this circumstance, fully explained by Turgot (*Réflexions*, § 84), has no influence at all on the principle, and may here be simply neglected.

[3] "If four bushels of wheat, the net product of an arpent of land, be worth

tion? Certainly not. The man who, when asked what determines a certain price, answers, "Demand and supply," offers a husk for a kernel. The answer may be allowable in a hundred cases, where it can be assumed that the one who asks the question knows sufficiently well what the kernel is, and can himself supply it. But it is not sufficient when what is wanted is an explanation of a problem of which we do not yet know the nature. If it were sufficient, we might be quite content to settle the whole problem of interest simply by the formula; demand and supply regulate the prices of all goods in such a way that a profit always remains over to the capitalist. For the interest problem throughout relates to phenomena of price; *e.g.* to the fact that the borrower pays a price for the "use of capital"; or to the fact that the price of the finished product is higher than the price of its costs, in virtue of which a profit remains over to the undertaker. But certainly no one would find this a satisfactory explanation.

We must therefore ask further, What deeper causes lie behind demand and supply, and govern their movements in such a way that a capital of £10,000 can regularly be exchanged for a rent-bearing piece of land in general, and a piece of land bearing £500 rent in particular? To this question Turgot gives no answer, unless we care to look on the somewhat vague words at the beginning of § 57 as such; and if so the answer cannot in any way be thought satisfactory: "Those who had much movable wealth could employ it not only in the cultivation of land, but also in the different departments of industry. The facility of accumulating this movable wealth, and of making a use of it quite independent of land, had the effect that one could value the pieces of land, and compare their value with that of movable wealth."

But if we take up the explanation at the point where Turgot broke off, and carry it a little farther, we shall dis-

six sheep, the arpent which produced them might have been given for a certain value—a greater value of course, but always easy to determine in the same manner as the price of all other commodities, *i.e.* first by discussion between the two contracting parties, and afterwards by the price current established by the competition of those who wish to exchange lands against cattle, and of those who wish to give cattle to get lands (§ 57). It is evident, again, that this price, or this number of years' purchase, ought to vary according as there are more or less people who wish to sell or buy lands, just as the price of all other commodities varies by reason of the different proportion between supply and demand" (§ 58).

cover that this interest, which Turgot thought to explain as the *result* of the exchange relation between land and capital, is in reality the *cause* of this exchange relation. That is to say, whether it is twenty or thirty or forty times the annual rent that is asked or offered for a piece of land, depends chiefly on the percentage which the capital that buys it would obtain if otherwise employed. That piece of land which yields £500 rent will be worth £10,000 if and because the rate of interest on capital amounts to 5 per cent. It will be worth £5000 if and because the interest rate is 10 per cent. It will be worth £20,000 if and because capital bears only 2½ per cent interest. Thus, instead of the existence and height of interest being explained by the exchange relation between land and capital, this exchange relation itself must be explained by the existence and height of interest. Nothing has been done, therefore, to explain interest, and the whole argument moves in a circle.

I should have confidence in finishing my criticism of Turgot's doctrine at this point, if I did not feel myself bound to be more than usually careful in all cases where the nature of reciprocal action between economic phenomena is concerned. For I know that, in the complexity of economical phenomena, it is exceedingly difficult to determine with certainty the starting-point of a chain of reciprocal causes and effects, and I am aware that, in deciding on such points, we are particularly exposed to the danger of being misled by dialectic. I should not like, therefore, to force on the reader the opinion that Turgot here made a mistake, without having removed every suspicion on the point by going over the proof again; particularly as this will give us a good opportunity of putting the character of our problem in a clearer light.

Accidents apart, a piece of land will yield its rent for a practically infinite series of years. The possession of it assures the owner and his heirs the amount of the yearly use, not for twenty or forty times only, but for many hundred times—almost for an infinite number of times. But as a matter of common experience this infinite series of uses, which, added together, represent a colossal sum of income, is regularly sold for a fraction of this sum—for twenty up to forty times the year's use—and this is the fact we wish explained.

In explanation it cannot be enough to point in a superficial way to the state of demand and supply. For if demand and supply are at all times in such a position that this remarkable result takes place, the regular recurrence must rest on deeper grounds, and these deeper grounds demand investigation.

In passing I may dismiss the hypothesis, which may have occurred to the reader, that the reason of the low purchase price is that the owner only takes into consideration those uses which he himself may hope to obtain from the land, and neglects all that lie outside and beyond these. If this hypothesis were correct, then, seeing that the average life of man, and therefore of landowners, has not varied very much in historical times, the proportion of the value of land to the rent of land must have remained tolerably constant. But this is by no means the case. Indeed we see that proportion varying from ten to fifty fold, in visible sympathy with the rate of interest at the time.

There must, therefore, be another reason for this striking phenomenon.

I think we should all agree in pointing to the following as the true reason;—in valuing a piece of land, we make a discounting calculation. Thus we value the many hundred years' use of a piece of land at only twenty times the annual use when the rate of interest is 5 per cent, and at only twenty-five times the annual use when the rate is 4 per cent, because we discount the value of the future uses; that is, we estimate them in to-day's value at a smaller amount, *pro rata temporis et usurarum*, exactly on the same principle as we estimate the present capital value of a limited or perpetual claim on rent.

If this is so, and I do not think it will be doubted, then the capital valuation of land to which Turgot appealed in explanation of the phenomenon of interest, is itself nothing more than one of the many forms in which that phenomenon meets us in economic life. For that phenomenon is protean. It meets us sometimes as the explicit payment of a loan interest; sometimes as payment of a hire which leaves a "net use" to the owner after deduction of a quota for wear and tear; sometimes as the difference in price between product and costs, which falls to the undertaker as profit; sometimes as the prior deduction by the creditor from the amount of the loan granted to the debtor; sometimes as the raising of the purchase money in cases of postponed payment; sometimes as the limitation of the purchase money for claims, prerogatives, and privileges not yet due; sometimes, finally—to mention an instance closely related, indeed essentially the same—as the lowering of the purchase money paid for uses inseparable from a piece of land, but only available at a later date.

To trace the profit that capital obtains in commerce and industry to the possibility of acquiring land in exchange for definite sums of capital, is, therefore, nothing else than to refer from one phenomenal form of interest to another which is as much in need of explanation as the first. Why do we obtain interest on capital? why do we discount the value of future rates of payment or rates of use? These are evidently only two different forms of the question which puts the same riddle. And the solution of it gains nothing from a kind of explanation that begins with the former question, only to come to a stand before the latter one.

CHAPTER IV

ADAM SMITH AND THE DEVELOPMENT OF THE PROBLEM

It has never, I think, been the good fortune of any founder of a scientific system to think out to the very end even the more important ideas that constitute his system. The strength and lifetime of no single man are sufficient for that. It is enough if some few of the ideas which have to play the chief part in the system are put on a perfectly safe foundation, and analysed in all their ramifications and complexities. It is a great deal if, over and above that, an equal carefulness falls to the lot of a few other favoured members of the system. But in all cases the most ambitious spirit must be content to build up a great deal that is insecure, and to fit into his system, on cursory examination, ideas which it was not permitted him to work out.

We must keep these considerations before us if we would rightly appreciate Adam Smith's attitude towards our problem.

Adam Smith has not overlooked the problem of interest; neither has he worked it out. He deals with it as a great thinker may deal with an important subject which he often comes across, but has not time or opportunity to go very deeply into. He has adopted a certain proximate but still vague explanation. The more indefinite this explanation is, the less does it bind him to strict conclusions; and a many-sided mind like Adam Smith's, seeing all the many different ways in which the problem can be put, but lacking the control which the possession of a distinct theory gives, could scarcely fail to fall into all sorts of wavering and contradictory expressions. Thus we have the peculiar phenomenon that, while Adam Smith has not laid down any distinct theory of interest, the germs of almost all the later and conflicting theories are to be found, with more or less distinctness, in his scattered observations. We find the same phenomenon in Adam Smith as regards many other questions.

The line of thought which seems to commend itself principally to him as explaining natural interest occurs in very similar language in the sixth and eighth chapters of book i. of the *Wealth of Nations*. It amounts to this, that there must be a profit from capital, because otherwise the capitalist would have no interest in spending his capital in the productive employment of labourers.[1]

General expressions like these have of course no claim to stand for a complete theory.[2] There is no reasoned attempt in them to show what we are to represent as the actual connecting links between the psychological motive of the capitalist's self-interest and the final fixing of market prices which leave a difference between costs and proceeds that we call interest. But yet, if we take those expressions in connection with a later passage,[3] where Smith sharply opposes the "future profit" that rewards the resolution of the capitalist to the "present enjoyment" of immediate consumption, we may recognise the first germs of that theory which Senior worked out later on under the name of the Abstinence theory.

In the same way as Adam Smith asserts the necessity of interest, and leaves it without going any deeper in the way of proof, so does he avoid making any systematic investigation of the important question of the source of undertaker's profit. He contents himself with making a few passing observa-

[1] "In exchanging the complete manufacture either for money, for labour, or for other goods, over and above what may be sufficient to pay the price of the materials and the wages of the workmen, something must be given for the profits of the undertaker of the work, who hazards his stock in the adventure. . . . He could have no interest to employ them unless he expected from the sale of their work something more than what was sufficient to replace his stock to him; and he could have no interest to employ a great stock rather than a small one unless his profits were to bear some proportion to the extent of his stock" (M'Culloch's edition of 1863, p. 22). The second passage runs: "And who would have no interest to employ him unless he was to share in the produce of his labour, or unless his stock was to be replaced to him with a profit" (p. 30).

[2] See also Pierstorff, *Lehre vom Unternehmergewinn*, Berlin, 1875, p. 6; and Platter, "Der Kapitalgewinn bei Adam Smith" (Hildebrand's *Jahrbücher*, vol. xxv. p. 317, etc.)

[3] Book ii. chap. i. p. 123, in M'Culloch's edition.

tions on the subject. Indeed in different places he gives two contradictory accounts of this profit. According to one account, the profit of capital arises from the circumstance, that, to meet the capitalist's claim to profit, buyers have to submit to pay something more for their goods than the value which these goods would get from the labour expended on them. According to this explanation, the source of interest is an increased value given to the product over that value which labour creates; but no explanation of this increase in value is given. According to the second account, interest is a deduction which the capitalist makes in his own favour from the return to labour, so that the workers do not receive the full value created by them, but are obliged to share it with the capitalist. According to this account, profit is a part of the value created by labour and kept back by capital.

Both accounts are to be found in a great number of passages; and these passages, oddly enough, sometimes stand quite close to each other, as, *e.g.* in the sixth chapter of the first book.

Adam Smith has been speaking in that chapter of a past time,—of course a mythical time,—when the land was not yet appropriated, and when an accumulation of capital had not yet begun, and has made the remark that, at that time, the quantity of labour required for the production of goods would be the sole determinant of their price. He continues: "As soon as stock has accumulated in the hands of particular persons, some of them will naturally employ it in setting to work industrious people, whom they will supply with materials and subsistence, in order to make a profit by the sale of their work, or by what their labour adds to the value of the materials. In exchanging the complete manufacture either for money, for labour, or for other goods, over and above what may be sufficient to pay the price of the materials and the wages of the workmen, something must be given for the profits of the undertaker of the work, who hazards his stock in this adventure."

This sentence, when taken with the opposite remark of the previous paragraph (that, in primitive conditions, labour is the sole determinant of price), very clearly expresses the opinion that the capitalist's claim of interest causes a rise in the price of the product, and is met from this raised price. But Adam Smith immediately goes on to say: "The value which the workman adds to the material, therefore, resolves itself in this case into two parts, of which the one pays the wages, the other the profits of the employer upon the whole stock of materials and wages which he advanced." Here again the price of the product is looked upon as exclusively determined by the quantity of labour expended, and the claim of interest is said to be met by a part of the return which the worker has produced.

We meet the same contradiction, put even more strikingly, a page farther on.

"In this state of things," says Adam Smith, "the whole produce of labour does not always belong to the labourer. He must in most cases share it with the owner of the stock which employs him." This is an evident paraphrase of the second account. But immediately after that come the words: "Neither is the quantity of labour commonly employed in acquiring or producing any commodity, the only circumstance which can regulate the quantity which it ought commonly to purchase, command, or exchange for. An additional quantity, it is evident, must be due for the profits of the stock which advanced the wages and furnished the materials of that labour." He could scarcely have said more plainly that the effect of a claim of interest is to raise prices without curtailing the wages of labour.

Later on he says alternately: "As in a civilised community there are but few commodities of which the exchangeable value arises from labour only, rent and profit contributing largely to that of the far greater part of them, so the annual produce of its labour will always be sufficient to purchase or command a much greater quantity of labour than was employed in raising, preparing, and bringing that produce to market" (first account, chap. vi.) "The produce of almost all other labour is liable to the like deduction of profit. In all arts and manufactures the greater part of the workmen stand in need of a master to advance them the materials of their work, and their wages and maintenance till it be completed. He shares in the produce of their labour, or in the value which it adds to the materials upon which it is bestowed; and in this consists his profit" (second account, chap. viii.)

"High or low wages and profit are the causes of high or low price; high or low rent is the effect of it" (first account, chap. xi.)

Contradictions like these on the part of such an eminent thinker admit, I think, of only one explanation;—that Adam Smith had not thoroughly thought out the interest problem; and—as is usual with those who have only imperfectly mastered a subject—was not very particular in his choice of expressions, but allowed himself to be swayed very much by the changing impressions which the subject may have made on him from time to time.

Adam Smith, then, has no perfected theory of interest.[1] But the suggestions he threw out were all destined to fall on fruitful soil. His casual remark on the necessity of interest was developed later into the Abstinence theory. In the same way the two accounts he gave of the source of interest were taken up by his followers, logically carried out, and raised into principles of independent theories. With the first account—that interest is paid out of an additional value which the employment of capital calls into existence—are connected the later Productivity theories. With the second account—that interest is paid out of the return to labour—are connected the Socialist theories of interest. Thus the most important of later theories trace their pedigree back to Adam Smith.

The position taken by Adam Smith towards the question may be called that of a complete neutrality. He is neutral in his theoretical exposition, for he takes the germs of distinct theories and puts them beside each other, without giving any one of them a distinct prominence over the others. And he is neutral in his practical judgment, for he maintains the same reserve, or rather the same contradictory hesitancy, both in praise and blame of interest. Sometimes he commends the capitalists as benefactors of the human race, and as authors of enduring blessing;[2] sometimes he represents them

[1] When Platter in the essay above mentioned (p. 71) comes to the conclusion that, "if Smith's system be taken strictly, profit on capital appears unjustifiable," it could only be by laying all the weight on the one half of Smith's expressions, and leaving the other out of account as contradictory to his other principles.

[2] Book ii. chap. iii.

as a class who live on deductions from the produce of other people's labour, and compares them significantly with people "who love to reap where they never sowed."[1]

In Adam Smith's time the relations of theory and practice still permitted such a neutrality, but it was not long allowed to his followers. Changed circumstances compelled them to show their colours on the interest question, and the compulsion was certainly not to the disadvantage of the science.

The special requirements of economic theory could not any longer put up with uncertain makeshifts. Adam Smith had spent his life in laying down the foundations of his system. His followers, finding the foundations laid, had now time to take up those questions that had been passed over. The development now reached by the related problems of land-rent and wages gave a strong inducement to pursue the interest problem. There was a very complete theory of land-rent; there was a theory of wages scarcely less complete. Nothing was more natural than that systematic thinkers should now begin to ask in earnest about the third great branch of income—the whence and wherefore of the income that comes from the possession of capital.

But in the end practical life also began to put this question. Capital had gradually become a power. Machinery had appeared on the scene and won its great triumphs; and machinery everywhere helped to extend business on a great scale, and to give production more and more of a capitalist character. But this very introduction of machinery had begun to reveal an opposition which was forced on economic life with the development of capital, and daily grew in importance,—the opposition between capital and labour.

In the old handicrafts undertaker and wage-earner, master and apprentice, belonged not so much to different social classes as simply to different generations. What the one was the other might be, and would be. If their interests for a time did diverge, yet in the long run the feeling prevailed that they belonged to one station of life. It is quite different in great capitalist industry. The undertaker who contributes the capital has seldom

[1] Book i. chap. vi. The sentence was written primarily about landowners, but in the whole chapter interest on capital and rent of land are treated as parallel as against wages of labour.

or never been a workman; the workman who contributes his thews and sinews will seldom or never become an undertaker. They work at one trade like master and apprentice; but not only are they of two different ranks, they are even of different species. They belong to classes whose interests diverge as widely as their persons. Now machinery had shown how sharp could be the collision of interest between capital and labour. Those machines which bore golden fruit to the capitalist undertaker had, on their introduction, deprived thousands of workers of their bread. Even now that the first hardships are over there remains antagonism enough and to spare. It is true that capitalist and labourer share in the productiveness of capitalist undertaking, but they share in this way, that the worker usually receives little—indeed very little—while the undertaker receives much. The worker's discontent with his small share is not lessened, as it used to be in the case of the handicraft assistant, by the expectation of himself in time enjoying the lion's share; for, under large production, the worker has no such expectation. On the contrary, his discontent is aggravated by the knowledge that to him, for his scanty wage, falls the harder work; while to the undertaker, for his ample share in the product, falls the lighter exertion—often enough no personal exertion whatever. Looking at all these contrasts of destiny and of interest, if there ever came the thought that, at bottom, it is the workers who bring into existence the products from which the undertaker draws his profit—and Adam Smith had come wonderfully near to such a thought in many passages of his widely read book—it was inevitable that some pleader for the fourth estate should begin to put the same question with regard to Natural interest as had been put many centuries earlier, by the friends of the debtor, with regard to Loan interest, Is interest on capital just? Is it just that the capitalist-undertaker, even if he never moves a finger, should receive, under the name of profit, a considerable share of what the workers have produced by their exertions? Should not the entire product rather fall to the workers?

The question has been before the world since the first quarter of our century, at first put modestly, then with increasing assertiveness; and it is this fact that the interest theory has to thank for its unusual and lasting vitality. So long as the problem interested theorists alone, and was of importance only for purposes of theory, it might have slumbered on undisturbed. But it was now elevated to the rank of a great social problem which the science neither could nor would overlook. Thus the inquiries into the nature of Natural interest were as numerous and solicitous after Adam Smith's day as they had been scanty and inadequate before it.

It must be admitted that they were as diverse as they were numerous. Up till Adam Smith the scientific opinion of the time had been represented by one single theory. After him opinion was divided into a number of theories conflicting with each other, and remaining so with rare persistence up till our own day. It is usually the case that new theories put themselves in the place of the old, and the old gradually yield the position. But in the present case each new theory of interest only succeeded in placing itself *by the side of* the old, while the old managed to hold their place with the utmost stubbornness. In these circumstances the course of development since Adam Smith's time presents not so much the picture of a progressive reform as that of a schismatic accumulation of theories.

The work we have now before us is clearly marked out by the nature of the subject. It will consist in following the development of all the diverging systems from their origin down to the present time, and in trying to form a critical opinion on the value, or want of value, of each individual system. As the development from Adam Smith onwards simultaneously pursues different lines, I think it best to abandon the chronological order of statement which I have hitherto observed, and to group together our material according to theories.

To this end I shall try first of all to make a methodical survey of the whole mass of literature which will occupy our attention. This will be most easily done by putting the characteristic and central question of the problem in the foreground. We shall then see at a glance how the theory differentiates itself on that central question like light on the prism.

What we have to explain is the fact that, when capital is

productively employed, there regularly remains over in the hands of the undertaker a surplus proportional to the amount of this capital. This surplus owes its existence to the circumstance that the value of the goods produced by the assistance of capital is regularly greater than the value of the goods consumed in their production. The question accordingly is, Why is there this constant surplus value?

To this question Turgot had answered, There must be a surplus, because otherwise the capitalists would employ their capital in the purchase of land. Adam Smith had answered, There must be a surplus, because otherwise the capitalist would have no interest in spending his capital productively.

Both answers we have already pronounced insufficient. What then are the answers given by later writers?

At the outset they appear to me to follow five different lines.

One party is content with the answers given by Turgot and Smith, and stands by them. This line of explanation was still a favourite one at the beginning of our century, but has been gradually abandoned since then. I shall group these answers together under the name of the Colourless theories.

A second party says, Capital produces the surplus. This school, amply represented in economic literature, may be conveniently called that of the Productivity theories. I may here note that in their later development we shall find the productivity theories splitting up into many varieties; into Productivity theories in the narrower sense, that assume a direct production of surplus on the part of capital; and into Use theories, which explain the origin of interest in the roundabout way of making the productive use of capital a peculiar element in cost, which, like every other element of cost, demands compensation.

A third party answers, Surplus value is the equivalent of a cost which enters as a constituent into the price, viz. abstinence. For in devoting his capital to production the capitalist must give up the present enjoyment of it. This postponement of enjoyment, this "abstinence," is a sacrifice, and as such is a constituent element in the costs of production which demands compensation. I shall call this the Abstinence theory.

A fourth party sees in surplus value the wage for work

contributed by the capitalist. For this doctrine, which also is amply represented, I shall use the name Labour theory.

Finally, a fifth party—for the most part belonging to the socialist side—answers, Surplus value does not correspond to any natural surplus whatever, but has its origin simply in the curtailment of the just wage of the workers. I shall call this the Exploitation theory.

These are the principal lines of explanation. They are certainly numerous enough, yet they are far from exhibiting all the many forms which the interest theory has taken. We shall see rather that many of the principal lines branch off again into a multitude of essentially different types; that in many cases elements of several theories are bound up in a new and peculiar combination; and that, finally, within one and the same theoretical type, the different ways in which common fundamental thoughts are formulated, are often so strongly contrasted and so characteristic that there would be some justification in recognising individual shades of difference as separate theories. That our prominent economic writers have exerted themselves in so many different ways for the discovery of the truth is an eloquent witness of its discovery being no less important than it is hard.

We begin with a survey of the Colourless theories.

CHAPTER V

THE COLOURLESS THEORIES

THE revolution spoken of at the end of last chapter, which was to elevate the long underrated question of interest into a social problem of the first rank, was not sudden enough to prevent a number of writers remaining content with the somewhat patriarchal treatment that the subject had received at the hands of Turgot and Adam Smith. It would be a great mistake to suppose that among these stragglers we should only meet with men of no independence, writers of second and third rank. Of course there is the usual crowd of little men who always appear in the wake of a pioneering genius, and find their mission in popularising the new doctrine. But besides these we find many a distinguished thinker who passes over our problem from motives very similar to those of Adam Smith.

It is easy to see that the opinions which those "colourless" writers, as I shall call them, have expressed on the subject of interest have exerted but little influence on the development of the theory as a whole. This circumstance will justify me in passing rapidly over the majority of them, and giving a complete account only of the few who may attract our interest either by their personality or by the peculiarity of their doctrine.

Any one familiar with the character of German political economy at the end of the past, and at the beginning of the present century, will not be astonished to meet in it a singularly large number of colourless writers. Their indifference to the subject is not without a certain variety. Some who remain faithful to Adam Smith copy also his vague suggestions about interest almost literally; in particular his remark that, if there were no interest, the capitalist would have no inducement to spend his capital productively. Thus Sartorius,[1] Lueder,[2] and Kraus.[3] Some take the same fundamental idea, but treat it more freely, as Hufeland[4] and Seuter.[5] Others assume that interest requires no explanation, and say nothing about it, as Pölitz,[6] and, somewhat later, Murhard.[7] Others, again, give reasons for it that are certainly peculiar, but these so superficial and trifling that they can scarcely lay claim to the honourable name of theories. Thus Schmalz, who argues in a circle and explains the existence of natural interest by the possibility of lending capital to others at interest.[8]

Count Cancrin's explanation of the matter is peculiarly naïve. For curiosity's sake, I give the short passage in his own words: "Every one knows," he says,[9] "that money bears interest, but why? *If two owners of real capital wish to exchange their products, each of them is disposed to demand* for the labour of storing, and *as profit, as much over the intrinsic value of the product as the other will grant him; necessity, however, makes them meet each other half way.* But money represents real capital: with real capital a profit can be made; and hence interest."

The words printed in italics are meant to explain the existence of natural interest, the others the existence of loan interest; and the author considers this explanation so satisfactory that in a later passage he refers back to it with

[1] *Handbuch der Staatswirthschaft*, Berlin, 1796, particularly §§ 8 and 23. Even his later *Abhandlungen die Elemente des Nationalreichthums und die Staatswirthschaft betreffend* (Göttingen, 1806) does not take an independent view of our subject.

[2] *Ueber Nationalindustrie und Staatswirthschaft*, 1800-1804 particularly pp. 82, 142.

[3] *Staatswirthschaft*, Auerswald's edition, 1808-11, particularly vol. i. pp. 24, 150; and the very naïve expressions, vol. iii. p. 126.

[4] *Neue Grundlegung*, Vienna, 1815, p. 221.

[5] *Die National-Oekonomie*, Ulm, 1823, p. 145. See also p. 164, where the causal connection is reversed and natural interest deduced from loan interest.

[6] *Staatswissenschaften im Lichte unserer Zeit*, part ii. Leipzig, 1823, p. 90. Here Pölitz only takes the trouble to show that profit, assumed as already existing, must fall to the owner of capital.

[7] *Theorie des Handels*, Göttingen, 1831.

[8] *Handbuch der Staatswirthschaft*, Berlin, 1808, §§ 110 and 120. See also § 129, where even contract "rents" are no better explained, but simply spoken of as facts. Schmalz's other writings are not more instructive.

[9] *Die Oekonomie der menschlichen Gesellschaften und das Finanzwesen*, Stuttgart, 1845, p. 19.

complacency: "Why capital bears interest, in the form of a definite rate per cent in the case of money values, in the form of the prices of commodities in the case of real capital, has been already made clear" (p. 103).

More attention is due to certain authors who give a stronger emphasis to Adam Smith's other suggestion that profit is a share in the product of labour diverted by the capitalist.

One of these writers, Count Soden,[1] sharply contrasts capital, as simple material on which "productive power" works, with the productive power itself. He traces profit to the fact that the owner of "capital-material" is able to "put the power of others in motion for himself, and therefore to share the profit on this power with the isolated producer, the wage-earner" (vol. i. p. 65). That some such sharing does take place Soden regards as a self-evident result of the relations of competition. Without giving himself the trouble of a formal explanation, the expression repeatedly escapes him that the small number of the capitalists, as compared with the great numbers of the wage-earners, must always make it possible for the capitalist to buy wage-labour at a price which leaves him a "rent" (pp. 61, 138). He thinks this quite fair (*e.g.* p. 65, onwards), and consequently gives his advice against attempting to raise wages by legal regulation. "For if, in the price thus regulated, the owner of the material comes to find that he gets no profit from the power of others, all material which he cannot himself work up he will leave dead" (p. 140). Soden, however, wishes that the "price" of wages should be brought up to their "true value." What level of wage it is that corresponds to this true value remains very obscure, in spite of the thorough discussion which the author devotes to the question of the value of the productive power (p. 132). The only thing certain is that, in his opinion, even when the productive power is compensated at its *full* value, there must still remain a rent to the capitalist.

The impression one gets from all this is, that the first part of the argument, where interest is explained to be a profit obtained from the power of others, would lead us to expect a very different conclusion from that come to in the second part;

[1] *Die National-Oekonomie*, Leipzig, 1805-1808. I quote from a reprint published in Vienna, 1815.

and that the reasons given for this change of front are much too vague to be satisfactory.

Lotz lays himself open to similar criticism.

This acute writer, in his *Handbuch der Staatswissenschaftslehre*, Erlangen, 1821, goes very exhaustively into the subject of interest. He argues with great vigour against the doctrine which Say had meantime put forward, that capital possesses an independent productive power. "In themselves all capitals are dead," and "there is no truth in the assertion of their independent labour": they are never anything else than tools of human labour (vol. i. p. 65, etc.) In the very notable passage which follows, the "rent" of capital is criticised from this point of view.

Since capitals are only instruments for furthering labour, and themselves do no labour, Lotz finds that the capitalist "from the return to labour, and from the amount of goods gained or produced by it, has no claim to anything more than the amount of expense which the furnishing of the capital has caused him; or, more plainly, the amount of the labourer's subsistence, the amount of the raw material given out to him, and the amount of the tools properly so called that are worn out by the worker during his work. This, strictly speaking, would be distinctively the rent appropriate to capital which the capitalist may claim from the labourer who works for him; and further, this is distinctively the appropriate quota of the quantity of goods produced by the labourer, or won from nature, that might belong of right to the capitalist. If this then be the appropriate sense of the term, there is no place for what is usually called profit, viz. a wage obtained by the capitalist for advancing his capital *such as guarantees a surplus over the expenses.* If labour returns more than the amount of the capitalist's expenditure, this return, and all the income that comes out of it, belongs distinctively to the labourer alone, as wages of his labour. For in point of fact it is not the capitalist who creates the labourer's products; all that the labourer, with the assistance of capital, may produce or win from nature belongs to himself. Or if the power which manifests its activity in the worker at his work be looked upon as a natural fund belonging to the entire industrial mass of mankind, then all that the labourer produces belongs to humanity as a whole" (p. 487, onwards).

In this acute and remarkable passage Lotz comes very near to the later Exploitation theory of the socialists. But all of a sudden he breaks away from this line of argument, and swings back into the old colourless explanation of Adam Smith by going on to say: "If, however, the capitalist were limited to a simple replacement of what he may have furnished, from his accumulated stock of wealth, to the worker during his work, and for his work—if the capitalist were so hardly treated, he would scarcely decide to advance anything from his stock on behalf of the worker and his work. He would perhaps never decide to accumulate capital at all; for there would not be many capitals accumulated if the accumulator had not the prospect of a wage for the trouble of this accumulating in the shape of the expected interest. If, therefore, the worker, who has none of the requisites and conditions necessary for the exercise of his power, is to hope and expect that owners will consent to furnish their capital, and so make it possible for him to exert the productive power that resides in him, or lighten the exertion for him, then he must of necessity submit to give up to the capitalists something of the return to his labour."

In what follows Lotz somewhat expands this vague explanation by suggesting, as a fair ground for the capitalist's claim, that, without the support of capital, the work which guarantees that there is a return to be divided could never have been done at all by the labourer, or, at any rate, could not have been so well done. This also gives him a standard for the "true and appropriate extent" of rent of capital; it should be calculated, that is to say, in proportion to the support which the worker has enjoyed at his work by the use of the capital. In explaining this method of calculation by several examples Lotz shows how nearly extremes may meet. A few pages before, he has said that the whole "return to labour, and all the income that comes out of it, belongs peculiarly to the labourer alone, as wages of his labour." He now goes on to show how in certain circumstances the owner of a labour-saving machine may claim for himself, and that rightly, nine-tenths of the return to labour!

It is easy to see that the contrast here between the starting-point and the conclusion is even more striking than it is with Soden, and that the argument relied on to explain and connect the two does not carry much more weight. At bottom it says nothing else than that the capitalist would *like* to get interest, and that the workers *may* consent to its deduction. But how far this "explanation" is from being really a theory of interest is forcibly illustrated if we put a parallel case in regard to the land-rent problem. Lotz's explanation does for the problem of interest exactly what would be done for the problem of rent, if one were to say that landowners must obtain a rent, because otherwise they would prefer to leave their ground uncultivated; and that it is a fair thing for the agricultural labourers to consent to the deduction of rent, because without the co-operation of the soil they could not get any return to divide, or could not get so good a return. Lotz, however, evidently never suspected that the essence of the problem is not even touched by any such explanation.[1]

A last group of Colourless writers takes a hesitating middle course between Adam Smith's views and the Productivity theory which Say had meantime put forward. They take some features from both, but do not expand any of them into a complete theory. From Say these authors usually take the recognition of capital as an independent factor in production; and they adopt perhaps one or other of Say's ways of speaking that suggest the "productive power" of capital. From Adam Smith they take the appeal to the motive of the capitalist's self-interest. But one and all of them avoid any precise formulation of the interest problem.

In this group we find Jakob,[2] who at times recognises

[1] In Lotz's former work, the *Revision der Grundbegriffe*, 1811-14, there are some rather interesting remarks on our subject, although they are full of inconsistency; among others, an acute refutation of the productivity theories (vol. iii. p. 100, etc.), an explanation of interest as "an arbitrary addition to the necessary costs of production," and as a "tax which the selfishness of the capitalist forces from the consumer" (p. 338). This tax is found, not necessary indeed, but "very fair." At p. 339 and at p. 323 Lotz considers it a direct cheating of the capitalist by the labourer if the former does not receive in interest as much as "he may be justified in claiming as the effect of those tools used up by the worker on his activity and on its gross return." It is very striking that in the second last of the passages quoted Lotz puts interest to the account of the consumer, and in the last of them to the account of the labourer; he thus exactly repeats Adam Smith's indecision on the same point.

[2] *Grundsätze der National-Oekonomie*, Halle, 1805; third edition, Halle, 1825. I quote from the latter.

as the ultimate source of all useful things only nature and industrial activity (§ 49), and traces the profit of capital to a capability on the part of labour to produce a surplus product (§§ 275, 280); but at other times points to profit as that "which is produced by a capital over its own value" (§ 277), designates capital by Say's term of "productive instrument" (§ 770), and often speaks of the owners of capital as immediate producers, who are called to take part in the original division of the product in virtue of the direct share which they have taken in the production of goods by contributing their capital.[1] Then we have Fulda,[2] who looks upon capital as a special though derived source of wealth, and, moreover, likens it to a machine which when properly employed not only pays for its own upkeep, but makes something more in addition; he does not attempt, however, to give any explanation of this (p. 135). Then comes Eiselen,[3] whose want of clearness at once comes out in his first recognising only two ultimate sources of wealth, nature and labour (p. 11), and then later looking upon nature, labour, and capital as "fundamental powers of production," from the co-operation of which the value of all products proceeds (§ 372). Eiselen, moreover, finds that the function of capital is to increase the return to labour and natural powers (§ 497 and other places); but in the end he can find nothing better to say in explanation of interest than that interest is necessary as an incentive to the accumulation of capital (§ 491; similarly §§ 517, 555, etc.)

Besides these we meet in the same group the gallant old master in political economy, Rau. It is singular that Rau, to the very end of his long scientific career, ignored the imposing number of distinct theories on interest which he saw springing up, and held by the simple way of explanation that had been customary in the days of his youth. Even in the eighth and last edition of his *Volkswirthschaftslehre*, which appeared in 1868, he contented himself with touching on the interest problem in a few cursory remarks, containing in substance the old self-interest motive introduced by Adam Smith. "If he (the capitalist) is to resolve to save wealth, accumulate it, and

[1] §§ 211, 711, 765, particularly marked in § 769.

[2] *Grundsätze der ökonomisch-politischen oder Kameralwissenschaften*, second edition, Tübingen, 1820.

[3] *Die Lehre von der Volkswirthschaft*, Halle, 1843.

make it into capital, he must get an advantage of another sort; viz. a yearly income lasting as long as his capital lasts. In this way the possession of a capital becomes to individuals . . . the source of an income which is called rent of capital, rent of stock, or interest."[1]

On Rau's works the rich development which the literature of interest had taken before 1868 has scarcely left a trace. Of Say's Productivity theory he has only adopted this much; that, like Say, he recognises capital to be an independent source of wealth; but he immediately weakens this concession by rejecting as inappropriate the expression "productive service," which Say used for the co-operation of this source of wealth, and by putting capital among "dead auxiliaries," in contrast to the producing forces of wealth (vol. i. § 84). And on one occasion, in a note, he quotes Senior's Abstinence theory, but without adding a single word either of agreement or criticism (vol. i. § 228).

When we turn from Germany to England our attention is first claimed by Ricardo.

In the case of this distinguished thinker we find the same phenomenon we have already noticed in the case of Adam Smith, that, without putting forward any theory of his own, he has had a deep influence on the development of the interest theory. I must classify him among the Colourless writers, for although he takes up the subject of interest at some length, he treats it only as a self-explanatory, or almost self-explanatory phenomenon, and passes over its origin in a few cursory remarks, to take up at greater length a number of concrete questions of detail. And although he treats these questions most thoroughly and intelligently, it is in such a way that their investigation throws no light on the primary theoretical question. But, exactly as in the case of Adam Smith, his doctrine contains propositions on which distinct theories could have been built, if only they had been worked out to all their conclusions. In fact, later on, distinct theories were built on them, and not the least part of their support consists in the authority of Ricardo, to whom the advocates of these theories were fond of appealing as their spiritual father.

The passages in which Ricardo makes reference to interest

[1] *Volkswirthschaftslehre*, vol. i. § 222. Similarly, but more generally, vol. i. § 138.

are very numerous. Apart from scattered observations, they are to be found principally in chapters i. vi. vii. and xxi. of his *Principles of Political Economy and Taxation.*[1] The contents of these passages, so far as they refer to our subject, may best be ascertained if we divide them into three groups. In the first group I shall place Ricardo's direct observations on the origin of interest; in the second, his views on the causes that determine its amount; in the third, his views on the connection of interest with the value of goods. It should be premised, however, that Ricardo, like the majority of English writers, makes no distinction between interest on capital and undertaker's profit, but groups both under the word Profit.

(1) The first group is very thinly represented. It contains a few passing remarks to the effect that there must be interest, because otherwise capitalists would have no inducement to accumulate capital.[2] These remarks have an evident connection with the analogous expressions of Adam Smith, with which we are familiar, and come under the same criticism. There is some warrant for seeing in them the primary germs from which the Abstinence theory has since been developed, but in themselves they do not represent a theory.

The same remark is true of another observation. In chap. i. § 5, p. 25, he says that, where production demands an employment of capital for a longer period, the value of the goods produced must be greater than the value of goods which have required exactly the same amount of labour, but where the employment of capital has extended over a shorter period; and concludes: "The difference in value is only a just compensation for the time that the profits were withheld." One might possibly find in these words a still more direct agreement

[1] London, 1817, third edition, 1821. I quote from M'Culloch's edition. John Murray, 1886.

[2] The most complete of these runs thus: "For no one accumulates but with a view to make his accumulation productive, and it is only when so employed that it operates on profits. Without a motive there could be no accumulation, and consequently such a state of prices" (as show no profit to the capitalist) "could never take place. The farmer and manufacturer can no more live without profit than the labourer without wages. Their motive for accumulation will diminish with every diminution of profit, and will cease altogether when their profits are so low as not to afford them an adequate compensation for their trouble, and the risk which they must necessarily encounter in employing their capital productively" (chap. vi. p. 68; similarly p. 67; chap. xxi. p. 175, and other places).

with the Abstinence theory, but in themselves they do not contain any finished theory.

(2) On the amount or rate of profit Ricardo's views (principally contained in chapters vi. and xxi.) are very interesting both as regards originality and self-consistency. As they arise out of his theory of land-rent, it will be necessary to give some account of that theory.

According to Ricardo, on the first settling of a country the most fruitful lands are taken into cultivation. So long as there is a superfluity of land of the "first quality" no rent is paid to the owner of the ground, and the whole revenue falls to the cultivators as wages of labour and profit of capital.

Later on, as population increases, the increasing demand for land products demands extended cultivation. This extended cultivation is of two kinds: sometimes the lands of inferior quality, despised up till now, are cultivated; sometimes the lands of first quality already in cultivation are cultivated with more intensiveness—farmed at a greater expenditure of capital and labour. In both cases—assuming that the state of agricultural *technique* remains unchanged—the increase in land products is only obtained at increased cost; and the last employed capital and labour are consequently less productive—less productive, that is to say, over the whole field, as the more favourable opportunities of cultivation are successively exhausted, and the less favourable must be resorted to.

The capitals thus employed in circumstances unequally favourable obtain at first unequal results. But these unequal results cannot permanently remain attached to particular capitals. The competition of capitalists will soon bring the rate of profit on all capitals engaged in agriculture to the same level. The standard, indeed, is given by the profit obtainable in the least remunerative employment of capital. All surplus return which the more favourably situated capitals yield in virtue of the better quality of the co-operating powers of the soil, falls into the lap of the landowners as rent.

The extent of profit and wage taken together is thus always determined by the return to the least productive employment of capital; for this return pays no rent, and is divided entirely as profit on capital and wage of labour.

Now of these two factors one, the wage of labour, follows

a hard and fast law. Wages are necessarily at all times equal to the amount of the necessary cost of subsistence of the worker. They are high if the value of the means of subsistence be high; low if the value of the means of subsistence be low. As then the capitalist receives what remains over, profit finds the line that determines its height in the height of wages at the time. In this connection between interest and wage Ricardo finds the true law of interest. He brings it forward with emphasis in a great many passages, and opposes it to the older view, particularly to that represented by Adam Smith, that the extent of profit is determined by the amount and competition of capitals.

In virtue of this law, Ricardo now goes on to argue, profit must tend to sink steadily with increasing economic cultivation. For in order to obtain means of subsistence for the increasing population, man must resort to conditions of cultivation that are always more and more unfavourable, and the decreasing product, after deduction of the wages of labour, leaves always less and less for profit. True, although the amount of the product diminishes, its value does not fall. For, according to Ricardo's well-known law, the value of products is at all times regulated by the quantity of labour employed in their production. Therefore if, at a later point of time, the labour of ten men brings forward only 150 quarters of corn, while at an earlier period it had brought forward 180, the 150 quarters will now have exactly the same value as the 180 before had, because in both is embodied the same quantity of labour—that is, the labour of ten men over a year. But now of course the value of the single quarter of wheat will rise. With it necessarily rises the amount of value which the worker requires for his subsistence, and, as a further result, his wages must also rise. But if, for the same amount of value which the lessened quantity of product represents, a higher wage must be paid to labour, there naturally remains over a less amount for profit.

Were man finally to extend cultivation to lands so unfruitful that the product obtainable was entirely required for the labourers' subsistence, profit would fall to zero. That is, however, impossible, because the expectation of profit is the one motive to the accumulation of capital, and this motive becomes weakened with the gradual lowering of profit; so that, before zero is reached, the further accumulation of capital, and with it the advance of wealth and of population, would come to a standstill.

The competition of capitalists, on which Adam Smith lays so much weight, can, according to Ricardo, only temporarily lower the profit of capital, when (in accordance with the well-known wage fund theory) the increased quantity of capital at first raises wages. But very soon the labouring population increases in proportion to the increased demand for labour, and wages tend to sink to the former level while profit tends to rise. The only thing that will finally reduce profit is when the means of support necessary for the increased population can be obtained only by the cultivation of less productive lands and at increased cost; and when, in consequence, the diminished product leaves a smaller surplus after paying the necessary wages of labour. This will not be in consequence of competition, but in consequence of the necessity of having recourse to less fruitful production. Only from time to time does the tendency of profit to sink with progressive economical development experience a check through improvements in agricultural *technique*, which allow of equal quantities of product being obtained with less labour than before.

If we take the substance of this theory we find that Ricardo explains the rate of profit from the rate of wages; the rate of wages is the cause, the rate of profit the effect.[1]

Criticism may approach this theory from different sides. It has, it need scarcely be said, no validity whatever for those who, like Pierstorff, hold Ricardo's rent theory to be fundamentally untrue. Further, that portion of the argument which rests on the wage fund theory will be exposed to all the objections raised to that theory. I shall put on one side, however, all those objections which relate to assumptions outside the interest theory, and direct my criticism simply to the theory itself.

[1] Ricardo puts the same causal relation very strongly in chap. i. § 4, when he gives the height of the "value of labour" as a secondary cause of the value of goods, in addition to the quantity of labour expended in the production,—having in his eye the influence exerted on the value of goods by the capitalist's claims to profit. The height of profit is to him only a dependent, secondary cause, in place of which he prefers to put the final cause of the whole relation, and this final cause he finds in the varying height of wages.

I ask, therefore, Assuming the correctness of the rent theory and of the wage fund theory, is the rate of profit, or, for that matter, the existence of profit, explained by Ricardo's theory?

The answer will be in the negative, and that because Ricardo has mistaken what are simply *accompanying circumstances* of the phenomenon for its *cause*. The matter stands thus.

It is quite right to say that wage, profit, and return of production do, after deduction of possible land-rent, stand in an iron connection. It is quite right to say that the profit of capital can never amount to more, and never to less, than the difference between return and wage. But it is false to interpret this connection as implying that the amount of the return and the amount of the wage are the determining, and the amount of profit simply the determined. Just as plausibly as Ricardo has explained the rate of profit as a result of the rate of wages might he have explained the rate of wages as a result of the rate of profit. He has not done so because he rightly recognised that the rate of wages rests on independent grounds, and grounds peculiar to the factor, labour. But what Ricardo recognised in the case of wages he has overlooked in the case of profit. Profit, too, has grounds that determine its amount arising out of circumstances peculiar to itself. Capital does not simply take what remains over; it knows how to exact its own proper share. Now an efficient explanation of profit would have to bring into prominence just those considerations that appear on the side of the factor "capital," and prevent the absorption of profit by wages just as effectually as, *e.g.* the labourer's necessary subsistence prevents the absorption of wages by interest. But Ricardo entirely fails to give this prominence to the specific grounds that determine the rate of interest.

Only once does he notice the existence of any such grounds, when he remarks that profit can never sink to zero, because, if it did so, the motive for the accumulation of capital, and with it the accumulation of capital itself, would come to an end.[1] But this thought, which, logically expanded, might have afforded material for a really original theory of interest, he

[1] Chap. vi. p. 67 and *passim*.

does not follow up. He continues to look for the circumstances that determine the rate of profit exclusively in the field of the competing factors; and he assiduously points out, as its decisive causes, sometimes the rate of wages, sometimes the degree of productivity of the most unproductive labour, sometimes even —in a way that breathes of the physiocrat, but still is in harmony with the whole doctrine just expounded—the natural fruitfulness of the soil.[1]

This criticism of Ricardo appears of course to be itself exposed to a very obvious objection. If, as we have assumed with Ricardo in the whole course of our argument, wage claims for itself an absolutely determined quantity,—the amount of the costs of subsistence, it appears as if, at the same time, the amount which remains over for profit is so strictly determined that there is no room for the working of any independent motives on the side of profit. Say, *e.g.* that the return to production ready for division is 100 quarters. If the workers occupied in producing these 100 quarters require 80 quarters, the share of capital is certainly fixed at 20 quarters, and could not be altered by any motive acting from the side of capital.

This objection, which is conceivable, will not, however, stand examination. For, to keep entirely to Ricardo's line of thought, the return which the least productive labour yields is not fixed but elastic, and is capable of being affected by any peremptory claims of capital and of labour. Just as effectually as the claims of the worker may and do prevent cultivation being extended to a point at which labour does not obtain even its own costs of subsistence, may the claims of capital prevent an excessive extension of the limits of cultivation, and actually do prevent it. For instance, suppose that these motives to which interest, generally speaking, owes its origin, and which Ricardo unfortunately does so little to explain, demand for a capital of definite amount a profit of 30 quarters, and that the workers employed by this capital need for their subsistence in all 80 quarters; then cultivation will require to call a halt at that point where the labour of so many men as can live on 80 quarters produces 110 quarters. Were the "motives of accumulation" to demand only a profit

[1] Chap. vi. towards end, p. 70.

of 10 quarters, then cultivation could be extended till such time as the least productive labour would produce 90 quarters. But the cultivation of land less productive than this will always be economically impossible, and at the same time the limit to the further increase of population will be for the moment reached.[1]

That the claims of capital may exert this limiting influence Ricardo himself allows, as we have seen, in the very extreme case where profit threatens to disappear altogether. But naturally those circumstances to which capital owes its existence in general put forth their energies not only in the very extreme cases, but permanently. They do not simply prevent the entire disappearance of profit; they keep it constantly in competition with the other factors, and help to determine its amount. So that profit no less than wages may be said to rest on independent determining grounds. To have entirely ignored these grounds is the decisive blunder of Ricardo.

The peculiar nature of this blunder explains also quite naturally the phenomenon that otherwise would be very striking; that the comprehensive investigations, which so distinguished a thinker as Ricardo devoted to the question of the rate of profit, remain so entirely unfruitful as regards the principal question, the causes of profit.

(3) Finally, a third group of observations relating to profit is interwoven with Ricardo's views on the value of goods. This is a subject which generally gives its writers opportunity to express themselves directly or indirectly as to the source whence profit comes. Does the capitalist's claim of profit make the exchange value of goods higher than it would otherwise have been, or not? If it does, profit is paid out of a special "surplus value," without taking anything from those who own the co-operating productive powers; in particular, without taking anything from the wage-worker. If not, it is got at the

[1] The careful reader will easily convince himself that the result remains the same, if we vary the form of the question, and look at the *value* instead of the *amount* of the product and wages. In that case, indeed, the value of the return remains fixed (see p. 90), while wages are an elastic quantity, and the proposition expressed in the text, changed only in expression, not in reality, will run thus: cultivation must call a halt at that point where the wages of labour, increased by the increasing costs of cultivation, leaves over to the capitalist from the value of the product no more than enough to satisfy his claims on profit.

expense of the other participants. On this Ricardo also has expressed himself, and his opinion is that an addition is made to the value of goods by the employment of capital; still he expresses himself in a somewhat cautious way.

He distinguishes between two different epochs of history. In the first, the primitive epoch—when there is very little capital and no private property in land—the exchange value of goods is exclusively determined by the quantity of labour expended on them.[1] In the second epoch, to which modern economy belongs, there emerges a modification through the employment of capital. The undertaker-capitalists ask, for the capital employed by them in production, the usual rate of profit, calculated according to the amount of the capital and the length of time during which it is employed. But the amount of capital and the duration of its employment are different in the different branches of production, and the claims of profit differ with them. One branch requires more circulating capital, which quickly reproduces itself in the value of the product; another requires more fixed capital, and this again of greater or less durability,—the rapidity of the reproduction in the value of the products being in inverse ratio to the durability. Now the various claims of profit are equalised by the fact that those goods the production of which has required a comparatively greater share in capital, obtain a relatively higher exchange value.[2]

In this passage one can see that Ricardo decidedly inclines to the view that interest arises out of a special surplus value. But the impression we get that Ricardo held this decided opinion is not a little weakened by certain other passages; partly by the numerous passages where Ricardo brings profit and wages into connection, and makes the increase of one factor come out of the loss or curtailment of the other; partly by the previous pure "labour principle" of the primitive epoch of industry, which is inconsistent with that view. It must be said too that he is much more interested and cordial in his exposition of this latter principle than in that of its capitalist modification; a circumstance which cannot but arouse the suspicion that he considered the original state of things the natural one. In fact, the later socialist writers

[1] Chap. i. § 1.

[2] Chap. i. §§ 4, 5.

have represented the "labour principle" as Ricardo's real opinion, and the capitalist modification which he conceded as simply an illogical conclusion.[1]

Thus also on the question whence profit comes we see Ricardo take an undecided position; not hesitating so markedly as his master, Adam Smith, but undecided enough to warrant his retention in the ranks of the Colourless theorists.

Ricardo's great contemporary, Malthus, has not expressed himself much more distinctly than Ricardo on the subject of interest. Yet there are certain expressions in his writings which allow us to separate him from the entirely Colourless writers, and class him among the Productivity theorists.

The epithet colourless applies, however, with peculiar appropriateness to Torrens.[2] This diffuse and short-sighted writer brings forward his views on the subject of interest for the most part in the course of an argument against the theory which Malthus had promulgated shortly before, that profit forms a constituent portion of the costs of production, and therefore of the natural price of goods. In opposition to this Torrens, with perfect correctness, but at intolerable length, points out that profit represents a surplus over costs, not a part of costs. He himself, however, has nothing better to put in place of Malthus's theory.

He makes a distinction between Market price and Natural price. Natural price is "that which we must give in order to obtain the article we want from the great warehouse of nature, and is the same thing as the cost of production" (p. 50); by which expression Torrens means "the amount of capital, or the quantity of accumulated labour expended in production" (p. 34). Market price and natural price in no way tend, as is usually affirmed, to a common level. For profit never makes any part of the expense of production, and is not therefore an element of natural price. But "market price must always include the customary rate of profit for the time being, otherwise industry would be suspended. Hence market price, instead of equalising itself with natural price, will exceed it by the customary rate of profit."

[1] So also Bernhardi, *Kritik der Gründe*, etc., 1849, p. 310, etc.

[2] An Essay on the *Production of Wealth*, London, 1821.

Torrens has thus eliminated profit from the determinants of natural price, and put it instead among the determinants of market price. This change, it is easy to see, is purely formal. It rests simply on the use of a different terminology. The economists whom he attacked had meant that profit is a determinant of the height of the average price of goods, and had called this average or permanent price "natural price." Torrens means exactly the same thing; only he calls the permanent price the "market price," and reserves the name of natural price for what is not a price at all, namely, the capital expended in production.

As to what really is the chief question—Why the actual prices of goods, whether they are called natural or market prices, leave over a profit to capital?—Torrens has almost nothing to say. He evidently considers profit to be a thing so self-explanatory that any detailed explanation of it is quite unnecessary. He contents himself with a few unsatisfactory formulas,—formulas, moreover, which contradict each other, as they point to lines of thought that are entirely distinct. One of these formulas is the often recurring observation that the capitalist must make a profit, otherwise he would have no inducement to accumulate capital, or lay it out in any productive undertaking (pp. 53, 392). Another, pointing in quite a different direction, is that profit is a "new creation" produced by the employment of capital (pp. 51, 54). But *how* it is created we are not told; he gives us a formula, not a theory.

But no member of the English school has been so unhappy in his treatment of the subject, and has done such ill service to the theory of interest, as M'Culloch.[1] He comes near quite a number of diverging opinions, but only gets deep enough in them to fall into flagrant self-contradiction; he does not expand any one of them sufficiently to form a theory that even approaches consistency. We find only one exception to this; but the theory which is there advanced is the most absurd that could possibly occur to any thinker. Even this, however, in later editions of his work he abandons, although not without allowing traces of it to remain and contrast equally with facts

[1] *Principles of Political Economy*, first edition, Edinburgh, 1825; fifth edition 1864.

and with the context. Thus M'Culloch's utterances on the subject are one great collection of incompleteness, irrationality, and inconsistency.

Since, however, M'Culloch's views have obtained extensive circulation, and command a certain respect, I cannot shirk the somewhat thankless task of justifying these strictures.

M'Culloch starts with the proposition that labour is the only source of wealth. The value of goods is determined by the quantity of labour required for their production. This he considers true not only of primitive conditions, but also of modern economic life, where capital, as well as direct labour, is employed in production; for capital itself is nothing else than the product of previous labour. It is only necessary to add to the labour which is embedded in the capital the labour immediately expended, and the sum of these determines the value of all products.[1] Consequently it is labour alone, even in modern economic life, which constitutes the entire cost of production.[2]

But only a few lines before this definition of costs as "identical with the quantity of labour," M'Culloch has included profit, as well as labour, among the costs;[3] and almost immediately after he has said that the quantity of labour *alone* determines value, he shows how a rise in the wages of labour, associated with a fall in profit, alters the exchange value of goods,—raising the value of those goods in the production of which capital of less than average durability is employed, and reducing the value of those goods in the production of which capital of more than average durability is employed.[4]

And, again, M'Culloch has no scruple in defining profit as an "excess of produce," as a "surplus," as "the portion of the

[1] Pp. 61, 205, 289 of first edition; fifth edition, pp. 6, 276.

[2] "The cost of producing commodities is, as will be afterwards shown, identical with the quantity of labour required to produce them and bring them to market" (first edition, p. 250). Almost in the same words in fifth edition, p. 250: "The cost or real value of commodities is, as already seen, determined by the quantity of labour," etc.

[3] "But it is quite obvious that if any commodity were brought to market and exchanged for a greater amount, either of other commodities or of money, than was required to defray the cost of its production, including in that cost the common and average rate of net profit at the time," etc. (first edition, p. 249; fifth edition, p. 250).

[4] First edition, p. 298; fifth edition, p. 283.

produce of industry accruing to the capitalists after all the produce expended by them is fully replaced,"—in short, as a surplus pure and simple, although not long before he had pronounced it a constituent part of the costs. Here are almost as many contradictions as propositions!

Nevertheless M'Culloch is at great pains, at least in the first edition of his *Principles*, to appear logical. To this end he avails himself of a theory by which he traces profit to labour. Profits are, as he emphasises with italics on p. 291 of his first edition, "only another name for the wages of accumulated labour." By this explanation he contrives to bring all those cases where profit exerts an influence on value under the law he has just enunciated, that the value of all goods is determined by labour. We shall see how he carries this out.

"Suppose," he says, "to illustrate the principle, that a cask of new wine, which cost £50, is put into a cellar, and that at the end of twelve months it is worth £55, the question is, Whether ought the £5 of additional value, given to the wine, to be considered as a compensation for the *time* the £50 worth of capital has been locked up, or ought it to be considered as the value of additional labour actually laid out on the wine?" M'Culloch concludes for the latter view, "for this most satisfactory and conclusive reason," that the additional value only takes place in the case of an immature wine, "on which, therefore, *a change or effect is to be produced*," and not in the case of a wine which has already arrived at maturity. This seems to him "to prove incontrovertibly that the additional value acquired by the wine during the period it has been kept in the cellar is not a compensation or return for time, but for the effect or change that has been produced on it. Time cannot of itself produce any effect; it merely affords space for really efficient causes to operate, and it is therefore clear it can have nothing to do with value."[1]

In these words M'Culloch, with almost startling naïvety, concludes his demonstration. He seems to have no suspicion that, between what he wished to show and what he has shown, there is a very great difference. What he had to show was that the additional value was caused by an addition of labour, of human activity; what he has shown at most is, that the

[1] First edition, p. 313.

additional value was not given by time, but by some kind of "change" in the wine. But that this change itself was effected by an addition of labour is not only not shown, but by hypothesis could not be shown; for during the whole intervening time the wine lay untouched in the cellar.

He himself appears, however, to be sensible, to some small extent, of the weakness of this first demonstration; for, "still better to illustrate this proposition," he adds example to example, although it must be said that, the more clear and exact these are meant to be as demonstrations of his thesis, the more obscure and impossible they actually are.

In the next illustration he supposes the case of an individual who has two capitals, "one consisting of £1000 worth of new wine, and the other consisting of £900 worth of leather, and £100 worth of money. Suppose now that the wine is put into a cellar, and that the £100 is paid to a shoemaker, who is employed to convert the leather into shoes. At the end of a year this capitalist will have two equivalent values—perhaps £1100 worth of wine and £1100 worth of shoes." Therefore, concludes M'Culloch, the two cases are parallel, and "both shoes and wine are the result of equal quantities of labour."[1]

Without doubt! But does this show what M'Culloch meant to show—that the additional value of the wine was the result of human labour expended on it? Not in the least. The two cases are parallel; but they are parallel also in this, that each of them includes an increment in value of £100, which is not explained by M'Culloch. The leather was worth £900. The £100 of money were exchanged for labour of equal value; and this labour, one would think, added £100 in value to the raw material. Therefore the total product, the shoes, should be worth £1000. But they are worth £1100. Whence comes the surplus value? Surely not from the labour of the shoemaker! For in that case the shoemaker, who was paid £100 in wages, would have added to the leather a surplus value of £200, and the capitalist, in this branch of his business, would have obtained a profit of fully 100 per cent, which is contrary to hypothesis. Whence then comes the surplus value? M'Culloch gives no explana-

[1] Pp. 313-315.

tion in the case of the leather, and still less, therefore, in the case of the wine, which was to have been explained by analogy with the leather.

But M'Culloch is indefatigable. "The case of timber," he says, "affords a still better example. Let us suppose that a tree which is now worth £25 or £30 was planted a hundred years ago at an expense of one shilling; it may be easily shown that the present value of the tree is owing entirely to the quantity of labour laid out on it. A tree is at once a piece of timber and a machine for manufacturing timber; and though the original cost of this machine be but small, yet, as it is not liable to waste or decay, the capital vested in it will, at the end of a distant period, have operated a considerable effect, or, in other words, will have produced a considerable value. If we suppose that a machine, which cost only one shilling, had been invented a hundred years since; that this machine was indestructible, and consequently required no repairs; and that it had all the while been employed in the weaving of a quantity of yarn, gratuitously produced by nature, which was only now finished, this cloth might now be worth £25 or £30. But, whatever value it may be possessed of, it is evident (!) it must have derived it entirely from the continued agency of the machine, or, in other words, from the quantity of labour expended on its production" (p. 317).

That is to say, a tree has cost a couple of hours' labour, worth a single shilling. At the present moment the same tree, without other human labour being expended on it in the interval, is worth not one shilling, but £25 or £30. And M'Culloch does not bring this forward as disproving, but as proving the proposition that the value of goods invariably adapts itself to the quantity of labour which their production has cost! Any further commentary is superfluous.[1]

[1] It would to some extent modify this judgment of M'Culloch if we could assume that, in the above argument, he has used the word Labour in that vague and confused sense in which he uses it later (note 1 to his edition of Adam Smith, Edinburgh, 1863, p. 435) as meaning "every kind of activity,"—not only that exerted by men, but that of animals, machines, and natural powers. Of course by such a watering down of its fundamental conception his theory of value would be stripped of every peculiar characteristic, and reduced to an idle play upon words; but at least he might be spared the reproach of logical nonsense. However, he cannot be allowed the benefit even of this small modifi-

In later editions of his *Principles* M'Culloch has dropped all these impossible illustrations of the proposition that profit is wage of labour. In the corresponding passage in the fifth edition (pp. 292-294) he mentions the illustration of the wine, which evidently causes him a certain amount of perplexity; but he contents himself with the negative statement that the surplus value is not produced by the activity of natural powers, as natural powers work gratuitously. The only positive statement he makes is, that the increment of value is a "result of the profit" which accrues to the capital required for carrying on the process; but he does not explain the nature of that profit. On p. 277, however, the proposition that profit is only another name for the "wages of anterior labour," remains unaltered.

I may conclude this criticism by quoting an expression of M'Culloch, which will illustrate his untrustworthiness in matters of theory.

To add to the chaos of his incoherent opinions, in one place he takes Adam Smith's old self-interest argument,[1] and as if not content with the confusion prevailing in his theory of interest, and anxious to throw his tolerably clear theory of wages into the same confusion, he pronounces the labourer himself to be a capital, a machine, and calls his wages a profit of capital in addition to a sum for wear and tear of the "machine called man!"[2]

Passing by another set of writers like Whately, Jones, and Chalmers, who contribute nothing of great consequence to our subject, we come to M'Leod.[3]

This eccentric writer is remarkable for the naïvety with which he treats the interest problem, not only in his earlier work of 1858, but in his later work of 1872, although in the

cation. For M'Culloch expresses himself too often, and too decidedly, to the effect that interest is to be traced to the *human labour* employed in the production of capital. Thus, *e.g.* in note 1 on p. 22 of his edition of Adam Smith, where he explains interest to be the wage of that labour which has been originally expended in the formation of capital, and where obviously the "labour" of the machine itself cannot possibly be understood; and, particularly, in the passage (*Principles*, fifth edition, pp. 292-294) where, in regard to the illustration of the wine, he expressly declares that its surplus value is not produced by the powers of nature as these work gratuitously.

[1] First edition, p. 221, in note; and similarly fifth edition, p. 240, at end.

[2] First edition, p. 319; second edition, p. 354; fifth edition, pp. 294, 295.

[3] *Elements of Political Economy*, London, 1858; *Principles of Economical Philosophy*, second edition, London, 1872.

fourteen years that intervened the problem had very greatly developed. For M'Leod there is absolutely no problem. Profit is simply a self-explanatory and necessary fact. The price of commodities sold, the hire of concrete capital lent, the interest on sums of money borrowed, "must," over and above costs, deterioration, and premium on risk, contain the "necessary" profit.[1] Why they should do so is not once asked, even in the most superficial way.

If on one occasion M'Leod describes the origin of loan interest, the immediate circumstances of the illustration in which he does so are selected in such a way that the obtaining of an "increase" from the capital lent admits of being represented as a natural self-intelligible thing, requiring no explanation. He makes the capitalist lend seed and sheep,[2] but even where the capital lent is one that does not consist of naturally fruitful objects, he considers the emergence of an increase as equally self-explanatory. That any one should think otherwise—that any one should even doubt the justifiability of profit, he appears, in spite of the wide dissemination of socialistic ideas in his time, to have no suspicion. To him it is perfectly clear that "when a man employs his own capital in trade he is entitled to retain for his own use all the profit resulting from such operations, whether these profits be 20 per cent, 100 per cent, or 1000 per cent; and if any one of superior powers of invention were to employ his capital in producing a machine, he might realise immense profits and accumulate a splendid fortune, and no one in the ordinary possession of their senses would grudge it him."[3]

At the same time M'Leod plays the severe critic on other interest theories. He rejects the doctrine that profit is a constituent of the costs of production.[4] He controverts Ricardo's statement that the height of profit is limited by the height of wages.[5] He condemns alike M'Culloch's strange Labour theory and Senior's acute Abstinence theory.[6] And yet these critical attacks never seem to have suggested to him one single view which might be put in place of the opinions he rejects.

[1] *Elements*, pp. 76, 77, 81, 202, 226, etc.
[2] *Ibid.* p. 62.
[3] *Ibid.* p. 216.
[4] *Economical Philosophy*, i. p. 638.
[5] *Elements*, p. 145.
[6] *Economical Philosophy*, i. p. 634; ii. p. 62.

This appears to me due to two peculiarities of his doctrine. The first of these lies in the extraordinary vagueness of his conception of capital. Capital, in its original and primary sense, he takes to mean "circulating power." It is only in a "secondary and metaphorical sense" that it is applied to commodities. But when so applied it embraces things so incongruous as tools and commodities, skill, capacities, education, land, and good character,[1]—a collection which, we must admit, makes it difficult to class the incomes that flow from all those different kinds of things under one category, and explain them by one definite theory. The second of these peculiarities is the exaggerated opinion he entertains of the theoretical value of the formula of supply and demand to explain the various phenomena of price. When he has succeeded in tracing back any phenomenon of value whatever to the relation of supply and demand,—or, as he likes to express it in his own terminology, to the relation between "the intensity of the service performed and the power of the buyer over the seller,"—he thinks that he has done enough. And thus, perhaps, he really thought it sufficient to say of interest on capital: "All value arises exclusively from demand, and all profit originates in the value of a commodity exceeding its costs of production."[2]

While in Germany and England there were a good many prominent writers who, for some considerable time, took an undecided attitude on the interest problem, we have only a few Colourless writers to record in the literature of France. The principal reason of this difference is that in France J. B. Say, who was one of the first to take up Adam Smith's doctrine, had already propounded a definite theory of interest, and popularised it simultaneously with Adam Smith's doctrine; while in Germany and England Adam Smith himself, and after him Ricardo, remained for a long time at the head of the general development of economic literature; and both of these, as we know, neglected the interest problem.

From French literature of that period there are, then, only three names which need be mentioned, two of them before the date of J. B. Say—Germain Garnier, Canard, and Droz.

[1] *Elements*, pp. 66, 69.

[2] *Principles of Economical Philosophy*, ii. p. 66.

Garnier,[1] still half entangled in the doctrine of the physiocrats, like them asserts the earth to be the only source of all wealth, and labour the instrument by which men obtain it from this source (p. 9). Capital he identifies with the "advances" that the undertaker must make, and profit he defines as the indemnification which he receives for these advances (p. 35). In one place he designates it with more significance as the "indemnification for a privation and a risk." He nowhere, however, goes any deeper into the matter.

To indicate Canard's [2] derivation of interest I must shortly refer to the general principles of his doctrine.

In the labour of man Canard sees the means to his support and development. One portion of human labour must be spent simply in the support of man; that Canard calls "necessary labour." But happily the whole labour of man is not necessary for this; the remainder, "superfluous labour," may be employed in the production of goods which go beyond the immediately necessary, and create for their producer a claim to get, by way of exchange, the command of just as much labour as the production of these goods has cost. Labour is thus the source of all exchange value; goods which have value in exchange are nothing else than accumulation of superfluous labour.

It is the possibility of accumulating superfluous labour that humanity has to thank for all economic progress. Through such accumulation lands are made fruitful, machines built, and, generally speaking, all the thousand and one means obtained which serve to increase the product of human labour.

Now the accumulation of superfluous labour is also the source of all rents. It may yield these rents by being employed in any of three ways. First, in manuring and improving the land; the net return arising from this is land-rent (*rente foncière*). Second, in the acquisition of personal skill, learning of an art or a handicraft; the skilled labour (*travail appris*) which is the result of such an expenditure must, beyond the wage of "natural" labour, yield a rent to that fund which had to be devoted to the acquisition of the knowledge. Finally, all the products of labour that proceed from these first two "sources of rent" must be divided out, so

[1] *Abrégé Elémentaire des Principes de l'Economie Politique*, Paris, 1796.

[2] *Principes d'Economie Politique*, Paris, 1801.

as to be employed by individuals in the satisfaction of their wants. This requires that a third class of owners should invest "superfluous labour" in the institutions of commerce. This accumulated labour also must bear a rent, the *rente mobilière*, commonly called money interest.

But as to why labour accumulated in these three forms should bear rent we are told almost nothing by Canard. Land-rent he accepts as a natural fact not requiring explanation.[1] In the same way he treats the *rente industrièlle*, contenting himself with saying that "skilled labour" *must* produce the rent of the capital that has been devoted to the acquisition of knowledge (p. 10). And for the *rente mobilière*, our interest on capital, he lays down a proposition which explains nothing, and embellishes it with details evidently intended to accompany an explanation. "Commerce, accordingly, like the other two sources of rent, presupposes an accumulation of superfluous labour which must, *in consequence*, bear a rent" (*qui doit par conséquent produire une rente*), p. 12. But there is nothing whatever to justify this *par conséquent*, unless Canard, perhaps, considers that the bare fact of labour having been accumulated is sufficient ground for its obtaining a rent; and so far he has not said so. He has certainly said that all rents are traceable to accumulated labour, but he has not said that all accumulated labour must bear a rent—a proposition which, in any case, is quite different from the other, and would have been a matter for proof as well as assertion.

If we take an analysis which follows later (p. 13), to the effect that all three kinds of rent must stand equal in importance, then undoubtedly we can make out a certain foundation for interest, although Canard has not put it into words; a foundation which would agree in essence with Turgot's Fructification theory. If it is a natural fact that capital invested in land bears rent, then all capitals otherwise invested must bear rent, or else everybody would invest in land. But if this be Canard's explanation—and it may at least be read between the lines—we have already, when

[1] "The earth has only been cultivated *because its product was able*, not only to compensate the annual labour of cultivation, but also to recompense the advances of labour which its first and original cultivation cost. This superfluity it is which forms the rent of land" (p. 5).

speaking of Turgot, shown its insufficiency as the sole explanation.

Droz, who writes some thirty years later (*Economie Politique*, Paris, 1829), has to choose between the English view, according to which labour is the sole productive power, and the theory of Say, in which capital represents an independent productive power. In each of these views, however, he finds something to object to, and accepts neither of them, but puts forward a third view, in which saving (*l'épargne*) takes the place of capital as an elementary productive power. He thus recognises three productive powers: the Labour of Nature, the Labour of Man, and the Saving which accumulates capitals (p. 69, etc.)

If Droz had followed this line of thought, belonging primarily to the theory of production, into the sphere of distribution, and made use of it to examine accurately the nature of income, he would have arrived at a distinctive theory of interest. But he did not go far enough for that. In his distribution theory he devotes almost all his attention to contract or loan interest, where there is not much to explain, and in a few words disposes of natural interest, where there is everything to explain. In these few words he gives himself no chance of going any deeper into the nature of interest by treating it as interest on loans which the capitalist pays to himself (p. 267). Thus Droz, in introducing the productive power of "saving," begins well, but all the same he does not escape from the category of the Colourless writers.

BOOK II

THE PRODUCTIVITY THEORIES

CHAPTER I

THE PRODUCTIVE POWER OF CAPITAL

SOME of the immediate successors of Adam Smith began to explain interest by the Productive Power of capital. J. B. Say led the way in 1803. A year after Lord Lauderdale followed, but independently of Say. The new explanation found acceptance. It was taken up by gradually widening circles of economists, and worked out by them with greater care; in course of which it became divided into several branches marked by considerable divergence. Although attacked in many ways, chiefly from the socialist side, the Productivity theory has managed to hold its own. Indeed, at the present time the majority of such writers as are not entirely opposed to interest, acquiesce in one or other modification of this theory.

The idea that capital produces its own interest, whether true or false, seems at least to be clear and simple. It might be expected, therefore, that the theories built on this fundamental idea would be marked by a peculiar definiteness and transparency in their arguments. In this expectation, however, we should be completely disappointed. Unhappily the most important conceptions connected with the Productivity theories suffer in an unusual degree from indistinctness and ambiguity; and this has been the abundant source of obscurity, mistakes, confusion, and fallacious conclusions of every kind. These occur so frequently that it would be unwise to let the reader meet them without some preparation. Once embarked on a sea of individual statements, it would be impossible to find our reckoning. It seems then necessary to mark out distinctly, in a few introductory remarks, the ground we mean to cover in stating and criticising these theories.

Two things here seem to stand particularly in need of clear statement. First, the meaning, or, more properly, the complex of meanings of the expression Productivity or Productive Power of capital; and second, the nature of the theoretic task assigned by these theories to this productivity.

First, What is meant by saying, Capital is productive?

In its most common and weakest sense the expression may be taken to mean no more than this,—that capital serves towards the production *of goods*, in opposition to the immediate satisfaction of needs. The predicate "productive," then, would only be applied to capital in the same sense as, in the usual classification of goods, we speak of "productive goods," in opposition to "goods for immediate consumption" (*Genussgüter*). Indeed the smallest degree of productive effect would warrant the conferring of that predicate, even if the product should not attain to the value of the capital expended in making it. It is clear from the first that a productive power in this sense cannot possibly be the sufficient cause of interest.

The adherents of those theories, then, must ascribe a stronger meaning to the term. Expressly or tacitly they understand it as meaning that, by the aid of capital, *more* is produced; that capital is the cause of a particular productive surplus result.

But this meaning also is subdivided. The words "to produce more" or "a productive surplus result" may mean one of two things. They may either mean that capital produces more *goods* or more *value*, and these are in no way identical. To keep the two as distinct in name as they are in fact, I shall designate the capacity of capital to produce more goods as its "Physical Productivity"; its capacity to produce more value as its "Value Productivity." It is perhaps not unnecessary to say that, at the present stage, I leave it quite an open question whether capital actually possesses such capacities or not. I only mention the different meanings which may be given, and have been given, to the proposition "capital is productive."

Physical productivity manifests itself in an increased quantity of products, or, it may be, in an improved quality of products. We may illustrate it by the well-known example given by Roscher: "Suppose a nation of fisher-folk, with no private ownership in land and no capital, dwelling naked in caves, and living on fish caught by the hand in pools left by the ebbing tide. All the workers here may be supposed equal, and each man catches and eats three fish per day. But now one prudent man limits his consumption to two fish per day for 100 days, lays up in this way a stock of 100 fish, and makes use of this stock to enable him to apply his whole labour-power to the making of a boat and net. By the aid of this capital he catches from the first perhaps thirty fish a day." [1]

Here the Physical Productivity of capital is manifested in the fact that the fisher, by the aid of capital, catches more fish than he would otherwise have caught—thirty instead of three. Or, to put it quite correctly, a number somewhat under thirty. For the thirty fish which are now caught in a day are the result of more than one day's work. To calculate properly, we must add to the labour of catching fish a quota of the labour that was given to the making of boat and net. If, *e.g.* fifty days of labour have been required to make the boat and net, and the boat and net last for 100 days, then the 3000 fish which are caught in the 100 days appear as the result of 150 days' labour. The surplus of products, then, due to the employment of capital is represented for the whole period by $3000-(150 \times 3)=3000-450=2550$ fish, and for each single day by $\frac{3000}{150}-3=17$ fish. In this surplus of products is manifested the physical productivity of capital.

Now how would the Value Productivity of capital be manifested? The expression "to produce more value," in its turn, is ambiguous, because the "more" may be measured by various standards. It may mean that, by the aid of capital, an amount of value is produced which is greater than the amount of value that could be produced without the aid of capital. To use our illustration: it may mean that the twenty fish caught in a day's labour by the aid of capital are of more value than the three fish which were got when no capital was employed. But the expression may also mean that, by the aid of capital, an amount of value is produced

[1] *Grundlagen der National-Oekonomie*, tenth edition, § 189.

which is greater than the value of the capital itself; in other words, that the capital gives a productive return greater than its own value, so that there remains a surplus value over and above the value of the capital consumed in the production. To put it in terms of our illustration: the fisher equipped with boat and net in 100 days catches 2700 fish more than he would have caught without boat and net. These 2700 fish, consequently, are shown to be the (gross) return to the employment of capital. And, according to the present reading of the expression, these 2700 fish are of more value than the boat and net themselves; so that after boat and net are worn out there still remains a surplus of value.

Of these two possible meanings those writers who ascribe value productivity to capital have usually the latter in their mind. When, therefore, I use the expression "value productivity" without any qualification, I shall mean by it the capacity of capital to produce a surplus of value over its own value.

Thus for the apparently simple proposition that "capital is productive" we have found no less than four meanings clearly distinguishable from each other. To get a satisfactory conspectus let me place them once more in order.

The proposition may signify four things:—

1. Capital has the capacity of serving towards the production of goods.

2. Capital has the power of serving towards the production of more goods than could be produced without it.

3. Capital has the power of serving towards the production of more value than could be produced without it.

4. Capital has the power of producing more value than it has in itself.[1]

[1] It would be very easy to extend the above list. Thus physical productivity might be shown to contain two varieties. The first,—the only one considered in the text,—is where the capitalist process of production *on the whole* (that is, the preparatory production of the capital itself, *and* the production by the aid of the capital when made) has led to the production of more goods. But it may also happen that the first phase of the total process, the formation of capital, shows so large a deficit that the total capitalist production ends by showing no surplus; while, all the same, the second phase taken by itself, the production *by aid* of the capital, produces a surplus in goods. Suppose, *e.g.* that the boat and net which last 100 days had required 2000 days for their production, then the fisher would receive for the use of boat and net which have cost in all

It does not require to be said in so many words that ideas so different, even if they should chance to be called by the same name, should not be identified,—still less substituted for one another in the course of argument. It should be self-evident, *e.g.* that, if one has proved that, speaking generally, capital has a capacity to serve towards the production of goods, or towards the production of more goods, he is not on that account warranted in holding it as proved that there is a power in capital to produce more value than could have been produced otherwise, or to produce more value than the capital itself has. To substitute the latter conception for the former in the course of argument would evidently have the character of begging the question. However unnecessary this reminder should be, it must be given; because, as we shall see, among the Productivity theorists nothing is more common than the arbitrary confusing of these conceptions.

To come now to the second point, of which at this introductory stage I am very anxious to give a clear statement,—the nature of the task assigned to the productive power of capital by the theories in question.

This task may be very simply described in the words;—the Productivity theories propose to explain interest by the productive power of capital. But in these simple words lie many meanings which deserve more exact consideration.

The subject of explanation is Interest on capital. Since there is no question that contract interest (loan interest) is founded in essential respects on natural interest, and can be easily dealt with in a secondary explanation, if this natural

2100 days of labour, only 100 × 30 = 3000 fish, while with the hand alone he could have caught in the same time 2100 × 30 = 6300 fish. On the other hand, if we look at the second phase by itself, then the capital, now in existence, of course shows itself "productive"; with its help in 300 days the fisher catches 3000 fish; without its help, only 300. If, on that account, we speak, even in this case, of a productive surplus result, and of a productive power of capital—as, in fact, we usually do—it is not without justification; only the expression has quite a different and a much weaker meaning. Further, with the recognition of the productive power of capital is often bound up the additional meaning, that capital is an *independent* productive power: not only the proximate cause of a productive effect, traceable in the last resort to the labour which produced the capital, but an element entirely independent of labour. . . . I have intentionally not gone into these varieties in the text, as I do not wish to burden the reader with distinctions of which, in the meantime at least, I do not intend to make any use.

interest first be satisfactorily explained, the subject of explanation may be further limited to Natural Interest on capital.

The facts about natural interest may be shortly described as follows.

Wherever capital is employed in production, experience shows that, in the normal course of things, the return, or share in the return, which the capital creates for its owner, has a greater value than the sum of the objects of capital consumed in obtaining it.

This phenomenon appears both in those comparatively rare cases where capital alone has been concerned in the obtaining of a return,—as, *e.g.* when new wine, by lying in store, becomes changed into matured and better wine,—and in the much more common cases where capital co-operates with other factors of production, land and labour. For sufficient reasons that do not concern us here, men engaged in economic pursuits are accustomed to divide out the total product into separate shares, although it is made by undivided co-operation. To capital is ascribed one share as its specific return; one share to nature as produce of the ground, produce of mines, etc.; one share, finally, to the labour that co-operates, as product of labour.[1] Now experience shows that that quota of the total product which falls to the share of capital—that is, the gross return to capital—is, as a rule, of more value than the capital expended in its attainment. Hence an excess of value—a "surplus value"—which remains in the hands of the owner of the capital, and constitutes his natural interest.

The theorist, then, who professes to explain interest must explain the emergence of Surplus Value. The problem, more

[1] Whether the shares allotted, in practical economic life, to the individual factors in production exactly correspond to the quota which each of them has produced in the total production, is a much disputed question that I cannot prejudge meantime. I have, on that account, chosen to use in the text modes of expression that do not commit me to any view. Moreover it is to be noted that the phenomenon of surplus value takes place, not only between individual shares in the return as thus allotted, and the sources of return that correspond to them, but also, *on the whole*, between the goods brought forward and the goods that bring them forward. The totality of the means of production employed in making a product—labour, capital, and use of land—has, as a rule, a smaller exchange value than the product has when finished—a circumstance that makes it difficult to trace the phenomenon of "surplus value" to mere relations of allotment inside the return.

exactly stated, will therefore run thus: Why is the gross return to capital invariably of more value than the portions of capital consumed in its attainment? Or, in other words, Why is there a constant difference in value between the capital expended and its return?[1] To take a step farther.

This difference in value the Productivity theories think to explain, and ought to explain, by the productive power of capital.

By the word "explain" I mean that they must show the productive power of capital to be the entirely sufficient cause of surplus value, and not merely name it as *one* condition among other unexplained conditions. To show that, without the productive power of capital, there could be no surplus value, does not explain surplus value any more than it would explain land-rent if we showed that, without the fruitfulness of the soil, there could be no land-rent; or than it would explain rain if we showed that water could not fall to the ground without the action of gravity.

If surplus value is to be explained by the productive power of capital, it is necessary to prove or show in capital a productive power of such a kind that it is capable, either by itself or in conjunction with other factors (in which latter case the other factors must equally be included in the explanation), of being the entirely sufficient cause of the existence of surplus value.

It is conceivable that this condition might be fulfilled in any of three ways.

1. If it were proved or made evident that capital possesses in itself a power which directly makes for the creating of value,—a power through which capital is able, as it were, to breathe value like an economic soul into those goods which it assists, physically speaking, to make. This is value productivity in the most literal and emphatic sense that could possibly be given it.

2. If it were proved or made evident that capital by its services helps towards the obtaining of more goods, or more useful goods; and if, at the same time, it was immediately evident that the more goods, or the better goods, must also be

[1] On the putting of the problem see my *Rechte und Verhaltnisse*, Innsbruck, 1881, p. 107, etc.

of more value than the capital consumed in their production. This is physical productivity with surplus value as a self-explanatory result.

3. If it were proved or shown that capital by its services helps towards the obtaining of more goods, or more useful goods; and if, at the same time, it were expressly proved that the more goods, or the better goods, must also be of more value than the capital consumed in their production, and why they should be of more value. This is physical productivity with surplus value expressly accounted for.

These are, in my opinion, the only modes in which the productive power of capital can be taken as sufficient foundation for surplus value. Any appeal to that productive power outside these three modes can, in the nature of the case, have no explanatory force whatever. If, *e.g.* appeal is made to the physical productivity of capital, but if it is neither shown to be self-evident, nor expressly proved, that a surplus value accompanies the increased amount of goods, such a productive power would evidently not be an adequate cause of surplus value.

The historical development of the actual productivity theories is not behind the above abstract scheme of possible productivity theories in point of variety. Each of the possible types of explanation has found its representative in economical history. The great internal differences that exist between separate typical developments strongly suggest that, for purposes of statement and criticism, we should arrange the productivity theories in groups. The grouping will be based on our scheme, but will not follow it quite closely. Those productivity theories which follow the first two types have so much in common that they may conveniently be treated together; while, within the third type, we find such important differences that a further division seems to be required.

1. Those productivity theories which claim for capital a direct value-producing power (first type), as well as those which start from the physical productivity of capital, but believe that the phenomenon of surplus value is self-evidently and necessarily bound up with it (second type), agree in this, that they derive surplus value immediately, and without explanatory middle term, from the asserted productive power. They

simply state that capital is productive; adding, perhaps, a very superficial description of its productive efficiency, and hastily conclude by placing surplus value to the account of the asserted productive power. I shall group these together under the name of the Naïve Productivity theories. The paucity of argument, which is one of their characteristics, is in many cases such that it is not even clear whether the author belongs to the first or the second type—one more reason for grouping tendencies that merge into one another under one historical consideration.

2. Those theories which take their starting-point in the physical productivity of capital, but do not regard it as self-evident that quantity of products should be bound up with surplus in value, and accordingly consider it necessary to pursue their explanation into the sphere of value, I shall call the Indirect Productivity theories. They are distinguished by the fact that, to the assertion and illustration of the productive power of capital, they add a more or less successful line of argument to prove that this productive power must lead (and why it must lead) to the existence of a surplus value which falls to the capitalist.

3. From these latter, finally, branches off a group of theories which, like the others, connect themselves with physical productivity, but lay the emphasis of their explanation on the independent existence, efficiency, and sacrifice of the *uses* of capital. These I shall call the Use theories. In the productive power of capital they do certainly see a condition of surplus value, but not the principal cause of its existence. As then they do not altogether merit the name of productivity theories, I prefer to treat them separately, and devote to them a separate chapter.

CHAPTER II

THE NAÏVE PRODUCTIVITY THEORIES

THE founder of the Naïve Productivity theories is J. B. Say.

It is one of the most unsatisfactory parts of our task to state what are Say's views on the origin of interest. He is a master of polished and rounded sentences, and understands very well how to give all the appearance of clearness to his thoughts. But, as a matter of fact, he entirely fails to give definite and sharp expression to these thoughts, and the scattered observations which contain his interest theory exhibit, unfortunately, no trifling amount of contradiction.

After careful consideration it seems to me impossible to interpret these observations as the outcome of *one* theory, which the writer had in his mind. Say hesitates between two theories; he makes neither of them particularly clear; but all the same the two are distinguishable. One of them is essentially a Naïve Productivity theory; the other contains the first germs of the Use theories. Thus, notwithstanding the obscurity of his views, Say takes a prominent position in the history of interest theories. He forms a kind of node from which spring two of the most important theoretical branches of our subject.

Of Say's two chief works, the *Traité d'Economie Politique*[1] and the *Cours Complet d'Economie Politique Pratique*,[2] it is on the former that we must rely almost exclusively for a statement of his views. The *Cours Complet* avoids suggestive expressions almost entirely.

According to Say all goods come into existence through the co-operation of three factors—nature (*agents naturels*),

[1] Published 1803. I quote from the seventh edition, Paris. Guillaumin and Co., 1861.

[2] Paris, 1828-29.

capital, and human labour power (*faculté industrielle*). These factors appear as the productive funds from which all the wealth of a nation springs, and constitute its *fortune*.[1] Goods, however, do not come into existence directly from these funds. Each fund produces, first of all, productive services, and from these services come the actual products.

The productive services consist in an activity (*action*) or labour (*travail*) of the fund. The industrial fund renders its services through the labour of the producing man; nature renders hers through the activity of natural powers, the work of the soil, the air, the water, the sun, etc.[2] But when we come to the productive services of capital, and ask how they are to be represented, the answer is less distinctly given. On one occasion in the *Traité* he says vaguely enough: "It (capital) must, so to speak, work along with human activity, and it is this co-operation that I call the productive service of capital."[3] He promises, at the same time, to give a more exact exposition later on of the productive working of capital, but in fulfilling this promise he limits himself to describing the transformations which capital undergoes in production.[4] Nor does the *Cours Complet* give any satisfactory idea of the labour of capital. It simply says, capital is set to work when one employs it in productive operations (*On fait travailler un capital lorsqu'un l'emploie dans des operations productifs*), i. p. 239. We learn only indirectly, from the comparisons he is continually drawing, that Say thinks of the labour of capital as being entirely of the same nature as the labour of man and of natural powers. We shall soon see the evil results of the vague manner in which Say applies the ambiguous word "service" to the co-operation of capital.

There are certain natural agents that do not become private property, and these render their productive services gratuitously —the sea, wind, physical and chemical changes of matter, etc. The services of the other factors—human labour-power, capital, and appropriated natural agents (especially land)—must be purchased from the persons who own them. The payment comes out of the value of the goods produced by these services, and this value is divided out among all those who have

[1] *Cours*, i. p. 234, etc.
[2] *Traité*, p. 68, etc.
[3] Book i. iii. p. 67.
[4] Book i. chap. x.

co-operated in its production by contributing the productive services of their respective funds. The proportion in which this value is divided out is determined entirely by the relation of the supply of and demand for the several kinds of services. The function of distributing is performed by the undertaker, who buys the services necessary to the production, and pays for them according to the state of the market. In this way the productive services receive a value, and this value is to be clearly distinguished from the value of the fund itself out of which they come.[1]

Now these services form the true income (*révenu*) of their owners. They are what a fund actually yields to its owner. If he sells them, or, by way of production, changes them into products, it is only a change of form undergone by the income.

But all income is of three kinds, corresponding to the triplicity of the productive services; it is partly income of labour (*profit de l'industrie*), partly land-rent (*profit du fonds de terre*), partly profit on capital (*profit* or *révenu du capital*). Between all three branches of income the analogy is as complete as it is between the different categories of productive service.[2] Each represents the price of a productive service, which the undertaker uses to create a product.

In this Say has given a very plausible explanation of profit. Capital renders productive services; the owner must be paid for these; the payment is profit. This plausibility is still further heightened by Say's favourite method of supporting his argument by the obvious comparison of interest with wage. Capital works just as man does; its labour must receive its reward just as man's labour does; interest on capital is a faithful copy of wages for labour.

When we go deeper, however, the difficulties begin, and also the contradictions.

If the productive services of capital are to be paid by an amount of value taken out of the value of the product, it is above all necessary that there be an amount of value in the product available for that purpose. The question immediately forces itself on us—and it is a question to which in any case the interest theory is bound to give a decisive answer—Why is there always that amount of value? To put it concretely,

[1] *Traité*, pp. 72, 343, etc.

[2] *Cours*, iv. p. 64.

Where capital has co-operated in the making of a product, why does that product normally possess so much value that, after the other co-operating productive services, labour and use of land, are paid for at the market price, there remains over enough value to pay for the services of capital — enough, indeed, to pay these services in direct proportion to the amount and the duration of the employment of capital?

Suppose a commodity requires for its production labour and use of land to the value of £100, and suppose that it takes so long to make the commodity that the capital advanced to purchase those services (in this case £100) is not replaced for a year, why is the commodity worth, not £100, but more—say £105? And suppose another commodity has cost exactly the same amount for labour and use of land, but takes twice as long to make, why is it worth, not £100, nor £105, but £110 — that being the sum with which it is possible adequately to pay for the productive services of the £100 of capital over two years?[1]

It will be easily seen that this is a way of putting the question of surplus value accommodated to Say's theory, and that it goes to the very heart of the interest problem. So far as Say has yet gone, the real problem has not been even touched, and we have yet to find what his solution is.

When we ask what ground Say gives for the existence of this surplus value, we find that he does not express himself with the distinctness one could wish. His remarks may be divided into two groups, pretty sharply opposed to each other.

In one group Say ascribes to capital a direct power of creating value; value exists because capital has created it, and the productive services of capital are remunerated *because* the surplus value necessary for this purpose is created. Here, then, the payment for the productive services of capital is the *result* of the existence of surplus value.

In the second group Say exactly transposes the causal relation, by representing the payment of the services of capital as the *cause*, as the reason for the existence of surplus value. Products have value because, and only because, the owners of

[1] In this illustration, besides the expenditure for labour and use of land, I do not introduce any separate expenditure for substance of capital consumed, because, according to Say, that entirely resolves itself into expenditure for elementary productive services.

the productive services from which they come obtain payment; and products have a value high enough to leave over a profit for capital, because the co-operation of capital is not to be had for nothing.

Omitting the numerous passages where Say speaks in a general way of a *faculté productive* and a *pouvoir productif* of capital, there falls within the first group a controversial note in the fourth chapter of the first book of his *Traité* (p. 71). He has been arguing against Adam Smith, who, he says, has mistaken the productive power of capital when he ascribes the value created by means of capital to the labour by which capital itself was originally produced. Take the case of an oil mill. "Smith is mistaken," he says. "The product of this preceding labour is, if you will, the value of the mill itself; but the value that is daily produced by the mill is another and a quite new value; just in the same way as the rented use of a piece of ground is a separate value from that of the piece of ground itself, and is a value which may be consumed without diminishing the value of the ground." And then he goes on: "If capital had not in itself a productive power, independent of the labour that has created it, how could it be that a capital, to all eternity, produces an income independent of the profit of the industrial activity which employs it?" Capital, therefore, creates value, and its capability of doing so is the *cause* of profit. Similarly in another place: "The capital employed pays the services rendered, and the services rendered produce the value which replaces the capital employed." [1]

In the second group I place first an expression which does not indeed directly refer to profit, but must by analogy be applied to it. "Those natural powers," says Say, "which are susceptible of appropriation become productive funds of value because they do not give their co-operation without payment." [2] Further, he constantly makes the price of products depend on the height of the remuneration paid to the productive services which have co-operated in their making. "A product will therefore be dearer just in proportion as its production requires, not only more productive services, but productive services that are more highly compensated. . . . The more

[1] Book ii. chap. viii. § 2, p. 395, note 1.

[2] Book i. chap. iv. at end.

lively the need that the consumers feel for the enjoyment of the product, the more abundant the means of payment they possess; and the higher the compensation that the sellers are able to demand for the productive services, the higher will go the price."[1]

Finally, there is a decided expression of opinion in the beginning of the eighth chapter of book ii. on the subject of profit. "The impossibility of obtaining a product without the co-operation of a capital compels the consumers to pay for that product a price sufficient to allow the undertaker, who takes on himself the work of producing, to buy the services of that necessary instrument." This is in direct contradiction to the passage first quoted, where the payment of the capitalist was explained by the existence of the surplus value "created," for here the existence of the surplus value is explained by the unavoidable payment of the capitalist. It is in harmony with this latter conception, too, that Say conceives of profit as a constituent of the costs of production.[2]

Contradictions like these are the perfectly natural result of the uncertainty shown by Say in his whole theory of value. He falls into Adam Smith and Ricardo's theory of costs quite as often as he argues against it. It is very significant of this uncertainty that Say in the passages already quoted (*Traité*, pp. 315, 316) derives the value of products from the value of the services which produce them; and at another time (*Traité*, p. 338) he does quite the opposite, in deriving the value of the productive funds from the value of the products which are obtained from them (*Leur valeur—des fonds productifs—vient donc de la valeur du produit qui peut en sortir*),—an important passage to which we shall return later.

What has been said is perhaps sufficient to show that no injustice is done to Say in assuming that he had not himself any clear view as to the ultimate ground of interest, but hesitated between two opinions. According to the one opinion interest comes into existence because capital produces it; according to the other, because "productive services of capital" are a constituent of cost, and require compensation.

Between the two views there is a strong and real antagonism,—stronger than one would perhaps think at first sight.

[1] Book ii. chap. i. p. 315, etc.

[2] *Traité*, p. 395.

The one treats the phenomenon of interest as above all a problem of production; the other treats it as a problem of distribution. The one finishes its explanation by referring simply to a fact of production: capital produces surplus value, therefore there is surplus value, and there is no occasion for further question. The other theory only rests by the way on the co-operation of capital in production, which it of course presupposes. It finds its centre of gravity, however, in the social formations of value and price. By his first view, Say stands in the rank of the pure Productivity theorists; by his second he opens the series of the very interesting and important Use theories.

Following the plan of statement indicated, I pass over Say's Use theory in the meantime, to consider the development taken by the Naïve Productivity theory after him.

Of development in the strict sense of the word we need scarcely speak. The most conspicuous feature of the Naïve Productivity theories is the silence in which they pass over the causal relation between the productive power of capital and its asserted effect, the "surplus value" of products. Thus there is no substance to develop, and the historical course of these theories, therefore, is nothing but a somewhat monotonous series of variations on the simple idea that capital produces surplus value. No true development is to be looked for till the succeeding stage—that of the Indirect Productivity theories.

The Naïve Productivity theory has found most of its adherents in Germany, and a few in France and Italy. The English economists whose bent does not seem favourable, generally speaking, to the theory of productivity, and who, moreover, possessed an Indirect Productivity theory ever since the time of Lord Lauderdale, have entirely passed over the naïve phase.

In Germany Say's catchword, the productivity of capital, quickly won acceptance. Although, in the first instance, no systematic interest theory was founded on it, it soon became customary to recognise capital as a third and independent factor in production, alongside of nature and labour, and to put the three branches of income—rent of land, wages of labour, and interest on capital—in explanatory connection with the three factors of production. A few writers who do so in an undecided kind of way, and add ideas taken from theories which trace interest to a different origin, have been already mentioned in the chapter on the Colourless theories.

But it was not long before Say's conception was applied with more definiteness to the explanation of interest. The first to do so was Schön.[1] The explanation he gives is very short. He first claims for capital, in fairly modest words, the character of being a "third and distinct source of wealth, although an indirect source" (p. 47). But at the same time he considers it proved and evident that capital must produce a "rent." For "the produce belongs originally to those who co-operated towards its making" (p. 82), and "*it is clear* that the national produce must set aside as many distinct rents as there are categories of productive powers and instruments" (p. 87). Any further proof is, very characteristically, not considered necessary. Even the opportunity he gets when attacking Adam Smith does not draw from him any more detailed reasoning for his own view. He contents himself with blaming Adam Smith, in general terms, for only considering the immediate workers as taking part in production, and overlooking the productive character of capital and land—an oversight which led him into the mistake of thinking that the rent of capital has its cause in a curtailment of the wages of labour (p. 85).

Riedel gives the new doctrine with more detail and with greater distinctness.[2] He devotes to its statement a special paragraph to which he gives the title "Productivity of Capital," and in the course of this he expresses himself as follows: "The productivity which capital when employed universally possesses is manifest on observation of the fact that material values which have been employed, with a view to production, in aiding nature and labour, are, as a rule, not only replaced, but assist towards a surplus of material values, which surplus could not be brought into existence without them. . . . The product of capital is to be regarded as that which in any case results from an employment of capital towards the origination of

[1] *Neue Untersuchung der National-Oekonomie*, Stuttgart and Tübingen, 1835.

[2] *National-Oekonomie oder Volkswirthschaft*, 1838.

material values, after deduction of the value of that assistance which nature and labour afford to the employment of capital. . . . It is always incorrect to ascribe the product of capital to the working forces of nature or labour which the capital needs in order that it may be employed. Capital is an independent force, as nature and labour are, and in most cases does not need them more than they need it" (i. § 366).

It is very significant that in this passage Riedel finds the productive power of capital "manifest on observation" of excess of value. In his view it is so self-evident that surplus value and productive power belong inseparably to each other, that from the fact of surplus value he argues back to the productive power of capital as its only conceivable cause. We need not, therefore, be surprised that Riedel considers that the existence of natural interest is amply accounted for when he simply mentions the catchword, "productivity of capital," and does not give any accurate explanation of it.

But the writer who has done more than any other to popularise the Productivity theory in Germany is Wilhelm Roscher.

This distinguished economist, whose most signal merits do not, I admit, lie in the sphere of acute theoretical research, has unfortunately given but little care to the systematic working out of the doctrine of interest. This shows itself, even on the surface, in many remarkable misconceptions and incongruities. Thus in § 179 of his great work[1] he defines interest as the price of the uses of capital, although evidently this definition only applies to contract and not to "natural" interest, which latter, however, Roscher in the same paragraph calls a kind of interest on capital. Thus also in § 148 he explains that the original amount of all branches of income "evidently" determines the contract amount of the same; therefore also the amount of the natural interest on capital determines the amount of the contract interest. Notwithstanding this, in § 183, when discussing the height of the interest rate, he makes its standard not natural interest but loan interest. He makes the price of the uses of capital depend on supply and demand "specially for circulating capitals"; the demand again depends on the number and solvability

[1] *Grundlagen der National-Oekonomie*, tenth edition, Stuttgart, 1873.

of the borrowers, specially the non-capitalists, such as landowners and labourers. So that from Roscher's statement it seems as if the height of interest were first determined by the relations of contract interest on the loan market, and then transferred to natural interest, in virtue of the law of equalisation of interest over all kinds of employment; while admittedly the very opposite relation holds good. Finally, in the theoretic part of his researches Roscher does not take up the most important question in point of theory, the origin of interest, but touches on it only slightly in his practical supplement on the politics of interest, where he discusses its legitimacy.

To judge by the contents of the following observations, which are a medley of the Naïve Productivity theory and of Senior's Abstinence theory, Roscher is an eclectic. In § 189 he ascribes to capital "real productivity," and in the note to it he praises the Greek expression *τοκος*, the born, as "very appropriate." In a later note he argues warmly against Marx, and his "latest relapse into the old heresy of the non-productivity of capital"; adducing, as convincing proof of its productivity, such things as the increase in value of cigars, wine, cheese, etc., "which, through simple postponement of consumption, may obtain a considerably higher value—both use value and exchange value—without the slightest additional labour." In the same paragraph he illustrates this by the well-known example of the fisher who first catches three fish a day by hand, then saves up a stock of 100 fish, makes a boat and net while living on his stock, and thereafter catches thirty fish a day by the assistance of this capital.

In all these instances Roscher's view evidently amounts to this, that capital directly produces surplus value by its own peculiar productive power; and he does not trouble himself to look for any intricate explanation of its origin. I cannot, therefore, avoid classing him among the Naïve Productivity theorists.

As already pointed out, however, he has not kept exclusively to this view, but has formally and substantially co-ordinated the Abstinence theory with it. He names as a second and "undoubted" foundation of interest the "real sacrifice which resides in abstinence from the personal enjoyment of capital";

he calls special attention to the fact that, in the fixing of the price for the use of the boat, the 150 days' privation of the fisherman who saved would be a weighty consideration; and he says that interest might be called a payment for abstinence in the same way as the wage of labour is called a payment for industry. In other respects too there are many ill concealed contradictions. Among other things, it agrees very badly with the productive power of capital which Roscher assumes to be self-evident, when in § 183 he declares the "use value of capital to be in most cases synonymous with the skill of the labourer and the richness of the natural powers which are connected with it."

Evidently the authority which the respected name of Roscher enjoys among German economists has stood him in good stead with his interest theory. If what I have said be correct, his theory has a very modest claim indeed to the cardinal theoretic virtues of unity, logic, and throughness; yet it has met with acceptance and imitation in many quarters.[1]

In France Say's Productivity theory obtained as much popularity as in Germany. It became unmistakably the fashionable theory, and even the violent attacks made on it after 1840 by the socialists, especially by Proudhon, did but little to prevent its spread. It is singular, however, that it was seldom accepted *simpliciter* by the French writers. Almost all who adopted it added on elements taken from one or even more theories inconsistent with it. This was the case—to name only a few of the most influential writers—with Rossi and Molinari, with Josef Garnier, and quite lately with Cauwès and Leroy-Beaulieu.

[1] I venture to pass over a goodly number of German writers who since Roscher's time have simply repeated the doctrine of the productive power of capital, without adding anything to it. Of these Friedrich Kleinwächter may be mentioned as one who has worked at the doctrine, if not with much more success, at least with greater thoroughness and care. See "Beitrag zum Lehre vom Kapital" (Hildebrand's *Jahrbücher*, vol. ix. 1867, pp. 310-326, 369-421) and his contribution to Schönberg's *Handbuch*. In the same category may be put Schulze-Delitzsch. For his views, which, like Roscher's, are somewhat eclectic, and not free from contradictions, see his *Kapitel zu einem Deutschen Arbeiterkatechismus*, Leipzig, 1863, p. 24.

In the German edition of 1884 there are three pages of criticism on Kleinwächter, which, by desire of Professor Böhm-Bawerk, I here omit.—W. S.

Since the Productivity theory experienced no essential change at the hands of these economists, I need not go into any detailed statement of their views, the less so that we shall meet the most prominent of them in a later chapter among the eclectics. I shall mention only one peculiarly strong statement of the last-named writer, for the purpose of showing how great a hold the Productivity theory has in French economics at the present day, in face of all the socialist criticism. In his *Essai sur la Répartition des Richesses*, the most important French monograph on the distribution of wealth—a book which has passed through two editions within two years—Leroy-Beaulieu writes, "Capital begets capital; that is beyond question." And a little later he guards himself against being supposed to mean that capital begets interest only in some legal sense, or through the arbitrariness of laws: "It is so naturally and materially; in this case laws have only copied nature" (pp. 234, 239).

From the Italian literature of our subject I shall, finally, instead of a number of writers, only mention one; but his method of treatment, with its simplicity in form and its obscurity in substance, may be taken as typical of the Naïve Productivity theory—the much read Scialoja.[1]

This writer states that the factors of production, among which he reckons capital (p. 39), share with, or transfer to their products their own "virtual" or "potential" value, which rests on their capacity towards production; and that, further, the share which each factor takes in the production of value is itself the standard for the division of the product among the co-operating factors. Thus in the distribution each factor receives as much value as it has created; if, indeed, this share may not be fixed *a priori* in figures (p. 100). In conformity with this idea he then declares natural interest to be that "portion" of the total profit of undertaking "which represents the productive activity of capital during the period of the production" (p. 125).

In turning now from statement to criticism, I must redistinguish between these two branches of the Naïve Productivity theory which I put together for convenience of historical

[1] *Principi della Economia Sociale*, Naples, 1840.

statement. It has been shown that all the views already examined agree in making surplus value result from the productive power of capital, without showing any reason why it should be so. But, as I have shown in last chapter, beneath this agreement in expression there may lie two essentially different ideas. The productive power of capital referred to may be understood, in the literal sense, as Value Productivity, as a capacity of capital to produce value directly; or it may be understood as Physical Productivity, a capacity of capital to produce a great quantity of goods or a special quality of goods, without further explanation of the existence of surplus value, it being regarded as perfectly self-evident that the great quantity of goods, or the special quality of goods, must contain a surplus of value.

In stating their doctrine most of the Naïve Productivity theorists are so sparing of words that it is more easy to say what they may have thought than what they actually did think; and often we can only conjecture whether a writer holds the one view or the other. Thus Say's "productive power" equally admits of both interpretations. It is the same with Riedel's "productivity." Scialoja and Kleinwächter seem to incline more to the former; Roscher, in his illustration of the abundant take of fish, rather to the latter. In any case it is not of much importance to determine which of these views each writer holds: if we submit both views to criticism, each will get his due.

The Naïve Productivity theory, in both its forms, I consider very far from satisfying the demands, which we may reasonably make on a theory purporting to be a scientific explanation of interest.

After the sharp critical attacks that have been directed against it from the side of the socialistic and the "sociopolitical" school, its inadequacy has been so generally felt, at least in German science, that in undertaking to prove this judgment I am almost afraid I may be thrashing a dead horse. Still it is a duty which I cannot shirk. The theories of which we are speaking have been treated with such a lack of thoroughness and such hastiness of judgment that, as critic, I must at least avoid a similar blunder. But my chief reason is that I mean to attack the Naïve Productivity theory with arguments which are essentially different from the arguments of socialistic criticism, and seem to me to go more nearly to the heart of the matter.

To begin with the first form.

If we are expected to believe that interest owes its existence to a peculiar power in capital directed to the creating of value, the question must at once force itself upon us, What are the proofs that capital actually possesses such a power? An unproved assurance that it does so certainly cannot offer sufficient foundation for a serious scientific theory.

If we run through the writings of the Naïve Productivity theorists, we shall find in them a great many proofs of a physical productivity, but almost nothing that could be interpreted as an attempt to prove that there is a direct value-creating power in capital. They assert it, but they take no trouble to prove it; unless the fact that the productive employment of capital is regularly followed by a surplus of value be advanced as a kind of empirical proof of the power of capital to produce value. Even this, however, is only mentioned very cursorily. It is perhaps put most plainly by Say, when, in the passage above quoted, he asks how capital could to all eternity produce an independent income, if it did not possess an independent productive power; and by Riedel when he "recognises" the productive power of capital in the existence of surpluses of value.

Now what is the worth of this empirical proof? Does the fact that capital when employed is regularly followed by the appearance of a surplus in value, actually contain a sufficient proof that capital possesses a power to create value?

It is quite certain that it does no such thing; no more than the fact that, in the mountains during the summer months, a rise of the barometer regularly follows the appearance of snow is a sufficient proof that a magic power resides in the summer snow to force up the quicksilver—a naïve theory which one may sometimes hear from the lips of the mountaineers.

The scientific blunder here made is obvious. A mere hypothesis is taken for a proved fact. In both cases there is, first of all, a certain observed connection of two facts, the cause of the facts being still unknown and being object of inquiry. There are in both cases a great many conceivable causes for the effect in question. In both cases accordingly a great many hypotheses might be put forward as to the actual cause; and it is only one among many possible hypotheses when the rising barometer is accounted for by a specific power of the summer snow, or when the surplus value of products of capital is accounted for by a specific power in capital to create value. And it is all the more a mere hypothesis since nothing is known in other respects as to the existence of the "powers" referred to. They have only been postulated for the purpose of explaining the phenomenon in question.

But the cases we have compared resemble each other not only in being examples of mere hypotheses, but in being examples of bad hypotheses. The credibility of a hypothesis depends on whether it finds support outside the state of matters which has suggested it; and, particularly, whether it is inherently probable. That this is not the case as regards the naïve hypothesis of the mountaineer is well known, and therefore no educated man believes in the story that the rise of the column of quicksilver is caused by a mysterious power of the summer snow. But it is no better with the hypothesis of a value-creating power in capital. On the one hand it is supported by no single fact of importance from any other quarter—it is an entirely unaccredited hypothesis; and, on the other hand, it contradicts the nature of things—it is an impossible hypothesis.

Literally to ascribe to capital a power of producing value is thoroughly to misunderstand the essential nature of value, and thoroughly to misunderstand the essential nature of production. Value is not produced, and cannot be produced. What is produced is never anything but forms, shapes of material, combinations of material; therefore things, goods. These goods can of course be goods of value, but they do not bring value with them ready made, as something inherent that accompanies production. They always receive it first from outside—from the wants and satisfactions of the economic world. Value grows, not out of the past of goods, but out of their future. It comes, not out of the workshop where goods come into existence, but out of the wants which those goods will satisfy. Value cannot be forged like a hammer, nor woven like a sheet. If it could, our industries would be spared those frightful convulsions we call crises, which have no other cause than that quantities of products, in the manufacture of which no rule of art was omitted, cannot find the value expected. What production can do is never anything more than to create goods, in the hope that, according to the anticipated relations of demand and supply, they will obtain value. It might be compared to the action of the bleacher. As the bleacher lays his linen in the sunshine, so production puts forth its activity on things and in places where it may expect to obtain value as its result. But it no more creates value than the bleacher creates the sunshine.

I do not think it necessary to collect more positive proofs in support of my proposition. It appears to me too self-evident to require them. But it is perhaps well to defend it against some considerations that at first sight—but only at first sight—seem to run counter to it.

Thus the familiar fact that the value of goods stands in a certain connection, though not a very close or exact connection, with the cost of their production, may give the impression that the value of goods comes from circumstances of their production. But it must not be forgotten that this connection only holds under certain assumptions. One of these assumptions is usually expressly stated in formulating the law that value depends on cost of production; while the other is usually tacitly assumed—neither of them having anything at all to do with production. The first assumption is that the goods produced are *useful*; and the second is that, as compared with the demand for them, they are *scarce*, and continue scarce.

Now that these two circumstances, which stand so modestly in the background of the law of costs, and not the costs themselves, are the real and ruling determinants of value, may be very simply shown by the following. So long as costs are laid out in the production of things which are adequately useful and scarce — so long, therefore, as the costs themselves are in harmony with the usefulness and scarcity of the goods—so long do they remain in harmony with their value also, and appear to regulate it. On the other hand, so far as costs are laid out on things which are not useful enough or scarce enough—as, say, in the making of watches which will not go, or the raising of timber in districts where there is naturally a superfluity of wood, or the making more good watches than people want—the value no longer covers the costs, and there is not even the appearance of things deriving their value from the circumstances of their production.

Another plausible objection is this. We produce, it may be, in the first instance, goods only. But since without the production of goods there would be no value, it is evident that in the production of goods we bring value into the world also. When a man produces goods of the value of £1000, it is quite evident that he has occasioned the existence of £1000 of value which would never have existed without the production; and this appears to be a palpable proof of the correctness of the proposition that value also comes into existence through production.

Certainly this proposition is so far correct, but in a quite different sense from that which is here given it. It is correct in the sense that production is *a* cause of value. It is not correct in the sense that production is *the* cause of value—that is to say, it is not correct in the sense that the complex of causes entirely sufficient to account for the existence of value is to be found in the circumstances of production.

Between these two senses lies a very great distinction, which may be better illustrated by an example. If a corn-field is turned up by a steam plough, it is indisputable that the steam plough is one cause of the grain produced, and at the same time is one cause of the value of the grain produced. But it is quite as indisputable that the emergence of value on the part of the grain is very far from being fully explained by saying that the steam plough has produced it. One cause of the existence of the grain, and at the same time of the value of the grain, was certainly the sunshine. But if the question were put why the quarter of corn possessed a value of thirty shillings, would anybody think it an adequate answer to say that the sunshine produced the value? Or when the old problem is put, whether ideas are innate or acquired, who would decide that they were innate from the argument that, if man were not born there would be no ideas, and that, consequently, there is no doubt that birth is the cause of the ideas?

And now to apply this to our present problem. Our productivity friends are wrong because they over-estimate their claim to be right. If they had been content to speak of a value-creating power of capital in the sense that capital supplies *one* cause of the emergence of value, there would have been nothing to object to. Next to nothing indeed would have been done towards explaining surplus value. It would only be stating explicitly what scarcely required to be stated at all; and in the nature of things our theorists would have been compelled to go on to explain the other and less obvious part-causes of surplus value. Instead of that, they imagine that they have given *the* cause of the existence of value. They assume that, in the words, "Capital, in virtue of its productive power, creates value or surplus value," they have given such a conclusive and complete explanation of its existence that no further explanation of any kind is needed, and in this they are grievously mistaken.

But from what has been said another important application may be drawn, and I give it here, although it is not directed against the Productivity theory. What is right for the one must be fair for the other; and if capital can possess no value-creating power because value is not "created," on the same ground no other element of production, be it land or be it human labour, possesses such a power. This has escaped the notice of that numerous school which directs the sharpest weapons of its criticism against the assumption that land or capital have any value-creating power, only with greater emphasis to claim that very power for labour.[1]

In my opinion those critics have only overturned one idol to set up another in its place. They have fought against one prejudice only to take up a narrower one. The privilege of creating value belongs as little to human labour as to any other factor. Labour, like capital, creates goods, and goods only; and these goods wait for and obtain their value only from the economical relations which they are meant to serve. The fact that there is a certain amount of legitimate agreement between quantity of labour and value of product has

[1] This view is widely accepted even outside the ranks of the Socialists proper. See, *e.g.* Pierstorff, *Lehre vom Unternehmergewinn*, p. 22.

its ground and reason in quite other things than a "value-creating" power in labour; in things which I have already suggested—of course in the most cursory way—in speaking of the incidental connection of value and costs. Labour does not and cannot give value.

All these prejudices have been a deplorable hindrance to the development of theory. People were misled by them into settling with the most difficult problems of the science much too easily. If the formation of value was to be explained they followed up the chain of causes a little way—often a very little way—only to come to a stop at the false and prejudiced decision that capital or labour had created the value. Beyond this point they gave up looking for the true causes, and made no attempt to follow the problem into those depths where we first meet with its peculiar difficulties.

To turn now to the second interpretation that may be given to the Naïve Productivity theory. Here the productive power ascribed to capital is, in the first instance, to be understood as Physical Productivity only; that is a capacity of capital to assist in the production of more goods or better goods than could be obtained without its help. But it is assumed as self-evident that the increased product, besides replacing the costs of capital expended, must include a surplus of value. What is the force of this interpretation?

I grant at once that capital actually possesses the physical productivity ascribed to it—that is to say, by its assistance more goods can actually be produced than without it.[1] I will also grant—although here the connection is not quite so binding—that the greater amount of goods produced by the help of capital has more value than the smaller amount of goods produced without its help. But there is not one single feature in the whole circumstances to indicate that this greater amount of goods must be worth more than the

[1] I purposely disclaim at this point any inquiry whether the physical productivity of capital thus conceded is an originating power in capital, or whether the productive results attained by the help of capital should not rather be put to the account of those productive powers through which capital itself originates; particularly to the account of the labour which made the capital. I do this to avoid diverting the discussion from that sphere where alone, in my opinion, the interest problem can be adequately solved,—that of the theory of value.

capital consumed in its production,—and it is this phenomenon of surplus value we have to explain.

To put it in terms of Roscher's familiar illustration, I at once admit and understand that, with the assistance of a boat and net, one may catch thirty fish a day, where without this capital one would only have caught three. I admit and understand, further, that the thirty fish are of more value than the three were. But that the thirty fish must be worth more than the proportion of boat and net worn out in catching them, is an assumption which, far from being self-evident, we are not in the least prepared for by the presuppositions of the case. If we did not know from experience that the value of the return to capital was regularly greater than the value of the substance of capital consumed, the Naïve Productivity theory would not give us one single reason for looking on this as necessary. It might very well be quite otherwise. Why should a concrete capital that yields a great return not be highly valued on that account—so highly that its capital value would be equal to the value of the abundant return that flows from it? Why, *e.g.* should a boat and net which, during the time that they last, help to procure an extra return of 2700 fish, not be considered exactly equal in value to these 2700 fish? But in that case—in all physical productivity—there would be no surplus value.

It is remarkable that, in certain of the most prominent representatives of the Naïve Productivity theory, there are to be found statements which would lead us to expect such a result, viz. the absence of a surplus value. Some of our authors directly teach that the value of real capital has a tendency to adapt itself to the value of its product. Thus Say writes (*Traité*, p. 338) that the value of the productive funds springs from the value of the product which may come from them. Riedel in § 91 of his *National-Oekonomie* lays down in detail the proposition that "the value of means of production"—therefore the value of concrete portions of capital—"depends substantially on their productive ability, or on a capacity assured them, in the unchanging principles of production, to perform a greater or less service in the producing of material values." And Roscher says in § 149 of the *Principles*: "Moreover land has this in common with other means of production that its price is essentially conditioned by that of its product."

What then, if, in accordance with these views, the value of real capital accommodates itself entirely to the value of the product, and becomes quite equal to it? And why should it not? But in that case where would be the surplus value?[1]

If then surplus value be actually bound up with the physical productivity of capital, the fact is certainly not self-evident; and a theory which, without a word of explanation, takes that as self-evident has not done what we expect of a theory.

To sum up. Whichever of the two meanings we give to the expression "productive power," the Naïve Productivity theory breaks down. If it asserts a direct value-creating power in capital, it asserts what is impossible. There is no power in any element of production to infuse value immediately or necessarily into its products. A factor of production can never be an adequate source of value. Wherever value makes its appearance it has its ultimate cause in the relations of human needs and satisfactions. Any tenable explanation of interest must go back to this ultimate source. But the hypothesis of value-creating power is an attempt to evade this last and most difficult part of the explanation by a quite untenable assumption.

If, however, the writers we are discussing understand by productivity, merely physical productivity, then they are mistaken in treating surplus value as an accompanying phenomenon that requires no explanation. In assuming that it is self-explanatory, and contributing no proof to the assumption, their theory leaves out the most important and difficult part of the explanation.

It is, however, very easy to understand the strong adherence given to the Naïve Productivity theory in spite of these defects. It is impossible to deny that at the first glance there is something exceedingly plausible about it. It is undeniable that capital helps to produce, and helps to produce "more." At the same time we know that, at the end of every production

[1] See also on this point my *Rechte und Verhältnisse*, p. 104, etc.; and particularly pp. 107-109.

in which capital takes part, there remains over a "surplus" to the undertaker, and that the amount of this surplus bears a regular proportion to the amount of capital expended, and to the duration of its expenditure. In these circumstances nothing really is more natural than to connect the existence of this surplus with the productive power that resides in capital. It would have been wonderful indeed if the Productivity theory had not been put forward.

How long one remains under the influence of this theory depends on how soon one begins to reflect critically on the meaning of the word "productive." So long as one does not reflect, the theory appears to be an exact representation of facts. It is a theory which, one might say with Leroy-Beaulieu, "N'a fait ici que copier la nature." But when one does reflect, this same theory shows itself to be a web of dialectical sophistry, woven by the misuse of that ambiguous term, "Productive Surplus Result" of capital.

That is why the Naïve Productivity theory is, I might say, the predestinated interest theory of a primitive and half-matured condition of the science. But it is also predestinated to disappear so soon as the science ceases to be "naïve." That up till the present day it is so widely accepted is not a matter on which modern political economy has any reason to congratulate itself.

CHAPTER III

THE INDIRECT PRODUCTIVITY THEORIES

THE Indirect[1] Productivity theories agree with the Naïve theories in placing the ultimate ground of interest in a productive power of capital. But in the working out of this fundamental idea they show a twofold advance. First, they keep clear of the mysticism of "value-creating powers," and, remaining on solid ground of fact, they always mean physical productivity when they speak of the "productivity of capital." Second, they do not consider it to be self-evident that physical productiveness must be accompanied by surplus in value. They therefore insert a characteristic middle term, with the special function of giving reasons why the increased quantity of products must involve a surplus in value.

Of course the scientific value of all such theories depends on whether the middle term will bear investigation or not; and since the writers of this group differ very considerably as regards this middle term, I shall be obliged in this chapter to state and criticise individual doctrines with much more minuteness than was necessary in the case of the almost uniform naïve theories. In doing so I certainly impose on myself and on my readers no small amount of trouble, but it is impossible to do otherwise without sacrificing honest and solid criticism. When a writer has anything particular to say, the honest critic must allow him to say it, and must answer him

[1] I use the unsatisfactory word Indirect for the German *Motivirte* (reasoned or motivated). The place taken by philosophy in German culture allows the use of many philosophical terms in general literature that we could not employ in English without pedantry. Our political economy, as we are often told, must use the language of the market and the shop.—W. S.

point by point: the particular must not be dismissed with a general phrase.

The series of the Indirect Productivity theories begins with Lord Lauderdale.[1]

In the theoretical history of interest Lauderdale has rather an important place. He recognises, as none of his predecessors did, that here is a great problem waiting on solution. He first states the problem formally and explicitly by asking, What is the nature of profit, and in what way does it originate? His criticism on the few writers who had expressed themselves on the subject of natural interest before his time is well weighed. And, finally, he is the first to put forward a connected and argued theory in the form of a theory, and not in the form of scattered observations.

He begins by pronouncing capital, in opposition to Adam Smith, to be a third original source of wealth, the others being land and labour (p. 121). Later on he goes very thoroughly into consideration of the method of its working as a source of wealth (pp. 154-206); and here at the very first he recognises the importance and difficulty of the interest problem, and takes occasion, in a remarkable passage, to put the problem formally.[2]

He is not satisfied with the views of his predecessors. He expressly rejects the doctrine of Locke and Adam Smith, who are inclined to derive interest from the increment of value which the worker produces by working with capital. He rejects also Turgot's doctrine, which, much too superficially, connects interest with the possibility of obtaining rent by the purchase of land.

Lauderdale then formulates his own theory in these words: "In every instance where capital is so employed as to produce a profit it uniformly arises either from its supplanting a portion of labour, which would otherwise be performed by the hand of man, or from its performing a portion of labour, which is

[1] *An Inquiry into the Nature and Origin of Public Wealth*, Edinburgh, 1804.

[2] "By what means capital or stock contributes towards wealth is not so apparent. What is the nature of the profit of stock, and how does it originate? are questions the answers to which do not immediately suggest themselves. They are indeed questions that have seldom been discussed by those who have treated on political economy, and important as they are, they seem nowhere to have received a satisfactory solution" (p. 155). I may here note that Lauderdale, like Adam Smith and Ricardo, does not distinguish between interest proper and undertaker's profit, but groups both under the name of profit.

beyond the reach of the personal exertion of man to accomplish" (p. 161).

In thus proclaiming the power of capital to supplant labourers as the cause of profit, Lauderdale refers, under a somewhat altered name, to the same thing as we have agreed to call the physical productivity of capital. For as a matter of fact Lauderdale himself, many times and with emphasis, calls capital "productive" and "producing," as on pp. 172, 177, 205.

Still the chief question remains, In what way does profit originate from the power of capital to supplant labourers? According to Lauderdale it is, that the owner of real capital[1] is able to secure for himself as his share, either wholly or at least in part, the wages of those workers who are replaced by the capital.

"Supposing, for example," says Lauderdale, in one of the many illustrations by which he tries to establish the correctness of his theory,[2] "one man with a loom should be capable of making three pairs of stockings a day, and that it should require six knitters to perform the same work with equal elegance in the same time; it is obvious that the proprietor of the loom might demand for making his three pairs of stockings the wages of five knitters, and that he would receive them; because the consumer, by dealing with him rather than the knitters, would save in the purchase of the stockings the wages of one knitter" (p. 165).

An objection obviously suggests itself which Lauderdale thus tries to weaken: "The small profit which the proprietors of machinery generally acquire, when compared with the wages of labour, which the machine supplants, may perhaps create a suspicion of the rectitude of this opinion. Some fire-engines, for instance, draw more water from a coal pit in one day than could be conveyed on the shoulders of 300 men,

[1] Compounds like *Kapitalstücke* and *Kapitalgüter* I usually translate "Real Capital."—W. S.

[2] Lauderdale with great patience and thoroughness applies his theory to all possible employments of capital. He distinguishes five classes of such employment—building and obtaining machinery, home trade, foreign trade, agriculture, and "conducting circulation." The illustration quoted in the text is from the first of these five divisions. I have chosen it because it most clearly illustrates the way in which Lauderdale puts before himself the connection of profit with the labour-replacing power of capital.

even assisted by the machinery of buckets; and a fire-engine undoubtedly performs its labour at a much smaller expense than the amount of the wages of those whose labour it thus supplants. This is, in truth, the case with all machinery."

This phenomenon, however, Lauderdale explains, should not mislead us. It simply arises from the fact that the profit obtainable for the use of any machine must be regulated by the universal regulator of prices, the relation of supply and demand. "The case of a patent, or exclusive privilege of the use of a machine . . . will tend further to illustrate this.

"If such a privilege is given for the invention of a machine, which performs, by the labour of one man, a quantity of work that used to take the labour of four; as the possession of the exclusive privilege prevents any competition in doing the work but what proceeds from the labour of the four workmen, their wages, as long as the patent continues, must obviously form the measure of the patentee's charge—that is, to secure employment he has only to charge a little less than the wages of the labour which the machine supplants. But when the patent expires, other machines of the same nature are brought into competition; and then his charge must be regulated on the same principle as every other, according to the abundance of machines, or (what is the same thing), according to the facility of procuring machines, in proportion to the demand for them."

In this way Lauderdale thinks he has satisfactorily established that the cause and source of profit lies in a saving of labour, or of the wages of labour.

Has he really succeeded in establishing this? Has Lauderdale in the foregoing passages really explained the origin of interest? A careful examination of his arguments will very soon enable us to answer this question in the negative.

No fault can be found with the starting-point that he takes for his argument. It is—to continue Lauderdale's own illustration—quite correct to say that one man with a knitting loom may turn out as many stockings in a day as six hand knitters. It is quite correct, also, to say that, where the loom is an object of monopoly, its owner may easily secure for its day's work the wage of five knitters, or, in the case of unlimited competition, of course a correspondingly less amount; and thus, after deducting the wages of the man who tends the machine, there remains over as the owner's share four days' wages of labour—under free competition, correspondingly less, but always something. Here it is shown that a share in value does really go to the capitalist.

But this share, thus proved to go to capital, is not the thing that was to be explained, the Net Interest or profit; but only the gross return to the use of capital. The five wages which the capitalist secures, or the four wages that he retains after paying the man who attends to the machine, are the total income that he makes by the machine. In order to get the net profit contained in that income we must, evidently, deduct the wear and tear of the machine itself. But Lauderdale, who in the whole course of his reasoning is always looking to profit, has either overlooked this—thus confusing gross and net interest—or he considers it quite self-evident that, after deducting from gross interest a proportion for wear and tear, something remains over as net interest. In the first case he has made a distinct blunder; in the second case he has assumed without proof that very point which is the most difficult, indeed the only difficult point to explain,—that, after deduction from the gross return of capital of so much of the real capital as has been consumed, something must remain over as surplus value, and why it should remain over. In other words, he has not touched on the great question of the interest problem.

As everything turns on this point, let me put it in its clearest light by means of figures. Suppose, for convenience, that the labourers get a pound a week, and that the machine lasts a year before it is entirely worn out. Then the gross use of the machine for a year will be represented by $4 \times 52 =$ £208. To ascertain the net interest contained in that we must evidently deduct the whole capital value of the machine now completely worn out by the year's work. How much will this capital value be? This evidently is the crucial point. If the capital value is less than £208, there is a net interest over. If it is equal to, or higher than £208, there can be no interest or profit over.

Now on this decisive point Lauderdale has given neither proof nor even assumption. No feature of his theory prevents us assuming that the capital value of the machine amounts to fully £208. On the contrary, if, with Lauderdale, we think of the machine as an object of monopoly, there is a certain justification in expecting that its price will be very high. I grant that experience goes to show that machines and real capital in general, be their monopoly price forced up ever so high, never cost quite so much as they turn out. But this is only shown by experience, not by Lauderdale; and by entirely shirking the explanation of that empirical fact he has left the heart of the interest problem untouched.

In that variation of the illustration where Lauderdale assumes that unrestricted competition ensues, it is true that we might consider the value of the machine as fixed (relatively at least) by the amount of its cost of production. But here again we are met by the doubt as regards the other determining factor, the amount of the gross use. Say, *e.g.* that the machine has cost £100, and that £100 is presumably its capital value, then whether there is any net interest over or not will depend on whether the daily gross return of the machine exceeds £$\frac{100}{365}$ or not. Will it exceed that? All that Lauderdale says on this point is that the claim of the capitalist "must be regulated on the same principle as everything else," the relation of supply and demand. That is, he says nothing at all.

And yet it was very necessary to say something, and, moreover, to prove what was said. For it is not in the least self-evident that the gross use is higher than the capital value of the machine, if that value is pressed down by free competition to the amount of its cost. It is just where unrestricted competition prevails in the use of the machine, that it presses down the value of the products of capital also—in this case, the stockings—and thus presses down the gross return to the machine. Now, so long as the machine produces more than it costs, there remains a profit to the undertaker; and the existence of a profit, one would think, will act as inducement to the further multiplication of the machines till such time as, through the increased competition, the extra profit entirely vanishes. Why should competition call a halt earlier?

Why, *e.g.* should it call a halt at the time when the gross use of a machine which costs £100 has sunk to £110 or £105, when a net interest of 10 per cent or 5 per cent is thereby assured? This calls for a satisfactory explanation of its own, and Lauderdale has not said a word about it.

His explanation has therefore shot beside the mark. What it actually explains is something that had no need of explanation, viz. the fact that capital gives a gross interest, a gross return. But what had great need of explanation, viz. the remainder of a net return *in* the gross return, remains as obscure as before.

The test by which Lauderdale attempts to confirm the accuracy of his theory, and on which he lays great weight, will not do much to change our opinion. He shows that where a machine saves no labour—where, *e.g.* the machine takes three days to make a pair of stockings, while the hand-worker does the same in two days—there is no "profit." This, according to Lauderdale, is an evident proof that profit does come from the power of capital to replace labourers (p. 164).

The reasoning is weak enough. It shows of course that the power of the machine to replace labour is an indispensable condition of the profit—which is tolerably self-evident, since, if the machine had not this property, it would have no use at all, and would not even belong to the class we call "goods." But it is very far from showing that interest is fully explained by this power. By using a strictly analogous test he might have proved a totally opposite theory, viz. that profit comes from the activity of the workman who tends the machine. If nobody tends the machine it stands still, and if it stands still it never yields any profit. Consequently it is the workman who creates the profit!

I have purposely taken the greater care in examining the blunders into which Lauderdale's method of explanation leads him, because the criticism applies not to Lauderdale alone, but to all those who, in trying to trace interest to the productivity of capital, have fallen into the same errors. And we shall see that the number of those who have thus been criticised in advance is not small, and embraces many a well-known name.

Lauderdale found his first important follower, though by no means his disciple, in Malthus.[1]

With his usual love of exact definition Malthus has carefully stated the nature of profit. "The profits of capital consist of the difference between the value of the advances necessary to produce a commodity and the value of the commodity when produced" (p. 293; second edition, p. 262).

"The rate of profit," he continues more exactly than euphoniously, "is the proportion which the difference between the value of the advances and the value of the commodity produced bears to the value of the advances, and it varies with the variations of the value of the advances compared with the value of the product."

After expressions like these the question would seem to suggest itself, Why must there be this difference between the value of the advances and the value of the product? Unfortunately Malthus does not go on to put this question explicitly. He has given all his care to the inquiry as to the rate of interest, and has left only a few rather inadequate indications as to its origin.

In the most complete of these Malthus, quite in the style of Lauderdale, points to the productive power of capital. "If by means of certain advances to the labourer of machinery, food, and materials previously collected, he can execute eight or ten times as much work as he could without such assistance, the person furnishing them might appear at first to be entitled to the difference between the powers of unassisted labour and the powers of labour so assisted. But the prices of commodities do not depend upon their intrinsic utility, but upon the supply and the demand. The increased powers of labour would naturally produce an increased supply of commodities; their prices would consequently fall, and the remuneration for the capital advanced would soon be reduced to what was necessary, in the existing state of society, to bring the articles, to the production of which they were applied, to market. With regard to the labourers employed, as neither their exertions nor their skill would necessarily be much greater than if they had worked unassisted, their remuneration would be nearly the

[1] *Principles of Political Economy*. London, 1820, third edition; Pickering, 1836.

same as before. . . . It is not, therefore," continues Malthus, making his point of view more precise by a polemical remark, "quite correct to represent, as Adam Smith does, the profits of capital as a deduction from the produce of labour. They are only a fair remuneration for that part of the production contributed by the capitalist, estimated exactly in the same way as the contribution of the labourer" (p. 80).

In this analysis the reader will have no difficulty in recognising the principal ideas of Lauderdale's Productivity theory, only put in a somewhat modified form and with somewhat less precision. There is only one feature that points in another direction; that is, the prominence—if we may use so strong a word—given to the fact that the pressure of competition must always leave over a share to the capitalist—as much as may be "necessary to bring the articles, to the production of which the capital was applied, to market." Malthus indeed has not said anything in further explanation of this new feature. But the fact of his mentioning it at all shows distinctly his feeling that, in the formation of profit, something besides the productivity of capital must be concerned.

The same idea comes out more forcibly in Malthus's direct statement that profit is a constituent part of the costs of production.[1]

The formal enunciation of this proposition, to which Adam Smith and Ricardo inclined without explicit mention of it,[2] was, as things have turned out, a literary event of some importance. It started the stirring controversy which was carried on for some decades with great vigour, first in England, and then in other countries, and this controversy was, indirectly, of great use in developing the interest theory. For when economists were eagerly discussing whether profit should belong to the costs of production or not, they could scarcely avoid making a more thorough investigation into its nature and origin.

The proposition that interest is a constituent portion of

[1] *Principles*, p. 84, and many other places; *Definitions in Political Economy* Nos. 40, 41.

[2] A note which may be found in Ricardo's *Principles* at the end of § 6, chap. i. (p. 30 of 1871 edition), has sometimes given the impression that Ricardo had by that time stated the above proposition explicitly. This, however, is not the case. He only suggested the idea to Malthus, who put it into words. See Wollenborg, *Intorno al costo relativo di Produzione*, Bologna, 1882, p. 26.

the costs of production is likely to be judged in an essentially different way by the theorist, and by the historian of theory. The former will pronounce it a gross mistake, as did Malthus's contemporary Torrens, and as lately Pierstaff has done in harsh terms—much too harsh, in my opinion.[1] Profit is not a sacrifice that production requires, but a share in its fruits. To pronounce it a sacrifice was only possible by a somewhat gross confusion of the national economic standpoint with the individual economic standpoint—the standpoint of the individual undertaker who, of course, feels the paying out of interest on borrowed capital as a sacrifice.

But still, even in this unfortunate form, there lies an idea which is full of significance, and which points beyond the inadequate Productivity theory; and this Malthus evidently had in his mind. It is the idea that the sacrifices of production are not exhausted in the labour which is employed in production, whether that labour be directly, or—as embodied in real capital—indirectly employed; that beyond this there is a peculiar sacrifice demanded from the capitalist which equally demands its compensation. Malthus of course was not able to indicate more accurately the nature of this sacrifice. Yet in this somewhat unusual mention of profit as a constituent of costs the historian of theory will recognise an interesting middle course between Adam Smith's first suggestion,—that the capitalist must have a profit, because otherwise he would have no interest in the accumulation of capital,—and the more precise theories; whether, with Say, these theories pronounce productive services to be a sacrifice demanding compensation and a constituent part of the costs of production, or, with Hermann, pronounce the use of capital to be that sacrifice, or, like Senior, find this sacrifice and cost in the capitalist's abstinence. In Malthus, indeed, the first notes of these more precise doctrines are yet too lightly sounded to drown the ruder explanation, which, like Lauderdale, he deduced from the productive power of capital.

But that neither the one explanation nor the other really passed into a substantial theory is shown by his remarks on the rate of profit (p. 294). Instead of deriving the current rate of interest, as one would naturally have expected, from

[1] *Lehre vom Unternehmergewinn*, p. 24.

the play of those same forces that bring interest into existence, he explains it as determined by influences of a different kind altogether; by the height of wages on the one hand and the price of products on the other.

He calculates in the following manner. Profit is the difference between the value of the costs advanced by the capitalist, and the value of the product. The rate of profit will, accordingly, be greater, the less the value of the costs and the greater the value of the product. But as the greatest and most important portion of the costs consist in wages of labour, we have as the two determinants which influence the rate of profit, the height of wages on the one hand and the price of products on the other.

However logical this way of explanation seems to be, it is easy to show that it does not, at any rate, go to the heart of the matter. To show what I mean, perhaps I may be allowed to make use of a comparison. Suppose we wish to name the cause that determines the distance between the car of a balloon and the balloon itself. It is clear at the first glance that the cause is to be found in the length of the rope that fastens the car to the balloon. What should we say if some one were to conduct the investigation thus: the distance is equal to the difference in the absolute height of the balloon and of the car, and is therefore increased by everything that increases the absolute height of the balloon and diminishes the absolute height of the car; and is diminished by everything that diminishes the absolute height of the balloon and increases the absolute height of the car? And now the explainer would call to the assistance of his explanation everything that could have any possible influence over the absolute elevation of the balloon and of the car—such as density of the atmosphere, weight of the covering of balloon and car, number of persons in the car, tenuity of the gases employed to fill it—only omitting the length of the rope that tied the two!

And just in this way does Malthus act. In page after page of research he inquires why wages are high or low. He is never tired of controverting Ricardo, and proving that the difficulty or ease of production from land is not the only cause of a high or a low wage, but that the abundance of capital which accompanies the demand for labour has also its influence on wage. In the same way he is never tired of asserting that the relation of supply and demand for products, by fixing their price higher or lower, is the cause of a high or a low profit. But he forgets to put the simplest question of all—the question on which everything hinges, What power is it that keeps wage of labour and price of product apart in such a way that, no matter what be their absolute level, they leave a space between them which is filled up by profit?

Only once, and then very faintly—even more faintly than Ricardo on a similar occasion—does Malthus hint at the existence of a power of this sort, when he remarks on p. 303 that the gradual diminution of the rate of profit must, in the long run, bring "the power and the will to accumulate capital" to a standstill. But he does not make any more use of this element to explain the height of profit than did Ricardo.

Finally, Malthus's explanation loses any force it had through the fact that, to determine the prices of products—price being one of his two standard factors—he cannot bring forward anything more substantial than the relation of supply and demand.[1] Here the theory finds a conclusion where it is, I grant, incontrovertible, but where at the same time it ceases to say anything. That the rate of interest is influenced by the relation between the demand and the supply of certain goods is, considering the fact that interest is itself a price, or a difference in price, a little too obvious.[2]

After Malthus the theory of the productive power of capital was only handed on in England by Read.[3] As Read, however, took elements from other theories, we shall have to speak of him again among the eclectics. But very similar views are to be found somewhat later in the writings of certain celebrated American economists, particularly Henry Carey and Peshine Smith.

Carey[4] offers one of the very worst examples of confused

[1] ". . . the latter case shows at once how much profits depend upon the prices of commodities, and upon the cause which determines these prices, namely, the supply compared with the demand" (p. 334).

[2] I think I may pass over Malthus's wearisome and unfruitful controversy against Ricardo's interest theory. It offers many weak points. Those who wish to read an accurate judgment on it will find it in Pierstorff, p. 23.

[3] *An Inquiry into the Natural Grounds of Right to Vendible Property or Wealth.* Edinburgh, 1829.

[4] His chief work is the *Principles of Social Science*, 1858.

thinking on a subject where there has already been much confusion. What he says on interest is a tissue of incredibly clumsy and wanton mistakes—mistakes of such a nature that it is almost inconceivable how they should ever have received any consideration in the scientific world. I should not express this opinion in such severe terms if it were not that Carey's interest theory even yet enjoys a reputation which I consider very ill deserved. It is one of those theories which, to my mind, cast discredit not only on their authors, but on the science that lets itself be seduced into credulous acceptance of them; not so much that it errs as for the unpardonably blundering way in which it errs. Whether I speak too harshly of it or not let the reader judge.

Carey has not given any abstract formulation to his views on the source of interest. Following his favourite plan of explaining economical phenomena by introducing simple situations of Robinson Crusoe life, he contents himself, in the present case, with giving a pictorial account of the origin of interest, so that we discover his opinion on its causes only by the characteristic features which he gives to imaginary transactions. It is from such pictures that we have to put together Carey's theory.

He deals with our subject ostensibly in the forty-first chapter of his *Principles*, under the title, "Wages, Profit, and Interest." After a few introductory words the following picture occurs in the first paragraph:—

"Friday had no canoe, nor had he acquired the mental capital required for producing such an instrument. Had Crusoe owned one, and had Friday desired to borrow it, the former might thus have answered him—

"'Fish abound at some little distance from the shore, whereas they are scarce in our immediate neighbourhood. Working without the help of my canoe, you will scarcely, with all your labour, obtain the food required for the preservation of life; whereas, with it, you will, with half your time, take as many fish as will supply us both. Give me three-fourths of all you take, and you shall have the remainder for your services. This will secure you an abundant supply of food, leaving much of your time unoccupied, to be applied to giving yourself better shelter and better clothing.'

"Hard as this might seem, Friday would have accepted the offer, profiting by Crusoe's capital, though paying dearly for its use."

Up to this point one can easily see that Carey's theory is a tolerably faithful copy of Lauderdale's. Like him Carey starts by making capital the cause of a productive surplus result. This forms the occasion for the capitalist receiving a price for the use of his capital, and this price—as appears from many passages — is without further examination identified by Carey, as it was by Lauderdale, with interest, although obviously it only represents the gross use of the capital. It makes no difference that Carey, unlike Lauderdale, does not look on capital as an independent factor in production, but only as an instrument of production. The essential feature remains that the surplus result from the production, associated with the employment of capital, is put down as the cause of interest.

But while Lauderdale is only open to the charge of having mixed up gross and net use, Carey plays fast and loose with a whole row of conceptions. Not only does he confuse net and gross use, but he confuses these two conceptions again with real capital itself, and that not occasionally but consistently. That is to say, he deliberately identifies the causes of a high or low interest with the causes of a high or low value of real capital, and deduces the height of the interest rate from the height of the value of real capital.

This almost incredible confusion of ideas shows itself in every passage where Carey treats of interest. For statement of his argument I shall use chap. vi. (on Value) and chap. xli. (on Wage, Profit, and Interest), where he expresses himself most connectedly on the subject.

According to Carey's well-known theory of value, the value of all goods is measured by the amount of the costs required for their reproduction. Progressive economical development, which is simply man's progressive mastery over nature, enables man to replace the goods he needs at a steadily decreasing cost. This is true, among other things, of those tools that form man's capital; capital shows, therefore, the tendency to fall steadily in value with the advance of civilisation. "The quantity of labour required for reproducing existing capital and for further extending the quantity of capital diminishes with every stage of progress. Past accumulations tend steadily to decline in value, labour rising not less steadily when compared with them" (iii. p. 130; so also i. chap. i. *passim*).

Accompanying this and as result of the decrease in the value of capital comes a fall in the price paid for its use. This proposition is not actually stated by Carey; he evidently thinks it too self-evident to require that,—as indeed, rightly understood, it is,—but it is assumed and referred to in his pictures of Crusoe's economical development. He relates how the owner of the first axe may have been able to demand for the loan of it more than half the wood that could be cut by it, while later, when better axes can be made at a cheaper price, a lower (relative) price is paid for their use (i. p. 193).

On these preliminary facts, then, Carey builds his great law of interest;—that, with advancing economical civilisation, the rate of profit on capital—that is, the rate of interest—falls, while the absolute quantity of profit rises. The way in which Carey arrives at this law can only be adequately appreciated by reading his own words. The reader may therefore pardon the somewhat lengthy quotation that follows.

"Little as was the work that could be done with the help of an axe of stone, its service to the owner had been very great. It was therefore clear to him that the man to whom he lent it should pay him largely for its use. He could, too, as we readily see, well afford to do so. Cutting with it more wood in a day than without it he could cut in a month, he would profit by its help were he allowed but a tenth of his labour's products. Being permitted to retain a fourth, he finds his wages much increased, notwithstanding the large proportion claimed as profit by his neighbour capitalist.

"The bronze axe being next obtained, and proving far more useful, its owner—being asked to grant its use—is now, however, required to recollect that not only had the productiveness of labour greatly increased, but the quantity required to be given to the production of an axe had also greatly decreased, capital thus declining in its power over labour, as labour increased in its power for the reproduction of capital. He, therefore, limits himself to demanding two-thirds of the price of the more potent instrument, saying to the woodcutter: 'You can do twice as much work with this as you now do with our neighbour's stone axe; and if I permit you to retain a third of the wood that is cut, your wages will still be doubled.' This arrangement being made, the comparative effects of the earlier and later distributions are as follows:—

	Total Product.	Labourer's Share.	Capitalist's Share.
First	4	1	3
Second	8	2·66	5·33

"The reward of labour has more than doubled, as a consequence of the receipt of an increased proportion of an increased quantity. The capitalist's share has not quite doubled, he receiving a diminished proportion of an increased quantity. The position of the labourer, which had at first stood as only one to three, is now as one to two; with great increase of power to accumulate, and thus to become himself a capitalist. With the substitution of mental for merely physical power, the tendency to equality becomes more and more developed.

"The axe of iron next coming, a new distribution is required, the cost of reproduction having again diminished, while labour has again increased in its proportions as compared with capital. The new instrument cuts twice as much as had been cut by the one of bronze, and yet its owner finds himself compelled to be content with claiming half the product; the following figures now presenting a comparative view of the several modes of distribution:—

	Total.	Labourer.	Capitalist.
First	4	1	3
Second	8	2·66	5·33
Third	16	8	8

"The axe of iron and steel now coming, the product is again doubled, with further diminution in the cost of reproduction; and now the capitalist is obliged to content himself with a less proportion, the distribution being as follows:—

Fourth	32	19·20.	12·80

"The labourer's share has increased, and, the total product having largely increased, the augmentation of his quantity is very great.

"That of the capitalist has diminished in proportion, but, the product having so much increased, this reduction of proportion has been accompanied by a large increase of quantity. Both thus profit greatly by the improvements that have been effected. With every further movement in the same direction the same results continue to be obtained—the proportion of the labourer increasing with every increase in the productiveness of effort—the proportion of the capitalist as steadily diminishing, with constant increase of quantity and equally constant tendency towards equality among the various portions of which society is composed. . . .

"Such is the great law governing the distribution of labour's products. Of all recorded in the book of science, it is perhaps the most beautiful, being, as it is, that one in virtue of which there is established a perfect harmony of real and true interests among the various classes of mankind" (iii. pp. 131-136).

I beg the reader to stop for a moment at this point of the quotation, and to decide exactly what it is that Carey has up to this point asserted, and, if not strictly speaking proved, has at least made quite clear. The object of Carey's inquiry was the price paid for the use of the axe—that is, its hire. The amount of this hire was compared with the amount of the *total return which a worker could obtain by the help of the axe.* The result of this comparison is the proposition that, with advancing civilisation, the hire paid for capital forms an always decreasing proportion of that total return. This and nothing else is the substance of the law which Carey up till now has expounded and proved, and which he often abridges in the words, "The proportion of the capitalist falls."

Let us hear Carey further. "That the law here given as regards the return to capital invested in axes is equally true in reference to all other descriptions of capital will be obvious to the reader upon slight reflection." He demonstrates its efficacy first in the reduction of the rent of old houses, on which there is nothing particular to remark, and then goes on. "So, too, with money. Brutus charged almost 50 per cent interest for its use, and in the days of Henry VIII the proportion allotted by law to the lender was 10. Since then it has steadily declined, 4 per cent having become so much the established rate in England that property is uniformly estimated at twenty-five years' purchase of the rent; so large, nevertheless, having been the increase in the powers of man that the present receiver of a twenty-fifth can command an amount of convenience and of comfort twice greater than could have been obtained by his predecessors who received a tenth. In this decline in the proportion charged for the use of capital we find the highest proof of man's improved condition" (iii. p. 135).

In these words Carey has suddenly performed a bold *volte-face.* He speaks as if the proof adduced in the foregoing passages referred to the *rate of interest*, and thenceforth treats it as an established fact that the depreciation of the *value of capital* brings about a depreciation of the *rate of interest*![1]

This change of front rests on as gross a piece of juggling as can well be imagined. In the whole course of the preceding argument Carey has never once mentioned the rate of interest, much less made it the subject of any proof. To apply the argument to the rate of interest Carey has now to make a double perversion of his conceptions—first, of the conception of "use"; second, of the conception of "proportion."

In the course of his argument he has always employed the phrase "use of capital" in the sense of "gross use." He who hires out an axe sells its gross use; the price which he receives for it is a hire or gross interest. But now all at once he employs the word use in the sense of *net* use, the use to which the net (money) interest corresponds. While the argument, therefore, was that gross interest has a tendency to fall (relatively), the conclusion drawn by Carey from his argument is that net use has this tendency.

But the second perversion is even more gross.

In the course of the argument the word "proportion" had always referred to the relation between the amount of the interest and the total return to the labour done by the help of capital. But now, in his application of the argument, Carey interprets the word proportion as expressing a relation between the amount of the use and the value of the parent

[1] *E.g.* iii. p. 119: "The proportion of the capitalist (profit or interest, as the following lines show) declines *because of the great economy of labour.*" P. 149: "Decrease of the costs of reproduction and reduction of the rate of interest *consequent on that,*" etc.

capital—in other words, the rate of interest. He speaks of a "proportion of 10 per cent," by which he does not mean as formerly 10 per cent of the *return* obtained by the assistance of the capital lent, but 10 per cent on the parent *capital*. And in the fall of the interest rate from 10 per cent to 4 per cent—"the decline in the proportion charged for the use of capital"—he sees a simple application of the law just proved, without a suspicion that the proportion spoken of earlier means something quite different from that now referred to.

In case the reader may think that this criticism is mere hair-splitting, I would ask him to consider the following concrete illustration, which I adapt as closely as possible to Carey's line of argument.

Suppose that with a steel axe a worker, in a year's time, can cut down 1000 trees. If only one such axe is to be had, and no other of the same kind can be made, its owner may ask and receive for the transference of its use a large part of the total return—say one-half. Thanks to the monopoly, the capital value which the single axe obtains in these circumstances will also be high; it may, *e.g.* amount to the value of as many trunks as a man can fell with it in two years—that is, 2000 trunks. The price of 500 trees which is paid for the year's use of the axe represents in this case a proportion of 50 per cent of the total yearly return, but a proportion of 25 per cent only of the value of the capital. This by itself proves that the two proportions are not identical; but let us look further.

Later on people learn to manufacture steel axes in any quantity desired. The capital value of the axes falls to the amount of the costs of reproduction at the time. Say that these costs are equal to eighteen days of labour; then a steel axe will be worth about as much as fifty trees, since the felling of fifty trees also costs eighteen days' labour. Naturally if the owner lend the axe he will now be content to take a much smaller proportion of the 1000 trees that represent the year's work; instead of receiving the half, as before, he now gets no more than a twentieth—that is, fifty trees. These fifty trees represent, on the one hand, 5 per cent of the total return, and, on the other hand, 100 per cent of the capital value of the axe.

What does this prove? The one proportion, 50 per cent of the gross return, represented only 25 per cent of the capital value of the axe; the smaller proportion, 5 per cent of the total return, represents 100 per cent of the capital value. In other words, while the proportion of the total return fell to a tenth part of what it was at first, the rate of interest represented by this proportion rose fourfold. So little necessity is there that the proportions which Carey lightly confuses with one another should run parallel; and so little does Carey's law of the "falling of the capitalist's proportion" show what he intended to show—the course pursued by the rate of interest.

It scarcely needs further proof that Carey's contributions to the explanation of interest are entirely worthless. The peculiar problem of interest, the explanation why it is that the return falling to the share of capital is worth more than the capital consumed in obtaining it, is not even touched. That this sham-solution has, nevertheless, found admission into the writings of many most respectable economists of our own and other nations is a proof of the very small degree of thoroughness and discrimination with which, unfortunately, our most difficult subject is usually treated.

Scarcely more correct—if at all—than Carey himself is his disciple E. Peshine Smith, whose *Manual of Political Economy* (1853) has lately obtained a wide circulation in Germany through Stöpel's translation.

Peshine Smith finds the origin of profit in a partnership between workman and capitalist. The object of the partnership is "to change the form of the commodities contributed by the capitalist, and increase their value by combining them with a new infusion of labour." The return, "the new thing produced," is divided, and divided in such a way that the capitalist receives more than the replacement of the capital he has contributed, and so makes a profit. Smith obviously considers it self-evident that it must be so. For without taking the trouble of a formal explanation, he points out, in quite general terms, that the bargain must promote the interests of both, and that "both the capitalist and the labourer expect to derive their respective shares in the advantages of their partnership." Beyond this he simply appeals to the fact: "In point of fact, they do so, however long may be the series of transformations and exchanges before the division is made" (p. 77).

A purely formal distinction of profit emerges according as, in the partnership, it is the capitalist or the labourer who takes the risk on himself. In the former case "the share in the product which the workman obtains is called wages; and the difference in value between the materials as turned over to the workman, the food, raiment, shelter, etc., furnished to the workman in kind, or commuted in wages, the deterioration of the tools employed, and the finished product, is termed profits. If the workman takes the risk upon himself, that share which he gives to the capitalist, in addition to replacing the capital he had borrowed, is called rent" (p. 77).

In this passage, where Smith speaks for the first time of profit, the superficial way in which he evades any deeper explanation of it clearly shows that he has not grasped his problem at all. Yet what he has said up till now, if not of much importance, is not incorrect.

But even this modest praise cannot be given to what follows, where he goes on to examine the influences which the growth of capital exerts on the rate of profit. Here he copies faithfully not only Carey's method of statement and his final conclusions, but even all his mistakes and blunders.

First of all, quite in Carey's style, he introduces a couple of economical pictures drawn from primitive conditions. A savage goes to the owner of a stone axe, and gets permission to use the axe under the condition that he builds one canoe for the owner of the axe, as well as one for himself. A generation passes away, and copper axes are substituted, by the aid of which three times as much work can be done as by the stone axe. Of the six canoes that the worker now builds in the same time as formerly he built two, he may retain four for himself, while two are claimed by the capitalist. The share of the labourer has thus increased both in proportion and in quantity; that of the capitalist has also increased in quantity, but has decreased in relative proportion,—it has fallen from a half to a third of the product. Finally, the celebrated "American axes" of the present day come into use. With them three times the work can now be done that used to be done by the copper axes, and of the eighteen canoes, or other products of labour, which the borrower of the axe can now make, he will have to pay four for the use of the axe, and fourteen are left him as the share of his labour. In this case again the share of the worker has proportionally advanced, and that of the capitalist diminished.

Arrived at this point, Smith begins to apply his rules to modern economic life and its forms.

First, for the form of contract with the savage is substituted the modern loan contract.

"The cases we have put represent the capitalist agreeing to make a fixed payment out of the product of the capital which he entrusts to the labourer, and of the mechanical force of the latter. In so doing he runs a risk that the labourer may not exert himself to his full ability, and that the residue after payment of wages, upon which he depends for profits, may be less than he calculates. To insure himself against this contingency, he naturally seeks to bargain for less wages than he is confident that the earnest and honest exertion of the workman's strength would enable him to pay, without impairing his expected profit. The workman, on the contrary, knowing what he *can* do, and unwilling to submit to any reduction, prefers to guarantee the profit which the capitalist desires, taking upon himself the risk that the product will leave a margin broad enough to provide for the wages which the capitalist is afraid to guarantee. The contract thus becomes one of hiring capital" (p. 80).

The careful reader will remark that in these words not only is the new form of contract substituted for the old,—to which there is no objection, but, quite unexpectedly, for the price of the use, which was the thing formerly mentioned, and which was a gross interest, is now substituted the "profit" (net interest),—to which there are very serious objections.

But Peshine Smith goes still farther. Without hesitation he substitutes for the proportion of the product the proportion of the parent capital, or the rate of interest. Carey had made this confusion blindly; Smith makes it with all deliberation, which is more singular and more difficult to excuse. "Men reckon their gains by a comparison between what they previously possessed and what is added to it. The capitalist reckons his profits not by his proportion of the product which has been won by the combination with labour, but by the ratio which the increment bears to the previous stock. He says he has made so much per cent on his capital; he rents it for so much per cent for a year. The difference is one of arithmetical notation, not of fact. When his proportion of the product is small, it being composed of the original capital and the increment, the ratio of the latter to the capital will also be small" (p. 82).

That is to say, a small proportion of product and a small rate of interest are substantially identical, and only different arithmetical notations for the same thing. For judgment of this strange doctrine I need only refer the reader to the illustration already given when criticising Carey. We there saw that the half of the product may represent 25 per cent of the capital, and that a twentieth part of the product may represent 100 per cent of the capital. This does seem something more than a mere difference in arithmetical notation!

Substituting one term for another in this way, Smith is able, finally, to proclaim Carey's "great law" that as civilisation advances the share of the capitalist—that is, the rate of interest—falls; and to verify it by the historical fact that in rich countries the rate of interest does fall. At the same time his own example illustrates how a tolerably true proposition may be deduced from very false reasoning.

In favourable contrast to the shallowness of the American writer is the homely but conscientious and thorough-going way in which the German investigator, Von Thünen, has dealt with our problem.[1]

Like Carey, Thünen investigates the origin of interest genetically. He goes back to primitive economical relations, follows the first beginnings of the accumulation of capital, and inquires in what manner and by what methods capital comes into existence in these circumstances, as well as under what laws it develops. Before beginning the inquiry itself he is careful to put down with minute exactitude all the assumptions of

[1] *Der isolirte Staat*, second edition, Rostock, 1842-63. The page numbers quoted in the text refer to the first division of the second part (1850).

fact with which he starts, as well as the terminology he means to use (pp. 74-90). This is valuable to Thünen as an aid to literary self-control, and is a characteristic example of his conscientious thoroughness.

From this introduction we find that Thünen starts by supposing a people living in a latitude of tropical fruitfulness, equipped with all the capacity, knowledge, and skill of civilisation, but still, so far, absolutely without capital, and without communication with other peoples; so that the accumulation of capital must come from within, and not be influenced at all from outside. Land has as yet no exchange value. All men are equal in position, equally capable, and equally saving, and get their means of support from labour.

The standard of value which Thünen makes use of for the scope of his inquiry is the labourer's means of subsistence, taking as unit the hundredth part ot the means of subsistence required by a labourer during a year. The year's need he calls *s*, the hundredth part he calls *c*; so that s = 100c.

"Suppose," he begins (p. 90), "that the worker, if diligent and saving, can produce by his hands 10 per cent more than he requires for his necessary subsistence—say 110c in the year. Then, aft^r deducting what he must spend for his own support, there remains over 10c.

"In the course, then, of ten years he may accumulate a store on which he can live for a year without working; or he may for the one whole year devote his labour to the making of useful tools—that is, to the creation of capital.

"Let us follow him now in the labour that creates the capital.

"With a hewn flint he manages to make wood into a bow and arrow. A fish bone serves for the arrow's point. From the stalk of the plantain, or the fibrous covering of the cocoanut, he makes string or packthread; the one he uses to string the bow, with the other he makes fishing nets.

"In the following year he applies himself again to the production of means of subsistence, but he is now provided with bow, arrows, and nets; with the help of those tools his work is much more remunerative, the product of his work much greater.

"Suppose that in this way the result of his work, after deducting what he must spend to keep the tools in an equally good state, rises from 110 to 150c, then he can lay by in one year 50c, and he only needs to devote two years now to the production of the means of subsistence, when he is free again to spend a whole year in the making of bows and nets.

"Now he himself can make no use of these, since the tools made in the previous year are sufficient for his needs; but he can lend them to a worker who up till now has worked without capital.

"This second worker has been producing 110c; if then he is lent the capital, on which the labourer who made it has expended a year's labour, his production, if he keeps up the value of the tools lent him and returns them, is 150c.[1]

"The extra production got by means of capital amounts therefore to 40c.

"This worker can consequently pay a rent of 40c for the borrowed capital, and this sum the worker who produced the capital draws in perpetuity for his one year's labour.

"Here we have the origin and ground of interest, and its relation to capital. As the wages of labour are to the amount of rent which the same labour, if applied to the production of capital, creates, so is capital to interest.

"In the present case the wage of a year's work is 110c; the rent brought in by the capital—that is, the result of a year's labour—is 40c.

"The ratio therefore is 110c : 40c = 100 : 36·4, and the rate of interest is 36·4 per cent."

The passage that follows refers not so much to the origin as to the rate of interest, and I shall only make a brief abstract of such of the leading ideas as may illustrate Thünen's conception still further.

According to Thünen, as capital increases, its productive efficiency declines, each new increment of capital increasing

[1] "But how can the object lent be kept and returned in equally good condition and equal in value? This, I admit, does not hold in the case of individual objects, but it certainly does in the totality of objects lent within a nation. If, *e.g.* any one hires out one hundred buildings for one hundred years, under the condition that the hirer annually erects a new building, the hundred buildings do retain equal value in spite of the annual wear and tear. In this inquiry we must necessarily direct our attention to the whole, and if here only two persons are represented as dealing with one another, it is simply a picture by which we may make clear the movement that goes on simultaneously over the whole nation" (note by Thünen).

the product of human labour in a less degree than the capital formerly applied. If, *e.g.* the first capital increased the return to labour by 40c—say from 110c to 150c—the capital next applied may bring a further increase of only 36c, a third capital 32·4c, and so on. This on two grounds.

1. If the most efficient of the tools, machines, etc., which constitute capital, are to be had in sufficient quantity, then the further production of capital must be directed to tools of less efficiency.

2. In agriculture the increment to capital, if it everywhere finds employment, leads to the cultivation of less fertile and less favourably situated lands, or to a more intensive cultivation that necessitates greater costs; and in these cases the capital last employed brings a less rent than that formerly employed (p. 195, and more in detail, p. 93).

In proportion as the extra return produced by the efficiency of capital declines, naturally the price that will and can be paid for the use of the capital transferred to the borrower also declines; and since there cannot be alongside each other two different rates of interest—one for the capital first applied and another for the capital applied later—the interest on capital as a whole adjusts itself to "the use of that portion of capital which is last applied" (p. 100). In virtue of these circumstances the rate of interest tends to sink with the increase of capital, and the reduction of rent that follows from this is to the advantage of the labourer, inasmuch as it raises the wage of his labour (p. 101).

We see then that Thünen very distinctly makes the productive efficiency of capital his starting-point. Not only is this productive efficiency the origin of interest, but the current degree of the efficiency exactly determines the rate of interest.

Now the value of this theory depends altogether on the way in which is explained the connection that exists between the greater productiveness of labour supported by capital and the obtaining of a surplus value by the owner of capital.

Thünen happily keeps clear of two dangerous pitfalls. He has no fiction of a value-creating power in capital; he only ascribes to it what it actually has, viz. the capacity to assist towards the production of more *products*—in other words, physical productivity. And second, he has escaped the fatal confusion of gross and net interest. What he calls net interest, the 40, 36, 32·4c, etc., which the capitalist receives, is really net interest, it being expressly assumed (p. 91) that the debtor, over and above that interest, fully replaces the value of the capital.

But by this very hypothesis Thünen has laid his interest theory open to attack from another side.

The connection of ideas which in Thünen's theory leads from the physical productivity of capital to the obtaining of surplus value by the capitalist may be put as follows:—

1. Labour supported by capital can obtain a greater amount of products. This assumption is undoubtedly correct.

2. The plus, which is traceable to the employment of capital, is made up, in Thünen's illustration, of two components: first, of the 40, 36, or 32·4c, which the capitalist receives in means of subsistence; and second, of the replacement of the real capital consumed in the employment. It is the two components *together* that make up the gross return to the employment of capital. A little calculation will show that this important proposition, although not plainly stated by Thünen, is really contained in his doctrine. According to Thünen, a year's labour unassisted by capital produces 110c. A year's labour assisted by capital is sufficient, not only to renew the capital so far as it has experienced wear and tear, but to produce 150c besides. The difference of the two results, which represents the plus due the employment of capital, presents, therefore, as a fact 40c *and* the upkeep of the capital. Still it must be confessed that Thünen has kept the existence of the second component very much in the background—not indeed mentioning it again except in two passages of p. 91, and entirely omitting to notice it in making out his later tables (pp. 98, 110, etc.) The exactness of these tables is thus marred in no slight degree. For it may be imagined that, when capitals representing six or ten years' labour are employed, the yearly labour spent in replacing them must absorb a considerable portion of the whole labour power of the user.

3. The excess production called forth by the employment

of capital[1] (= renewal + 40 or 36 or 32·4c, as the case may be) falls to the capitalist as such. This assumption of Thünen's is, in my opinion, on the whole correct, even if the war of prices may often modify the share of the capitalist in individual cases.

4. This gross production of capital that falls to the capitalist is regularly more valuable than the real capital consumed in obtaining it, so that a net production, a net interest, an excess value remains. This proposition forms the natural conclusion to the chain of thought. Thünen has not put it any more than the others in the form of a general theoretical proposition. It only appears in the fact that his illustration shows a regular surplus value in the amount received by the capitalist over the amount given out by him, and this of course—seeing that the illustration chosen is meant to be a typical one—comes pretty much to an express formulation of the theoretical proposition; all the more so that Thünen was bound to maintain and explain a permanent surplus value of the return to capital over the sacrifice of capital, if he meant to explain the interest which *is* this very surplus value.

At this point we come to the last and the decisive stage in Thünen's argument. Hitherto we have found nothing essential to object to, but just at this critical point the weakness of his theory betrays itself.

When we ask, In what way does Thünen explain and give reasons for the existence of this surplus value? it must be answered that he does not explain it, but assumes it. Indeed the decisive assumption has merely slipped in at that very insignificant passage where Thünen says that the possession of a capital enables the worker to produce a surplus product of 40, 36, and so on, *after deduction of what is necessary to give back the capital "in equally good condition" and "equal in value."*

If we look more closely at this apparently harmless proposition, we find it to contain the assumption that capital possesses power (1) to reproduce itself and its own value, and (2) over and above that, to produce something more. If, as is here assumed, the product of capital is always a sum of which

[1] To avoid misunderstandings I should emphasise that Thünen assumes the surplus production of the capital last applied to be the standard for the whole amount of capital.

one constituent alone is equal to the whole sacrifice of capital, then it needs no explanation that the whole sum must be worth more than that sacrifice, and Thünen is quite right not to trouble with any further explanation. But the question is, Was Thünen justified in assuming any such efficiency in capital?

To my mind this question must be answered distinctly in the negative. It is true that, in the concrete situation first supposed by Thünen, that assumption may appear to us quite plausible. We find nothing at all out of place in assuming, not only that the hunter equipped with bow and arrows is able to bring down forty more head of game than he could without those weapons, but that he might also have time enough over to keep his bow and arrows in good condition, or to renew them; so that his renewed capital was worth as much at the end of the year as it was at the beginning. But is it allowable for any one to make analogous suppositions in regard to a complicated condition of economical affairs—that is, a condition in which capital is too various, and the division of labour too complete, to allow of the capital being renewed by the labourer who has been using it? If this labourer must pay for the renewal of the capital, is it self-evident that the excess in products obtained by the help of the capital will exceed the costs of the renewal, or the value of the capital consumed?

Certainly not. There are, on the contrary, two conceivable possibilities by which the surplus value might be swept away. First, it is conceivable that the great productive utility assured by possession of the capital increases the economical estimate of this capital so much that its value comes up to the value of the expected product; that, *e.g.* bows and arrows which, during the whole term of their existence, secure the obtaining of 100 head more of game become equal in value to the 100 head. In that case the hunter, in order to replace the weapons worn out, would be obliged to give to the maker of the weapons the whole surplus return of 100 head (or the value of the 100 head), and would retain nothing to pay surplus value or interest to the man who lent him the weapons.

Or, second, it is conceivable that the competition in the making of weapons is so severe that it presses down their price below that very high economical estimate. But will this same competition not also, of necessity, press down the claims which the capitalist may impose when lending the weapons? Lauderdale has assumed such a pressure; so has Carey; and our experience of economical life leaves no doubt that such a pressure will be exerted. Now here we ask, as we did in the case of Lauderdale, Why should the pressure of competition on the capitalist's share never be so strong as to press down its value to the value of the capital itself? Why is it that there is not so great a quantity of any particular form of capital produced and employed that its employment returns just enough to replace the capital and no more? But if this were to happen, the surplus value, and with it the interest, would, in this case also, disappear.

There are, in short, three possibilities in the relation between the value of the product of capital and the value of the capital that produces that product. Either the value of the product raises the value of the real capital to the level of its own value; or, through competition, the value of the real capital brings down the value of the return to capital to its own value; or, finally, the share of capital in the product remains steadily above the value of the real capital. Thünen presupposes the third of these possibilities without either proving or explaining it; and thus, instead of explaining the whole phenomenon which is ostensibly the subject of explanation, he has assumed it.

Our final judgment must, therefore, be expressed as follows. Thünen gives a more subtle, more consistent, more thorough version of the Productivity theory than any of his predecessors, but he too stumbles at the most critical step; where the problem is to deduce surplus value from the physical productivity of capital,—from the surplus in products,—he includes among his assumptions the thing he has to explain.[1]

[1] Not to burden the statement in the text by more difficulties than I am compelled to bring before the reader, I shall put a few considerations supplementary to the above criticism as a note. Thünen makes two essays which, possibly, may be interpreted as attempts to justify the above assumption, and thus to give a real explanation of interest. The first essay is the remark he very often makes (pp. 111, 149), that capital obtains its highest rent when a certain amount of it has been laid out, and that rent sinks when that limit is overstepped; so that capitalist producers have no interest in pushing their production beyond this point. It is possible to read this proposition as explanatory of the fact that

Thünen's method marks a high level of solid and well considered investigation. Unfortunately this level was not long maintained, even in the literature of his own nation. In his successors, Glaser[1] and Roesler,[2] who wrote on the

the supply of capital can never be so great as to press down the net interest to zero. But this consideration of the totality of profits made by capitalists has no deciding influence, perhaps no influence at all on the action of individual capitalists; it cannot, therefore, prevent the further growth of capital. Every one ascribes, and rightly ascribes, to the increase of capital formed by his own individual saving, an infinitely small effect on the height of the general interest rate. On the other hand, every one knows that this individual saving has a very notable effect in increasing the income that he individually gets in the shape of interest. For this reason every one who has the inclination, and who has the chance, will save, undisturbed by any such considerations; just as every landowner improves his land and betters his methods of cultivation, even when he knows, as a matter of theory, that if all owners were to do the same it would necessarily be followed, if the state of population remain unchanged, by a fall in the price of products and, notwithstanding reduced costs, by a fall in rent.

The second attempt might be found in Thünen's note quoted above on p. 166, at that place where he speaks of the renewal of the capital by the borrower. There Thünen points out that "in this inquiry we must necessarily direct our attention to the whole." It is conceivable that this warning might be taken as an attempt to prove that the phenomenon supposed in the text, where the user of capital renews it by his own labour, and beyond that obtains a surplus product, maintains its validity in *all* economic circumstances, provided the people as a whole be substituted for the individual. That is to say, even if the single individual cannot by his own personal labour renew the capital consumed by him, it will hold, as regards the whole people, that by the use of capital men are able to obtain a surplus product, and *besides*, with a portion of the saved labour, to replace the capital consumed. In this line of thought, then, we might see a support of the objection I made in the text, where I pronounced Thünen's hypothesis to be applicable only to the simplest cases, and to be inadmissible in complicated ones. I do not think that this warning—to look at the whole—was meant by Thünen in the sense I have just indicated. But if it was, it does not take anything from the force of my objection. For in questions of distribution—and the question of interest is a question of distribution—it is not right in every circumstance to look at the whole. From the fact that society, as a whole, is able by the help of capital to renew this capital itself, and over and above that, to produce more products, it does not follow at all that there should be interest on capital. For this plus in products might just as well accrue to the labourers as surplus wage (they being certainly as indispensable to the obtaining of it as the capital) as to the capitalist in the shape of interest. The fact is that interest, as surplus value of individual return over individual expenditure of capital, depends on the *individual* always obtaining particular forms of capital at a price which is less than the value of the surplus product obtained by means of them. But the consideration of society as a whole will not by itself guarantee this to the individual; at any rate it is not self-evident that it will do so. If it were so surely there would not be so many theories over a self-evident thing!

[1] *Die allgemeine Wirthschaftslehre oder National-Oekonomie*, Berlin, 1852.

[2] *Kritik der Lehre vom Arbeitslohn*, 1861. *Grundsätze der Volkswirth-*

same lines, we see a distinct falling off in thoroughness of conception and strictness of method.

In the interval, however, the Productivity theories had become the object of serious and weighty attacks. Rodbertus, in a quiet but effective criticism, had accused them of confusing questions of distribution and questions of production; pointing out that, in assuming the portion of the total product called profit to be a specific product of capital, they had committed a *petitio principii ;* at the same time enunciating his own formula that the sole source of all wealth was labour. Then Lasalle and Marx had varied this theme, each in his own way; the one with vehemence and wit, the other bluntly and ruthlessly.

These attacks called out a reply from the camp of the Productivity theorists, and with this we shall conclude a chapter already too long. It comes from the pen of a still youthful scholar, but it commands our full consideration; partly from the position of its author, who, as a member of the Staatswissenschaftliche Seminar in Jena, and therefore in close scientific relation with the leading representatives of the historical school in Germany, may well be taken as representing the views ruling in that school; partly from the circumstances which called out that reply. For, as it was written with full knowledge of the weighty attacks which Marx in his great book had directed against the productivity of capital, and in refutation of these attacks, we are justified in expecting it to contain the best and the most cogent that its author, after full critical consideration, was able to say in favour of the Productivity theory.

The reply is to be found in two essays of K. Strasburger, published in 1871 in Hildebrand's *Jahrbücher für National-Oekonomie und Statistik.*[1]

The substance of his theory Strasburger has condensed in the second of these essays as follows:—

"Capital supplies natural powers which, while accessible to

schaftslehre, 1864. *Vorlesungen über Volkswirthschaft*, 1878. In the German edition Professor Böhm-Bawerk has devoted several pages to statement and criticism of these two writers; but in the present edition he wishes me to omit them as of little importance.—W. S.

[1] "Zur Kritik der Lehre Marx' vom Kapitale" and "Kritik der Lehre vom Arbeitslohn," vols. xvi. and xvii. of above.

every one, can often be applied to a definite production only by its help. Not every one possesses the means of subordinating those natural powers. The power of the man who works with a small capital is spent in doing things that are done for another man who is amply supplied with capital by natural powers. On this account the work of natural powers, if effected through the medium of capital, is no gift of nature; it is taken into account in exchange; and he who has no capital must give over the product of his own labour to the capitalist for the work of the natural powers. Capital, therefore, produces values, but the rôle it plays in production is quite different from that played by labour."

And a little farther on (p. 329) he says: "What has been already said will show how we understand the productivity of capital. Capital produces values inasmuch as it gets natural powers to do work which otherwise would have to be done by man. The productivity of capital, therefore, rests upon its activity in production being distinct from that of living labour. We have said that the work of natural powers is considered in exchange as an equivalent of human labour. Marx maintains the contrary. He thinks that, if one worker is assisted in his work by natural powers more than another, he creates more use values—the quantity of his products is greater; but that the action of the natural powers does not raise the exchange value of the commodities produced by him. For refutation of this view it is sufficient to remember what we have already noted above—that it is not every one who possesses these means of subordinating natural powers; those who possess no capital must buy its work by means of their own labour. Or if they work by the help of another man's capital, they must give over to him a share of the value produced. This share of the value newly produced is profit: the drawing of a certain income by the capitalist is founded on the nature of capital."

If we condense the substance of this still further we get the following explanation.

While it is true that natural powers are in themselves gratuitous, it is often only by the help of capital that they can be made of use. Now since capital is only available in limited quantity, its owners are able to obtain a payment for the co-operation of the natural powers thus made available. This payment is profit. Profit, therefore, is explained by the necessity of paying a price to the capitalists for the co-operation of natural powers.

What success has this theory in explaining the phenomena under discussion?

Strasburger's premises may be readily conceded. I grant at once that many natural powers can only be utilised through the mediation of capital; and I also grant that, the amount of capital being limited, the owner of it may be able to get paid for the co-operation of the natural powers thus made available. But what I cannot grant is, that these premises tell us anything at all of the origin of interest. It is a hasty and unreasoned assumption of Strasburger that the existence of interest follows from these premises, so long as these premises, in their very nature, lead to entirely different economical phenomena. It should not be difficult to expose Strasburger's mistake.

Only one of two things is here possible: either capital can only be had in such a limited quantity that the capitalists can obtain a payment for the powers of nature made available; or it can be had in unlimited quantity. Strasburger's theory assumes the former of these to be the case. Accepting this we ask, How does the capitalist, in practical business life, actually obtain payment for the natural powers?

It would be a hasty *petitio principii* to answer, Simply by pocketing the profit. A very little consideration will make it clear that, if interest comes from the payment of natural powers, it can only make its appearance as a secondary result of more complicated economical processes. That is to say, since natural powers reside in capital, it is obvious they can only be made use of at the same time as the services of capital are made use of. But, further, since capital has come into being through the expenditure of labour, and when used either perishes in a single use or wears itself out gradually, it is clear that, wherever the services of capital are made use of, the labour that is embedded in the capital must be paid for also. The payment for natural powers, therefore, can only accrue to the capitalist as a constituent portion of a gross return, which, over and above that payment, contains a second payment for expenditure of labour.

To be still more exact. The economical process by which the capitalist receives payment for natural powers is the sale of the services of his capital at a higher price than that which represents the expenditure of labour made in producing the concrete capital in question. If, *e.g.* a machine which lasts for a year is made at the expenditure of 365 days of labour, and if the customary day's wage is half a crown, to sell the daily services of the machine for half a crown would only just pay for the labour embedded in the machine, and leave nothing over for the natural powers that it makes available. No payment for these natural powers emerges until the daily services of the machine are paid for by more than half a crown —say by 2s. 9d.

Now this general process may take place under several different forms.

One of these forms is when the owner of the capital uses it himself in production as an undertaker. In this first case, the payment of the total services of capital consists in that proportion of the product which remains over after deducting the other expenses of production, such as use of ground and direct labour. This constitutes the "gross return to capital." If this gross return, calculated by the day, amounts to 2s. 9d., and if 2s. 6d. only is required to pay for the labour which has created the capital used up in a day, the surplus of 3d. a day represents the payment for natural powers. It must not be taken for granted, however, that this surplus is profit on capital. On that we shall decide later.

In a second and more direct way, the services of capital may obtain payment by hiring. If our machine obtains a day's hire of 2s. 9d., in exactly the same way 2s. 6d. will represent the payment of the labour expended in making the machine, and the surplus of 3d. again represents the payment for natural powers.

But there is still a third way in which a man may part with the services of capital—that is, by parting with the capital itself; which, economically, amounts to a cumulative parting with all the services which that capital is able to perform.[1] Now in this case will the capitalist be content if he is compensated for the labour embedded in the machine?

[1] See Knies, *Kredit*, part ii. pp. 34, 37.

Will he not also demand a compensation for the natural powers that are made available by its use? Of course he will. There is absolutely no ground to conceive why he should get paid for natural powers in the case of a successive parting with the machine's services, and not in the case of a cumulative parting with them; especially when, with Strasburger, we have assumed that the quantity of capital is so limited that he can compel such a payment.

What form, then, will the payment for natural powers take in this case? Quite naturally they will take this form: the price of the machine will rise above that amount which represents the customary payment of the labour employed in making the machine. Therefore, if the machine has cost 365 days of labour at 2s. 6d. a day, its purchase price will amount to *more* than 365 half-crowns. And since there is no reason why, in cumulative parting with the services of capital, natural powers should be paid for at a cheaper rate than in successive partings, we may, as in our former suppositions, assume in this case also a payment for natural powers at 10 per cent of the labour payment. Consequently the capital price would be fixed at $365 + 36 \cdot 5 = 401 \cdot 5$ half-crowns, or £50 : 3 : 9.

Now what about interest under these suppositions? There is no difficulty in answering this. The owner of the machine, who employs it in his own undertaking, or hires it out, draws 2s. 9d. a day for its services during the year which it lasts. That yields a total income of 365 × 2s. 9d. = £50 : 3 : 9. But since the machine itself is worn out through the year's use, and its capital value amounted to quite £50 : 3 : 9, there remains as surplus, as pure interest, nothing. Although, therefore, the capitalist has got paid for natural powers, there is no interest; a clear proof that the cause of interest must lie in something else than payment for natural powers.

An objection may very probably be made at this point. It may be said, It is not possible for the value of real capital to remain so high that its producers obtain in the price a premium for natural powers; in such a case the production of capital would be too remunerative, and would certainly call out a competition that, in the long run, would press down the value of the real capital to the value of the labour employed in its production. *E.g.* if a machine that had cost 365 days' labour should, in consequence of natural powers being made available by it, fetch a price of £50 : 3 : 9; then, supposing the usual wage in other employments to be 2s. 6d. a day, the labour directed to the making of such machines would be more remunerative than any other kind of labour; as a consequence there would be a great rush into this branch of production, and the manufacture of those machines would be multiplied till the increased competition had pressed down their price to 365 half-crowns per machine. At the same time the advantage obtainable by the labourer from their use would be pressed down to the normal standard.

I grant at once the possibility of such an occurrence. But I ask, on the other hand, If the machines have become so numerous, and competition so strong that their producer is glad to sell them at a bare compensation for his labour, and can calculate nothing for the use of the natural powers which he makes available, how should he, in hiring out these machines, or employing them himself, be able all at once to demand something for natural powers? There is only one alternative. Either the machines are scarce enough to allow of a calculation for natural powers; in which case their scarcity will serve as well in selling as in hiring, and the capital value of the machines will rise to the point of absorption of gross interest, if no other thing prevents it. Or the machines are made in such quantity that any calculation for natural powers is made impossible by the pressure of competition; in which case it will be as true for the hiring as for the selling, and gross interest will fall till it is once more absorbed in the cost of replacement—always supposing, again, that there is not some factor, outside of the payment for natural powers, which keeps the two quantities apart.

Thus Strasburger, like many of his predecessors, has missed the very point which was to be explained. He shows, perhaps, why the gross interest which capital yields is high—in our illustration, why the machine yields 2s. 9d. instead of half-a-crown per day—but he does not show why the value of the capital itself does not rise in the same proportion. He does not explain why a machine which yields 2s. 9d. per day for 365 days is not valued at 365 × 2s. 9d. = £50 : 3 : 9, but only at 365 half-crowns = £47. But the writer who means to explain net interest must explain just this difference between the value of the capital itself and the sum of its total gross productiveness.

It is characteristic of the Indirect Productivity theories that after almost seventy years' development they should end nearly at the same point as that from which they started. What Strasburger teaches in the year 1871 is in substance almost exactly what Lauderdale taught in 1804. The "power of capital to replace labourers," which power, on account of its scarcity and in the measure of its scarcity, enables the capitalist to obtain a payment, is only different in name from the natural powers which the possession of capital makes available, and which, equally in the measure of the scarcity of capital, compel a payment. Here as there is the same confounding of gross interest and capital value on the one side, and gross interest and net interest on the other; the same misinterpretation of the true effects of premises assumed; the same neglect of the true causes of the phenomenon under discussion.

In this return to the starting-point is seen the whole barrenness of the development that lies between. This barrenness was no accident. It was not simply an unfortunate chance that no one found the Open Sesame which had the power to discover the mysterious origination of interest in the productivity of capital. It was rather that on the road to the truth a wrong turning had been taken. From the first it was a hopeless endeavour to explain interest wholly and entirely from a productive power of capital. It would be different if there were a power that could make value grow directly, as wheat grows from the field. But there is no such power. What the productive power can do is only to create a quantity of products, and perhaps at the same time to create a *quantity* of value, but never to create *surplus* value. Interest is a surplus, a remainder left when product of capital is the minuend and value of consumed capital is the subtrahend. The productive power of capital may find its result in increasing the minuend. But so far as that goes it cannot increase the minuend without at the same time increasing the subtrahend in the same proportion. For the productive power is undeniably the ground and measure of the value of the capital in which it resides. If with a particular form of capital one can produce nothing, that form of capital is worth nothing. If one can produce little with it, it is worth little; if one can produce much with it, it is worth much, and so on;—always increasing in value as the value that can be produced by its help increases; *i.e.* as the value of its product increases. And so, however great the productive power of capital may be, and however greatly it may increase the minuend, yet so far as it does so, the subtrahend is increased in the same proportion, and there is no remainder, no surplus of value.

I may be allowed, in conclusion, one more comparison. If a log is thrown across a flooded stream the level of water below the log will be less than the level of water above the log. If it is asked why the water stands higher above the log than below, would any one think of the flood as the cause? Of course not. For although that flood causes the water above the log to stand *high*, it tends at the same time, so far as that is concerned, to raise the level of the water below the log just as high. It is the cause of the water being "high"; what causes it to stand "higher" is not the flood, but the log.

Now what the flood is to the differences of level, the productive power of capital is to surplus value. It may be an adequate cause of the value of the product of capital being high, but it cannot be the adequate cause that the product is higher in value than the capital itself, seeing that it feeds and raises the level of the capital in the same way as it does that of the product. The true cause of the "plus" in this case also is—a log, and a log which has not been so much as mentioned by the Productivity theories proper. It has been sought by other theories in various things; sometimes in the sacrifice of a use, sometimes in the sacrifice of abstinence, sometimes in a sacrifice of work devoted to make capital, sometimes simply in the exploiting pressure of capitalist on labourer; but so far as we have gone there has been no satisfactory recognition of its nature and action.[1]

[1] Many readers may wonder why a writer who shows himself so very decidedly opposed to the Productivity theory, does not at all avail himself of the abundant and powerful support given by the socialist criticism; in other words, why

I do not dismiss the theory with the argument that capital itself is the product of labour, and thus its productivity, whatever else it be, is not an originating power. The reason simply is that I attribute to this argument only a secondary importance in the theoretical explanation of interest. The state of the case seems to me to be as follows. No one will question that capital, once made, manifests a certain productive effect. A steam-engine, *e.g.* is in any case the cause of a certain productive result. The primary theoretic question suggested by this state of matters now is, Is that productive capacity of capital —of capital made and ready—the quite sufficient cause of interest? If this question were answered in the affirmative, then of course, in the second place, would come the question whether the productive power of capital is an independent power of capital, or whether it is only derived from the labour which has produced the capital; in other words, whether (manual) labour, through the medium of capital, should not be considered the true cause of interest. But having answered the first question in the negative, I have no occasion to enter on the secondary question, whether the productive power of capital is an originating power or not. Besides, in a later chapter I shall have the opportunity of taking a position on the latter question.

BOOK III

THE USE THEORIES

CHAPTER I

THE USE OF CAPITAL

THE Use theories are an offshoot of the Productivity theories, but an offshoot which quickly grew into an independent life of its own.

They attach themselves directly to that idea on which the Productivity theories proper got into difficulties,—the idea that there is an exact causal connection between the value of products and the value of their means of production. If, as economists began to recognise, the value of every product is, as a rule, identical with the value of the means of production expended in making it, then every attempt to explain surplus value by the productive power of capital must fail; for the higher that power raises the value of the product, the higher must it raise the value of the capital itself as identical with it. The latter must follow the former with the fidelity of a shadow, and there should be no possibility of the slightest space between them.

Nevertheless there is a space.

This line of thought suggested almost of itself a new way of explanation. If, on the one hand, it is true that the value of every product is identical with the value of the means of production sacrificed in making it, and if, on the other hand, it is observed that, notwithstanding this, the product of capital is regularly greater than the value of the real capital thus sacrificed, the conviction almost forces itself on us that this real capital may not represent *all* the sacrifice that is made to obtain a product. Perhaps, besides this real capital, there is something else that must be expended at the same time; a something which claims a part of the value of the product,—the surplus value we are inquiring about.

This Something was sought and found. Indeed, we might say that more than one was found. Three distinct opinions were put forward as to its nature; and out of the one fundamental idea there grew three distinct theories—the Use theory, the Abstinence theory, and the Labour theory. Of these the one that kept most closely by the Productivity theories, and indeed made its first appearance simply as an extension of them, is the Use theory.

The fundamental idea of the Use theory is the following. Besides the *substance* of capital, the *use* (*Gebrauch* or *Nutzung*) of capital is an object of independent nature and of independent value. To obtain a return for capital it is not enough to sacrifice substance of capital alone; the use of the capital employed must be sacrificed also during the period of the production. Now since, as a matter of theory, the value of the product is equal to the sum of the values of the means of production spent in making it, and since, in conformity with this principle, the substance of capital and the use of capital, taken together, are equal to the value of the product, this product naturally must be greater than the value of the substance of capital by itself. In this way the phenomenon of surplus value is explained as being the share that falls to the part sacrifice, the "use of capital."

This theory of course assumes that capital is productive, but less emphatically, and in a way that is quite free from ambiguity. It assumes that the accession of capital to a given amount of labour assists in obtaining a relatively greater product than labour, unsupported by capital, could obtain. It is not necessary, however, that the capitalist process of production *on the whole*, embracing as it does both the making and the employing of capital, should be profitable. If, *e.g.* a fisherman makes a net by 100 days' labour, and with the net catches 500 fish in the 100 days during which the net lasts, while another fisherman without any net has been able to catch three fish a day for the 200 days, evidently the total process has not been a profitable one. Notwithstanding the employment of capital, only 500 fish have been caught by an outlay of 200 days' labour, while in the other case 600 fish have been caught. Nevertheless, according to the Use theory—as also according to facts—the net once made must bear interest. For, once made, it helps to catch more fish than could be caught without a net, and this fact is sufficient to assure the surplus return of 200 fish being calculated as due to its assistance. But it is only calculated as such in association with its use. There will be ascribed, therefore, a part return of, perhaps 190 fish, or their value, to the substance of the net; the remainder will be ascribed to the use of the net. Thus emerges a surplus value and an interest on capital.

If this very moderate amount of physical productivity on the part of capital is sufficient, according to the Use theory, to cause surplus value, it is self-evident that this theory in no way assumes any direct value productivity; indeed, rightly understood, it really excludes it.

The relation of the Use theories to the productive power of capital will not, however, be found stated so clearly in the writings of their representatives as I have thought necessary to state it. On the contrary, indeed, appeals to the productive power of capital long accompany the development of the Use theory proper, and we are very often left in doubt whether the author relies, for his explanation of surplus value, more on the productive power of capital or on the arguments peculiar to the Use theory. It is only gradually that the Use theories have cut themselves clear of this confusion with the Productivity theory, and developed in complete independence.[1]

In what follows I mean, first, to show the historical development of the Use theories. Criticism of them I shall divide into two parts. Such critical remarks as refer simply to individual defects in individual theories I shall include at once with the historical statement. My critical estimate of the school as a whole will follow in a separate chapter.

[1] The hesitating way in which many of the Use theorists have expressed themselves is to blame in great part for the fact that, up till now, so little attention has been paid to the independent existence of these theories. Their representatives were usually classed with the adherents of the Productivity theories proper, and it was considered that the former had been confuted when only the latter had been. From what I have said above it will be seen that this is quite erroneous. The two groups of theories rest on essentially distinct principles.

CHAPTER II

HISTORICAL STATEMENT

THE development of the Use theory is associated for the most part with three names. J. B. Say first suggested it; Hermann worked out the nature and essence of the Uses, and so put the theory on a firm foundation; Menger gave it the most complete form of which, in my opinion, it is capable. All the writers that come between take one or other of these as their model, and although some of them are well worthy of attention, they are of secondary importance to those just mentioned.

There are two things that strike us in looking over the list of these writers. The first is that, with the single exception of Say, the working out of the Use theory has been done entirely by German science. And the other is that in Germany this theory seems to have attracted the marked preference of our most thorough and acute thinkers. At least we find represented here a remarkable number of the best names in German science.

We have already considered at length the doctrine of Say, the founder of this school.[1] In his writings Productivity theory and Use theory grow up side by side; so much so that neither seems to come before or be subordinate to the other; and the historian of theory has no alternative but to consider Say as the representative of both theories. As basis for what follows I shall recapitulate very briefly the line of thought followed in such of his ideas as belong properly to the Use theory.

The fund of productive capital provides productive services.

[1] See above, p. 120.

These services possess economical independence, and are the objects of independent valuation and sale. Now as these services are indispensable for production, and at the same time are not to be obtained from their owners without compensation, the prices of all products of capital, under the play of supply and demand, must adjust themselves in such a way that, over and above the compensation to the other factors in production, they contain the ordinary compensation for these productive services. Thus the "surplus value" of the products of capital, and with it interest, originates in the necessity of paying independently for this independent sacrifice in production, the "services of capital."

The most signal weakness of this doctrine, apart from its being continually traversed by contradictory expressions of the Naïve Productivity theory, lies, perhaps, in the confusion in which Say leaves the conception of productive services. A writer who makes the independent existence and remuneration of such services the axis on which his interest theory turns is, at least, bound to express himself clearly as to what should be understood by these terms. Not only has Say omitted to do this, as we have already seen, but the few indications that he does give point in an entirely wrong direction.

From the analogy that Say repeatedly draws between the services of capital on the one hand, and human labour, as also the activity of the "natural fund," on the other, we might conclude that, by the services of capital, Say would wish us to understand the putting in motion of the natural powers that reside in real capital; *e.g.* the physical actions of beasts of burden, of machines, the setting free of the heating power in coal, etc. But if this is what he means, then the whole argument is on the wrong track. For this putting in motion of natural powers is nothing else than what, in another place, I have called the "Material Services" (*Nutzleistungen*) of goods.[1] It is what our current science, with its unsuggestive and lamentably obscure vocabulary, has termed the *Nutzung* of capital, meaning the gross use of capital. It is this that is remunerated by the undiminished gross return sometimes called Hire.[2] In a word, it is the substance of gross interest, not of

[1] See my *Rechte und Verhaltnisse*, p. 57. More exactly also below.

[2] It will be well to remember that the word Hire (*Miethzins* in German) is

net interest, and it is net interest with which we are here concerned. If this is what Say actually meant by his *services productifs*, then his whole theory has missed the mark; for it is only gross interest that emerges from the necessity of paying for productive services, not net interest; and it is net interest that is the object of explanation. But if by the *services productifs* he meant anything else, he has left us absolutely in the dark regarding the nature of it, and the theory built on its existence is, to say the least of it, incomplete.

In any case, then, Say's theory is not satisfactory. Yet it pointed out a new way which, when properly followed, led much nearer the heart of the interest problem than the barren Productivity theories had.

The two writers who come next after Say can scarcely be said to have done much towards any such development. One of them, indeed, Storch, fell very far short of the point to which Say had brought the theory.

Storch [1] professes to follow Say, and often quotes him, but he only takes Say's results. He does not use his argument, and he has not supplied the want by one of his own. It is a characteristic symptom of the barren way in which Storch deals with our subject that he does not explain loan interest by natural interest, but natural by loan interest.

He starts by saying (p. 212) that capital is a "source of production"—although a secondary source—along with nature and labour, the two primary sources of goods. The sources of production become sources of income inasmuch as they often belong to different persons; and they must first, through a loan contract be put at the disposal of the person who unites them

properly used of the lending of a durable article where the sum paid monthly or yearly includes wear and tear. If we pay 20s. a month for the hire of a piano, it is understood that the piano suffers so much by our use, and that the 20s. covers that deterioration. We are not expected to repair the damage done to the piano, nor to pay an extra sum for repairing it. That is to say, the 20s. per month is a gross interest, which includes the replacement of the capital. If in three years the music-seller gets £36 in hires for an ordinary piano, it is evident that this is far more than interest. The true interest (net interest) is found by deducting the capital value of the piano. Say that that value was £30, and that in three years' time the piano is worn out; then £6 is the interest obtained by the music-seller over a period of three years on a capital sum of £30. But this distinction, evident at a first glance in a concrete example, has been overlooked, as we see, by more than one economist.—W. S.

[1] *Cours d'Economie Politique*, vol. i. Paris, 1823.

in productive co-operation. For this they receive remuneration, and this remuneration goes as income to the lender. "The price of a loaned piece of land is called rent; the price of loaned labour is called wages; the price of a loaned capital is called sometimes interest, sometimes hire."[1]

After Storch has thus given us to understand that lending out of productive powers is the regular way of getting an income, he adds, by way of postscript, that a man can obtain an income even if he himself employs the productive powers. "A man who cultivates his own garden at his own expense unites in his own hands the land, the labour and the capital. Nevertheless" (the word is significant of Storch's conception) "he draws from the first a land rent; from the second a subsistence; from the third an interest on capital." The sale of his products must return him a value which is, at least, equivalent to the remuneration he would have got from the land, labour, and capital if he had lent them; otherwise he will stop cultivating the garden, and lend out his productive powers.[2]

But why should it be possible for him to get a remuneration for the productive powers, particularly for the capital he lends? Storch does not take much trouble to answer this question. "Since every man," he says on p. 266, "is compelled to eat before he can obtain a product, the poor man finds himself in dependence on the rich, and can neither live nor work if he does not receive from him some of the food already in existence, which food he promises to replace when he has completed his product. These loans cannot be gratuitous, for, if they were, the advantage would be entirely on the side of the poor man, and the rich would have no interest whatever in making the bargain. To get the rich man's consent, then, it must be agreed that the owner of the accumulated surplus or capital draws a rent or a profit, and this rent will be in proportion to

[1] These last words are a quotation from Say.

[2] Even in discussing the question of the rate of interest this perversion of the relation of natural and loan interest reappears. On p. 285 Storch makes interest determined by the proportion between the supply of the capitalists having capitals to lend, and of the undertakers wishing to hire these capitals. And on p. 286 he says that the rate of the income of those persons who themselves employ their productive powers adapts itself to that rate which is determined by the demand and supply of *loaned* productive powers.

the amount of the capital advanced." This is an explanation which, in economical precision, leaves almost everything to be desired.

Of a second follower of Say, Nebenius, it cannot at any rate be said that the theory received any harm at his hands.

In his celebrated work on Public Credit,[1] Nebenius has devoted a brief consideration to our subject, and given a somewhat eclectic explanation of it. In the main he follows Say's Use theory. He accepts his category of the productive services of capital,[2] and bases interest on the fact that these services obtain exchange value. But in course of the argument he brings out a new element, in pointing to "the painful privations and exertions"[3] which the accumulation of capital requires. In the long run he shows ample agreement with the Productivity theory. Thus on one occasion he remarks that the hire which the borrower has to pay for a capital which he employs to advantage may be considered as the fruit of that capital itself (p. 21); and, on another occasion, he emphasises the fact that, "in the reciprocal valuation by which the hire is determined, it is the productive power of the capitals that forms the chief element" (p. 22).

Nebenius, however, does not enter on any more exact explanation of his interest theory; nor does he analyse the nature of the productive services of capital, obviously taking the category without question from Say.

At this point I may mention a third writer who rose into prominence later—writing long after Hermann—but never got beyond Say's standpoint; Carl Marlo, in his *System der Weltökonomie*.[4]

[1] *Oeffentliche Credit*. I quote from the second edition, 1829.

[2] See, *e.g.* pp. 19, 20.

[3] "On the one hand, the necessity and the usefulness of capital for the business of production in its most multifarious forms, and on the other, the hardship of the privations to which we owe its accumulation; these lie at the root of the exchange value of the services rendered by capital. They get their compensation in a share of the value of the products, to the production of which they have co-operated" (p. 19).

"The services of capital and of industry necessarily have an exchange value; the former because capitals are only got through more or less painful privations or exertions, and people can be induced to undergo such only by getting an adequate share. . . ." (p. 22)

[4] Kassel, 1850-57.

In striking contrast with the imposing plan of this work, and the supreme importance which, from its very nature, the interest problem should have had in it, is the extremely slight treatment which the problem actually received. One may search these bulky volumes in vain for any connected and thorough inquiry into the origin of interest; indeed for any real interest theory at all. If it were not that Marlo in the course of his polemic against his opponents—particularly against the doctrine that labour is the sole source of value [1]—had to some extent marked out his standpoint, what he said positively on the question of interest would not be enough to indicate, in the very slightest degree, what his opinions were,—to say nothing of introducing the uninitiated to the nature of the problem.

Marlo's views are a mixture of Use and Productivity theories taken from Say. He recognises, with special emphasis on the necessity of their working together,[2] two sources of wealth—natural power and labour power—and from this comes his conception of capital as "perfected natural power." [3] Corresponding to the two sources of wealth are two kinds of income—interest and wages. "Interest is the compensation for the productive or consumptive use of parent-wealth." "If we apply forms of wealth as instruments of work, they contribute to production, and so render us a service. If we apply them to purposes of consumption we not only consume the wealth itself, but also the service which it might have rendered if productively employed. If we employ wealth belonging to other people, we must compensate the owners for the productive service which it might have rendered. The compensation for this is variously called interest or rent. If we employ our own goods we ourselves draw the interest which they bear." [4] It is a poor epitome of Say's old theory.

This unsatisfactory repetition of old arguments is still more wonderful when we consider that in the interval a very great stride had been taken towards the perfecting of the Use theory by Hermann's *Staatswirtschaftliche Untersuchungen*, published in 1832.

[1] i. sect. ii. p. 246, etc., and many other places.

[2] ii. p. 214, and other places.

[3] ii. p. 255.

[4] ii. pp. 633, 660.

This work forms the second milestone in the development of the Use theory. Out of Say's scanty and contradictory suggestions—which he accepts with flattering recognition [1]—Hermann has built up a stately theory; the same care expended on its foundations as on its details. And it is of no small importance that this well-constructed theory has become a vital part of Hermann's entire system. It permeates the whole of his lengthy work from end to end. There is not a chapter in it where a considerable space is not given to its statement or application. There is not a passage in it where the author allows himself to be untrue to the position which his acceptance of the Use theory compels him to take.

In what follows I can only briefly state the principal points of Hermann's theory, although it certainly deserves our more thorough acquaintance. In doing so I shall confine myself for the most part to the second edition of the *Staatswirtschaftliche Untersuchungen* (1874), in which the theory is substantially unchanged, and is at the same time put more definitely and in a more complete shape.

The foundation of Hermann's theory is his conception of the independent use of goods. Quite in contrast to Say, who tries to gloss over the nature of his *services productifs* with a few analogies and metaphors, Hermann takes all possible care in explaining his fundamental conception.

He introduces it first in the theory of Goods, where he speaks of the different kinds of usefulness that goods have. "Usefulness may be transitory or it may be durable. It is partly the nature of the goods, partly the nature of the use that determines this point. Transitory, often momentary usefulness belongs to freshly cooked food, and to many kinds of drink. The doing of a service has only a momentary use value, yet its result may be permanent, as is the case in tuition, in a physician's advice, etc. Land, dwellings, tools, books, money, have a durable use value. Their use, for the time that they last (called in German their *Nutzung*),[2] can be conceived of as a good in itself, and may obtain for itself an exchange value which we call interest."

[1] See first edition, p. 270, in the note.

[2] "Ihr Gebrauch während dessen sie fortbestehen, wird ihr Nutzung gennant," etc.

But not only are durable goods, but transitory and consumable goods also, capable of affording a durable use. Since this proposition is of cardinal importance in Hermann's theory, I give his exposition of it in his own words:—

"Technical processes are able, throughout all the change and combination of the usefulness of goods, to preserve the sum of their exchange values undiminished, so that goods, although successively taking on new shapes, still continue unchanged in value. Iron ore, coal, labour, obtain, in the form of pig iron, a combined usefulness to which they all three contribute chemical and mechanical elements. If, then, the pig iron possesses the exchange value of the three exchange goods employed, the earlier sum of goods persists, bound up qualitatively in the new usefulness, added together quantitatively in the exchange value.

"To goods that are of transitory material, technical processes, through this change of form, add economical durability and permanence. This persistence of usefulness and of exchange value which is given to goods otherwise transitory by technical change of form, is of the greatest economical importance. The amount of durable useful goods becomes thereby very much greater. Even goods of perishable material and of only temporary use, by constantly changing their shapes while retaining their exchange value, become re-created so that their use becomes lasting. Thus, as it is in the case of durable goods, so it is in the case of goods changing their form qualitatively, while retaining their exchange value; this use may be conceived of as a good in itself, as a use (*Nutzung*) which may itself obtain exchange value." I shall return to this notable passage later on.

Hermann then makes use of this analysis to introduce his conception of capital, which is based altogether on that of its use.

"Lasting or durable goods, and perishable goods which retain their value while changing their shape, may thus be brought under one and the same conception; they are the durable basis of a use which has exchange value. Such goods we call capital." [1]

The bridge between these preliminary conceptions and

[1] P. 111. Hermann of course does not always remain quite faithful to the conception here given. In this passage he calls the goods which form the basis

Hermann's interest theory proper is formed by the proposition that, in economic life, the uses of capital do regularly receive the exchange value, of which, as independent quantities, they are capable. Hermann does not treat this proposition with the emphasis adequate to its importance. Although everything further depends on it, he neither puts it formally, nor gives it any detailed explanation. Explanation, indeed, there is in plenty, but it is rather to be read between the lines than in them. It amounts to this, that the "uses" possess exchange value because they are economical goods—a piece of information which is concise indeed, but may be accepted as satisfactory without further commentary.[1]

His explanation of interest then proceeds as follows.

In almost all productions uses of capital, possessing exchange value, form an indispensable portion of the expenses of production. These expenses are made up of three parts :—

1. Of the outlay of the undertaker—that is, the expenditure of wealth previously existing; as, for instance, principal, secondary, and auxiliary materials, his own labour and that of others, wear and tear of workshops, tools, etc.

2. Of the undertaker's active intelligence and care in the initiation and carrying on of the undertaking, etc.

3. Of the uses of fixed and floating capital necessary for the production all the time of their employment up till the sale of the product.[2]

of a durable use capital; but later on he is fond of representing capital as something different from the goods—as it were something hovering over them. Thus, *e.g.* when he says on p. 605: "Above all we must distinguish the object in which a capital exhibits itself from the capital itself. Capital is the basis of a durable use which has definite exchange value; it continues to exist undiminished so long as the use retains this value, and here it is all the same whether the goods which form the capital are useful simply as capital or in other ways—that is, generally speaking, it is all the same in what form the capital exhibits itself." If the question be put, What then is capital, if it is not the substance of the goods in which it "exhibits" itself? it might be difficult enough to give a straightforward answer, and one that would not be simply playing with words.

[1] Hermann evidently considers the exchange value of uses too self-evident to need any formal explanation from him. Even the extremely scanty explanation mentioned above is usually given only indirectly, although at the same time quite plainly; thus when on p. 507 he says: "For the use of land the corn producer can obtain no compensation in price, so long as it is offered to any one in any quantity as a free gift."

[2] Pp. 312, etc., 412, etc.

Now since, economically, the price of the product must cover the total costs of production, that price must be high enough to cover "not only the outlays, but also the sacrifice that the undertaker makes in the uses of capital, as also in his intelligence and care;" or, as it is usually expressed, over and above the compensation for outlays, the price must yield a profit (profit of capital and profit of undertaking). And more exactly explaining his idea, Hermann adds;—this profit "is by no means merely an advantage that comes by accident in the struggle that determines price." Rather we should say that profit is as much a compensation for goods possessing exchange value that are really sacrificed in the product as the outlays are. The only difference is that the undertaker makes these outlays in order to procure and hold together certain productive elements already existing, while the uses of the capital employed and his own superintendence of the business are new elements in the work, provided by himself during the production. He makes use of the outlays in order to obtain the highest possible remuneration for these new elements that he adds. "This remuneration is profit" (p. 314).

To make this explanation of profit complete, one thing is still wanting; it should be made clear how it is that, in production, there must be sacrifice of the uses of capital, besides that of the outlays of capital. This Hermann supplies in another place, where at the same time he points out, with great circumstantiality, that all products may ultimately be traced to exertions of labour and uses of capital. In doing so he makes some interesting statements about the character of the "use of goods," as he conceives of it, and it may be well to give this passage also in full.

He is making an analysis of the sacrifices that are required for the procuring of salt fish. He enumerates labour of catching, use and wear and tear of tools and boats, labour of procuring salt; and again the use of all kinds of tools, casks, and so on. Then he breaks up the boat into wood, iron, cordage, labour, and use of tools; the wood again, into use of the forest and labour; the iron, into use of the mine, and so on. "But this succession of labours and uses does not exhaust the sum total of the sacrifices made in procuring salt fish. There must besides be taken into calculation the period of time during which each element of exchange value is embodied in the product. For from that moment when a labour or a use is employed in the making of a product, the disposal of it in any other way is made impossible. Instead of being made use of in itself, it is simply made to co-operate in the making and delivery of the product to the consumers. To get a proper idea of this, it is to be remembered that labours and uses, so soon as they are employed in the making of a product, enter into floating capital quantitatively, as a constituent element, with the exchange value that they possessed at the time of their employment. With this value they become floating capital. But it is just this amount of value that a man abstains from using in any other way till the product is paid for by the buyer. As with the getting, working up, storing, and conveying, the floating capital grows through ever new labours and uses expended on it, it is itself wealth, the use of which is handed over to the consumers with every new accession of value up to the delivering over of the product to the buyer. And what must be paid for by the buyer is not simply the renunciation of that use which the undertaker might have made of the wealth for his own gratification. No; it is actually a new and peculiar use which is handed over to him along with the wealth itself; the putting together and keeping together, the storing and keeping ready for use, of all the technical elements of the production, from the acquiring of its first basis in natural goods, on through all technical changes and commercial processes, till the product is handed over in the place, at the time and in the quantity desired. This holding together of the technical elements of the product is the service, the objective use of floating capital."[1]

If we compare the form which Hermann has given to the Use theory with the doctrine of Say, we find them alike in their rough outlines. Both recognise the existence of independent work done by capital. In the fact that capital is made use of in production, both see a sacrifice independent of and separate from the expenditure of the substance of capital. And both explain interest as the necessary compensation for this independent sacrifice. Still, Hermann's doctrine shows

[1] P. 286, etc.

a substantial advance on Say's. Say had, in fact, given the mere outlines of a theory, inside which the most important features were left blank. His *services productifs* are nothing but an ambiguous name, and the very important consideration of how the sacrifice of these services constitutes an independent sacrifice in production—independent, that is, of the substance of capital sacrificed—is very much left to the reader's fancy. In trying, with true German thoroughness, to work out and make clear these two cardinal points, Hermann has definitely filled in the outlines he took from Say, and in doing so has given to the whole the rank of a solid theory.

A negative merit in Hermann, not to be under estimated, is that he severely abstains from the secondary explanations (explaining interest by productivity) that are so offensive in Say. The expression "productivity" is perhaps as often in his mouth, but he uses it in a sense that, if not happy, is at least not misleading.[1]

Hermann of course has not managed to keep his formulation of the Use theory free from all inconsistencies. In particular it remains doubtful, in his case also, what is the nature of the connection between the exchange value of the uses of capital and the price of the products of capital. Is the price of products high because the exchange value of uses is high? Or, on the contrary, is the exchange value of the uses high because the price of products is high? This point, over which Say falls into the wildest contradictions,[2] Hermann has not made entirely clear. In the passage given above, and in many others, he obviously inclines to the former view, and so represents the price of products as affected by the value of the uses of capital.[3] But at the same time there are many expressions which assume just the opposite. Thus (p. 296) he remarks that the determining of the price of products "is itself the first to react on the price of the labours and uses." And similarly on another occasion (p. 559) he ascribes a determining influence on the price of the incomplete products, not to the constituent costs which have gone to create the incomplete product, but to the finished products

[1] See below, p. 204. [2] See above, p. 125.

[3] See also p. 560: "The uses of capital are therefore a ground of the determination of prices."

which are their final result. It was reserved for Menger to make this difficult question entirely clear.

Thus far we have looked only at Hermann's doctrine of the origin of interest. But we cannot pass over the quite peculiar views that he propounds on the causes of the different rates of interest.

Hermann starts from the proposition already referred to, that "the total quantity of products," resolved into its simple constituents, is "a sum of labours and uses of capital." If we allow this, it becomes clear, in the next place, that all acts of exchange must consist in the exchange of labours and uses of capital possessed by one for labours and uses possessed by another, these labours and uses being either direct or embodied in products. Whatever, then, a man receives for his own labour in other people's labours and uses is the exchange value of labour, or wage; and "whatever a man receives in the labours and uses of other men, when he offers his own uses for sale, forms the exchange value of these uses, or the profit of capital." The wages of labour and the profit of capital must therefore, between them, exhaust the total quantity of all products coming to market.[1]

On what, then, depends the rate of profit; or, which is the same thing, the rate of the exchange value of the uses of capital? First, naturally, on the amount of other people's labours and uses obtainable for these. But this itself depends again, for the most part, on the proportion in which the two participants in the total product, labour and uses of capital, are supplied and demanded as against each other. And of course every increase in the supply of labour tends to diminish wages and to raise profit; and every increase in the supply of uses, to raise wages and lower profit. But, again, the supply of either of these two factors may be increased by two circumstances; either by increase of the available amount or by increase of its productiveness. These circumstances act in the following way.

"If the *amount* of capital increases, more uses are offered for sale, more equivalent values are sought for them. Now these equivalent values can only be labours or uses. So far

[1] Under capital Hermann includes land.

as, in exchange for the increased uses, other uses of capital are demanded, a greater amount of equivalent values is actually disposable. Since then supply and demand are equally increased, the exchange value of the uses cannot alter. But if, as is here assumed, the quantity of labour, on the whole, is not increased, the owners of capital find, for the increased amount of uses which they seek to exchange against labour, only the amount of labour they got before—that is, they get an unsatisfactory equivalent value. The exchange value of uses will therefore sink in comparison with labour; with the same exertions, the labourer will buy more uses. In the exchange of use against use the capitalists now receive the same equivalent value as formerly, but in the exchange of uses against labour they receive less. The amount of profit, therefore, in proportion to the total capital—that is, the rate of profit—must fall. The total quantity of goods produced is indeed increased, but the increase has been divided among capitalists and labourers.

"If the *productiveness* of capital increases, or if in the same time it furnishes more means of satisfying needs, the owners of capital offer for sale more useful goods than before, and ask therefore for more equivalent values. They obtain these so far as each one seeks other uses in exchange for his own increased use. Here the supply has risen with the demand. The exchange value must therefore remain unaltered—that is, the uses of equal capitals for equal times exchange with each other—although the character of these uses as regards usefulness is higher than before. But under the assumption that labour is not increased, all the uses with which the capitalist wishes to buy labour do not obtain their former equivalent value; this must raise the competitive demand for labour, and must lower the exchange value of uses as against labour. The labourers now receive more uses for the same amount of labour as before, and find themselves therefore better off; the owners of capital do not themselves enjoy the whole fruit of the increased productiveness of capital, but are compelled to share it with the workers. But the lowering of the exchange value of the uses does not cause the owners of capital any loss, since the reduced value can obtain more means of enjoyment than the higher value formerly obtained."

On analogous grounds, which we need not further pursue, Hermann shows that the rate of profit rises if the amount or the productiveness of labour decreases.

The most striking feature in this theory certainly is, that Hermann finds a reason for the decline of interest in the increase of the productive power of capital. In this he goes in direct opposition, on the one hand, to Ricardo and his school, who found the principal cause of the declining rate of interest in the decrease of the productiveness of capitals when driven to worse lands; but, on the other hand, to the Productivity theorists also, who, from the nature of their theory, were bound to accept a direct proportion between the degree of productivity and the rate of interest.[1]

Whether the substance of Hermann's Use theory be tenable or not, I leave in the meantime an open question. But that Hermann's application of it to explain the height of the interest rate is not correct is, I think, demonstrable even at the present stage of our inquiries.

It appears to me that, in this part of his doctrine, Hermann has made too little distinction between two things that should have been kept very clearly distinct,—the ratio between total profit and total wage, and the ratio between amount of profit and amount of capital, or the rate of interest. What Hermann has put forward admirably explains and proves a lowering or raising of total profit in proportion to wages of labour; but that explains and proves nothing as regards the height of profit, or the rate of interest.

The source of the oversight lies in this: the abstraction—in other respects quite justifiable—in virtue of which he sees nothing in products but the labours and uses out of which they come, Hermann has extended to the sphere of exchange value, where it should never have been applied. Accustomed to look on uses and labours as representatives of all goods, Hermann thought he might look at these representatives even where the matter at issue concerned the high or low exchange value of any one amount. He calculates thus: uses and labours are the representatives of all goods. Consequently if the use buys as many uses as before, but at the same time buys less labours,

[1] *E.g.* Roscher, § 183. Roesler, who accepts Hermann's results, although he ascribes them to somewhat different causes, is the only exception.

its exchange value is evidently smaller. Now this is not true. The exchange value of goods (in the sense of "power in exchange," which is the sense that Hermann always gives to the word) is measured, not only in the quantities of one or two definite kinds of goods that can be got in exchange for it, but *in the average of all goods;* among which, in this case, are to be counted all products, each product having equal rights with the goods called "labour" and with the goods called "use of capital." Thus exchange value is understood in practical life and in economics, and thus also it is understood by Hermann himself. On p. 432 he expressly declares: "Among such differences of the goods in which price is paid, the establishment of an average price, such as we desired for the fixing of exchange value, is not to be thought of, but the conception of exchange value is not impossible on that account. It is arrived at by considering all the average prices which, in the same market, are paid for one good in all goods; it is a series of comparisons of the same good against many other goods. We shall call the exchange value of a good, as thus determined, the 'real value' of the good, to distinguish it from the average amount of the money prices, or the money value."

Now it is not difficult to show that the power in exchange of the use of capital as against products moves in quite a different direction from its power in exchange against other uses and labours. For instance, if the productiveness of all uses and labours rises to exactly double, the power in exchange between uses and labours, as regards each other, is not disturbed; on the other hand, the power in exchange of both as against the products which result from them is very seriously disturbed: it is, that is to say, doubled.

As regards the rate of interest, the question obviously is, What is the proportion between the exchange power of the uses of capital and the exchange power of a quite definite class of product, viz. that real capital which furnishes the "use"? If the power in exchange of the *use* of a machine be twenty times less than the exchange power of the *product* machine, the use of the machine "buys" £10, while the machine itself obtains £200 as its equivalent value, and the proportion corresponds to a 5 per cent rate of interest. If the exchange value of the use of a machine again is only ten times less than that of the product machine, the one buys £20 while the other buys £200, and the proportion corresponds to a 10 per cent rate of interest.

Now there is no obvious ground for assuming that the exchange value of real capital is determined in a different way from the exchange value of other products, and, as we have seen, the exchange value of products as against the exchange value of uses, generally speaking, can be altered in another proportion than the exchange value between uses and labour *as regards each other* is altered. It follows then that the ratio between the power in exchange of the uses of capital and the power in exchange of real capital (in other words, the rate of interest) may take a different course from the proportion of exchange value between uses and labour. Hermann's rule therefore is not sufficiently proved.[1]

In conclusion, let me say just a word on the position that Hermann assumes towards the "productivity of capital." I have already said that he often uses the expression, but never with the meaning given to it by the Productivity theory. He is so far from saying that interest is produced directly from capital, that he maintains high productive power to be a cause of the lowering of interest. He expressly guards himself also (p. 542) against being supposed to say that profit is a compensation for "dead use." He asserts that capital, to give its due results, demands "plan, care, superintendence, intellectual activity generally." For the rest, he has not himself attached any particularly clear conception to the expression "productivity." He defines it in the words: "The totality of the ways in which capital is employed, and the relation of the product to the expenditure, constitute what is called the productivity of capital."[2] Does he mean by this the relation of the *value* of the product to the *value* of the expenditure? If so, then high productivity would only accompany high interest, whereas high productivity certainly occasions low interest. Or does he mean the relation of the *quantity* of the product to the *quantity* of the expenditure? But in economic life

[1] A note which occurs here in the German edition is omitted by the author's instructions.—W. S.

[2] P. 541; p. 212 of first edition.

quantity, speaking generally, is of no importance. Or does he mean the relation of the *quantity* of the product to the *value* of the expenditure? But quantity on one side and value on the other are incommensurable. The fact of the matter, it appears to me, is that Hermann's definition will not stand strict interpretation. On the whole, it is just possible that he may have had in his mind a kind of physical productivity.

In Germany many writers of note have accepted Hermann's Use theory, and given it their strong support.

One very clear-headed follower of his is Bernhardi.[1] Without developing the theory any further,—for he contents himself with quoting Hermann's doctrine incidentally, and expressing agreement with it,[2]—he shows his originality and profound thinking by a number of fine criticisms, directed principally against the English school.[3] He has, too, a word of censure for the school that stands at the opposite extreme, the blind Productivity theorists, with their "strange contradiction" of ascribing to the dead tool an independent living activity (p. 307).

Mangoldt again takes the same ground as Hermann, and diverges from him only in unimportant particulars. Thus he gives even less importance to the "productivity of capital" in the formation of interest.[4] He would go so far as abolish that expression as incorrect, although he does not scruple to use it himself "for the sake of brevity."[5] Thus, too, where Hermann puts the height of interest in inverse ratio to the productivity of capital, Mangoldt puts it in direct ratio; indeed, he accepts Thünen's formula, and puts it in direct ratio to the "last applied dose of capital."

Similarly Mithoff, in his account of the economical distribution of wealth, lately published in Schönberg's *Handbuch*,[6] follows Hermann in all essential respects.

Schäffle takes a peculiar position on the Use theory. One of the most prominent promoters of that critical movement

[1] *Versuch einer Kritik der Gründe die für grosses und kleines Grundeigenthum angeführt werden*, St. Petersburg, 1849.

[2] *E.g.* p. 236, etc.

[3] P. 306, etc.

[4] *Volkswirtschaftslehre*, Stuttgart, 1868; particularly pp. 121, 137, 333, 445, etc.

[5] Pp. 122, 432.

[6] Schönberg's *Handbuch*, i. pp. 437, 484, etc.

which came into existence with the rise of scientific Socialism, Schäffle was one of the first to pass through the fermentation of opinion which might have been expected when two such different conceptions encountered each other. This fermentation has left very characteristic traces on his utterances on the subject of interest. I shall show later on that in Schäffle's writings may be found no less than three distinctly different methods of explaining interest. One of these belongs to the older, two to the later "critical" conception. The first of them falls within the group of the Use theories.

In his first great work, the *Gesellschaftliche System der menschlichen Wirtschaft*,[1] Schäffle states his entire theory of interest according to the terminology of the Use theory. Profit of capital is with him a profit from the "use (*Nutzung*) of capital": loan interest is a price paid for that use, and its rate depends on the supply and demand of the uses of loan capital: the uses are an independent element in cost, and so on. But there are unmistakable signs that he is not far from giving up the theory he professedly holds. He repeatedly gives the word "use" a signification very far from that attached to it by Hermann. He explains the use of capital as a "working" (*Wirken*) of an economical subject by means of wealth; as a "using" (*Benutzung*) of wealth for fruitful production; as a "devoting," an "employment" of wealth, as a "service" of the undertaker—expressions which would lead us to see in the Use, not so much a material element in production issuing from capital, as a personal element proceeding from the undertaker.[2] This impression is, moreover, confirmed by the fact that Schäffle repeatedly speaks of profit as premium for an economical vocation. Further, he argues positively against the view that profit is a *product* of the use of capital contributed to the process of production (ii. p. 389). He charges Hermann with having coloured his theory too much by the idea of an independent productivity in capital (ii. p. 459). But, on the other hand, he often uses the word "use" in such a way that it can only be interpreted in the objective, and therefore in Hermann's sense; as, *e.g.* when he speaks of the supply and demand of the uses of loan capital. On one occasion he

[1] Third edition, Tübingen, 1873.

[2] *Ges. System*, third edition, i. p. 266; ii. p. 458, etc.

explicitly admits that in the use, besides the personal element, there may be contained a material element, which he calls the *Gebrauch* of capital (ii. p. 458). And notwithstanding his condemnation of Hermann, he himself does not scruple now and then to ascribe "fruitfulness" to the use of capital. Thus he neither entirely accepts the ground of the Use theory nor entirely rejects it.

Even in his later systematic work, the *Bau und Leben des sozialen Körpers*,[1] Schäffle's views have not developed into a completely clear and consistent theory. While he has got beyond the old Use theory in one respect, in another he has come nearer to it. In the *Bau und Leben* he always looks upon interest as a "return to the use (*Nutzung*) of capital," which use at all times maintains an economical value. In this he gives up the subjective meaning of use, and now treats it unambiguously as a purely objective element contributed by goods. He speaks of the uses as "functions of goods," as "equivalents of useful materials in living labour," as "living energies of impersonal social substance." Even in the socialist state this objective use would retain its independent value, and thereby preserve its capacity to yield interest. The phenomenon of interest can only disappear if, in the socialist state, the community, as sole owner of capital, should contribute the valuable use of capital gratuitously; in which case the return from it would go to the advantage of the entire social body (iii. p. 491). On the other hand, Schäffle rather diverges from the old Use theory in not acknowledging the use of capital as an ultimate and original element in production, and in tracing all costs of production to labour alone (iii. pp. 273, 274). But in doing so he chances on another line of explanation, which I shall have to discuss at length in another connection.

While these followers of Hermann have not developed his theory so much as broadened it, Knies may fairly claim to have improved it in some essential respects. He has made no change in its fundamental ideas, but he has given these fundamental ideas a much clearer and more unambiguous expression than Hermann himself gave them. That Hermann's theory was very much in want of such improvement was

[1] Second edition, Tübingen, 1881.

shown by the many misunderstandings of it. I have already remarked that Schäffle considered Hermann a Productivity theorist. Still more remarkable is it that Knies himself thought he saw in Hermann, not a forerunner, but an opponent.[1]

Knies was not always a Use theorist. In his *Erörterungen über den Kredit*,[2] published in 1859, he looked on credit transactions as barter transactions, or, according to circumstances, buying transactions, in which what one party gives is given in the present, and what the other gives as equivalent is given in the future (p. 568). One of the ulterior results of this conception was that interest must not be looked on as an equivalent of a use transferred in the loan, but—almost as Galiani had put it long before[3]—as a part-equivalent of the parent loan itself. But since then Knies has expressly withdrawn this conception, considering that there is no call for such an innovation, and that, on the contrary, there is much to deter one from accepting it.[4] Later still, in a fully argued-out analysis, he has expressed himself quite directly to the effect, that any consideration of the different values which present and future goods of the same class may possess on account of the greater urgency of immediate need is, though "not quite unfruitful," still distinctly insufficient to explain the principal point in the phenomenon of interest.[5]

In place of this, in his comprehensive work *Geld und Kredit*, Knies has laid down an unusually clear and thoroughly reasoned Use theory.[6]

Although the purpose of this work only called for investigation into Contract interest, Knies yet treats the subject from such a general standpoint that his views on Natural interest may easily be supplied from what he says on the other.

In fundamental ideas he agrees with Hermann. Like him he conceives of the use (*Nutzung*) of a good as "that use

[1] Knies, *Geld und Kredit*, ii. part ii. p. 35. See also Nasse's *Rezension* in vol. xxxv. of the *Jahrbücher für National-Oekonomie und Statistik*, 1880, p. 94.

[2] *Zeitschrift für die gesammte Staatswissenschaft*, vol. xv. p. 559.

[3] See above, p. 49.

[4] *Der Kredit*, part i. p. 11.

[5] *Ibid.* ii. p. 38. I may perhaps express the conjecture that the respected author was led to the above polemic by the contents of a work which I had written in his economical *Seminar* a few years before, and in which I had laid down the views contested.

[6] *Das Geld*, Berlin, 1873. *Der Kredit*, part i. 1876; part ii. 1879.

(*Gebrauch*) which lasts through a period of time, and is limitable by moments of time"; a use to be kept quite distinct from the good itself which is the "bearer of the use"; and a use capable of economical independence. To the question which most concerns the Use theory, whether an independent use and its transfer are conceivable and practicable in the case of *perishable* goods, he devotes a searching inquiry, which ends with a distinct answer in the affirmative.[1] Another cardinal question of the Use theory is, whether and why the independent use of capital must possess an exchange value, and obtain a compensation in the form of interest. This question, as we have seen, Hermann does not leave without answer, but he has laid so little stress on the answer, and put it in such an insignificant form, that it has not unfrequently been quite overlooked.[2] In contrast to this, Knies has carefully reasoned it out, and concludes that "the emergence and the economical justification of a price for use, in the shape of interest, is founded on the same relation as that on which the price of material goods is founded." The use is an instrument for the satisfaction of human need just as much as the material good is; it is an object that is "economically valuable and that is economically valued."[3] When I add that Knies has avoided not only any relapse into the Productivity theory, but even the very appearance of such a relapse, and that he has appended to his theory some very notable criticisms, particularly of the socialistic interest theory, I have said enough to point out how deeply Hermann's theory is indebted to a thinker equally distinguished for his acuteness and for the conscientiousness of his research.

We now come to that writer who has put the Use theory into the most perfect form in which it could well be put—Karl Menger, in his *Grundsätze der Volkswirthschaftslehre*.[4]

The superiority of Menger to all his predecessors consists in this, that he builds his interest theory on a much more complete theory of value,—a theory which gives an elaborate and satisfactory answer to the very difficult question of the

[1] *Das Geld*, pp. 61, 71, etc. I shall return to the details of this inquiry later on, when criticising the Use theory as a whole. [2] See above, p. 196.

[3] *Kredit*, part ii. p. 33, and other places. [4] Vienna, 1871.

relation between the value of products and that of their means of production. Does the value of a product depend on the value of its means of production, or does the value of the means of production depend on that of their product? As regards this question economists up till Menger's time had been very much groping in the dark. It is true that a number of writers had occasionally used expressions to the effect that the value of the means of production was conditioned by the value of their anticipated product; as, for instance, Say, Riedel, Hermann, Roscher.[1] But these expressions were never put forward in the form of a general law, and still less in the form of an adequate logical argument. Moreover, as must have been noticed, expressions are to be found in these writers which indicate quite the opposite view; and with this opposite view the great body of economic literature fully agrees in recognising as a fundamental law that the cost of goods determines their value.

But so long as economists did not see clearly on this preliminary question, their treatment of the interest problem could scarcely be more than uncertain groping. How could any one possibly explain in clear outline a difference in value between two amounts—expenditure of capital and product of capital—if he did not even know on which side of the relation to seek for the cause, and on which side for the effect?

To Menger, then, belongs the great merit of having distinctly answered this preliminary question. In doing so he has definitely and for all time indicated the point at which, and the direction in which, the interest problem is to be solved.

His answer is this. The value of the means of production ("goods of higher rank," in his terminology) is determined always and without exception by the value of their products ("goods of lower rank"). He arrives at this conclusion by the following argument.[2]

[1] See above, pp. 130, 190.

[2] I regret that I must deny myself the pleasure of introducing in this place more than the barest outlines of Menger's value theory. Holding as I do that his theory is among the most valuable and most certain acquisitions of modern economics, I feel that it cannot be at all adequately appreciated from any such sketch. In my next volume I shall have the opportunity of going more thoroughly into the subject. Meanwhile, for more exact information on the propositions

Value is the importance "which concrete goods, or quantities of goods, receive for us through the fact that we are conscious of being dependent, for the satisfaction of our wants, on having these goods at our disposal." The amount of value that goods possess always depends on the importance of those wants, which depend for their satisfaction on our disposal over the goods in question. Since goods of "higher rank" (means of production) are only of service to us through the medium of those goods of "lower rank" (products) which result from them, it is clear that the means of production can only have an importance as regards the satisfaction of our wants so far as their *products* possess such an importance. If the only use of means of production were to consist in the making of valueless goods, these means of production could evidently in no way obtain value for us.

Further, since that circle of wants the satisfaction of which is conditioned by a product is obviously identical with that circle of wants the satisfaction of which is conditioned by the sum of the means of production of the product, the degree of importance which a product possesses for the satisfaction of our wants, and that which the sum of its means of production possesses, must be essentially identical. On those grounds the anticipated value of the product is the standard not only for the existence, but also for the *amount* of the value of its means of production. Finally, since the (subjective) value of goods is also the basis for their price, the price, or, as some people call it, the "economical value" of goods, is regulated by the same principle.

This being the foundation, the interest problem assumes the following shape.

A capital is nothing else than a sum of "complementary goods" of higher rank. Now if this sum derives its value from the value of its anticipated product, how is it that it never quite reaches that value, but is always less by a definite proportion? Or, if it is true that the anticipated value of the product is the source and the measure of the value of its means of production, how is it that real capital is not valued as highly as its product?

which I have given in very condensed form in the text, I must refer to Menger's own unusually luminous and convincing statement in the *Grundsätze*, particularly p. 77 onward.

To this Menger gives the following acute answer.[1]

The transformation of means of production into products (or, shortly, Production) always demands a certain period of time, sometimes long, sometimes short. For the purposes of production it is necessary that a person should not only have the productive goods at his disposal for a single moment inside that period of time, but should retain them at his disposal and bind them together in the process of production over the whole period of time. One of the conditions of production, therefore, is this: the disposal over quantities of real capital during definite periods of time. It is in this Disposal that Menger places the essential nature of the use of capital.

The use of capital, or the disposal over capital, thus described, in so far as it is in demand and is not to be had in sufficient quantity, may now obtain a value, or, in other words, may become an economical good. When this happens,—as is usually the case,—then, over and above the other means of production employed in the making of a concrete product (over and above, *e.g.* the raw materials, auxiliary materials, labour, and so on), there enters into the sum of value contained in the anticipated product, the disposal over those goods that are required for the production, or the use of capital. And since, on that account, in this sum of value there must remain something for the economical good we have called "use of capital," the other means of production cannot account for the full amount of the value of the anticipated product. This is the origin of the difference in value between the concrete capital thrown into production and the product; and this at the same time is the origin of interest.[2]

In this doctrine of Menger the Use theory has at last attained to its full theoretical clearness and maturity. In it there is no falling back on old errors; there is nothing that could even recall the old Productivity theories and their dangers; and with that the interest problem has definitely passed from a production problem, which it is not, to a value problem, which it is. The value problem is, at the same time, so clearly and so sharply put, its outlines so happily filled in by the

[1] Pp. 133-138.

[2] Mataja in his *Unternehmergewinn* (Vienna, 1884) is in substantial agreement with Menger. This valuable work, unfortunately, reached me too late to allow me to make any thorough use of it.

exposition he gives of the value relation between product and means of production, that Menger has not only distanced his predecessors in the Use theory, but has laid a permanent foundation on which all earnest work at the problem of interest must, for the future, be built.

The work of the critic as regards Menger, therefore, is different from that as regards any of his predecessors. In considering the previous doctrines I have purposely laid on one side the question whether the fundamental principle of the Use theory was warranted or not. I have only examined them in the way of asking whether they presented this principle with more or less completeness, with more or less internal consistency and clearness. In fact, up till now I have, to some extent, tested the concrete Use theories by the ideal Use theory, but I have not tested the ideal Use theory itself. In the case of Menger, however, it is only this latter test that needs to be applied. As regards his theory only one critical question remains to be put, but that the most decisive one: Can the Use theory give us a satisfactory explanation of the interest problem?

I shall try to answer this question in such a way that it will not merely be a special criticism of Menger's formulation of the theory, but will warrant us in forming an opinion on the whole theoretical movement that reaches its highest development with Menger.

In doing so I am conscious of having undertaken one of the most difficult tasks in criticism. Difficult through the general nature of the matter, which has for so many decades baffled the endeavours of the most prominent minds; difficult, in particular, because I shall be compelled to oppose opinions put forward, after most careful consideration, by the best minds of our nation, and supported with most marvellous ingenuity; difficult, finally, in this, that I shall be compelled to oppose ideas that were once vehemently contested in long past times, then won most brilliant victory over their opponents, and since then have been taught and believed in as dogmas. For what follows, then, I must particularly ask the reader to grant me an unbiassed hearing, patience, and attention.

CHAPTER III

PLAN OF CRITICISM

ALL the Use theories rest on the following assumption. Not only does real capital itself possess value, but there is a Use (*Nutzung*) of capital which exists as an independent economical good, possessing independent value; and this latter value, together with the value of the capital, makes up the value of the product of capital.

Now in opposition to this I maintain:—

1. There is no independent "use of capital," such as is postulated by the Use theorists; there can, therefore, be no independent value of the kind asserted, and the phenomenon of "surplus value" cannot thus be accounted for. The assumption is nothing but the product of a fiction which is in contradiction of actual fact.[1]

2. Even if there were a "use of capital" of such a nature as is assumed by the Use theorists, the actual phenomena of interest would not be satisfactorily explained thereby.

The Use theories, therefore, rest on a hypothesis which contradicts actual facts, and is, besides, insufficient to explain the phenomena in question.

In proceeding to prove these two theses, I feel that I stand in a somewhat unfortunate position as regards the former. While the discussion of the second thesis opens up virgin soil, un-

[1] To guard against a misunderstanding which I should very much deprecate, let me say in so many words that I have no intention of denying the existence of "uses of capital" in general. What I must deny is the existence of that special something which our theorists point to as the "use" of capital, and which they endow with a variety of attributes that, in my opinion, go against the nature of things. But this is anticipating.

disturbed as yet by the strife of economists, the first seems to put me in the position of attacking a *res judicata*,—a case long ago carried up through all courts, and long ago decided conclusively against me. It is, indeed, essentially the same question as was in dispute centuries ago between the canonists and the defenders of loan interest. The canonists maintained: Property in a thing includes all the uses that can be made of it; there can, therefore, be no separate use which stands outside the article and can be transferred in the loan along with it. The defenders of loan interest maintained that there was such an independent use. And Salmasius and his followers managed to support their views with such effectual arguments that the public opinion of the scientific world soon fell in with theirs, and that to-day we have but a smile for the "short-sighted pedantry" of these old canonists.

Now fully conscious that I am laying myself open to the charge of eccentricity, I maintain that the much decried doctrine of the canonists was, all the same, right to this extent;—that the independent use of capital, which was the object of dispute, has no existence in reality. And I trust to succeed in proving that the judgment of the former courts in this literary process, however unanimously given, was in fact wrong.

In the next few chapters, then, I hope to prove my first thesis—that there is no "use of capital" of the kind postulated by the Use theorists.

The first thing we have to do is of course to define the subject of discussion. What then is this Use, this *Nutzung*, the independent existence of which is maintained by the Use theorists and denied by me?

As to the nature of the Use there is no agreement among the theorists themselves. Menger in particular gives an essentially different reading of the conception from that of his predecessors. In view of this I find it necessary to divide my inquiry into at least two parts, the first of which has to do with the conception given by the Say-Hermann school, while the second will deal with Menger's conception.

CHAPTER IV

THE USE OF CAPITAL ACCORDING TO THE SAY-HERMANN SCHOOL

Among the writers of the Say-Hermann school there obtains no exact agreement in the description and definition of the Use. But this want of agreement appears to me traceable, not so much to any real difference of opinion about the subject, as to their common failure to give any clear account of its nature. They hesitate in their definitions, not because they have different objects in view, but because, of the one object that all have in view, they have only uncertain vision. One proof of this lies in the fact that the individual Use theorists get into contradiction with their own definitions almost as often as with those of their colleagues. In this chapter we shall gather together provisionally the more important readings of the conception.

Say speaks of the "productive services" of capital, and defines them as a "labour" which capital performs.

Hermann in one place (p. 109) defines the *Nutzung* of goods as their *Gebrauch*. He repeats this on p. 111, where he says that the *Gebrauch* of goods of perishable material may be thought of as a good in itself, as a *Nutzung*. If *Gebrauch* here is simply identified with *Nutzung*, this is not the case in a passage on p. 125, where Hermann says that the *Gebrauch* is the employment of the *Nutzung*. On p. 287, finally, he explains "the holding together of the technical elements of the product" as the "service," the "objective *Nutzung*" of floating capital.

Knies also identifies *Gebrauch* and *Nutzung*.[1]

Schäffle in one place defines *Nutzung* as the "employment" of goods (*Gesell. System*, iii. p. 143); similarly on p. 266 as "acquisitive employment." On p. 267 he calls it "the

[1] *Geld*, p. 61: "*Nutzung*=the *Gebrauch* of a good lasting over a period of time, and limitable by moments of time."

working of an economical subject by means of wealth, a using of wealth towards fruitful production." On the same page it is called a "devotion" of wealth to production; with which it is a little inconsistent that, on the next page, he speaks of a devotion of the *Nutzung* of capital—that is, of the devotion of a devotion. In the *Bau und Leben*, finally, Schäffle explains the uses in one place (iii. p. 258) as "functions of goods"; somewhat later (p. 259) as "equivalents of useful materials in living labour"; while on p. 260 the *Nutzung* is defined as the "releasing of the utility (*Nutzen*) from material goods."

If we look more closely at this somewhat chequered array of definitions and explications we may see in them two interpretations of the conception of use, a subjective and an objective. These two interpretations correspond pretty exactly with the double sense in which the word Use or *Nutzung* is generally employed in ordinary speech. It indicates, on the one hand, the subjective activity of the one who uses, and is called in German indifferently *Benutzung* or *Gebrauch* in the subjective sense of that equally ambiguous word; or, more significantly, *Gebrauchshandlung*. And, on the other hand, it indicates an objective function of the goods that are used; a service issuing from the goods. The subjective interpretation appears vaguely in Hermann's identification of *Nutzung* and *Gebrauch*, and very strongly in Schäffle's earlier work. The objective interpretation distinctly predominates with Say; almost as distinctly with Hermann, who, indeed, in one place speaks explicitly of the "objective use" of capital; and even Schäffle inclines to it in his latest work when he speaks of the use as a "function of goods."

It is easy to see that of the two interpretations it is simply and solely the objective that accords with the character of the Use theory. For, taking it only on the most obvious grounds, it is absolutely impossible to give a subjective meaning to those uses of capital which the borrower buys from the lender, and pays with loan interest. These cannot be acts of use performed by the lender, for he does not perform any such. Nor can they be acts of use performed by the borrower, for, although he may intend to perform such actions, he does not of course require to buy his own actions from the lender. To speak, therefore, of a transference of the uses of capital in the loan, has a meaning only if we understand by the word "uses" *objective* elements of use of some kind or other. I think, then, that I am justified in leaving out of account, as inconsistencies that contradict the spirit of their own theory, those subjective interpretations of use that are to be found sporadically in individual Use theorists, and in confining myself exclusively to the objective interpretations which have been adopted by the majority, and which, since Schäffle's change of front, are the only recognised interpretations. By Use, then, in the sense given it by the Say-Hermann school, we have to think of an objective useful element which proceeds from goods, and acquires independent economical existence as well as independent economical value.

Now nothing can be more certain than that there are, in fact, certain objective useful services of goods that obtain economical independence, and may, not unfitly, be designated by the name of Uses (*Nutzungen*). I have already, in another place, treated of these in detail, and done my utmost to describe their true nature as exactly and thoroughly as possible.[1] Singularly enough, this attempt of mine stands almost alone in economic literature. I say "singularly enough" deliberately, for it does seem to me a very wonderful thing that, in a science which from beginning to end turns, as on its axis, on the satisfying of needs by means of goods,—on the relation of use between men and goods,—no inquiry has ever been made into the technical character of the use of goods. Or that, in a science where pages, chapters, even monographs have been written on many another conception, not a couple of lines should have been devoted to the definition or explanation of the fundamental conception "use of a good," and that the expression should be dragged into every theoretical research in all the confusion and ambiguity which it has in ordinary life.

Since for our present purpose everything depends on us getting a reliable idea of the useful functions which goods serve, I must at this point go into the matter with some exactitude; only begging the reader not to look on what follows as a digression, but as strictly germane to the subject.[2]

[1] See my *Rechte und Verhältnisse vom Standpunkte der volkwirthschaftlichen Güterlehre*, Innsbruck, 1881, p. 51.

[2] I take the liberty in the next chapter of repeating, partly in the same words, the argument of my *Rechte und Verhältnisse*, which was written some time ago with a view to the present work.

CHAPTER V

THE TRUE CONCEPTION OF THE USE OF GOODS

ALL material goods (*Sachgüter*) are of use to mankind through the action of the natural powers that reside in them. They are a part of the material world, and for that reason all their working, including their useful working, must bear the character that working generally has in the material world; it is a working of natural powers according to natural laws. What distinguishes the working of material *goods* from the working of other kinds of natural *things*, harmless or hurtful, is the single circumstance, that the results of such working admit of being directed towards the advantage of man, this direction also being under the rule of natural laws. That is to say, all things are endowed simply with working natural powers, but experience shows that these powers only admit of being directed to a definitely useful end, when the matter which possesses these powers has taken on certain forms that are favourable to them being so directed. All matter on the surface of the earth, for instance, among other forms of energy, possesses an amount of energy corresponding to its distance from the centre of the earth. But while men can do nothing with this form of energy when stored up in a mountain, that same energy is useful to them when the matter possessing it has taken on some form they wish—that is, some form in which the energy is available; say, that of a clock pendulum, or a paper weight, or a hammer. The energy of chemical affinity which carbon possesses is identical in every molecule of it. We get a direct economic utility, however, from the results of this energy only when the carbon has taken such forms as that of wood or coal; not when it exists as part of one of the constituents of the air. We may therefore say that the nature of material *goods*, as opposed to those material *things* that are not useful, is that they are such special forms of matter as admit of the natural powers they possess being directed to the advantage of man.

From this follow two important inferences, of which one concerns the character of the useful functions of material goods, and the other concerns the character of the use (*Gebrauch*) of goods.

The function of goods can consist in nothing else than in a giving off, or rendering up, or putting forth of power; or, to use the terminology of physical science, the passing of energy into work. On the natural side it shows a complete parallelism with the character of the useful function performed by a manual labourer. In the same way as a porter or a navvy is of use, when he puts forth the natural power residing in his body in the form of rendering useful services, so are material goods of use through concrete forthputting of the natural powers inherent in them and capable of direction—physically speaking, through the forthputting in work of the available forms of energy they possess. It is by the passing of available energy into work that the "use" of goods is obtained by man.[1]

The use (*Gebrauch*) of a thing then is realised in this way: man takes the peculiar forms of energy of the good at the proper time, supplies the conditions necessary to render them available where they previously existed in an unavailable form, and then brings these forms of energy into proper connection with that object in which the useful effect is to take place. For instance, in order to "use" the locomotive the stoker fills the boiler with water, applies heat, and thus obtains in an available form the heat energy of the steam, which is transferred into energy of motion of the locomotive. This last-

[1] I may remind the reader that, according to the scientific conception of energy—energy being that quality the possession of which confers upon a body the power of doing work—it may exist either as available or unavailable energy; that is, the body may possess energy of which a use can be made, or it may possess energy of which no use can be made. Thus the storage of energy in certain material bodies in an unavailable form, and the change of this unavailable into available energy, by means of which work is done that has a direct influence on the satisfaction of human wants, is just the physical conception applied to economics.—W. S.

named energy is then transferred by connection to the carriages that convey persons or goods. Or one brings a book into the necessary relation with his eye for the image, which is continually being formed by reflection, to fall on the retina; or brings the house which continually offers shelter into proper relation with his whole person. But any "use" of material goods which does not consist in the receiving from them of useful results due to their inherent powers or forms of energy, is absolutely unthinkable.

I think I need have no fear of the propositions I have just advanced meeting with any scientific opposition. The conception laid down is no longer strange in our economic literature;[1] and in the present state of the natural sciences the acceptance of it has indeed become a peremptory necessity. If by any chance it should be objected that this conception is one that belongs to the natural sciences and is not an economic one, I answer that in these questions economic science must leave the last word to natural science. The principle of the unity of all science demands it. Economic science does not explain the facts that belong to its province to the very bottom, any more than any other science does. It solves only one portion of the causal connection that binds together the phenomena of things, and leaves it to other sciences to carry the explanation farther. Not to mention other limiting sciences, the sphere of economic explanation lies between the sphere of psychological explanation on the one hand, and that of the natural sciences on the other. To give a concrete example. Economic science will explain thus far the circumstance that bread has an exchange value: it will point out that bread is able to satisfy the want of sustenance, and that men have a tendency to ensure the satisfaction of their wants, if necessary by making a sacrifice. But that men have this tendency, and why they have it, is not explained by economic science but by psychology. To explain that men want sustenance and why, falls within the domain of physiology. Finally, it also falls within the sphere of

[1] Schäffle, in particular, in the third volume of his *Bau und Leben*, very beautifully puts the same point of view. Schäffle, I may say, forms an honourable exception among economists as regards this objectionable habit of not taking any trouble with the principles that regulate the working of goods.

physiology to explain that bread is able to satisfy that want, and why it is able to do so, but physiology does not finish the explanation within its own sphere; it has to call in assistance from the more general physical sciences.

Now it is clear that all explanations given by economic science have a value only under this condition, that they are continuous with the related sciences. The explanations of economics cannot rest on anything that a science related to it is bound to declare untrue or impossible; otherwise the thread of the explanation is broken from the first. It must on that account keep exactly in touch with the related sciences at the points where they limit it, and one such point is just this question as to the working of material goods.

The one thing of which I have, perhaps, some reason to be afraid is, that the employment of this physical conception in regard to a certain limited class of material goods, especially to the so-called "ideal goods," may be somewhat startling at the first glance to some readers. That, *e.g.* a fixed and stationary dwelling-house, a volume of poems, or a picture of Raphael should be of use to us through the forthputting of inherent properties connected with one or other of the forms of energy, or, as we may shortly express it, the forthputting of its natural powers, may at first, I admit, be a little strange. Objections like these, however, which have their origin more in feeling than in understanding, may be removed by a single consideration. All the things that I have named enter into the relation which makes them "goods" only in virtue of the peculiar natural powers which they possess, and possess, indeed, in peculiar combination. That a house shelters and warms, is nothing else than a result of the forces of gravity, cohesion, and resistance, of impenetrability, of the non-conducting quality of building materials. That the thoughts and feelings of the poet reproduce themselves in us is mediated, in a directly physical way, by light, colour, and form of written characters; and it is this physical part of the mediation which is the office of the book. There must of course have been a poet soul in whom ideas and feelings waked, and, again, it is only in a spirit and through spiritual forces that they can be reawakened; but the way of spirit to spirit lies some little distance through the natural world, and over this distance even the spiritual must make use of the vehicle of natural powers. Such a natural vehicle is the book, the picture, the spoken word. Of themselves they give only a physical suggestion, nothing more; the spiritual we give of our own on accepting the suggestion; and if we are not prepared beforehand for a profitable acceptance of it,—if we cannot read, or, reading, cannot understand, or cannot feel,—it remains simply a physical suggestion.

With these explanations perhaps I may consider it established beyond question that material goods exert their economical use through the forthputting of the natural powers residing in them.

The individual useful forthputtings of natural powers that are obtainable from material goods I propose to designate as "Material Services."[1] In itself, indeed, the word Use (*Nutzung*) would not be inappropriate, but to adopt it would be to surrender our conception to all the obscurity that now, unfortunately, hangs over that ambiguous expression.[2]

The conception of Material Services is, in my opinion,

[1] I have already introduced this term *Nutzleistung* in my *Rechte und Verhältnisse;* before that I used it in a work written in 1876 but not printed. It is employed by Knies several times in the second portion of his *Kredit*, but unfortunately in the same ambiguous sense in which on other occasions he uses the word *Nutzung*.

NOTE BY TRANSLATOR.

After much deliberation Material Service is the nearest rendering I can give to the word *Nutzleistung*, introduced by Professor Böhm-Bawerk. Every translator finds the difficulty of rendering scientific terms from one language into another, but this difficulty is greater in political economy, where we are bound to use words "understanded of the people." The word *Nutzleistung* is one of these happy combinations which, as compounded of two familiar words, do not strike a German as peculiar or clumsy, and are yet strict enough to satisfy scientific requirements. But our language does not admit of many such combinations—the literal translation "use rendering" at once shows the impossibility in the present case —and in a translation one does not feel justified in coining a new word. In rendering the word thus it becomes necessary to eliminate a note that follows in the German edition, where Professor Böhm-Bawerk congratulates himself on having escaped Say's *services productifs*, which might be objected to on the ground that "only a person, not a thing, can render services." The prefix "material" seems to me fairly to meet this objection, as the total expression now implies a service —a forthputting of natural powers in the service of man—rendered by a material object.—W. S.

[2] After this clause, in the German edition, come the words: "Und andererseits scheint mir der Name Nutzleistung in der That ausserordentlich prägnant zu sein: es sind im eigenstlichen Wortsinn nützliche Kräfteleistungen, die von den Sachgütern ausgehen."—W. S.

destined to be one of the most important elementary conceptions in economic theory. In importance it does not come behind the conception of the economic Good.[1] Unfortunately up till now it has received little attention and little development. From the nature of our task it is indispensable that we should repair this neglect, and follow out some of the more important relations into which the material services enter in economic life.

First of all, it is clear that everything which would lay claim to the name of a "good" must be capable of rendering material services, and that, with the exhausting of this capability, it ceases to have the quality of a good; it falls out of the circle of "goods" back into the circle of simple "things." An exhaustion of this capability must not be thought of as an exhaustion of the capability to exert or to put forth energy in general; for what we have called the "natural powers" of the material are as imperishable as the material itself. But although these powers or forms of energy never cease to exist in some form or other, they may very well cease to be available for material services in this way, that the original good, in the course of doing work, has undergone such a change,—be it separation, dislocation, or uniting of its parts with other bodies, —that, in its changed form, its energy is no longer available for human use. For instance, when the carbon of the wood burned in the blast furnace has combined with oxygen in the combustion process, its powers cannot again be employed to smelt iron, although these powers are constant, and continue to work according to natural laws. The broken pendulum retains its energy due to gravity just as it did before, but the loss of the pendulum form does not allow of this energy being directed to regulate the clock. The exhaustion of capability to render material services we are accustomed to call the using up or Consumption of goods.

[1] It is unfortunate that in English economics we have devoted so little attention to this most elementary conception, on which Menger, in particular, has bestowed so much pains. The poverty of our scientific nomenclature shows this defect very markedly: the word "commodity" is really the only singular equivalent we have for the familiar and suggestive word "goods," although I personally have not scrupled to translate the German *Gut* by the English "good." There is, indeed, reason for Mr. Ruskin's sarcasm that our most famous treatise on Wealth does not even define the meaning of the word "wealth."—W. S.

While all goods thus agree and must agree in this, that they have to render material services, they differ essentially from one another in the number of services that they have to render. On this rests the familiar division of goods into perishable and non-perishable, or better, into perishable and durable.[1] Many goods are of such a nature that, to render the uses peculiar to them, they must give forth their whole power, as it were, at a blow, in one more or less intense service, so that their first use quite exhausts their capability of service, and is their *consumption*. These are the so-called perishable goods, such as food, gunpowder, fuel, etc. Other goods, again, are, in their nature, capable of rendering a number of material services in the way of giving off these services successively, within a shorter or longer period of time; and thus after a first, or even after many acts of use, they may retain their capability of rendering further services, and so retain their character of goods. These are the durable goods, such as clothing, houses, tools, precious stones, land, etc.

Where a good successively gives off a number of material services, it may do so in one of two ways: either the services following each other evidently separate themselves from each other, as clearly marked single acts, in such a way that they are easily distinguished, limited, and counted,—as, *e.g.* the single blows of a coining press, or the operations of the automatic printing press of a great newspaper; or they issue from the goods in unbroken, similar continuance,—as, *e.g.* the shelter silently given over long periods of time by a dwelling-house. If, however, it is desired, in cases of this sort, to separate and divide the continuous amount of services—and practical need often requires this—the expedient is adopted that is generally taken in the dividing of continuous quantities; the dividing line that does not suggest itself in the phenomena under consideration is borrowed from some outside circumstance, *e.g.* from the lapse of a definite time; as when one delivers over to the hirer of a house the services to be rendered by the house during the year.

Another essential feature that meets us in the analysis of

[1] Even the so-called non-perishable goods are perishable, however gradually they perish.

material services is their capability of obtaining complete economical independence. The source of this phenomenon is that in very many, indeed in most cases, the satisfaction of a concrete human want does not demand the exhaustion of the entire useful content of a good, but only the rendering of a single material service. In virtue of this the single service in the first instance obtains an independent importance as regards the satisfaction of our wants, and then in practical economic life this independence is fully recognised. We give the recognition (1) wherever we make an independent estimate of the value of isolated services; and (2) wherever we make them into independent objects of business transactions. This latter happens when we sell or exchange single services, or groups of services, apart from the goods from which they proceed. Economical custom and law have created a number of forms in which this is effectuated. Among the most important of these I may name the relations of tenancy, of hire, and of the old *commodatum*;[1] further, the institution of easements, of fee farm, of copyhold (*emphyteusis* and *superficies*). A little consideration will convince us that, as a fact, all these forms of transaction agree in this, that one portion of the services of which a good is capable is divided off and transferred separately, while the rest of the anticipated services, be they many or few, remain with the ownership of the body of the good, in the hands of the owner of the good.[2]

Finally, it is of great theoretic importance to determine the relations that exist between the material services and the goods from which they proceed. On this point I may put down three cardinal propositions, all of which appear to me so obvious that we may dispense here with any detailed proof of them; more especially as I have gone thoroughly into the subject on another occasion.[3]

1. It seems to me clear that we value and desire goods only on account of the material services that we expect from them. The services, as it were, form the economical substance

[1] Not of the loan; see below.

[2] See also my *Rechte und Verhältnisse*, p. 70, etc.

[3] In my *Rechte und Verhältnisse*, p. 60, where, in particular, I have stated the character of the material services as primary elements of our economic transactions, and have deduced the value of goods from the value of the material services.

with which we have to do. The goods themselves form only the bodily shell.

2. It follows from the above, and appears to me equally beyond doubt, that, where entire goods are obtained and transferred, the economical substance of such transactions always lies in the acquisition and the transference of material services; indeed of the totality of these services. The transference of the goods themselves constitutes only a form—certainly a form that, in the nature of things, is very prominent, but still only an accompanying and limiting form. To buy a good can mean nothing, economically speaking, but to buy all its material services.[1]

3. From this, finally, comes the important conclusion that the value and price of a good is nothing else than the value and price of all its material services thrown together into a lump sum; and that accordingly the value and price of each individual service is contained in the value and price of the good itself.[2]

Before going farther let me illustrate these three propositions by a concrete example. I think all readers will agree with me when I say that a cloth manufacturer values and demands looms only because he expects to get from the looms the useful energies peculiar to them; that not only when he hires a loom, but when he buys it, he looks, as a fact, to the acquisition of its services; and that the ownership he acquires at the same time in the body of the machine only serves as greater security that he will obtain these services. Even if this ownership in point of law appears to be the primary thing, economically it is certainly only the secondary. And, lastly, it will be granted, I think, that the use which the whole machine renders is nothing else than the use of all its material services thrown together into one sum; and that similarly the value and price of the whole machine is nothing else, and can be nothing else, than the value and price of all its material services thrown together into one sum.

[1] This idea, though put somewhat differently, is explicitly recognised by Knies, *Der Kredit*, part ii. pp. 34, 77, 78. He expressly calls the selling price of a house the price of the permanent use of a house in opposition to the hire price, which is the price of the temporary uses of the same good. See also his *Geld*, p. 86. Schäffle too (*Bau und Leben*, second edition, iii.) describes goods as "stores of useful energies" (p. 258).

[2] For more exact statement, see my *Rechte und Verhältnisse*, p. 64.

CHAPTER VI

CRITICISM OF THE SAY-HERMANN CONCEPTION

Having, then, sufficiently explained the nature and the constitution of the use of goods, let us come back to the principal point under consideration—the critical examination of the conception of "use" put forward by the Use theorists.

And first we ask, May it not be the case that the Uses (*Nutzungen*) of the Say-Hermann school are identical with our Material Services (*Nutzleistungen*)? There can be no doubt that they are not identical. That *something* which the school in question calls "use" is intended to be the basis and the equivalent of net interest. The material services, on the contrary, are sometimes (in the case of durable goods) the basis of gross interest, embracing the net interest and a part of the capital value itself; sometimes (in the case of perishable goods) the basis of the entire capital value. If I buy the material services of a dwelling-house, I pay a year's rent for the services of one year; this is a gross interest. If I buy the material services of a cwt. of coal, I pay, for the services of the single hour in which the coal burns to ashes, the whole capital value of the coal. On the other hand, what the Use theorists call "use" is paid for quite differently. The "use" that a cwt. of coal gives off during a whole year attains no higher price than, say, a twentieth part of the capital value of the coal. Use and Material Service must, therefore, be two quite distinct amounts. From this, among other things, it is clear that those writers who defined and pointed out the existence of what we have called material services, under the idea that they were defining the basis of net interest, and pointing to it, were under a serious delusion. This criticism applies particularly to the *services productifs* of Say, and to Schäffle's earlier definitions of use.

And now we come to the decisive question. If what the Use theorists called "uses" (*Nutzungen*) are anything else than the "material services" of goods, does their conception represent anything real? Is it conceivable that between, beside, or among these material services we get some other useful thing from goods?

I can give no other answer to this question than the most emphatic No. And I think every one will be compelled to give this answer who admits that material goods are objects of the material world; that material results cannot be produced otherwise than through manifestations of natural powers; and that even the "utility" of a thing is an activity. Granted these premises,—none of which are likely to be opposed,—it appears to me that no other kind of use in material goods is conceivable than that which comes through the forthputting of their peculiar natural powers—that is, through the rendering of Material Services.

But it is not even necessary to appeal to the logic of the natural sciences. I appeal simply to the common sense of the reader. Take an example or two to remind us of what we mean when we say that goods are "of use." A thrashing machine, there is no doubt, is of use economically in helping to thrash corn. How does it, how can it, render this use? Not otherwise than through putting forth its mechanical powers one after another, till such time as the worn-out mechanism refuses to put forth any more power of the same kind. Can any reader picture to himself the effect that the thrashing machine exerts in separating the corn from the ear under any other form than that of a forthputting of mechanical power? Can he imagine one single use that the machine could exert in thrashing, not through putting forth of power, but through some other kind of *Nutzung*? I doubt it very much. The thrashing machine either thrashes by putting forth its physical powers, or it does not thrash at all.

It would be useless too to attempt to make out another kind of use or *Nutzung* by pointing to different kinds of *mediate* uses that can be got from the thrashing machine. Our grain when thrashed is certainly worth more than it was before being thrashed, and the increment of value is a use we get from the machine. But it is easy to see that this is not a use *in addition to* the material services of the machine, but a use *through* these services; that it is just the use of the machine. Take an exactly similar case. Suppose some one were to give me £50, and with it I were to buy myself a riding-horse. No one would say that I had received two presents —£50 *and* a riding-horse. We have just as little right to conceive of the mediate use of the material services as a second and different useful service of the goods.[1]

This becomes quite clear in the case of perishable goods. What do I get from a cwt. of coal? The heat-creating powers that it gives off during combustion, and which I pay for by the capital price of the coal, and, beyond that, nothing—absolutely nothing. And what I call my "use" of the coal consists in this, that I put these material services, as they issue from the coal, into connection with some one object in which I wish to effect a change through heat; the use lasts as long as these services issue from the burning coal.

And when I lend a man a cwt. of coal for a year, what does my debtor get from it? Just the heat-creating power that issues from the coal during a couple of hours, and besides that, in this case also, nothing—absolutely nothing. And his use of the coal likewise is exhausted in the same number of hours. It may perhaps be asked, Can he not, then, in virtue of the loan agreement, use the coal over a whole year? The owner, I admit, could have nothing to say against it, but nature has; and nature says inexorably that the use shall be over in a couple of hours. What then remains of the contract is, that the debtor is obliged at the expiry of the year, but not till then, to replace the loan by *another* cwt. of coal. But it is surely a most extraordinary confusion of ideas that the fact of a man having to give a cwt. of coal at the expiry of a year in place of another cwt. of coal that has been burnt, should be taken

[1] A hair-splitting critic might perhaps point out that the possession of good machines assists the maker to secure, say, a good credit, a good name, good custom, etc. The careful reader will have no difficulty in answering such objections. To the same category belongs the "use through exchange."

to mean that, in the burned cwt. of coal, there continues to exist an objective use for a whole year!

For any "use of goods," then, other than their natural material services, there is no room either in the world of fact or in the world of logical ideas.

Possibly many readers will consider this analysis sufficiently convincing. But the matter is too important, and the antagonistic views too deeply rooted, to admit of it resting here: and, accordingly, I shall try to bring forward still further evidence against the existence of the use postulated by the Use theorists. Of course the nature of my contention, as a negative one, does not allow of a positive proof. I cannot put before the mind the non-existence of a thing in the same way as I might put the existence of a thing. Nevertheless there is no lack of decisive evidence on the point, and indeed it is offered by my opponents themselves.

There are two criterions of a true proposition: that it is obtained by a correct process of reasoning, and that it leads to correct conclusions. In the case of the assertion we are combating—the assertion that there is an independent use—neither of these criterions applies, and what I mean to prove now is this:—

1. That in all the reasoning by which the Use theorists thought they had proved the existence of this Use, an error or a misunderstanding has crept in.

2. That the assumption of an Independent Use necessarily leads to conclusions that are untenable.

After what has been already demonstrated, that there is no place for any objective Use or *Nutzung* besides the Material Services, the proof of the above points should afford the fullest evidence that can be brought forward for my thesis.

CHAPTER VII

THE INDEPENDENT USE: AN UNPROVED ASSUMPTION

OF the prominent representatives of the Use theory, two have taken particular pains to prove the existence of an independent use, Hermann and Knies. I shall therefore make their argument the chief subject of critical examination. Besides these writers, however, the contribution made by Say, the Nestor of the Use theory, and by Schäffle, deserve our consideration. To begin with the last two writers, a few words will show the misunderstanding into which they have fallen.

Say ascribes to capital the rendering of productive services, or, as he often expresses it, the rendering of "labour," and this labour is, according to him, the foundation of interest. The expressions Services and Labour may perhaps be objected to as more applicable to the actions of persons than of impersonal goods. But there is no doubt that Say is substantially right; capital does perform "labour." It appears to me, however, just as much beyond doubt that the labour which capital actually performs consists in what I have called the Material Services of goods, and these form the foundation of gross interest, or, as the case may be, of the capital value of goods. Say appears quietly to assume that capital, besides these, gives off services distinct from what we have defined as the material services, and that such services may be the separate foundation of a net interest, but he does not give the slightest proof of it—possibly because he had never remarked the chameleon-like ambiguity of his conception of the *services productifs*.

Very much the same is true of Schäffle. I need not speak

of the subjective interpretations of his earlier work, which are inconsistent with the character of the Use theory, and which have been quietly withdrawn in the latest edition of his *Bau und Leben*. In the later work, however, he calls goods "stores of useful energies" (iii. p. 258), and he calls uses "functions of goods," "equivalents of useful materials in living labour" (iii. pp. 258, 259), "living energies of impersonal social substance" (p. 313). This is all quite correct; but the function of goods, the forthputting of useful energies, is nothing else than our Material Services, and these, as we have shown, find their equivalent not in net interest, as Schäffle assumes, but in gross interest, or, in the case of perishable goods, in their capital value. Say and Schäffle, therefore, have misunderstood what it was they had to prove, and their arguments are therefore entirely beside the mark.

The way in which Hermann arrives at his independent "use" (*Nutzung*) has quite a psychological interest.

His first introduction of the conception occurs when speaking of the use of durable goods. "Land, dwellings, tools, books, money, have durable use value. Their use, for the time that they last, may be conceived of as a good in itself, and may obtain for itself an exchange value which we call interest."[1] Here no special evidence is adduced for the existence of an independent use possessing an independent value, and indeed there is no need to prove it; every one knows that, as a fact, the use of a piece of ground, or the use of a house, can be independently valued and sold. But what must be emphasised is, that the thing which every reader will understand in this connection, and must understand, as use, is the *gross* use of durable goods; the basis of rent in the case of land, of hire in the case of houses—the same thing, in short, as we have called the material services of goods. Further, the independent existence of this "use" alongside of the good that renders the use, is only explained by the fact that the use in question does not exhaust the good itself. We are forced to admit that the use is something different from the good itself and independent of it, because the good continues to exist alongside it, in the sense that a portion of the use which it is capable of affording remains intact.

[1] *Staatswirthschaftliche Untersuchungen*, second edition, p. 109.

The second step that Hermann takes is to draw an analogy between the use of durable and the use of perishable goods, and to try to show that, in the case of the latter also, there is an independent use with independent value existing alongside the value of the good. He finds[1] that perishable goods, through technical change of form, preserve their usefulness, and although in changed shape, "may obtain permanence for their use." If, *e.g.* iron-ore, coal, and labour are transformed into pig iron, in being so transformed they contribute the chemical and mechanical elements for a new usefulness which emerges from their combination; and if, in such case, the pig iron possesses the exchange value of the three goods of exchange employed in its making, then the former sum of goods persists, qualitatively bound up in the new usefulness, quantitatively added together in the exchange value. "But if in this way goods that are perishable are capable of a lasting use, then," continues Hermann, "it is the same with goods that change their form qualitatively while retaining their exchange value, as it is with durable goods; this use may be conceived of as a good in itself, as a use (*Nutzung*) which may itself obtain exchange value."

In this Hermann has of course reached the goal he set before him, of proving that, even in perishable goods, there is a use which exists alongside of the good itself. Let us look, however, a little more closely at the basis of his argument.

First of all, it should be noticed that the sole support of this demonstration is a conclusion drawn from analogy. The existence of an independent use in perishable goods can in no way appeal, like the use of durable goods, to the testimony of the senses, and to practical economic experience. No one has seen an independent use detaching itself from a perishable good. If we think that it is to be seen in the case of every loan inasmuch as a loan is nothing else than a transfer of the use of perishable goods, we are wrong; here we do not see an independent use; we only infer that there is one. What we see is simply that the borrower receives £100 at the beginning of the year, to give back at the end of it £105. That in this case £100 is given for the sum that was lent, and £5 for the use of the same, is not an immediate sensuous observation;

[1] P. 110, etc. See the quotation above, p. 194.

it is a construction put by us on our observation. At all events, where the existence of an independent use in perishable goods is in question, no appeal can be made to the case of the loan; for so long as the existence of that independent use *is* questioned, of course the justification of interpreting the loan as a transfer of use must also be questioned, and to try to prove the one by the other is obviously begging the question.

If, therefore, the "independent use of perishable goods" is to be anything more than an unproved assertion, it can only be through the force of the argument from analogy that Hermann has introduced,—not indeed in form but in substance,—in the passage just quoted. The argument there is as follows: Durable goods are capable, as every one knows, of affording a use independent of the goods themselves; if we look closely we can see that perishable goods, like durable goods, allow of a durable use; consequently perishable goods are, and must be, capable of affording a use independent of the goods themselves.

The conclusion thus drawn is false, for, as I shall prove immediately, the analogy fails just at the critical point. I admit at once that perishable goods, through technical change of form, really become capable of durable use. I grant that coal and iron ore are first used in the production of iron. I grant that the use which the iron then affords is nothing but a further result of the powers of those first things; which first things are therefore used in the shape of iron for the second time, and again in the nail that is made out of the iron for the third time, and in the house which the nail helps to hold together for the fourth time; that is to say, are used in a lasting way. Only it must be carefully noted that the durableness in this case rests on quite another ground, and possesses quite another character from that of durable goods properly so called. The durable goods are used over and over again in this way that, in each act of use, only a part of their useful content is exhausted, while another part is left undisturbed for future acts of use. But the perishable goods are used over and over again by exhausting the *whole* of them over and over again—by exhausting the whole useful content of that form which the goods have at the time; but since this useful content then takes on a new shape, the exhaustive use is repeated in it again. The two kinds of use are as distinct as the continuous outflow of water from a reservoir is distinct from the continuous flow of water from one vessel to another and back again; or, to take an example from the economical world, they are as distinct as the obtaining of successive proceeds from selling land piece by piece is distinct from the obtaining of successive proceeds by spending the price of the *whole* piece of ground in a new purchase, and selling this new purchase over again.

A few words more will bring out more sharply the halting nature of Hermann's analogy.

Between the "durable use" which Hermann points out in perishable goods, and durable goods proper, there is really a perfect analogy, but Hermann, instead of drawing this parallel, has drawn another. We have here to do with one of those points in which the neglect that our science has been guilty of in regard to the conception of the "use of goods" has revenged itself on the science. If Hermann had more accurately examined the conception of use (*Gebrauch*) he would have perceived that under that name two very distinct things are coupled together—things which, for want of a better expression, I shall distinguish as the immediate and mediate use of goods. The immediate use (the only one which perhaps has any claim to the name of "use") consists in the receiving of the material services of a good. The mediate use (which perhaps it would be more proper not to call "use" at all) consists in receiving the material services of *those other goods* that only come into existence through the material services of the first "used" good; then again the services of the goods that proceed from the material services of these latter goods, and so on. In other words, the "mediate use" consists in receiving the more distant members of that chain of causes and effects which takes its beginning in the first immediate use—members that possibly go on evolving to the crack of doom.

Now I should not like to say that it is exactly false to call the use of these distant results of a good a use of the good itself; in any case the two kinds of use have an entirely different character. If any one likes to call my riding on a horse a use of the hay that my horse has eaten, it is manifest, at all events, that this is an entirely different kind of use from the immediate use of the hay, and in some essential respects is subject to totally different conditions.

If we wish therefore to draw an analogy between the use of two goods, or of two kinds of goods, we must evidently confine ourselves strictly to similar kinds of use. We may compare the immediate use of one good with the immediate use of another, or the mediate use of one good with the mediate use of another; but not the immediate use of one good with the mediate use of another,—particularly if we wish to deduce further scientific conclusions from the comparison. It is here that Hermann has gone wrong. Durable goods as well as perishable goods permit of two kinds of use. Coal, a perishable good, has its immediate use in burning; its mediate use, as Hermann has quite correctly pointed out, in the use of the iron which is smelted by its aid. But this is the case also with every durable good. *E.g.* every spinning frame, besides its immediate use which consists in the production of yarn, has also a mediate use which consists in the use of the yarn for making cloth, in the use of cloth for making clothing, in the use of clothing itself, and so on. Now the proper comparison would obviously be between the immediate use of the durable goods and the momentary use of the perishable goods,[1] or between the durable mediate use of the perishable and the similarly durable mediate use of the durable goods. But Hermann has made a mistake in the parallels; he has drawn his analogy where there is really none—between the immediate use of durable goods and the mediate use of the perishable; misled by the circumstance that both kinds of use are "durable," and overlooking the fact that, in the two cases, this "durableness" rests on grounds that are utterly and entirely distinct.

This much, I trust, has at all events been made clear by the present analysis, that the analogy which Hermann draws between the "durable" use of durable and of perishable goods is not complete. But beyond this it is easy to show that the dissimilarity comes in exactly at the critical point. Why is

[1] To prove the appropriateness of this analogy we need only picture to ourselves the graduation of transition from the durable goods,—such as land, precious stones,—down through always less durable goods,—as tools, furniture, clothes, linen, tapers, paper collars, and so on,—till we come to the entirely perishable goods—matches, food, drink, etc.

it that we can see in durable goods an independent use with an independent value by the side of the good itself? Not simply because the use is a durable one, but because the use that has already been made of the good leaves something over of the good, and of the value of the good; because in that portion of the immediate useful content that has been released and in the portion that is not yet released we have two different things that exist beside each other, each of them having simultaneously an economic value of its own. But in the case of perishable goods the exact opposite of all this is the case. Here the use of the moment entirely exhausts the useful content of the form which the good had at the moment, and the value of this use is always identical with the entire value of the good itself. At no one moment have we two valuable things alongside of each other; only one and the same valuable thing two times in succession. When we use coal and iron ore in making iron, we consume them; for this use we pay the entire capital value of these goods, and not one atom of them is saved, or continues to exist and have an independent value beside and after this consumption. And it is just the same when the iron is consumed again for the making of nails. It is consumed; the whole capital value of the iron is paid for it; and not the smallest fragment of it continues to exist alongside. There never are in one single moment the thing *and* its use beside each other; only the things "coal and iron-ore," "iron," and "nails," *after one another*, and *through* their successive use. But such being the case, it can be shown us neither by analogy nor in any other way how the "use" of a perishable article can attain to an existence and to a value independent of the article itself.

The fact is, Hermann's analogical reasoning is no more correct than an argument like the following would be. From a great water tank in an hour's time I can draw off a gallon of water every second. Each of the 3600 gallons thus poured out has an independent existence of itself, and is a perfectly distinct thing; distinct from the water that has been drawn and from the water that remains in the tank. But suppose I have only one gallon of water, and go on pouring this from one vessel in to another; as in the former case, a gallon of water is poured out every second for the space of an hour.

Therefore in this case also it must be 3600 independent gallons that are poured out from our vessels!

But, lastly, Hermann takes a third step, and resolves the use of durable goods into two elements; one element that alone deserves the name "use" (*Gebrauch* or *Nutzung*) and a second element which he calls "using up" (*Abnutzung*). I must confess that this last step reminds me very forcibly of the old anecdote of Munchausen, in which Munchausen lets himself down by a rope from the moon by always cutting the rope above his head, and knotting it again below him. Very much in the same way Hermann has at first treated of the whole (gross) use of durable goods as use (*Nutzung*), till such time as he has based a conclusion from analogy on it, and through it has demonstrated a use in perishable goods also. No sooner has he got this length than he tears his primary conception of use in pieces, nowise disturbed by the fact that with it he destroys the peg to which he has attached his later conception of independent use, and that this conception now hangs in the air.

I shall return later on to the further inconsistencies involved in this. In the meantime I content myself with saying that the contention which looks so fascinating at the first glance proves on closer examination to have no better support than a false analogy.

It would be an obvious omission in my criticism if it were not to include the thorough and conscientious efforts of Knies on this subject. The work of this distinguished thinker has a twofold similarity to Hermann's doctrine; like Hermann, his arguments are remarkably convincing at first sight, and this power they owe to an effective employment of analogies—analogies, however, which, like those of Hermann, I feel bound to declare false.

Knies chances on our subject when discussing the economical nature of the loan. He agrees with the view that the essence of the loan consists in a transfer of the *use* of the sum lent; and when trying, with his usual carefulness, to find reasons for this conception, he is compelled to go into the question of the existence or non-existence of an independent use in perishable goods.

In some introductory considerations he starts from the idea that there are economical "transfers" which do not coincide with the transfer of the rights of property. The transferences of the simple use of goods seem to be of this sort. He goes on to note the distinction between perishable and non-perishable goods, and then turns to a detailed consideration of the transfer of the uses of non-perishable goods—a consideration which, with him as with Hermann, is made to serve as bridge to explain the delicate phenomena in the use of perishable goods. Here he puts down the distinction that must be drawn between the *Nutzung* as "that *Gebrauch* of a good which lasts over a period of time, and is measured by moments of time," and the good itself as the "bearer of the *Nutzung*." The economical principle of the transfers in question is that the intention is to transfer a *Nutzung*, but not the bearer of a *Nutzung*. But the nature of things necessitates that the transfer of the *Nutzungen* of goods always involves certain concessions in regard to the bearer of the *Nutzung*. The owner of a leased piece of ground, *e.g.* must, from physical considerations, deliver it over to the lessee, if the lessee is to get the use of it. The amount of these concessions, and the inevitable risk of loss as well as of deterioration of the good which bears the use, vary just as things vary, and as the particular circumstances of the individual case vary. In hire, for instance, a certain amount of deterioration, and the consent of the owner to this deterioration, are quite necessary.[1]

Then, after explaining the meaning of the legal categories of fungible and non-fungible goods, Knies puts the following question (p. 71), Is it not then actually possible, must it not, indeed, be understood as the intention of a compact, that the use (*Nutzung*) of a fungible, and even of a perishable good should be transferred?

In this sentence Knies implicitly asks whether there is not an independent use of perishable goods. He answers the question by putting the following case.

"A cwt. of corn is a fungible and perishable good of this kind. The owner, in certain circumstances, cannot part with this cwt., and is not inclined to exchange it, or sell it,—perhaps

[1] *Geld*, p. 59, etc.

because he is obliged to consume (*verbrauchen*), or wishes to consume it himself at the end of six months. But up till that date he does not need it. This being so he might of course very well allow himself to transfer the use (*Gebrauch*) of it to some one else for the next six months, if only at the expiry of that time he could get back his good. Say, then, that there is another man who desires the corn, but cannot barter for it or buy it. He will point out that he could not get any use (*Nutzung*) from the corn, as a perishable good, unless through the consumption (*Verbrauch*) of the corn itself, say as seed; but that he would be able to replace another cwt. from the harvest obtained by means of this use (*Nutzung*) transferred to him. The owner may find this perfectly satisfactory for his economical interests, since the transaction here refers to a fungible good.

"In this statement there is not a particle of an idea containing anything at all impossible, far-fetched, or artificial. But such a transaction taken by itself—that is, the transfer of a cwt. of corn under the condition of the borrower giving back a cwt. of corn at the end of six months—belongs undoubtedly to those things that are called loans. . . . In conformity with this we put the loan in the category of transfers of a Use (*Nutzung*)—that is, of the use (*Nutzung*) of fungible goods which pass over into the control and for the use of the owner, and are replaced by a similar quantity. Naturally, in the case of the loan, it is of the greatest consequence to understand clearly that, however liberal the concessions may be as regards the *bearer* of the use, still it is not in the concessions that the principle of the transaction lies. Rather are these concessions always determined in conformity with the overruling necessity of obtaining the use at the time. And just on this account, in the case of a perishable good, they are extended so far as to give the owner the power of consumption, while all the same there is even here no other principle in the matter than the transfer of a use. In the loan, therefore, the transfer of the right of property is unavoidable, but still only as an accompanying circumstance."

I admit at once that these analyses are calculated to make an entirely convincing impression on one who does not look very closely into them. Not only has Knies shown unusual skill in drawing the analogy which the old opponents of the canonists used to draw, between lease and hire on the one side and the loan on the other, but he has enriched it by a new and effective feature. For by the allusion he makes to the unavoidable concessions, in regard to the "bearer of the use," that are made in the case of all transfers of use, he has managed to change the element that seemed completely to destroy the analogy between the loan and the hire (the complete transfer of the property in the goods lent) into a further support of it.

If, however, we do not allow ourselves to be carried away by these brilliant analogies, but begin to reflect critically on them, we shall easily see that their admissibility, and with it the strength of the proof, depends on an affirmative answer being given to a previous question. The previous question is, Whether in perishable goods there *is* any independent use to transfer by way of loan? And we shall look more exactly at the kind of evidence that Knies specially brings forward as regards this question—a question that is the key to his whole theory of the loan.

At this point I think we shall make the astonishing discovery that Knies has not said a word in proof of the existence, or even the conceivableness of an independent use, but has evaded the great difficulty of his theory by using the word *Nutzung* in a double sense.

I shall try to show how he does so. On p. 61 he himself identifies the *Nutzung* of a good with its *Gebrauch*. He knows besides (p. 61 again) that in perishable goods there is no other possible *Gebrauch* but a *Verbrauch*. He must, therefore, also know that in perishable goods the *Nutzung* is identical with the *Verbrauch*. But, on the other hand, he uses the word *Nutzung* in stating the problem, and then in the concluding sentence—"In conformity with this we put the loan in the category of transfers of a *Nutzung*"—he evidently uses the word in a sense that is not identical with *Verbrauch*, but means a durable *Nutzung*. In the course of the passage quoted he mixes up step by step the *Nutzung* in the first sense with the *Nutzung* in the second sense, till he arrives at this concluding sentence, where, from a number of propositions that are only correct if they refer to *Nutzung* in the first sense, is drawn the conclusion that there is a *Nutzung* in the second sense.

The first proposition runs: "The owner, in certain circumstances, cannot part with this cwt., and is not inclined to exchange it, or sell it,—perhaps because he is obliged to consume (*verbrauchen*), or wishes to consume it himself at the end of six months. But up till that date he does not need it."

In this proposition the kind of use that is thought of, and, in the nature of things, the only kind that can be thought of, is quite correctly indicated as the *Verbrauch* of the good. Then he continues: "He might of course very well allow himself to transfer the *Gebrauch* of it to some one else for the next six months, if only at the expiry of that time he could get back his good."

Here begins the ambiguity. What is the meaning of *Gebrauch* here? Does it mean *Verbrauch?* Or does it mean a kind of *Nutzung* that lasts over a period of six months? Obviously the *Gebrauch* is conceivable only as the *Verbrauch*, but the words "*Gebrauch* for the next six months" are calculated to suggest a durable *Gebrauch*, and with this begins the *quid pro quo.*

Now follows the third proposition: "Say then that there is another man who desires the corn, but cannot barter for it or buy it. He will point out that he could not get any *Nutzung* from the corn, as a perishable good, unless through the *Verbrauch* of the corn itself, say as seed; but that he would be able to replace another cwt. from the harvest obtained by means of this *Nutzung* transferred to him. The owner may find this perfectly satisfactory for his economical interests, since the transaction here refers to a fungible good."

This proposition contains the crowning confusion. Knies makes the suitor for the loan point out distinctly that a *Nutzung* of perishable goods cannot be anything else than identical with their *Verbrauch*, but in the same breath he uses and places the words *Nutzung* and *Verbrauch* in such a way that the two conceptions are kept separate from one another, and appear *not* to be identical. He thus smuggles into his argument—and the oftener he does it the less likely is it to be noticed—the suggestion of a durable *Nutzung* in perishable goods. Thus when it is said that the harvest is "obtained by means of this *Nutzung* transferred," one might quite well imagine that the *Nutzgebrauch* of the seed is here again only the same thing as the *Nutzverbrauch* which obtained the harvest. But, thanks to the agreement of the "*Nutzung* transferred" with the "transfer of the *Nutzung*," which we have been constantly hearing about, and which had meant the opposite of the "transfers of the *bearer* of the *Nutzung*," we are forced involuntarily to think of a durable *Nutzung* after the analogy of the *Nutzung* of durable goods. Any scruple we may have about the conceivableness of such a *Nutzung* is the more easily silenced that we are told, at the same time, that through it the harvest is obtained — that is, that something very real indeed is accomplished—a proof of the existence of a *Nutzung* which the reader, once caught in the tangle, naturally puts to the account of the "durable *Nutzung*."

And now from this confused argument Knies draws his conclusions. After saying that "in this statement there is not a particle of an idea containing anything at all impossible, far-fetched, or artificial"—which, indeed, if we grant his assumptions, is quite correct, but admits of no conclusion in favour of his thesis if, for the words *Gebrauch* or *Nutzung*, we substitute in each ambiguous passage the word *Nutzverbrauch*—he draws the conclusion, Therefore the loan belongs to the class of transfers of a simple *Nutzung*.

This conclusion is simply fallacious. The thing he had to prove has not been proved. Nay, more; the thing that was to be proved is introduced quietly in the deduction, as something that had been assumed; the *Nutzung*, in the peculiar sense attached to it, is spoken of as if it were a familiar fact, without one word being said in support of what was to be proved, the existence of such a *Nutzung*. But the difficulty of discovering this fundamental flaw in the argument is very much aggravated by two circumstances: first, that the false *Nutzung* sails under the flag of the true *Nutzung*, and we forget to protest against the existence of the so-called *Nutzung*, because, thanks to the dialectical skill of the author, we do not keep it separate and distinct from the true *Nutzung*, which unquestionably does exist; and second, through the very naïveté of the suggestion. That is to say, without in point of fact once entering on the problem whether a durable *Nutzung* in perishable goods is conceivable or not, Knies represents the owner and the suitor for the loan as negotiating over the transfer of the *Nutzung* in a tone of certainty, which implies that the existence of the *Nutzung* is beyond question,—and the reader almost involuntarily shares in the certainty!

If we look back and compare the efforts that the writers of the Say-Hermann school have made to prove their peculiar Use of capital, we shall perceive, among all their difference of detail, a substantial agreement which is very suggestive.

All the authors of that school, from Say to Knies, when they begin to speak of the use of capital, first of all allude to the material services which capital actually renders. Then under cover of this they get the reader to admit that the "use of capital" does really exist; that it exists as an independent economic element, and even possesses an independent economical value. That this independence is not the independence of a second whole beside the good itself, but only that of an independent and separable part of the content of the good, the rendering of the service being always attended by a diminution in the value of the good itself; and that the remuneration of this service is a gross interest—all this is kept in the background.

But no sooner have they got the length of recognising the "independent use of capital" than they substitute, for the true material services of capital (under cover of which they arrived at the independent use), the imaginary use of their own making, impute to it an independent value *outside the full value* of the good, and end by drawing away the true use that had served as a ladder for the false. This way of working is seen in Say and Schäffle only in a hasty and abbreviated form, in quietly changing what is the substance of gross interest into what is the substance of net interest; but Hermann and Knies work it out in complete detail before our eyes. Blunders like these show us how urgent is the necessity that the "revision of fundamental conceptions," so much desiderated, should even at this late date be applied to the apparently insignificant conception of the Use of goods. I have tried to do my part in giving a first contribution to it, and I believe that in the present chapter I have proved my first proposition,—that in all the reasoning by which the Use theorists of the Say-Hermann school thought they had proved the existence of the asserted use, an error or a misunderstanding has crept in.

Not only, however, is the assumption of that independent use absolutely unproved, but, as I mean to show in the next chapter, it leads necessarily to internal contradictions and untenable conclusions.

CHAPTER VIII

THE INDEPENDENT USE: ITS UNTENABLE CONCLUSIONS

It is customary among the Use theorists, and even among others,[1] to make a distinction between a gross *Nutzung*, which is the basis of gross interest (rent or hire), and a net *Nutzung*, which is the basis of net interest. It is singular enough that we have all been in the habit of innocently repeating this distinction, without it ever occurring to any one that there was in it an irreconcilable contradiction.

If we are to believe the unanimous assurance of our theorists, *Nutzung* should be taken as synonymous with *Gebrauch* in the objective sense of the word. Now, if there is a net and a gross *Nutzung*, are we to understand that there are two *Nutzungen*, two *Gebräuche* of the same good—not, it must be remembered, two successive or two alternative kinds of *Gebrauch*, but two simultaneous cumulative *Gebräuche* that

[1] It is as well to put it in so many words that, in this polemic on the conception of Use, I am in opposition, not only to the Use theorists properly so called, but to almost the entire literature of political economy. The conception of the Use of capital which I dispute is that commonly accepted since the day of Salmasius. Even writers who explain the origin of interest by quite different theories—*e.g.* Roscher, by the Productivity theory; or Senior, by the Abstinence theory; or Courcelle-Seneuil or Wagner, by the Labour theory—always conceive of loan interest as a remuneration for a transferred Use or Usage of capital, and occasionally they conceive even of natural interest as a result of the same use or usage. The only distinction between them and the Use theorists properly so called is this, that the former employ these expressions naïvely, using terms that have become popular, and do not trouble themselves as to the premises and conclusions of the Use conception,—which sometimes entirely contradict the rest of their interest theory; while the Use theorists build their distinctive theory on the conclusions of that conception. The almost universal acceptance of the error I am opposing may further justify my prolixity.

are obtained beside or in each other in every transaction, however elementary, where a *Gebrauch* enters?

That one good gives off two uses, the one after the other, can be understood. That one good permits of two kinds of use alternatively—as wood for building and for burning—can also be understood. It is quite conceivable even that one good should permit of two kinds of use simultaneously, the one beside the other, and that these furnish two distinct utilities; *e.g.* that a picturesque rustic bridge should at once serve as medium of traffic, and as object of æsthetic satisfaction.

But when I hire a house or a lodging, and make use of it for purposes of habitation, to imagine that in one and the same series of acts of use I am receiving and profiting by two different uses, a wider one for which I pay the whole hire, and a narrower one for which I pay the net interest contained in the hire; or to imagine that in every stroke of the pen that I put on paper, in every look that I throw on a picture, in every cut that I make with my knife, in short, in every use, however simple, that I get from a good, I get always two uses, in or beside each other;—this is in contradiction alike with the nature of things and with healthy common sense. If I look at a picture, or live in a house, I make one use of the picture or house; and if in this connection I speak of two things, whether *Gebrauch* or *Nutzung*, I am giving a wrong name to one of them.

To which of them do I give the wrong name?

On this point, again, the current view is a very strange one. The theorists we are speaking of certainly appear to have felt in some degree the impropriety of assuming two uses to exist alongside each other. For although as a rule they employ the word *Nutzung* to express two things, they sometimes make an attempt to put one of them out of sight. Indeed, the gross *Nutzung* is eliminated when it is split up into net *Nutzung* plus partial replacement of capital. Thus Roscher, whom we are justified in quoting as the representative of the current opinion, says:[1] "The *Nutzung* of a capital must not be confounded with its partial replacement. In house rent, for instance, over and above the payment for the *Gebrauch* of the house, there must be contained a sufficient sum for repairs, indeed

[1] *Grundlagen*, tenth edition, p. 401, etc.

enough for the gradual accumulation of capital sufficient to put up a new building." It follows that the thing for which we pay net interest is in truth a *Gebrauch,* and it is erroneous and inaccurate to apply the name to that for which we pay gross interest. I do not believe that it would be possible to put the representatives of this wonderful view in a more embarrassing position than by challenging them to define what they mean by *Gebrauch.* What else can it mean than the receiving or, if we like to give it an objective significance, the proffering of the Material Services of which a good is capable? Or, if there is any objection to my expression, let us say "useful services" with Say, or "releasing of a use from material goods" or "receiving of useful effects" with Schäffle, or however else we like to put it. But define the word as we may, one thing appears to my mind beyond dispute. When A makes over to B a house for temporary habitation, and B inhabits it, then A has given over to B the *Gebrauch* of the house, and B has taken the *Gebrauch* of the house; and if B pays anything for the *Gebrauch,* he does not pay a single penny of hire or rent for anything else than this;—that he may avail himself of the useful properties and powers of the house. In other words, he has paid for the *Gebrauch* transferred to him.

It may be said, Yes, perhaps so; but has not B consumed a portion of the value of the house itself? and if so, did he not get transferred to him a part of the value of the house itself, in addition to the use of the house? One who would argue thus might be expected to hold the somewhat singular view that two aspects of one event are two events. The truth of the matter is that the hirer has received the *Gebrauch* of the house, and only the *Gebrauch;* but in using it, and through using it, he has diminished its value. He has received a "store of energies," from which he is at liberty to "release" so many; he has done nothing but "release" or use them; but, naturally, the value of the remainder of the energies has been diminished thereby. To construe that as meaning that the hirer has received two things alongside each other, *Gebrauch* and partial value of capital, appears to me very much as if, in buying a fourth horse to match three he had already, a man were to consider it an acquisition of two separate things—first, a horse, and second, the complement of the team of four; and as if he were then to maintain that, of the £50 he paid, only one portion, say £25, was the price of the horse, while the remaining £25 was the price of the complement of the team! It is the same thing as if one were to say of a workman who had put up the cross on the steeple and thereby finished the building of the steeple, that he had performed two acts—first, had put up the cross, and second, had finished the building of the steeple; and were further to say that, if the workman took an hour to do the whole job, not more than three-quarters of an hour were needed for the erection of the cross, since a part of the whole time expended, say a quarter of an hour, must be put to the account of the second act, the completion of the building of the steeple!

But if, notwithstanding all this, some one thinks that he sees in *Gebrauch*, not the gross *Nutzung*, but another something which is ill to define, let him say in what the *Gebrauch* of a meal consists. In eating? It cannot be so, for that is a gross *Nutzung*, that swallows up the whole value of the capital, and of course we cannot confuse that with the true *Gebrauch*. But in what then does it consist? In an aliquot part of eating? or in something entirely different from eating? I am glad to think that the duty of answering this question does not fall to me, but to the Use theorists.

If, then, we are not to give the words *Gebrauch* and *Nutzung* a meaning that is equally opposed to language and to life, to the representations of practice and of science, we cannot deny the gross *Nutzung* the property of being a true *Nutzung*. But if there cannot be two *Nutzungen*, and if in any case the gross *Nutzung* must be recognised as that which correctly conveys the conception of *Nutzung*, then there is no need to argue further against the net *Nutzung* of the Use theorists.

But let us leave all that on one side, and confine our attention to the following. Whether the gross *Nutzung* be a true *Nutzung* or not, at any rate it is undoubtedly something. And the Use theorists would like to make out the net *Nutzung* to be something likewise. Now these two quantities, if they both actually exist, must at all events stand in some relation to each other. The net *Nutzung* must either be part of the gross *Nutzung* or it is no part of it; there is no third course. Now let us see. If we look at durable goods it seems probable that the net *Nutzung* is a part of the gross; for since the remuneration of the former, the net interest, is contained in the remuneration of the latter, the gross interest, so must also the first object of purchase be contained in the second, and be a part of it. This indeed even the Use theorists themselves maintain when they analyse the one sum of the gross *Nutzung* into net *Nutzung* plus partial replacement of capital. But look now at perishable goods. The net interest I pay in this case is *not* paid for their consumption (*Verbrauch*), for if, on the moment of the consumption, I replace the perishable goods by their fungible equivalent, I do not require to pay any interest. What I pay interest for is only the *delay* in the replacement of the equivalent; that is, I pay it for something that is not contained in the consumption—that most intense form of gross use—but stands quite outside it. Are we to conclude then that the net *Nutzung* is at once part and not part of the gross *Nutzung?* How can the Use theorists explain this contradiction?

I might draw out to much greater length the number of riddles and contradictions into which the assumption of the independent *Nutzung* leads us. I might ask the Use theorists what, for instance, I should represent to myself as the ten years' *Nutzung*, or the ten years' *Gebrauch*, of the bottle of wine that I drank on the first day of the first year? An existence it must have, for I can buy or sell it on a loan of from one to ten years. I might point out what a singular assumption it is, even verging on the ludicrous, that, on the moment when a good by its complete consumption actually ceases to be of use, it should really be only beginning to afford a perpetual use; that one debtor, who at the end of a year pays back a bottle of wine he borrowed, has consumed less than another who only returns the bottle of wine at the end of ten years, inasmuch as the former has consumed the bottle of wine and its one year's use, the latter the bottle of wine and its ten years' use; while all the time it is evident to everybody that both parties have obtained the same use from the bottle of wine, and that the obligation that emerges, to pay back *another* bottle of wine sooner or later, has absolutely nothing to do with the shorter or longer duration of the objective uses of the *first* bottle. But I think that more than enough has been said to carry conviction.

To sum up, I consider that three things have been here proved. I think it has been proved, firstly, that the nature of goods, as material bearers of useful natural powers, precludes the conceivability of any *Nutzung* that does not consist in the forthputting of their useful natural powers—that is, any *Nutzung* that is not identical with what I have called the Material Services of goods—those services being the basis not of net, but of gross interest; or, in the case of perishable goods, their entire capital value.

I think that it has been proved, secondly, that all attempts on the part of the Use theorists to demonstrate the existence or the conceivability of a net *Nutzung* different from the material services, are erroneous or based on a misunderstanding.

I think it has been proved, thirdly, that the assumption of the net *Nutzung* postulated by the Use theorists necessarily leads to absurd and contradictory conclusions.

I think, therefore, that I am entirely justified in maintaining that the net *Nutzung*, on the existence of which the Use theorists of the Say-Hermann school base their explanation of interest, does not in truth exist, but is only the product of a misleading fiction.

But in what way did this remarkable fiction enter into our science? And how came it to be taken for reality? By recurring for a little to the history of the problem I hope to dispel any doubts that may linger in the minds of my readers; and, in particular, I trust we may get an opportunity of estimating at its true value any prejudice that might still linger as a consequence of the former victory of Salmasius's theory.

CHAPTER IX

THE INDEPENDENT USE: ITS ORIGIN IN LEGAL FICTION

We have here to deal with one of those not uncommon cases where a fiction, originating in the sphere of law and originally used for practical legal purpose by people who were fully conscious of its fictitious character, has been transferred to the sphere of economics, and the consciousness of the fiction has been lost in the transfer. Jurisprudence has at all times required fictions. To make comparatively few and simple principles of law suffice for the whole varied actuality of legal life, jurisprudence is often compelled to look upon cases as quite similar with each other that in reality are not similar, but may be appropriately dealt with in practice as if they were so. It was in this way that the *formulae fictitiae* of the Roman civil process originated; thus also the legal "persons," the *res incorporales*, and innumerable other fictions of the science of law.

Now it sometimes happened that a fiction which had grown very venerable became in the end petrified into a thoroughly credited dogma. If for hundreds of years people had been accustomed to treat a thing, both in theory and practice, as if it really were essentially the same as something else, then, other circumstances being favourable, it might end in their quite forgetting that there was a fiction. So it is, as I have pointed out in another place, with the *res incorporales* of Roman law; and so too it has been with the independent *Nutzung* of perishable and fungible goods. Let us follow, step by step, the course whereby the fiction became petrified into a dogma.

There are some goods the individuality of which is of no

importance,—goods that are only taken account of by their kind and amount, *quae pondere, numero, mensura consistunt.* These are called in law fungible goods.[1] Since no importance attaches to their individuality, the replacing goods perfectly supply the place of the replaced goods. For certain purposes of practical legal life these goods could be treated without difficulty as identical. Particularly was this the case in such legal transactions as related to the giving away and getting back of fungible goods. Here it suggested itself as convenient to conceive of the giving back of an equal amount of fungible goods as a giving back of the very same goods; in other words, to feign identity between the fungible goods given back and those given away.

So far as I know, the old Roman sources of law do not put this fiction formally. They say quite correctly of it that, in the loan, *tantundem* or *idem genus,* not simply *idem* is given back. But at any rate the fiction is there. If, *e.g.* the so-called *depositum irregulare,* where the depositary was allowed to employ on his own account the sum of money given over to his safe keeping, and to replace the deposit in other pieces of money, was treated as a *depositum,*[2] this construction can only be explained by supposing that the lawyers invoked the assistance of the fiction whereby the pieces of money replaced were considered identical with those given in for safe keeping. Modern jurisprudence has occasionally gone farther, and spoken explicitly of a "legal identity" between fungible goods.[3]

From this first fiction it was but a step to a second. If it once came to be thought that, in the loan and in similar transactions, the same goods were given back that the debtor had received, the further idea was logically bound to follow, that the debtor had retained the goods lent him during the whole period of the loan, had kept them unbroken, and had used them unbroken; that the use obtained from them was therefore a durable use; and that where interest was paid it was paid just for this durable use.

[1] The common German word is *vertretbar,* which might be loosely translated here by "representative" or "replaceable." But the word "fungible" is perhaps worth adopting in English economics.—W. S.

[2] See L. 31, Dig. loc. 19, 2, and L. 25, § 1, Dig. dep. 16, 3.

[3] Goldschmidt, *Handbuch des Handelsrechtes,* second edition, Stuttgart, 1883, vol. ii. part. i. p. 26 in the note.

This second step in the fiction the jurists did make. They knew quite well, to begin with, that they were only dealing with a fiction. They knew quite well that the goods given back are not identical with the goods received; that the debtor does not hold and possess these goods during the whole period of the loan;—the fact being that, to attain the purpose of the loan, the debtor must, as a rule, very soon entirely part with the goods. Lastly, they knew quite well that, for the same reason, the debtor does not get any durable use out of the goods lent. But for the practical purposes and requirements of both parties it was the same as if everything actually were what it pretended to be, and therefore the jurists could employ the fiction. They gave expression to this fiction in the sphere of their science when, on the ground of it, they confirmed the expression for loan interest that had already found a home in the speech of the people, *usura*, money paid for use; when they taught that interest was paid for the use of the sum lent; and when they made out a usufruct even in perishable goods. This usufruct of course was only a quasi-usufruct, the lawyers being quite aware that they were only dealing with a fiction. On one occasion they even expressed this pointedly, in correcting a legislative act that had given the fiction too realistic an expression.[1]

Finally, after many centuries of teaching that the *usura* was money paid for use, and in an age when the better part of the living spirit of classical jurisprudence had fled, and had consequently been replaced by a greater reverence for transmitted formulas, the justification of loan interest was sharply attacked by the canonists. One of their strongest weapons was the discovery of this fiction in regard to the uses of perish-

[1] Ulpian, it is well known, in Dig. vii. 5, L. 1, *De usufructu earum rerum quae usu consumuntur vel minuuntur*, quotes a decree of the Senate which established the bequeathing of a usufruct in perishable goods. On this Gaius remarks: "Quo senatus consulto non id effectum est, ut pecuniae usufructus proprie esset; nec enim naturalis ratio auctoritate senatus commutari potuit; sed, remedio introducto, caepit quasi usufructus haberi." I do not agree with Knies (*Geld*, p. 75) that Gaius took exception simply to the formal flaw that there could only be a regular usufruct in goods belonging to another person, while the legatee holds the perishable goods left him as his own property, *res suae*. The appeal to the *naturalis ratio* could hardly have been made in order to rehabilitate a defective formal definition of usufruct; it is infinitely more probable that it was made on behalf of a truth of nature that was seriously violated by the decree.

able goods. For the rest, their argument appeared so convincing that one could scarcely see how loan interest was to be saved, if the premiss were granted that there is no such thing as an independent use of perishable goods. Thus the fiction all at once attained an importance it never had before. To believe in the actual existence of the *usus* was the same thing as to approve of interest; not to believe in it seemed to force one to condemn it. To save interest in this dilemma, people were inclined to give the legal formula more honour than it deserved; and Salmasius and his followers exerted themselves to find reasons which would allow them to take the formula for the fact. The reasons they did find were just good enough to convince people eager to be convinced,—as already won over by a demonstration that was in other respects excellent,—that Salmasius, on the whole, had right on his side; while his opponents, who were evidently wrong as regards the chief point, were suspected even on those points where they were occasionally right. So it happened—not for the first, and certainly not for the last time—that under the pressure of practical exigencies an abortive theory was born, and the old fiction of the lawyers proclaimed as fact.

Thus it has remained ever since, at least in political economy. While the newer jurisprudence drew back for the most part from the doctrine of Salmasius, modern political economy has held by the old stock formula taken from the legal *répertoire*. In the seventeenth century the formula had served to support the practical justification of interest; in the nineteenth it did as good service in affording a theoretical explanation of it, which people would have been embarrassed to get otherwise. This puzzling "surplus value" had to be explained. It appeared to hang in the air. Something was wanted to hang it from. And there, in the most welcome way, the old fiction offered itself. As beseemed its rising claims as a theory, it was dressed out in all sorts of new accessories, and so was worthy at last, under the name of *Nutzung*, to take the highest place of honour, and become the foundation stone of a theory of interest as distinctive as it is comprehensive.

It may be the good fortune of these pages to break the spell under which the custom of centuries has laid our conception. It may be that the net *Nutzung* of capital will be relegated finally to that domain from which it never should have emerged—the domain of fiction, of metaphor, which, as Bastiat once remarked with only too much truth, has so often turned the science from the right path. With it many a deeply rooted conviction will have to be given up—not the Use theory only, in the narrower and proper sense of the word, which makes the *Nutzung* the chief pillar in the explanation of interest, but a number of other convictions also, which are commonly accepted outside the rank of the Use theorists, and which employ that conception along with others. Among other things will go the favourite construction of the loan as a transfer of uses, as having its analogue in rent and hire.

But what is to be put in its place?

To answer that does not, strictly speaking, belong to our present critical task; it is a matter for the positive statement which I have reserved for the second volume of this work. It may, however, with some justice be expected that, when I assume the doctrine of the canonists as regards one of its principal points, I should at least indicate how we are to escape the obviously false conclusions of the canonists. Consequently I shall briefly indicate my own view on the nature of the loan; of course under the reservation of returning to more exact treatment of it in my next volume, and meantime asking my readers to postpone their final verdict on my theory till such time as I have stated it in detail, and connected it with the entire theory of interest.

I may best take up the subject at the old canonist dispute. In my opinion the canonists alone were wrong in their conclusions, while both parties were wrong in the reasoning which led them to their conclusions. The canonists remained in the wrong, because they made only one mistake in their reasoning. Salmasius made two mistakes, but of these the second cancelled the harm done by the first, so that after a very tumultuous course his argument ended in reaching the truth. I explain this as follows:—

Both parties agree in regarding it as an axiom that the capital sum replaced on the expiry of the loan contract is the equivalent, and, indeed, is the exact and full equivalent, of the capital sum originally lent. Now this assumption is so false that the wonder is how it has not long ago been exposed as a superstition. Every economist knows that the value of goods does not depend simply on their physical qualities, but, to a very great extent, on the circumstances under which they become available for the satisfaction of human needs. It is well known that goods of the same kind, *e.g.* grain, have a very different value in varying circumstances. Among the most important of the circumstances that influence the value of goods, outside of their physical constitution, are the time and place at which they become available. It would be very strange if goods of a definite kind had exactly the same value at all places where they might be found. It would be strange, for instance, if a cwt. of coal at the pit-brow had exactly the same value as a cwt. of coal at the railway terminus, and if that again had exactly the same value as a cwt. of coal at the fireside. Now it would be quite as strange if £100 which are at my disposal to-day should be exactly equivalent to £100 which I am to receive a year later, or ten or a hundred years later. On the contrary it is clear that, if one and the same quantity of goods falls to the disposal of an economical subject at different points of time, its economical position will, as a rule, come under a different influence, and, in conformity with that, the goods will obtain a different value. It is impossible to agree with Salmasius and the canonists, and assume it as a self-evident principle that there is a complete equivalence between the present goods given in loan and the goods of like number and kind returned at some distant period. Such an equivalence, on the contrary, can only be a very rare and accidental exception.

It is very evident from what source both parties obtained the quite unscientific view of the equivalence between the sum of capital given out and that received back. It is from the old legal fiction of the identity between fungible goods of similar kind and number. If, on the strength of this fiction, the loan is conceived of as if it meant that the same £100, which the creditor advances to the debtor, is given back by the debtor to the creditor on the expiry of the loan, then of course this replacement must be looked on as entirely equivalent and just. It was the common mistake of the canonists and of their opponents that they fell into this trap laid for them in the first part of the legal fiction. It was the sole mistake of the canonists and the first mistake of Salmasius. The further development was simply this:—

The canonists remained in error because this was their only mistake. Once they had made it they began at the wrong time to be sharp-sighted, and to expose the assumed independent use of the loaned goods as a fiction. With that fell away every support that could properly have been given to interest, and they were bound—falsely, but logically—to pronounce it wrong. But the first error that Salmasius had made, in the fiction of the identity between the capital received and the capital paid back, he rectified by a second; he retained that fiction as regards the loan of *money*, and held that in this case the borrower possessed the "use" of the loaned goods all the time of the loan.

The truth is in neither reading. *The loan is a real exchange of present goods against future goods.* For reasons that I shall give in detail in my second volume, present goods invariably possess a greater value than future goods of the same number and kind, and therefore a definite sum of present goods can, as a rule, only be purchased by a larger sum of future goods. Present goods possess an agio in future goods. *This agio is interest.* It is not a separate equivalent for a separate and durable use of the loaned goods, for that is inconceivable; it is a part equivalent of the loaned sum, kept separate for practical reasons. The replacement of the capital + the interest constitutes the full equivalent.[1]

[1] The germs of this view, which I consider the only correct one, are to be found in Galiani (see above, p. 49), in Turgot (see above, p. 56), and latterly in Knies, who, however, has since expressly withdrawn it as erroneous.

CHAPTER X

MENGER'S CONCEPTION OF USE

Up till now my analyses have gone to prove that there is no independent use of goods of the kind conceived of by the Say-Hermann side of the Use theory, and by nearly all the economists of the present day in their train. It still remains to be proved that there cannot be an independent use even in that essentially different shape that Menger sought to give the conception.

While the Say-Hermann school represented the "net use" as an objective element of use, separating itself from goods, Menger explains it as a Disposal; indeed, as "a disposal over quantities of economical goods within a definite period of time."[1] This disposal being for economic subjects a means to better and more complete satisfaction of their wants, it acquires, according to Menger, the character of an independent good, which, on account of its relative scarcity, will usually be at the same time an economical good.[2]

Now, to go no farther, it seems to be putting a very daring construction on things to say that the disposal over goods, that is, a relation to a good, is itself a good. I have on another occasion[3] stated at length the reasons for which I consider it

[1] *Grundsätze*, p. 132, etc. [2] *Ibid.* p. 132, etc.

[3] See my *Rechte und Verhältnisse*, particularly p. 124. See also the acute remarks of H. Dietzel in the tract *Der Ausgangspunkt der Sozialwirthschaftslehre und ihr Grundbegriff* (*Tübinger Zeitschrift für die gesammte Staatswissenschaft, Jahrgang*, 39), p. 78, etc. On the other hand, I cannot agree with Dietzel in some further criticisms that he makes on Menger on p. 52, etc. He has two objections to Menger's fundamental definition of economical goods as "those goods the available quantity of which is less than human need." First, he says, in trade generally we must recognise "the tendency to assimilate need and available quantity," on account of which "in every normal case" a

theoretically inadmissible to recognise relations as real Goods, in the sense given to that term by economic theory. These reasons, I believe, have the same validity as regards this "disposal" over goods.

To maintain its position in face of these weighty deductive objections Menger's hypothesis must have some very strong and positive support. I doubt if it has sufficient support of this kind. The special character of my present contention prevents us from the first from obtaining any direct evidence, such as might be given by the senses, that "disposal" really is a good. The only thing we have to consider is whether the hypothesis is accredited by a consensus of sufficiently numerous and significant *indirect* supports. And this I must doubt.

It appears to me that there is, distinctively, only one indirect support for it, and that is, the existence of a surplus value which is unexplained otherwise. As astronomers, from certain otherwise unexplained disturbances in the orbits of known planets, have concluded for the existence of disturbing and as yet unknown planetary bodies, so does Menger postulate

number of the most important economical objects must fall out of the circle of economical goods. And second, he says, Menger's definition of his conception is not definite enough, and leaves room for all sort of things that have not the character of economical goods, such, for instance, as useful "technical knowledge." I onsider that both objections are based on a misunderstanding. As a matter of fact trade can never quite assimilate the available quantity of economical goods to the need for them ; it can of course meet the demand that has power to pay, but never the need. However commerce may flood a market with exchangeable goods, while it will very soon succeed in supplying the amount that people can buy, it will never supply all they wish to possess for the purpose of supplying their wants to the saturation point—that point where the last and most insignificant wish is gratified. As to the second objection, Menger's definition seems to me to mark out the circle of economic goods both correctly and sufficiently. We must not overlook the fact that what determines the conception of the "good" has a share in determining the conception of the "economical good." Things like qualities, skill, rights, relations, cannot, I admit, be economical goods, even if they are only to be had in insufficient quantity, but that is because they are not true goods—that is to say, they are not really effectual means of satisfying human wants, and at best can only be called so by a metaphor. But where we have true goods, such of them as are insufficient in quantity are at the same time economical goods. If, therefore, Menger, in some individual cases, does come into collision with truth—as I maintain he does in regard to the economical good "disposal"—it is not because he has made a mistake in defining the attribute "economical," but only because he has occasionally treated the conception of the "good" a little too loosely.

the existence of a "bearer" of the surplus value which otherwise is unexplained. And since the disposal over quantities of goods for definite periods of time appears to him to stand in a regular connection with the emergence and the amount of surplus value, he does not hesitate to put forward the hypothesis that this disposal is the "bearer" sought for, and, as such, an independent good of independent nature. If the possibility of any other explanation had ever occurred to this distinguished thinker, I am persuaded that he would have withdrawn his hypothesis at once.

Now is this one indirect point of support sufficient to prove that "disposal" is an independent good?

There are two reasons for answering this in the negative. The one is that the phenomena of surplus value can be explained in an entirely satisfactory way without this hypothesis, and indeed can be explained on lines that Menger himself has laid down in his now classical theory of value; the proof of this I hope to give in my next volume. But the following consideration is of itself, in my opinion, quite convincing.

According to Menger's theory the loan is looked upon as a transference of disposal over goods. The longer then the period of the loan, the greater of course is the quantity of the transferred good, the disposal. In a loan for two years more disposal is transferred than in a loan for one year; in a three years' loan more disposal than in a two years' loan; in a hundred years' loan almost an unlimited amount of disposal is transferred. Finally, if the replacement of the capital is not only postponed for a very long time, but is altogether dispensed with, surely a quite infinite amount of disposal is transferred to the borrower. This, for instance, will be the case if goods are not lent, but given.

We now ask in such a case, How much value is received by the one to whom the gift is made? There can be no doubt that he receives as much value in capital as is possessed by the thing given. And the value of the permanent disposal that inheres in the thing, and is presented along with it?—Is evidently contained in the capital value of the thing itself. From which I draw the conclusion—and I do not think I am perpetrating any fallacy in so concluding—that if the plus, viz. the value of the permanently inhering disposal, is contained in the capital value of the good itself, the minus contained in it, the *temporary* disposal over a good, must be contained in the value of the good itself. The temporary disposal, therefore, cannot be, as Menger assumes, an independent bearer of value alongside the value of the good in itself.[1]

[1] If we put the illustration a little differently it may show more forcibly that the value of the disposal is contained in the value of the good. Suppose that A first lends B a thing for twenty years without interest—presents him therefore with the good called "disposal for twenty years," and then, a couple of days after the loan contract is concluded, presents him with the thing itself. Here he has in two actions given away the twenty years' disposal and the thing itself. If the "disposal" were a thing of independent value in addition to the thing itself, the total value of the gift would obviously be greater than the value of the thing itself, which just as obviously is not the case.

CHAPTER XI

FINAL INSUFFICIENCY OF THE USE THEORY

In Chapter III. I indicated that I proposed to maintain two theses. The first of these I think I may regard as proved, viz. that the use assumed by the Use theory as having an independent existence has really no existence at all. But even if it had, the actual phenomena of interest would not be sufficiently explained thereby. The proof of this second thesis will not require many words.

The Use theory, in virtue of its special line of explanation, is led to make a distinction between a value which goods have in themselves, and a value which the use of goods has. In this it starts with the tacit assumption that the usual estimated value, or selling value of real capital, represents the value of the goods themselves, exclusive of the value of their use; the explanation of surplus value being based on this very circumstance, that the value of the use joins itself, as a quite new element, to the value of the substance of capital, and that the two together make up the value of the product.

But this assumption contradicts the actual phenomena of the economical world.

It is well known that a bond only obtains a price equivalent to its full course value if it is provided with all the coupons belonging to it; in other words, if the disposal over all its future "uses"—to adopt the language of a Use theorist—is transferred to the buyer at the same time with the bond. But if one of the coupons is missing, the buyer will always make a corresponding reduction in the price that he pays for the bond. An analogous experience occurs with all other goods. If, in selling an estate that otherwise would have fetched £10,000, I retain the use of the estate for one or more years, or, if I sell another such estate which is burdened, perhaps in virtue of a legacy, with so many years' claim by a third party to its produce, there is no doubt that the price obtainable for the estate will fall below the amount of £10,000 by a sum that corresponds to the "uses" retained, or claimed by the third party.

These facts, which may be multiplied at will, in my opinion admit of being interpreted in only one way,—that the usual estimated value or selling value of goods embraces not only the value of the "goods in themselves," but also that of their future "uses," supposing there are any such.

But if this is so, then the "use" fails to explain the very thing which it was intended by the Use theory to explain. That theory would explain the fact that the value of a capital of £100 expands in its product to £105, by saying that a new and independent element of the value of £5 had been added to it. This explanation falls to the ground, as the Use theory must recognise, the moment it is seen that, in the capital value of £100, the future use itself has been considered and is contained. However unreservedly one may admit the existence of such uses, the riddle of surplus value is not read by them; the form of the question is only a little changed. It will now run: How comes it that the value of the elements of a product of capital, viz. *substance of capital and uses of capital*, which before were worth together £100, expands in the course of the production to £105? The fact is, that instead of one riddle we have now two. The first, that given by the nature of the phenomena of every interest theory, runs: Why does the value of the elements expand by the amount of the surplus value? To this the Use theory has added a second riddle of its own, In what way do the future "uses" of a good and the value of the "good in itself" together make up the present capital value of the good?—and no Use theorist has faced the difficulties of such a problem.

Thus the Use theory ends by putting more problems than it started with.

But if it has not had the good fortune to solve the interest problem, the Use theory has contributed more than any other to prepare the way towards it. While many other theories went wandering in ways that were quite unfruitful, the Use theory managed to gather together many an important piece of knowledge. I might compare it with some of the older theories of natural science; with that combustion theory of ancient times that worked with the mystical element Phlogiston; or with that older theory of heat that worked with a Warm Fluid. Phlogiston and warm fluid turned out to be fabulous essences, just as the "net use" turns out to be. But the symbol which in the meantime our theorists put in the place of the unknown something, helped in the same way as the x of our equations to discover a number of valuable relations and laws revolving about that unknown something. It did not point out the truth, but it helped to bring about its discovery.

BOOK IV

THE ABSTINENCE THEORY

CHAPTER I

SENIOR'S STATEMENT OF THE THEORY

N. W. SENIOR must be regarded as the founder of the Abstinence theory. It appeared first in his lectures delivered before the University of Oxford, and later in his *Outlines of the Science of Political Economy.*[1]

Rightly to estimate Senior's theory we must for a moment recall the position which the doctrine of interest held in England about the year 1830.

The chief writers of the modern school of political economy, Adam Smith and Ricardo—the former with less, the latter with greater distinctness—had pronounced labour to be the only source of value. Logically carried out, this could leave no room for the phenomenon of interest. All the same, interest existed as a fact, and exerted an undeniable influence on the relative exchange value of goods. Adam Smith and Ricardo took notice of this exception to the "labour principle," without seriously trying either to reconcile the disturbing exception with the theory, or to explain it by an independent principle. Thus with them interest forms an unexplained and contradictory exception to their rule.

This the succeeding generation of economical writers began to perceive, and they made the attempt to restore harmony between theory and practice. They did so in two different ways. One party sought to accommodate practice to theory. They held fast by the principle that labour alone creates value, and did their best to represent even interest as the result and wage of labour,—in which, naturally, they were not very

[1] Extracted from the *Encyclopaedia Metropolitana*, London, 1836. I quote from the fifth edition, London, 1863.

successful. The most important representatives of this party are James Mill and M'Culloch.[1]

The other party with more propriety tried to accommodate theory to fact. This they did in various ways. Lauderdale pronounced capital, as well as labour, to be productive, but his views found little acceptance among his countrymen. Ever since the time of Locke English economists were much too thoroughly acquainted with the idea that capital itself is the result of labour to be willing to recognise in it an independent productive power. Others again, with Malthus at their head, found a way of escape in explaining profit as a constituent part of the costs of production alongside of labour. Thus, formally at least, was the phenomenon of interest brought into harmony with the ruling theory of value. Costs, they said, regulate value. Interest is one of the costs. Consequently the value of products must be high enough to leave a profit to capital after labour has received its remuneration.

It must be admitted that this explanation left substantially everything to be desired. It was too evident that profit was a surplus over the costs, and not a constituent part of them; a result and not a sacrifice.

Thus neither of the economic positions which were then taken on the theory of interest was quite satisfactory. Each had some adherents, but more opponents; and these opponents found a welcome opening for attack in the sensible weaknesses of the doctrine. The opportunity was amply utilised. The one party was forced to see its assertion translated into the ridiculous statement that the increment of value which a cask of wine gets through lying in a cellar can be traced to labour. The other party was forced, by inexorable logic, to confess that a surplus is not an outlay. And while the two parties were thus at variance over the proper foundation of interest, a third party began to make itself heard, if only modestly at first,—a party which explained interest as having no economical foundation, as being merely an injury to the labourer.[2]

Amid this restless and barren surging of opinions came Senior, proclaiming a new principle of interest, viz. that interest is a reward for the capitalist's Abstinence.

[1] See above, p. 97, and below, book vii.

[2] Ever since Hodgskin's writings (1825). See below, book vi.

Isolated statements expressing the same idea had indeed appeared frequently before Senior's time. We may see it foreshadowed in the often recurring observation of Adam Smith and Ricardo that the capitalist must receive interest, because otherwise he would have no motive for the accumulation and preservation of capital; as also in the nice opposition of "future profit" to "present enjoyment" in another part of Adam Smith's writings.[1] More distinct agreement is shown by Nebenius in Germany and Scrope in England.

Nebenius found the explanation of the exchange value of the services of capital, among other things, in this, that capitals are only got through more or less painful privations or exertions, and that men can only be induced to undergo these by getting a corresponding advantage. But he does not discuss the idea any further, and shows himself in the main an adherent of a Use theory which shades into the Productivity theory.[2]

Scrope puts the same idea still more directly.[3] After having explained that, over and above the replacement of the capital consumed in production, there must remain to the capitalist some surplus, because it would not be worth his while to spend his capital productively if he were to gain nothing by it, he explicitly declares (p. 146): "The profit obtained by the owner of capital from its productive employment is to be viewed in the light of a compensation to him for abstaining for a time from the consumption of that portion of his property in personal gratification." In what follows it must be confessed that he treats the idea as if it was peculiarly "time" that was the object of the capitalist's sacrifice; argues in a lively way against M'Culloch and James Mill, who had declared "time" to be only a word, an empty sound, which could do nothing, and was nothing; and does not even hesitate to declare that time is a constituent part of the costs of production: "The cost of producing any article comprehends (1) the labour, capital, and time required to create and bring it to market" (p. 188),—a strange falling off, which scarcely need be seriously discussed.

Now this same idea, which his predecessors merely touched on, Senior has made the centre of a well-constructed theory of

[1] See above, p. 71.   [2] See above, p. 192.

[3] *Principles of Political Economy*, London, 1833.

interest: and whatever we may think of the correctness of its conclusions, we cannot deny it this credit that, among the confused theories of that time, it was remarkable for its systematic grasp, its consistent logic, and the thorough manner in which it puts its materials to the best advantage. An epitome of the doctrine will confirm this judgment.

Senior distinguishes between two "primary" instruments of production, labour and natural agents. But these cannot attain to complete efficiency if they are not supported by a third element. This third element Senior calls Abstinence, by which he means "the conduct of a person who either abstains from the unproductive use of what he can command, or designedly prefers the production of remote to that of immediate results" (p. 58).

His explanation why he does not take the usual course of pronouncing capital to be the third element in production is rather ingenious. Capital is, he says, not a simple original instrument; it is in most cases itself the result of the co-operation of labour, natural agents, and abstinence. Consequently, if we wish to give a name to the peculiar element—the element separate from the productive powers of labour and nature—which becomes active in capital, and stands in the same relation to profit as labour stands to wage, we cannot name anything but abstinence (p. 59).

Of the manner in which this element takes part in the accumulation of capital, and at the same time, indirectly, in the results of production, Senior repeatedly gives ample illustrations. I give one of the shortest in his own words:—

"In an improved state of society the commonest tool is the result of the labour of previous years, perhaps of previous centuries. A carpenter's tools are among the simplest that occur to us. But what a sacrifice of present enjoyment must have been undergone by the capitalist who first opened the mine of which the carpenter's nails and hammer are the product! How much labour directed to distant results must have been employed by those who formed the instruments with which the mine was worked! In fact, when we consider that all tools, except the rude instruments of savage life, are themselves the product of earlier tools, we may conclude that there is not a nail among the many millions annually fabricated in England which is not to a certain degree the product of some labour for the purpose of obtaining a distant result, or, in our nomenclature, of some abstinence undergone before the conquest, or perhaps before the Heptarchy" (p. 68).

Now the "sacrifice," which lies in the renunciation or postponement of enjoyment, demands indemnification. This indemnification consists in the profit of capital. But admitting this one must ask, In the economical world is the capitalist able to enforce what may be called his moral claim on indemnification? To this important question Senior gives the answer in his theory of price.

The exchange value of goods depends, according to Senior, partly on the usefulness of the goods, partly on the limitation of their supply. In the majority of goods (exception being made of those in which any natural monopoly comes into play) the limit of supply consists only in the difficulty of finding persons who are willing to submit to the costs necessary for making them. In so far as the costs of production determine the amount of supply they are the regulator of exchange value; and indeed chiefly in this way, that the costs of production of the buyer—that is, the sacrifice with which the buyer could himself produce or procure the goods—constitute the "maximum of price," and the cost of production of the seller the "minimum of price." But these two limits approximate each other in the case of that majority of goods which come under free competition. In their case therefore the costs of production simply make up a sum that determines the value.

But the costs of production consist of *the sum of the labour and abstinence* requisite for the production of goods. In this sentence we come to the theoretical connection between the doctrine of interest and that of price. If the sacrifice Abstinence is a constituent part of the costs of production, and these costs of production regulate value, the value of goods must always be great enough to leave a compensation for the abstinence. In this way the surplus value of products of capital, and with it natural interest on capital, is formally explained.

To this last exposition Senior adds a criticism of the interest theory of several of his predecessors which almost deserves to be called classical. He exposes among other things in a forcible way the blunder which Malthus had committed in putting profit among costs. But not content with criticising, he explains very beautifully how Malthus had fallen into the mistake. Malthus had rightly perceived that, beyond the sacrifice of labour, there is another sacrifice made in production. But since there was no term by which to designate it, he had called the sacrifice by the name of its compensation, in the same way as many people call wage of labour (which is the compensation for the sacrifice of labour) a constituent part of cost, instead of calling the labour itself by that name. Torrens, again, who had already blamed Malthus for his mistake, had himself committed a sin of omission. He had rightly eliminated "profit" from the costs of production, but was himself quite unable to fill the gap.

CHAPTER II

CRITICISM OF SENIOR

SINCE the first formulation which the Abstinence theory received from Senior is still the best, we shall be able to form a critical judgment on the whole subject most suitably by taking up Senior's theory. Before stating my own views, I think it advisable to mention certain other criticisms which have obtained a wide currency in our science, and in which, I believe, Senior's doctrine has been judged much too harshly. To begin with a late critique. Pierstorff, in his able *Lehre vom Unternehmergewinn*, expresses himself in terms of extreme disapprobation of Senior's theory. He goes so far as to declare that Senior's way of looking at things, in contrast to that of his predecessors, indicates a degeneration, a renunciation of earnest scientific research; and charges him with having "substituted for the economical basis of phenomena an economical and social theory cut to suit his purpose" (p. 47).

I must confess that I scarcely understand this expression of opinion, particularly as coming from a historian of theory who should know how to estimate excellence even when it is purely relative. Senior's theory of interest is infinitely superior to that of his predecessors in depth, systematic treatment, and scientific earnestness. The words "renunciation of earnest scientific research" into the interest problem might apply to the methods of such men as Ricardo or Malthus, M'Culloch or James Mill. These writers sometimes do not put the problem at all; sometimes solve it by an obvious *petitio principii;* sometimes solve it by peculiarly absurd methods. Even Lauderdale, whom Pierstorff unfortunately has not discussed, notwithstanding an earnest attempt at its solution, remains standing in the outer courts of the problem, and by a gross misunderstanding entirely fails to explain the interest phenomenon by his value theory. Unlike him, Senior, with deep insight, has recognised not only that there is a problem, but also the direction in which it is to be solved, and where the difficulties of the solution lie. Setting aside all sham solutions, he goes to the heart of the matter, to its foundation in the surplus value of products over expenditure of capital; and if he has not found the whole truth, it certainly is not for want of scientific earnestness. One would have thought that the pointed and well weighed critical observations which Senior so plentifully intersperses with his text should have protected him from so harsh a judgment.

Just as wide of the mark seem to me the well-known words in which Lassalle, twenty years ago, in his tumultuously eloquent but absurdly rhetorical way, jeered at Senior's doctrine: "The profit of capital is the 'wage of abstinence.' Happy, even priceless expression! The ascetic millionaires of Europe! Like Indian penitents or pillar saints they stand: on one leg, each on his column, with straining arm and pendulous body and pallid looks, holding a plate towards the people to collect the wages of their Abstinence. In their midst, towering up above all his fellows, as head penitent and ascetic, the Baron Rothschild! This is the condition of society! how could I ever so much misunderstand it!"[1]

This brilliant attack notwithstanding, I believe that there is a core of truth in Senior's doctrine. It cannot be denied that the making, as well as the preservation of every capital, does demand an abstinence from or postponement of the gratification of the moment; and it appears to me to admit of as little doubt that this postponement is considered in, and enhances the value of those products that, under capitalist production, cannot be obtained without more or less of such postponement. If, *e.g.* two commodities have required for their production exactly the same amount of labour, say 100 days, and that one commodity is ready for use immediately that the labour is finished, while the other—say new wine—must lie for a year; experience certainly shows that the commodity which becomes ready for use later will stand higher in price

[1] *Kapital und Arbeit*, Berlin, 1864, p. 110.

than that which is ready at once, by something like the amount of interest on the capital expended.

Now I have no doubt that the reason of this enhancement is nothing else than that there must be in this case a postponement of the gratification obtainable from the labour performed. For if the commodity immediately ready for use and that ready later on were to stand equally high in value, everybody would prefer to employ his 100 days in that labour which pays its wages immediately. This tendency is bound to call forth an increased supply of the goods immediately ready for use, and this again must bring down their price as compared with that of the goods ready later on. And as the wages of labour have a tendency to equalise themselves over all branches of production, in the end there is assured to the producers of these later goods a plus over the normal payment of labour; in other words, an interest on capital.

But it is just as certain—and on this ground Lassalle is for the most part right as against Senior—that the existence and the height of interest by no means invariably correspond with the existence and the height of a "sacrifice of abstinence." Interest, in exceptional cases, is received where there has been no individual sacrifice of abstinence. High interest is often got where the sacrifice of the abstinence is very trifling—as in the case of Lassalle's millionaire—and low interest is often got where the sacrifice entailed by the abstinence is very great. The hardly saved sovereign which the domestic servant puts in the savings bank bears, absolutely and relatively, less interest than the lightly spared thousands which the millionaire puts to fructify in debenture and mortgage funds. These phenomena fit badly into a theory which explains interest quite universally as a "wage of abstinence," and in the hands of a man who understood polemical rhetoric so well as Lassalle they only furnished so many pointed weapons of attack against that theory.

After much consideration I am inclined to think that the actual defects from which Senior's theory suffers may be reduced to three.

First, Senior has made too sweeping a generalisation on an idea quite right in itself, and has used it too much as a type.

There is no doubt in my mind that the element, postponement of gratification, which Senior puts in the foreground, does as a fact exert a certain influence on the origination of interest. But that influence is neither so simple, nor so direct, nor so exclusive as to permit of interest being explained as merely a "wage of abstinence." More exact proof of this is not possible here, and must be left for my second volume.

Second, Senior has expressed that part of his theory which is substantially correct in a fashion at all events open to attack. I consider it a logical blunder to represent the renunciation or postponement of gratification, or abstinence, as a second independent sacrifice in addition to the labour sacrificed in production.

Perhaps the best way of treating this somewhat difficult subject will be to put it in the form of a concrete example, and then try to grasp the principle.

Take the case of a man living in the country who is considering in what kind of labour he should employ his day. There are, perhaps, a hundred different courses open to him. To name only some of the simplest—he could fish, or shoot, or gather fruit. All three kinds of employment agree in this, that their result follows immediately,—even by the evening of the same work-day. Suppose that our country friend decides on fishing, and brings home at night three fish. What sacrifice has it cost him to obtain them?

If we leave out of account the trifling wear and tear of the fishing gear, it has cost him evidently one day's work, and nothing else. It is possible, however, that he looks at this sacrifice from another point of view. It is possible that he measures it by the gratification he might have got if he had spent his work-day otherwise, which gratification he must now do without. He may calculate thus: If I had spent to-day in shooting instead of fishing I might have shot three hares, and I must now do without the gratification obtainable from these.

I believe that this way of reckoning sacrifice is not incorrect. Here the man simply looks at work as a means to an end, and taking no notice of the mean—the primary sacrifice of work—fixes his attention on the end which was sacrificed through the mean. It is a method of calculation very common in economic life. Say that I have definitely set aside £30 for expenditure, but am hesitating between two modes of spending it. In the end I make up my mind to spend it on a pleasure trip instead of the purchase of a Persian carpet. Evidently the real sacrifice which the pleasure trip will cost me may be represented under the form of the Persian carpet which I have to do without.

In any case it appears to me obvious that, in reckoning the sacrifice made for any economic end, the direct sacrifice in means—that sacrifice which is first made—and the indirect sacrifice, which takes the shape of other kinds of advantage that *might* have been obtained in other circumstances by the means sacrificed, can be calculated only alternatively and never cumulatively. I may consider the sacrifice of my pleasure trip to be *either* the £30 which it has directly cost me, *or* the Persian carpet which it has indirectly cost me, but never as the £30 *and* the carpet. Just in the same way our rustic may consider, as the sacrifice which the catching of the three fish costs him, either the day's work directly expended, or the three hares indirectly sacrificed (or, say, the gratification he gets from eating them), but never the day's work *and* the gratification obtained through shooting the hares. So much I think is clear.

But besides these occupations, which recompense him for his day's work at the end of the day, there are others open to our labourer which produce a result that cannot be enjoyed till a later date. He might, *e.g.* sow wheat, getting the produce of it after a year's time; or he might plant fruit trees, from which he could have no return for ten years. Suppose he chooses the latter. If we again leave out of account the land and the trifling wear and tear of tools, what has he sacrificed to obtain the fruit trees?

To me there seems no doubt about the answer. He has sacrificed a day's work, and nothing more. Or, if the indirect way of computation be preferred, instead of the day's work he may calculate the other kinds of gratification that might have been got by spending the day in other ways—say the immediate enjoyment of three fish, or of three hares, or of a basket of fruit. But at all events it seems to me obvious in this case also, that, if the gratification which might have been got through the work is reckoned as sacrifice, then not the smallest portion of the work itself can be reckoned in the sacrifice; while, if the work is reckoned as sacrifice, there cannot be added to that in the calculation the smallest fragment of the other kinds of enjoyment that were renounced. To do otherwise would be to make a double reckoning, which would be just as false as if the man in our former illustration had reckoned the cost of the pleasure trip as the £30 actually paid, and besides as the Persian carpet which he might have bought with the £30.

It is a double calculation of this kind that Senior has made. He has not done so, I admit, in the gross way of calculating, in addition to the labour, the entire gratification he might have had from the labour; but in reckoning the postponement or abstinence from gratification independently of the labour he has gone farther than was allowable. For it is clear that in the sacrifice of labour is already included the sacrifice of the *whole* advantage that might have been got from employing the labour in other ways,—the whole advantage, containing all the partial or secondary shades of advantage that may depend on the principal advantage. The man who sacrifices £30 on a pleasure trip sacrifices, not *in addition to* but *in* the £30, both the Persian carpet that he might have bought with it and the satisfaction which he might have found in its possession; sacrifices too, among other things, the special advantage he might have had in the durability of this possession, and the length of time over which the gratification was spread. And just in the same way the labourer who sacrifices one day of work of the year 1889 in the planting of trees, makes a sacrifice, *in* and not *in addition to,* this day of work, not only of the three fish which he might have caught by the day's labour, but also of the peculiar enjoyment which he has, say, in a fish-dinner; as also of the advantage which springs from the fact that he might have had this gratification in the year 1889. The special reckoning of the postponement of gratification, therefore, contains a double calculation.

It is not perhaps too much to hope that most of my readers will agree with the foregoing arguments. Nevertheless I cannot consider the subject yet threshed out. There is no doubt that Senior's way of putting the matter has something very fascinating and persuasive about it, and if the case made use of in our illustration is put in a certain light favourable to

Senior's conception, the argument against me may appear absolutely convincing. This argument I have still to reckon with.

Put parallel cases as follows. If I employ to-day in catching fish, these fish cost me one day of labour. That is clear. But if I employ to-day in planting fruit trees, which will not bear fruit for ten years' time, then not only have I "taken it out" of myself (to use a significant colloquialism) for a whole day, but, over and above that, I have to wait for ten years for any result from my labour, although that waiting perhaps costs me much self-denial and mental pain. Therefore it would seem that in this latter act I make a sacrifice which is more than a day of labour; it is the exertion and toil of one day, and besides that, the burden of postponing the result of my work for ten years.

Plausible as this argument is, its basis is none the less fallacious. Let me first show, by following it out to some of its conclusions, that there is a fallacy, and then point out the source of the fallacy. Later on I shall have another opportunity of reviewing all that has been said and reducing it to principles.

Imagine the following case. I work for a whole day at the planting of fruit trees in the expectation that they will bear fruit for me in ten years. In the night following comes a storm and entirely destroys the whole plantation. How great is the sacrifice which I have made, as it happens, in vain? I think every one will say—a lost day of work, and nothing more. And now I put the question, Is my sacrifice in any way greater that the storm does not come, and that the trees, without any further exertion on my part, bear fruit in ten years? If I do a day's work and have to wait ten years to get a return from it, do I sacrifice more than if I do a day's work, and, by reason of the destructive storm, must wait to all eternity for its return? It is impossible to make such an assertion. And yet Senior would have it so; for while in the first case the sacrifice is stated to be a day's work and nothing more, in the second case it is a day's work plus a ten years' abstinence from its result! What a singular position too, according to Senior's view, must the progression of sacrifice attain as the time of use recedes! If labour immediately pays its own wages the sacrifice is only the labour expended. If it pays them in a year, the sacrifice is labour plus a year's abstinence. If it pays them in two years, the sacrifice is labour plus two years' abstinence. If it pays them twenty years afterwards, then the sacrifice grows to labour plus twenty years' abstinence. And if it never pays them at all? Must not, then, the sacrifice of abstinence reach its highest conceivable point, infinity, and form the climax of the upward progression? Oh no! Here the sacrifice of abstinence sinks to zero; the labour is the only thing counted as sacrifice, and the total sacrifice is not the greatest, but the least in the entire series!

I think that these conclusions plainly indicate that in all cases the only real sacrifice consists in the labour put forth, and that, if we thought ourselves compelled to acknowledge a second sacrifice besides that, viz. the postponement of gratification, we must have been misled by a specious presentation of the case.

But I must confess that the mistake is one we are very apt to fall into. What is it that misleads us?

The source of it is simply this, that the element of Time is not really indifferent; only it exerts its influence in a somewhat different way from that imagined by Senior and by people generally. Instead of affording material for a second and independent sacrifice, its importance rather lies in determining the amount of the one sacrifice actually made. To make this quite clear I must run the risk of being a little tedious.

The nature of all economic sacrifices that men make consists in some loss of wellbeing which they suffer; and the amount of sacrifice is measured by the amount of this loss. It may be of two kinds: of a positive kind, where we inflict on ourselves positive injury, pain, or trouble; or of a negative kind, where we do without a happiness or a satisfaction which we otherwise might have had. In the majority of economical sacrifices which we make to gain a definite useful end, the only question is about one of these kinds of loss, and here the calculation of the sacrifice undergone is very simple. If I lay out a sum of money, say £30, for any one useful end, my sacrifice is calculated simply by the gratification which I might have got by spending the £30 in other ways, and which I must now do without.

It is otherwise with the sacrifice of labour. Labour presents two sides to economical consideration. On the one hand it is, in the experience of most men, an effort connected with an amount of positive pain, and on the other, it is a mean to the attainment of many kinds of enjoyment. Therefore the man who expends labour for a definite useful end makes on the one hand the positive sacrifice of pain, and on the other, the negative sacrifice of the other kinds of enjoyment that might have been obtained as results of the same labour. The question now is, Which is the correct way, in this case, of calculating the sacrifice made for the concrete useful end?

The point we have to consider is, What would have been the position as regards our pleasure and pain if we had not expended the labour with a view to this particular end, but had disposed of it in some other reasonable way? The difference between the two evidently shows the loss of well-being which the attainment of our useful purpose costs us. If we make use of this method of estimating difference, we may very soon convince ourselves that the sacrifice made by labour is sometimes to be measured by the positive pain, sometimes by the negative loss of gratification, but never by both at once.

The question then comes to this, Whether, if we had put forth the day's labour otherwise, we could have got a satisfaction greater than the pain which the one day's labour causes us, or not? Suppose we feel the pain of a day's labour as an amount which may be indicated by the number 10. We actually employ the day in catching three fish, and these fish give us a gratification expressed by the number 15. And we ask what is the amount of sacrifice which the catching of the three fish costs us. What we shall have to decide is, whether, if we had not gone fishing, it would have been possible to us to get by a day's work another kind of satisfaction greater than the number 10. If no such possibility is open to us—say that shooting would only bring us a gratification represented by the number 8, while the labour-pain was, as before, 10—then evidently we should either fish or remain idle. What our three fish cost us in this case is the labour-pain indicated by the number 10, which pain we have undergone for the sake of the fish, and which pain we would otherwise not have undergone. There is no question here of any loss of other kinds of enjoyment, for the simple reason that we could not have got them. If, on the other hand, it is possible, by labouring for a day at other kinds of work, to get a gratification greater than the pain represented by the number 10—if we could, *e.g.* by a day's shooting obtain three hares of the value of 12, then it is quite reasonable to expect that we should not in any case remain idle, but possibly go shooting instead of fishing. What our fish really cost us now is not the positive labour-pain expressed by the number 10—for this we should have undergone at any rate—but the negative loss of an enjoyment which we might have had, indicated by the number 12. But of course we must never calculate the want of enjoyment and the pain of labour cumulatively; for if we had not preferred catching fish, we could not have spared ourselves the pain of labour and yet have had the gratification of shooting. And just as little, if we choose to fish, do we *by that choice* make a double sacrifice.

What has been said gives us the materials for a general rule which practical men are in the habit of applying with perfect confidence. It may be put in the following words.

If we apply labour to a useful end, the sacrifice made in doing so is always to be reckoned to the account of that one of the two kinds of loss of wellbeing which is the greater in amount; to labour-pain, if there is no kind of gratification in prospect which outweighs it; to gratification, where there is the possibility of such; but never in both at the same time.

And further, since in the economic life of to-day we have an infinite number of possibilities of turning our work to fruitful account, the first of these two cases almost never occurs. At the present time, then, we estimate by far the greater number of cases not by the pain of work, but by the profit or advantage we have renounced.

Here we have at last reached the point where we see the real influence of the element Time on the amount of the sacrifice. It is a fact—the grounds on which it rests do not concern us here—that in circumstances otherwise equal we prefer a present enjoyment to a future. Consequently, if we have to choose between applying a means of satisfaction, say labour, to the satisfaction of a present want, and applying it towards the satisfaction of a future want, the attraction of the immediate gratification will make it difficult to decide in favour of the future use. If, however, we do decide for the future use, in measuring the amount of sacrifice made for it by the greatness of the use foregone, the attraction of the moment which adheres to the use foregone will weigh down the scale, and make our sacrifice appear harder than it would otherwise have appeared. It is not that we make a second sacrifice in this. Whether we have to choose between two present or two future uses, or between a present and a future use, we always make the one sacrifice only, labour. But since, according to our analysis, we usually measure the amount of the sacrifice by the amount of the use foregone, the attraction of the earlier satisfaction is considered and has its influence on this valuation, and helps to make the calculation of the *one* sacrifice higher than it would otherwise have been. This is the true state of the facts to which Senior in his theory gave a faulty construction.[1]

The reader will, I trust, pardon me keeping him so long at this abstract discussion. From the point of theory, however, it contains the weightiest arguments against a doctrine that must be taken seriously,—a doctrine which up till now has often been rejected, but never, in my opinion, refuted. For myself, I hold it the lesser evil to be over-scrupulous in inquiry before passing sentence, than to pass sentence without full inquiry.

Lastly, the third fault of Senior's theory seems to me that he has made his interest theory part of a theory of value in which he explains the value of goods by their costs.

Now, even admitting the correctness of this theory, the "law of costs" avowedly holds only as regards one class of goods, those which can be reproduced in any quantity at will. In so

[1] Even in that minority of cases where the sacrifice of labour is measured in *pain* of labour, the time element of postponement of gratification cannot form a second and independent sacrifice. For the pain of labour only enters into the valuation, as we have seen, when the pain in question is greater than any kind of use which can be got out of the labour, inclusive of all the attractions of the moment that may happen to be in it; and when, consequently, the choice can only reasonably be thought of as lying between the concrete future uses, towards which the labour would actually be directed, and entire cessation from labour. Since there is here no question of any other kind of earlier enjoyment of goods, such an enjoyment cannot of course be, in any way, an element in the valuation of sacrifice.

far, then, as Senior makes his theory of interest an integral part of a value theory which is merely partial, it can only be, in the most favourable circumstances, a partial interest theory. It might explain those profits that are made in the production of goods reproducible at will, but logically every other kind of profit would escape it altogether.

Senior's Abstinence theory has obtained great popularity among those economists who are favourably disposed to interest. It seems to me, however, that this popularity has been due, not so much to its superiority as a theory, as that it came in the nick of time to support interest against the severe attacks that had been made on it. I draw this inference from the peculiar circumstance that the vast majority of its later advocates do not profess it exclusively, but only add elements of the Abstinence theory in an eclectic way to other theories favourable to interest. This is a line of conduct which points, on the one hand, to a certain undervaluing of the strength of its position as a theory; its advocates do not hesitate to discredit it rather rudely by piling up along with it a great many heterogeneous and contradictory explanations. And, on the other hand, it points to a preference for that practical and political standpoint which is satisfied if only a sufficient number of reasons are brought forward to prove the legitimacy of interest, although it should be at the expense both of unity and logic.

Thus we shall meet the majority of the followers of Senior among the eclectics. I may name, provisionally, among English economists, John Stuart Mill and the acute Jevons; among French writers, Rossi, Molinari, and Josef Garnier; among Germans, particularly Roscher and his numerous following; then Schüz and Max Wirth.

Among those writers who hold by the Abstinence theory pure and simple, I merely name the most prominent. Cairnes places himself essentially at Senior's standpoint in his spirited treatment of the costs of production.[1] The Swiss economist Cherbuliez[2] explains interest to be a remuneration for the "efforts of abstinence," and so stands on the boundary line

[1] *Some Leading Principles of Political Economy*, 1874, chap. iii.

[2] *Précis de la Science Economique*, Paris, 1862; particularly vol. i. pp. 161, 402, etc.

between the Abstinence theory and a peculiar variety of those Labour theories which we have to discuss in the next book. In Italian literature Wollemborg has lately followed the lead of Senior and Cairnes in acute inquiry into the nature of costs of production.[1] Among the Germans is Karl Dietzel, who, however, touches on the problem only occasionally and cursorily.[2]

None of these writers have added any essentially new feature to Senior's Abstinence theory, and it is not necessary to go minutely into what they have said on the subject. But I must make more careful mention of a writer whose theory made a great stir in its day, and maintains an important influence even yet; I mean Frédéric Bastiat.

[1] *Intorno al Costo Relativo di Produzione*, etc., Bologna, 1882.

[2] *System der Staatsanleihen*, Heidelberg, 1855, p. 48: "The lender of capital bases his claim on compensation for the using of the capital transferred by him, first, on the fact that he has given up the chance of giving value to his own labour power by embodying it in the object; and second, that he has refrained from consuming it, or its value, at once, in immediate enjoyment. This is the ground on which interest on capital rests; the subject, however, has no further concern for us in this place."

CHAPTER III

BASTIAT'S STATEMENT

BASTIAT'S much discussed theory of interest may be characterised as a copy of Senior's Abstinence theory forced into the forms of Bastiat's Value theory, and thereby much deteriorated. The fundamental thought in each is identical. The postponement of gratification, which Senior calls Abstinence, and Bastiat calls sometimes Delay, sometimes Privation, is a sacrifice demanding compensation. But beyond this they diverge from each other in some respects.

Senior, who deduces the value of goods from their cost of production, simply says that this sacrifice is a constituent element of the costs, and is done with it. Bastiat, who bases the value of goods on "exchanged services," elevates the postponement also to the rank of a service. "Postponement in itself is a special service, since on him who postpones it imposes a sacrifice, and on him who desires it confers an advantage."[1] This service, according to the great law of society, which runs "service for service," must be specially paid. The payment takes place where the capitalist has borrowed his capital from another person by means of loan interest (*intérêt*).

But even outside of loan interest this service must be compensated; for, speaking generally, every one who receives a satisfaction must also bear the collective burdens which its production requires, including the postponement. This postponement is looked upon as an "onerous circumstance," and

[1] *Harmonies Economiques* (vol. vi. of complete works), third edition, Paris, 1855, p. 210. See also the pages immediately preceding, 207-209, and generally the whole of Chapter VII.

forms therefore, quite universally, an element in the valuation of the service, and at the same time in the formation of the value of goods. This is, in a few words, the substance of what Bastiat says with rhetorical diffuseness and copious repetitions.

I called this doctrine a deteriorated copy of Senior's. If we put on one side all those defects that belong to Bastiat's interest theory not as such, but only in virtue of its being embodied in his value theory—which to my mind is exceedingly faulty—the deterioration shows itself chiefly in two respects.

The first is that Bastiat confines his attention and his arguments almost entirely to a secondary point, the explanation of contract interest, and for that neglects the principal thing, the explanation of natural interest. Both in his *Harmonies Economiques* and in the monograph which he specially devoted to the interest problem, *Capital et Rente*, he is never tired of discoursing by the page on the interpretation and justification of loan interest.

But he applies his theory to the explanation of natural interest only once, and then only in passing, in the passages already quoted (*Harmonies*, third edition, p. 213); and these leave a great deal to be desired in point of clearness and thoroughness.

The results of this negligence make themselves felt principally in this, that the chief thing in the exposition of interest, the sacrifice of postponement, is not nearly so clearly put by Bastiat as by Senior; for when Bastiat opposes the owner of capital to the borrower of capital, the sacrifice which he speaks of as made by the owner is generally that of doing without the productive use that meantime might have been made of the capital lent.[1] This has quite a good signification

[1] "Si l'on penètre le fond des choses, on trouve qu'en ce cas le cédant se prive en faveur du cessionaire ou d'une satisfaction immédiate qu'il récule de plusieurs années, ou d'un instrument de travail qui aurait augmenté ses forces, fait concourir les agents naturels, et augmenté, a son profit, le rapport des satisfactions aux efforts" (vii. p. 209). "Il ajourne la possibilité d'une production. . . . Je l'emploierai pendant dix ans sous une forme productive" (xv. p. 445). So often in the tract *Capital et Rente*, *e.g.* p. 44. James, who has made a plane, and has now lent it to William for a year, makes this the ground for his claim of interest: "I expected some advantage from it, more work done and better paid, an improvement in my lot. I cannot lend you all that for nothing."

if it means nothing more than what Salmasius had once tried to prove against the canonists, that, if by employing capital a man can make a natural profit, there is both reason and justification for claiming an interest on the capital when loaned. But to point to that sacrifice is evidently quite inappropriate as an explanation of natural interest, and the phenomenon of interest in general is not satisfactorily explained thereby, the existence of natural interest being already assumed in it as a given fact.

For the deeper explanation of interest it is evident that that other sacrifice on which Senior dwells is the only one that has any importance,—the sacrifice that consists in postponing the satisfaction of needs. Now Bastiat of course speaks of this sacrifice also, but by confusing it with the former sacrifice he gets his doctrine into a tangle; indeed it seems to me that he not only confuses his readers, but himself. At least there are to be found in his writings, especially in his *Capital et Rente*, not a few passages in which he starts with his Abstinence theory, but comes suspiciously near the standpoint of the Naïve Productivity theorists. The course of explanation suggested, in the often quoted passage in the *Harmonies*, was to show how under capitalist production the surplus value of the product arises from the necessity of buyers of the product paying for the "onerous circumstance" of the postponement of gratification, as well as for the labour embodied in the product. Instead of following out this line of explanation, he not unfrequently looks upon it as self-evident that capital, in virtue of the productive power that resides in it, must give its owner an "advantage," a "gain," an enhanced price, and a bettering of his lot; in a word, a profit.[1] But that, as we know already, is not to explain interest, but to assume it.

[1] Thus Bastiat in *Capital et Rente*, p. 40, assumes that the borrowed sack of corn puts the borrower in a position to produce a *valeur supérieure*. On p. 43 he calls the reader's attention, in italics, to the fact that the "principle that is to solve the interest problem" is the power that resides in the tool to increase the productivity of labour. Again he says, on p. 46, "Nous pouvons conclure qu'il est dans la nature du capital de produire un intérêt." On p. 54, "L'outil met l'emprunteur à même de faire des profits." Indeed it is the aim of the brochure, as we gather from the introduction to it, to defend the "productivity of capital" against the attacks of the socialists.

As a fact, Bastiat has often been accused of having entirely missed the chief point, the explanation of natural interest; the accusation is not, I think, quite justified, but, as we can see, it is very easily explained.[1]

This is the first point in which Bastiat's theory does not improve on Senior's. The second consists in a wonderful addition he makes. Besides the explanation of interest just stated, he gives another—of so different a nature, and at the same time so evidently mistaken, that I cannot even make a guess as to how Bastiat saw any relation between it and his principal explanation.

Every branch of production, he explains, is an aggregate of efforts. But between various efforts an important distinction is to be drawn. One category of efforts is connected with services which we are presently engaged in rendering. A second category of efforts, on the other hand, is connected with an indefinite series of services. To the first category, for instance, belong the daily efforts of the water-carrier, which are directed immediately to the fetching of water; or, in the sphere of agriculture, the labours of sowing, weeding, ploughing, harrowing, reaping, threshing, which are collectively directed to obtain a single harvest. To the second category belongs the labour which the water-carrier expends in making his barrow and water cask; which the farmer expends on his hedging, harrowing, draining, building, improvements generally: all those labours which, as the economists say, go to the formation of a fixed capital, and result in benefit to a whole series of consumers, or a whole series of harvests.[2]

Bastiat now raises the question, How, according to the great law of "service for service," are these two categories of efforts to be estimated or rewarded? As regards the first category, he finds this very simple. These services must be compensated, on the whole, by those who profit by them. But that does not apply in the case of the second category, those services which lead to the formation of a fixed capital; for the number of those who profit by this capital is indefinite. If the producer were to get paid by the first consumers it would not be just; for, in the first place, it is unreasonable that the

[1] See, *e.g.* Rodbertus, *Zur Beleuchtung*, i. p. 116, etc.; Pierstorff, p. 202.
[2] P. 214.

first consumers should pay for the last; and in the second place, there must come a point of time when the producer would have at once the stock of capital not yet consumed, and also his compensation, which again involves an injustice.[1] Consequently, Bastiat concludes with a mighty logical *salto mortale*, the distribution among the indefinite series of consumers is only managed thus: the capital itself is not distributed, but the consumers are burdened with the interest of the capital instead—a way of getting out of it which Bastiat explains to be the only conceivable one for the solution of the problem in question,[2] and one which, offered spontaneously by the "ingenious natural mechanism of society," saves us the trouble of substituting an artificial mechanism in its place.[3] Thus Bastiat explains interest as the form in which an advance of capital is redistributed over a sum of products: "C'est là, c'est dans la répartition d'une avance sur la totalité des produits, qu'est le principe et la raison d'être de l'Intérêt" (vii. p. 205).

It must have occurred to every one while reading these lines that, in this analysis, Bastiat has fallen into some errors almost inconceivably gross. It is, first, an error to say that it is not possible to distribute the capital itself over the purchasers. Every business man knows that it is possible; and knows too that it is done, and how it is done. He simply calculates the probable duration of the capital laid out, and, on the basis of this calculation, charges every single period during which the capital is employed, and every single product, with a corresponding quota for wear and tear and replacement of the capital sum. When the purchasers pay the quota for replacement of the fixed capital in the price of the finished commodities, "the capital itself" is of course distributed over them. Perhaps not with absolute "justice," because there may be an error in the calculated duration of the capital, and in the calculated quota for wear and tear which is based on that; but, on the average, the prices successively

[1] P. 216.

[2] ". . . et je défie qu'on puisse imaginer une telle répartition en dehors du mécanisme de l'intérêt" (p. 217).

[3] "Réconnaissons donc que le mécanisme social naturel est assez ingénieuz pour que nous puissions nous dispenser de lui substituer un mécanisme artificiel" (p. 216, at end).

paid will, in any case, cover the capital sum that is to be replaced.

And it is a second gross error to assume that the producers receive interest instead of receiving back the capital itself, which, he says, cannot be distributed. The fact is, as every one knows (1), that, in the quota for replacement, they receive back the capital itself, and (2) so long as a part of this capital lasts they receive interest besides. Interest, therefore, rests on an entirely distinct foundation from the replacement of capital. It is really difficult to understand how Bastiat could make a mistake in such simple and well-known matters.

In conclusion, I may note in passing that Bastiat has borrowed his practical law of interest from Carey: the law that with the increase of capital the absolute share obtained by the capitalist in the total product increases, and the relative share diminishes.[1] In his attempts to prove this law—which from the point of view of theory are quite worthless—like Carey he carelessly confuses the conception of "percentage of total product" with the conception of "percentage on capital" (rate of interest).

On the whole, Bastiat's interest theory seems to me to be quite unworthy of the reputation which it has, at least in certain circles, so long enjoyed.

[1] P. 223.

BOOK V

THE LABOUR THEORIES

CHAPTER I

THE ENGLISH GROUP

UNDER the title of the Labour theories I group together a number of theories which agree in explaining interest as a wage for labour rendered by the capitalist.

As to the nature of the "labour" which furnishes the basis for the capitalist's claim of wage there is very material divergence among the various views. Thus I am compelled to distinguish three independent groups of Labour theories, and as it happens that their respective circles of adherents are marked out very much by nationality, I shall call them the English, the French, and the German group.

The English writers, chiefly represented by James Mill and M'Culloch, explain interest by tracing it to that labour through which real capital itself comes into existence.

James Mill[1] chances on the interest problem in his doctrine of price. He has put down the proposition that the costs of production regulate the exchange value of goods (p. 93). At the first glance capital and labour are seen to be constituents of the cost of production. But on looking closer Mill sees that capital itself comes into existence through labour, and that all costs of production may be traced therefore to labour alone. Labour then is the sole regulator of the value of goods (p. 97).

With this proposition, however, the well-known fact, discussed already by Ricardo, that postponement also has an influence on the price of goods, does not appear to agree. If, for instance, in one and the same season a cask of wine and

[1] *Elements of Political Economy*, third edition, London, 1826. I was not able, unfortunately, to get sight of the first edition of 1821.

twenty sacks of meal have been produced by the same amount of labour, they will of course, at the end of the season, have an equal exchange value. But if the owner of the wine lays it in a cellar and keeps it for a couple of years, the cask of wine will have more value than the twenty sacks of meal—indeed, more value by the amount of two years' profit.

Now, James Mill gets rid of this disturbance of his law by explaining profit itself as a wage of labour; as a remuneration for indirect labour. "It is no solution to say that profits must be paid, because this only brings us to the question, Why must profits be paid? To this there is no answer but one, that they are the remuneration for labour, labour not applied immediately to the commodity in question, but applied to it through the medium of other commodities, the produce of labour."

This idea is more exactly elucidated by the following analysis. "A man has a machine, the produce of a hundred days' labour. In applying it the owner undoubtedly applies labour, though in a secondary sense, by applying that which could not have been had but through the medium of labour. This machine, let us suppose, is calculated to last exactly ten years. One-tenth of the fruit of a hundred days' labour is thus expended every year, which is the same thing in the view of cost and value as saying that ten days' labour has been expended. The owner is to be paid for the hundred days' labour which the machine costs him at the rate of so much per annum, that is, by an annuity for ten years equivalent to the original value of the machine.[1] It thus appears (!) that profits are simply remuneration for labour. They may, indeed, without doing any violence to language (!), hardly even by a metaphor, be denominated wages; the wages of that labour which is applied, not immediately by the hand, but mediately, by the instruments which the hand has produced. And if you may measure the amount of immediate labour by the amount of wages, you may measure the amount of secondary labour by that of the return to the capitalist."

In this way James Mill thinks that he has satisfactorily

[1] The author (as is evident from a parallel passage on p. 100) means annuities which replace the original value of the machine in ten years, and at the same time pay interest at the rate fixed by the condition of the market.

explained interest, and at the same time maintained in its integrity his law that labour alone determines the value of goods. It is pretty obvious, however, that he has not succeeded in doing either.

It may be allowed to pass that he calls capital "hoarded" labour; that he calls the employment of capital employment of a mediate secondary labour; and that he considers the wearing out of the machine as a giving out of the hoarded labour by instalments. But why then is every instalment of hoarded labour paid by an annuity which contains more than the original value of that labour, namely, the original value plus the usual rate of interest thereon? Allowing that the remuneration of capital is the remuneration of mediate labour, why is the mediate labour paid at a higher rate than the immediate; why does the latter receive the bare rate of wages while the former receives an annuity higher by the amount of the interest? Mill does not solve this question. He takes the fact that a capital, according to the state of competition in the market, has equal value with a certain number of annual payments that *already include the interest*, and uses this fact as a fixed centre, as if he had not taken upon himself to explain the profit, and therefore also the extra profit, that is contained in the annuity.

He says, I admit, in an explanatory tone, Profit is wage of labour. But he has a very false idea of the explanatory power of this phrase. It might perhaps be satisfactory if Mill could show that there is here a labour which has not yet received its normal wage, and will only receive it in the profit; but it is in no way satisfactory to explain profit as an extra wage for a labour that has already been paid at the normal rate by means of the sum for amortisation contained in the annuities. It is always open to ask, Why should mediate labour be more highly paid than immediate labour? And this is a question towards the solution of which Mill has given not the slightest hint. Moreover by this artificial construction he even loses the advantage of remaining consistent with his Labour theory; for evidently the law that the amount of labour determines the price of all goods is rudely upset if a part of the price is traceable, not to the *amount* of the labour expended, but to the greater *height* of the *wage* that it receives! In this respect, therefore, Mill's theory comes considerably short of its professed object.

A very similar theory was put forward by M'Culloch, in the first edition of his *Principles of Political Economy* (1825), but omitted in later editions. I have stated it already on an earlier occasion, and need add nothing more to that statement.[1] Finally, the same idea was given out cursorily by Read in England and Gerstner in Germany, but these writers we shall have to consider later on among the eclectics.

THE FRENCH GROUP

A second group of Labour theorists pronounce interest to be the wage of that labour which consists in the saving of capital (*Travail d'Epargne*). This theory is carried out most thoroughly by Courcelle-Seneuil.[2]

According to Courcelle-Seneuil, there are two kinds of labour—muscular labour and the labour of Saving (p. 85). The latter conception he expounds as follows. In order that a capital once made should be conserved, there is need of a continual effort of foresight and saving, in so far as, on the one hand, one looks to future needs, and, on the other hand, refrains from present enjoyment of capital with the view of being able to satisfy future needs by means of the capital thus saved. In this "labour" lies an act of intelligence—the foresight, and an act of will—the saving that "refrains from enjoyment for a given period of time."

Of course, at the first glance, it appears singular to give to saving the name of Labour. But this impression, in the author's opinion, only arises from our usually looking too much at the material side of things. If we reflect dispassionately for a moment we will recognise that it is just as painful to a man to refrain from the consumption of an article when made, as to labour with his muscles and his intellect to obtain an article that he wishes; and that it really requires a special un-natural exertion of intellect and will to maintain capital in

[1] See above, p. 97. The doubtful honour of priority in this theory belongs to James Mill.

[2] *Traité théorique et pratique d'Economic Politique*, i. Paris, 1858.

existence—an act of will which is contrary to the natural bias toward pleasure and idleness.

After attempting to strengthen this line of argument by pointing to the habits of savages, the author concludes with this formal deliverance: "We consider then that saving is really, and not simply metaphorically, a form of industrial labour, and consequently a productive power. It demands an exertion which, it is true, is purely of a moral kind, but it is all the same painful. It has therefore as much right to the character of labour as an exertion of the muscles has."

Now the labour of saving demands remuneration in the same way as muscular labour. While the latter is paid by the *salaire*, the former obtains its payment in the shape of interest. The following passage explains the necessity of this, and shows in particular why the wage of the labour of saving must be a permanent one: "The desire, the temptation to consume, is a permanent force; its action can only be suspended by combating it with another force which, like itself, is permanent. It is clear that every one would consume as much as possible if he had no interest (*si'l n'avait pas intérêt*) to abstain from consuming. He would cease to abstain from the moment that he ceased to have this interest, so that it must continue without interruption, in order that capitals may always be conserved. That is why we say that interest" (*l'intérêt:* note the play upon words) "is the remuneration of this labour of saving and of conservation; without it capitals, whatever be their form, could not continue; it is a necessary condition of industrial life" (p. 322).

The height of this wage is regulated "according to the great law of supply and demand"; it depends, on the one side, on the wish and the ability to expend a sum of capital reproductively; and on the other, on the wish and the ability to save this sum.

To my mind all the pains which its author has taken to represent the Labour of Saving as a real labour cannot efface the stamp of artificiality which this theory bears on its very face. The non-consuming of wealth a labour; the pocketing of interest by those who toil not nor spin, a suitable wage for work;—what a chance for any Lassalle who cares to play upon the impressions and emotions of the reader! But, instead of stating rhetorically that Courcelle is wrong, I prefer to show on rational grounds why he is wrong.

First of all, it is clear that Courcelle's theory is only Senior's Abstinence theory clad in a slightly different dress. As a rule, where Senior says "abstinence," or "sacrifice of abstinence," Courcelle says "labour of abstinence," but really both writers make use of the one fundamental idea in the same way. Thus at the outset Courcelle's Labour theory is open to a great many of those objections raised to Senior's Abstinence theory, on the ground of which objections we have already pronounced that theory to be unsatisfactory.

But further, the new form which Courcelle gives it is open to special objections of its own.

It is quite correct to say that foresight and saving do cost a certain moral pain. But the *presence* of labour in anything by which an income is obtained is far from justifying us in explaining that income as a *wage* of labour. To do so we must be able to show that the income is really obtained for the labour, and only in virtue of the labour. Now this will be best shown if we find that the income emerges where labour has been expended; that it is wanting where there has been no labour; that it is high where much of the labour has been expended, and low where little has been expended. But of any such harmony between the alleged cause of interest and the actual emergence of interest, it would be difficult to discover a trace. The man who carelessly cuts the coupons of £100,000, or gets his secretary to cut them, draws a "wage of labour" of £4000 or £5000. The man who, with actual pain of foresight and saving, has scraped together £50, and put them in the savings bank, scarcely gets a couple of pounds for his "labour"; while the man who, with as much pain, has saved £50, but cannot risk them out of his hand because of some claim that may be made on him at any moment, gets absolutely no wage at all.

What is the reason of this? Why are wages apportioned so differently—differently as between individual classes of saving labourers; differently as compared with the wage payment of muscular labour? What is the reason that the owner of £100,000 gets £5000 for his "year's labour"; that the manual labourer, who suffers pain and saves nothing, gets

£50; that the artisan, who suffers pain and saves £50 thereby, gets the sum of £52 for "muscular labour" and "labour of saving" together? A theory which pronounces interest to be wages of labour must undertake to make its explanation more exact. Instead of this, the nice question of the rate of interest is simply dismissed by Courcelle with a general reference to the great law of supply and demand.

Without meaning to be ironical, one might say that Courcelle would have had almost as much justification, theoretically speaking, if he had pronounced the bodily labour of pocketing the interest, or of cutting the coupons, to be the ground and basis of interest. These also are "labours" which the capitalist performs, and if it should be thought strange that, according to the law of supply and demand, this sort of labour is paid at such an unusually high rate, it is scarcely more strange than the fact we have just been considering—that the intellectual labour of inheriting a million of money is annually paid by so many thousands of pounds. One might say of this latter kind of labour, So few people have the "wish and the ability" to lay up millions of capital, that, in the existing demand for capital, the wages of such people must be very high; and similarly it might be said of the former, So very few people have the "wish and the ability" to pocket thousands of pounds in interest. Of "wish" there will be no lack in either case; but of ability—well, that rests in both cases principally on the fact of a person being so fortunate as to possess a million of capital!

If after what has been said a direct refutation of Courcelle's Labour theory still seems necessary, let me put the following case. A capitalist lends a manufacturer £100,000 at 5 per cent for a year. The manufacturer employs the £100,000 productively, and by doing so receives a profit of £6000. From this he deducts £5000 as interest due to the capitalist, and keeps £1000 as undertaker's profit to himself. According to Courcelle the £5000 which the capitalist receives are the wage for providing for future wants, and for the act of will which resists the temptation to consume the £100,000 immediately—an act of will directed to the refraining from enjoyment. But has not the manufacturer performed exactly the same, or even a greater labour? Was the manufacturer, when he had the £100,000 in his hands, not tempted to consume it immediately? Could he not, for instance, have squandered the capital, and gone through the bankruptcy court? Has he then not also withstood the temptation and asserted his will in refraining? Has he not by prudence and foresight done more than the capitalist to provide for future needs, in as much as he not only thought of future needs in general, but gave his stock of materials that positive treatment which changed them into products, and thus actually fitted them to satisfy human wants? And yet the capitalist for the labour of conserving his £100,000 receives £5000, and the manufacturer, who has performed the same intellectual and moral labour on the same £100,000 in still greater degree, gets nothing; for the £1000 which constitute his undertaker's profit are payment for quite another kind of activity.

It may be objected that the manufacturer would not have dared to use the £100,000, seeing that it was not his property; in his saving, therefore, there is no merit to deserve payment. But in this theory merit has nothing to do with the case. The wage of saving is great if only the sum saved and conserved be great, without the slightest consideration whether the conservation has demanded much moral striving or little. But that the debtor has actually conserved the £100,000, and has overcome the temptation to consume it, admits of no denial. Why then does he get no "wage of saving"? To my mind there can be no doubt about the explanation of these facts. It is that people get interest, not because they work for it, but simply because they are *owners*. Interest is not an income from labour, but an income from ownership.

Quite recently Courcelle-Seneuil's theory has been, somewhat timidly, followed by Cauwes.[1]

This writer states it, but not as his sole interest theory, and not without certain clauses and turns of expression which show that he finds this conception of the "labour of saving" not quite beyond question. "Since the conservation of a capital presupposes an exertion of the will, and in many

[1] *Précis du Cours d'Economic Politique*, second edition, Paris, 1881, 1882.

cases even industrial or financial combinations of some difficulty, one might say that it represents a veritable labour such as has sometimes, and not without justification, been called *Travail d'Epargne*" (i. p. 183). And in another place Cauwes meets the doubt whether interest be due to the capitalist, since the loan costs no labour to justify the claim of interest, in the words: "In the loan, it may be, there is no labour; but the labour consists in the steadfast will to preserve the capital, and in the protracted abstinence from every act of gratification or consumption of the value represented by it. It is, if the expression does not seem too bizarre, a labour of saving that is paid by interest."[1] But besides this Cauwes brings forward other grounds for interest, particularly a statement of the productivity of capital, and thus we shall meet him again among the eclectics.

A slight approach to Courcelle's Labour theory is to be found in a few other French writers; as in Cherbuliez,[2] who pronounces interest to be wage for the "efforts of abstinence"; and in Josef Garnier, who gives a very parti-coloured explanation, in the course of which he uses the catchword "labour of saving."[3] But these last named do not carry the conception any farther.

THE GERMAN GROUP

The idea that in France afforded material for a very artificial and elaborate theory of interest has been made use of—of course on freer lines—by a prominent school of German economists, the Katheder Socialists, to use a term which has been acclimatised.[4] The Labour theory of the German Katheder Socialists is, however, only loosely connected with the French theory in having the same fundamental idea. Both in origin and in manner of development it is entirely independent.

The origin of the German Labour theory may be found in a somewhat incidental remark that occurs in one of the

[1] ii. p. 189; also i. p. 236.

[2] See above, p. 286.

[3] *Traité d'Economie Politique*, eighth edition, Paris, 1880. P. 522: "Le loyer rémunère et provoque les efforts ou le travail d'épargne et de conservation."

[4] The name they themselves use is the "Social Political-School of National Economy."

writings of Rodbertus-Jagetzow. There he speaks of a conceivable state of society where there should be private property, but no *rent-bearing* private property; in which, therefore, all existing income would be income from labour in the shape of salary or wages. Such would be the state of things if the means of production, land and capital, were the common property of the whole society, private rights of property being still recognised over the income which each one would receive—in goods only—in proportion to his labour.

On this Rodbertus remarks in a note that, in economical respects, property in the means of production must be looked upon in an essentially different light from property in an income that accrues only in the shape of goods. As regards income-goods, all that is required is that the owner consume them economically. But property in land and capital is, besides, a kind of office that carries national economic functions with it,—functions which consist in directing the economical labour and the economical means of the nation in consonance with the national need, and therefore in exerting those functions which, in the ideal state of collective ownership, would be exerted through national officers. The most favourable view then that one can take of rent from this standpoint—land-rent and capital rent alike—is that it represents the salaries of such officers; that it represents a form of salary where the officer is strongly, even pecuniarily interested in the proper use of his functions.[1]

Everything points to the belief that Rodbertus in no way intended in these words to put forward a formal theory of interest.[2] But the idea latent in them was seized on and developed by some of the prominent Katheder Socialists.

It was first taken up by Schäffle. As early as the third edition of his older work, the *Gesellschaftliche System*, 1873, he embodied the idea, that interest is a remuneration for services

[1] *Zur Erklarung und Abhülfe der heutigen Kreditnoth des Grundbesitzes*, second edition, 1876, ii. p. 273, etc.

[2] This follows from the tone of the passage, which suggests a simile and a comparison rather than a strict explanation; from its position in a note; from the fact of Rodbertus having another and a different theory; finally, from an explicit explanation which he makes in stating this other theory, that interest in the present day has not the character of (indirect) salary, but that of an immediate share in the national product (*Zur Beleuchtung*, p. 75).

rendered by the capitalist, in his formal definition of interest. "Profit," he says, "is to be looked upon as the remuneration that the undertaker may claim for a national economic function inasmuch as, independently of any national organisation, he binds together the productive powers economically by means of the speculative use of capital."[1] This conception turns up repeatedly in different connections in the same book, and as a rule it occurs in those passages where interest is looked at from a broader point of view. Schäffle even defends it in one place as the only warrantable theory, and rejects in its favour the other interest theories in a body.[2] But, singularly enough, when he deals with the nicer details of the doctrine, the height of the interest rate and so on, he does not avail himself of this fundamental idea, but makes use of the technical machinery of the Use theory; although it must be admitted that he brings the Use theory very near to the Labour theory by the subjective colouring he gives to the conception of Use.[3]

In his later work, the *Bau und Leben*, the conception of interest as the compensation for a "functional performance" on the part of the capitalist comes out more distinctly. This conception makes it possible for Schäffle to justify interest at least in the present day, and in so far as we are not able to replace the costly services of private capital by a more suitable organisation.[4] But even here the details of the phenomena of interest are not explained by means of this conception, and we still find reminiscences of the Use theory, although the conception of Use has now become objective.[5] Thus Schäffle, as it were, struck the key-note, but only the key-note, of a Labour theory; he has not carried it out in detail like Courcelle-Seneuil.

[1] ii. p. 458. [2] ii. p. 459, etc. [3] See above, p. 206.

[4] "Thus I cannot, in any case, agree with the absolute condemnation of capital and of profit as 'pure appropriation of surplus value'; it is a function of cardinal importance which private capital, whatever be its motives, now performs when it assists what Rodbertus called 'business left to itself,'" (second edition, iii. p. 386). "Historically then even capitalism may be fully warranted and profit justified. To remove the latter without having found a better organisation of production would be senseless." "We may therefore practically condemn profit as appropriation of 'surplus value' only if we are able to replace the economic service of private capital by a public organisation positively established, more complete, and less greedy of surplus value" (*Mehrwerth schluckende*), iii. p. 422.

[5] See above, p. 207.

Wagner goes a little farther, but still only a little farther. With him too the capitalists are "functionaries of the whole community for the accumulation and employment of that national fund which consists of the instruments of production,"[1] and profit is an income they draw for this function, or, at least, *in* this function (p. 594). But the work of the capitalist, as consisting in the "accumulation and employment of private capitals," in "disposing activities and saving activities," he characterises more distinctly than Schäffle as "labours" (iii. pp. 592, 630) which form a part of the total costs expended in the production of goods, and in so far form a "constitutive element of value" (p. 630). In what way this element contributes to the formation of value in goods; how, from its efficacy, are derived the proportion between interest and sums of capital, the height of interest, and so on, Wagner tells us as little as Schäffle. He too has only struck the key-note of the Labour theory, though perhaps a little more distinctly.

This being the case, I should not venture to say positively whether the Katheder Socialists by this line of thought intended to give a theoretical explanation of interest, or only a justification of interest from the social-political side. In favour of the first view, there is (1) the embodying of the labour motive in the formal definition of interest; (2) the circumstance that Wagner at least has declared himself so positively against all other interest theories that, if he has not adopted the Labour theory, he has left interest, theoretically, quite unexplained; (3) that Wagner expressly pronounces the "labour of the capitalist" to be a constituent of the costs of production, and a "constitutive element of value"—a phrase which it is difficult to interpret otherwise than as meaning that the theoretical cause of the phenomenon of "surplus value" is the compensation demanded as return for the labour expended by the capitalist.

In favour of the second view, that the Katheder Socialists have pointed to the "capitalists' services" only as a ground for *justifying* the present existence of interest without meaning thereby to *explain* its existence, there is (1) the absence of any theoretical detail; (2) the circumstance that Schäffle, at least so

[1] *Allgemeine oder theoretische Volkswirthschaftslehre*, part i. *Grundlegung*, second edition. Leipzig and Heidelberg, 1879, pp. 40, 594.

far as he gives any explanation of details, makes use of another theory of interest; and (3) the great preponderance which, in the writings of the Katheder Socialists, is generally laid on the political element as against the theoretical.

In the circumstances it may be best to put my criticism hypothetically.

If it is the case that the Katheder Socialists, in pointing to the capitalists' "labours," wished to justify the existence of interest only from the social-political side, what they have said is, in the highest degree, worthy of attention. To go farther into this side of the question, however, is beyond my present task.

If it is the case, however, that the Katheder Socialists, in pointing to the capitalists' "labours," intended to explain interest theoretically, I should have to pass the same judgment on them that I passed on the French version of the Labour theory, viz. that the explanation is entirely inadequate.

It has so often been the case in the historical development of dogma that justification of interest from the social-political side is confused with theoretical explanations of interest, that it may be worth while to bring out very clearly and once for all the difference between the two. For this purpose let me put a parallel case which may at the same time give me an opportunity of showing at a glance the inadequacy of the Labour theory.

With the first acquisition of land there is generally connected a certain exertion or labour of the acquirer. Either it is that he must first make the ground productive, or that he must take a certain amount of trouble to gain possession of it; and this latter, in certain circumstances, may not be trifling, as, *e.g.* when it is preceded by a prolonged search for a locality suitable for settlement. The land now bears to its acquirer a rent. Can the existence of rent be *explained* by the fact of the labour originally expended? With the exception of Carey, and some few writers who share his perverse views, no one has ventured to maintain this. No one can maintain it who is not entirely blind to the connection of things. It is perfectly clear that, when a fruitful carse bears rent, it is not because its occupation has at one time or other cost labour. It is perfectly clear that if a rocky hillside bears no rent it is not because it has been occupied without trouble. It is, again, beyond doubt that two equally fruitful and equally well-situated pieces of land bear equal rents, even if the one that is fruitful by nature is simply taken occupation of at a trifling expenditure of labour, while the other has to be made productive by a great expenditure of labour. Further, it is clear that, if 200 acres bear twice as much rent as 100 acres, it is not because their first occupation was twice as troublesome. And finally, every one can see that, if rent rises with increasing population, the rising rent has nothing in the world to do with the original expenditure of labour. In short, it is clear that the emergence and the amount of rent do not in the least correspond with the emergence and amount of the labour originally expended in the occupation. It is impossible, then, that the principle which will explain the phenomenon of rent can be found in the original expenditure of labour.

Essentially different, however, is the question whether the existence of rent cannot be *justified* by this expenditure of labour. In this case one may quite well take up the position that he who makes a piece of ground productive, or even does no more than occupy it as the first pioneer of civilisation, has merited a wage as lasting as the advantage that thereby accrues to human society; that it is just and reasonable that he who has put a piece of ground under cultivation for all time should for all time receive a part of its productiveness in the shape of rent. I shall not maintain that this way of looking at the institution of private property in land, and of private land-rents based on that institution, must be conclusive in all circumstances, but it certainly may be so in some circumstances. It is, *e.g.* very probable indeed that a colonial government, anxious to expedite the settling of its territory, does wisely when it offers, as premium for the labour of cultivation and of first occupation, the ownership of lands brought into cultivation, and with that the right to a permanent rent. In this way the consideration of the labour put forth by the first occupant may furnish quite a plausible justification, and a conclusive social-political motive for the introduction and retention of rent, while none the less it is an entirely insufficient explanation of it.

It is exactly the same with the relation in which the capitalists' "saving and disposing activities" stand to interest.

In so far as, in those activities, we see the most effectual means to the accumulation and proper employment of a sufficient national capital, and in so far as we could not expect that these activities would be forthcoming from private persons in sufficient amount, if such persons were not led to expect permanent advantages, these services may furnish a very substantial justification and a conclusive legislative reason for the introduction and maintenance of interest. But it is an entirely different question whether the existence of interest can also be theoretically explained by pointing to that "labour." If it can be so explained, then there must be shown some normal relation between the alleged result, the interest of capital, and the asserted cause, the expenditure of labour on the part of the capitalist. But in the actual world we should look for any such relation in vain. A million bears £50,000 of interest, whether the saving and employment of the million has cost its owner much, little, or no trouble. A million bears ten thousand times as much interest as a hundred, even if there should be infinitely more anxiety and vexation in the saving of the hundred than in the saving of the million. The borrower who guards another man's capital and employs it, notwithstanding this "expenditure of labour," receives no interest; the owner receives it although his labour be nil. Schäffle himself once was fain to confess: "A distribution of wealth according to amount and desert of work, obtains neither among the capitalists as compared with each other, nor among the workers as compared with the capitalists. The distribution is neither guided by any such principles nor yet does it harmonise with them accidentally."[1]

But if experience shows that interest stands outside of any relation to the labour performed by the capitalist, how in reason can the principle of its explanation be found there? I believe the truth is too plainly told in the facts to need any long demonstration. Just as surely as interest bears no proportion to the labour put forth by the capitalist, does it stand in exact proportion to the fact of possession and to the amount of possession. Interest on capital, to repeat my former words, is not an income from labour, but an income from ownership.[2]

[1] *Bau und Leben*, iii. p. 451.

[2] It is much to be regretted that of Wagner's theoretical political economy

Thus the Labour theory of interest in all its varieties is seen to be incapable of giving a theoretical explanation that will stand examination. No unbiassed person indeed could expect any other result. No one but a person who takes particular delight in far-fetched explanations could for a moment doubt that the economic power of capital has some other ground behind it than a "capacity for labour" on the part of the capitalist. It is impossible to doubt that interest, not in name only but in reality, is something different from a wage of labour.

That economists should fall into various kinds of Labour theories can only be explained by the custom prevalent ever since Adam Smith and Ricardo of tracing all value to labour. To enable them to force interest also into the unity of this theory, and ascribe to it the origin which they supposed to be the only legitimate one, they did not hesitate at the most far-fetched and artificial explanations.[1]

the part which specially deals with the theory of interest has not yet appeared. It may be that this distinguished thinker would have given such explanations as make my present polemic,—which I have been careful to make hypothetical,—superfluous.

[1] As appendix to this chapter I should like, shortly, to refer to J. G. Hoffmann. He also interprets interest as wage for certain labours. "Even those rents," he says, meaning rents from capital, "are only a wage for labour, and indeed for labour of great public benefit; for with the obtaining of this wage is bound up, essentially and peculiarly, the duty of free activity in the public welfare, in science and skill, in everything that lightens, ennobles, and adorns human life" (*Ueber die wahre Natur und Bestimmung der Renten aus Boden—und Kapitaleigenthum, Sammlung der kleiner Schriften staatswirthschaftlichen Inhalts*, Berlin, 1843, p. 566). As regards Hoffmann, even more than as regards the Katheder Socialists, we are justified in doubting whether the words quoted were meant as a theoretic explanation of interest. If they were so, his theory is unquestionably more inadequate than all the other Labour theories; if they were not, it lies outside my task to question their justification.

BOOK VI

THE EXPLOITATION THEORY

CHAPTER I

HISTORICAL SURVEY

We come now to that remarkable theory the enunciation of which, if not the most agreeable among the scientific events of our century, certainly promises to be one of the most serious in its consequences. It stood at the cradle of modern Socialism and has grown up along with it; and to-day it forms the theoretical centre around which move the forces of attack and defence in the struggle of organising human society.

This theory has as yet no short distinctive name. If I were to give it one from a characteristic of its chief professors, I should call it the Socialist theory of interest. If I were to try to indicate by the name the theoretic purport of the doctrine itself,—which to my mind would be more appropriate,—no name seems more suitable than that of the Exploitation theory. This accordingly is the name I shall use in the sequel. Condensed into a few sentences, the essence of the theory may be provisionally put thus.

All goods that have value are the product of human labour, and indeed, economically considered, are *exclusively* the product of human labour. The labourers, however, do not retain the whole product which they alone have produced; for the capitalists take advantage of their command over the indispensable means of production, as secured to them by the institution of private property, to secure to themselves a part of the labourers' product. The means of doing so are supplied by the wage contract, in which the labourers are compelled by hunger to sell their labour-power to the capitalists for a part of what they, the labourers, produce, while the remainder of the product falls as profit into the hands of the capitalists, without any exertion on their part. Interest is thus a portion of the product of other people's labour, obtained by exploiting the necessitous condition of the labourer.

The way had been prepared for this doctrine long beforehand; indeed it had become all but inevitable, owing to the peculiar turn taken by the economic doctrine of value since the time of Adam Smith, and particularly since the time of Ricardo. It was taught and believed that the value of all, or at least of by far the greater part of economical goods, is measured by the quantity of labour incorporated in them, and that this labour is the cause and source of the value. This being the case, it was inevitable that, sooner or later, people would begin to ask why the worker should not receive the whole value of which his labour was the cause. And whenever that question was put it was impossible that any other answer could be given, on this reading of the theory of value, than that one class of society, the drone-like capitalists, appropriates to itself a part of the value of the product which the other class, the workers, alone produce.

As we have seen, this answer is not given by the founders of the Labour-value theory, Adam Smith and Ricardo. It was even evaded by some of their first followers, such as Soden and Lotz, who laid great emphasis on the value-creating power of labour, but, in their total conception of economic life, kept close to the footsteps of their master. But this answer was none the less involved in their theory, and it only needed a suitable occasion and a logical disciple to bring it sooner or later to the surface. Thus Adam Smith and Ricardo may be regarded as the involuntary godfathers of the Exploitation theory. They are indeed treated as such by its followers. They, and almost they alone, are mentioned by even the most pronounced socialists with that respect which is paid to the discoverers of the "true" law of value, and the only reproach made them is that they did not logically follow out their own principles, and so allowed themselves to be prevented from developing the Exploitation theory out of their theory of value.

Any one who cares to hunt up ancient pedigrees of theories might discover in the writers of past centuries many an expression that fits in with the line of thought taken by the Exploitation theory. Not to speak of the canonists, who arrived at the same results more by accident than anything else, I may mention Locke, who on one occasion points very distinctly to labour as the source of all wealth,[1] and at another time speaks of interest as the fruit of the labour of others;[2] James Steuart, who expresses himself less distinctly, but takes the same line;[3] Sonnenfels, who occasionally describes capitalists as a class who do no labour, and thrive by the sweat of the labouring classes;[4] or Büsch, who also,—treating indeed only of contract interest,—regards it as "a return to property obtained by the industry of others."[5]

These are instances which could very likely be multiplied by careful examination of the older literature. The birth of the Exploitation theory, however, as a conscious and coherent doctrine, must be assigned to a later period.

Two developments preceded and prepared the way for it. First, as mentioned above, it was the development and popularising of the Ricardian theory of value which supplied the scientific soil out of which the Exploitation theory could naturally spring and grow. And, secondly, there was the triumphant spread of capitalist production on a large scale; for this large production, while creating and revealing a wide gulf of opposition between capital and labour, placed in the foremost rank of great social questions the problem of interest as an income obtained without personal labour.

Under those influences the time seems to have become ready for the systematic development of the Exploitation theory

[1] *Civil Government*, book ii. chap. v. § 40: "Nor is it so strange, as perhaps before consideration it may appear, that the property of labour should be able to overbalance the community of land; for it is labour indeed that put the difference of value on everything; and let any one consider what the difference is between an acre of land planted with tobacco or sugar, sown with wheat or barley, and an acre of the same land lying in common without any husbandry upon it, and he will find that the improvement of labour makes the far greater part of the value. I think it will be but a very modest computation to say that of the products of the earth useful to the life of man nine-tenths are the effect of labour, nay, if we will rightly estimate things as they come to our use, and cast up the several expenses about them, what in them is purely owing to nature, and what to labour, we shall find that in most of them ninety-nine hundredths are wholly to be put on the account of labour."

[2] *Considerations of the Consequences of the Lowering of Interest*, 1691, p. 24. See above, p. 45.

[3] See above, p. 46.

[4] *Handlungswissenschaft*, second edition, p. 430.

[5] *Geldumlauf*, book iii. p. 26.

about the twentieth year of this century. Among the first to give it explicit statement—in a history of theory I leave out of account the "practical" communists, whose efforts, of course, were based on similar ideas—were Hodgskin in England and Sismondi in France.

Hodgskin's writings—a little known *Popular Political Economy* and an anonymous publication under the significant title "Labour defended against the Claims of Capital"[1]—do not seem to have had any extensive influence. Thus Sismondi becomes all the more important in the development of the theory.

In naming Sismondi as representative of the Exploitation theory, I must do so with a certain reservation. It is that, although his theory contains all the other essential features of that system, he expresses no condemnatory opinion on interest. He is the writer of a transition period. Though really acquiescing in the new theory, he has not yet broken with the old so completely as to accept all the very extreme conclusions of the new position.

For our purpose the book which we have chiefly to consider is his great and influential *Nouveaux Principes d'Economic Politique*.[2] In it Sismondi connects with Adam Smith. He accepts with warm approval (p. 51) Adam Smith's proposition that labour is the sole source of all wealth;[3] complains that the three kinds of income,—rent, profit, and wages,—are fre-

[1] I may give a few characteristic passages: "All the benefits attributed to capital arise from coexisting and skilled labour." After stating that, by the help of tools and machines, more products and better products can be created than without them, he adds the following consideration: "But the question then occurs, What produces instruments and machines, and in what degree do they aid production independent of the labourer, so that the owners of them are entitled to by far the greater part of the whole produce of the country? Are they or are they not the product of labour? Do they or do they not constitute an efficient means of production separate from labour? Are they or are they not so much inert, decaying, or dead matter of no utility whatever, possessing no productive power whatever, but as they are guided, directed, and applied by skilful hands?" (p. 14)

The numerous writers with socialistic tendencies mentioned by Held in the second book of his *Zur sozialen Geschichte Englands* (Leipzig, 1881) have little direct concern with the theory of interest.

[2] First edition, 1819. Second edition, Paris, 1827. I quote from the latter.

[3] A proposition, however, which Adam Smith himself did not always very consistently adhere to. Besides labour he not seldom mentions land and capital as sources of goods.

quently ascribed to three different sources, land, capital, and labour, while in reality all income springs from labour alone, these three branches being only so many different ways of sharing in the fruits of human labour (p. 85). The labourer, by whose activity all goods are produced, has not been able "in our stage of civilisation" to obtain possession of the means necessary to production. On the one hand, land is generally in the possession of some other person who requires from the labourer a part of the fruit of his labour as compensation for the co-operation of this "productive power." This part forms the land-rent. On the other hand, the productive labourer does not as a rule possess a sufficient stock of the means of subsistence upon which to live during the course of his labour. Nor does he possess the raw materials necessary to production or the often expensive tools and machines. The rich man who has all these things thus obtains a certain command over the labour of the poor man, and, without himself taking part in that labour, he takes away, as compensation for the advantages which he places at the disposal of the poor man, the better part of the fruits of his labour (*la part la plus importante des fruits de son travail*). This share is the profit on capital (pp. 86, 87). Thus, by the arrangements of society, wealth acquires the capacity of reproducing itself by means of the labour of others (p. 82).

But although the labourer produces by his day's labour very much more than the day's needs, yet, after the division with the landowner and the capitalist, there seldom remains to him much more than his absolutely necessary maintenance, and this he receives in the form of wages. The reason for this lies in the dependent position in which the labourer is placed in relation to the undertaker who owns the capital. The labourer's need for maintenance is much more urgent than the undertaker's need for labour. The labourer requires his maintenance in order to live, while the undertaker requires his labour only to make a profit. Thus the transaction turns out almost invariably to the disadvantage of the labourer. He is in nearly all cases obliged to be satisfied with the barest maintenance, while the lion's share in the results of a productivity which is increased by the division of labour falls to the undertaker (p. 91, etc.)

Any one who has followed Sismondi thus far, and has noticed among others the proposition that "the rich spend what the labour of others has produced" (p. 81), must expect that Sismondi would end by condemning interest, and declaring it to be an unjust and extortionate profit. This conclusion, however, Sismondi does not draw, but with a sudden swerve wanders into some obscure and vague observations in favour of interest, and finishes by entirely justifying it. First of all he says of the landowner that, by the original labour of cultivating, or even by occupation of an unowned piece of land, he has earned a right to its rent (p. 110). By analogy he ascribes to the owner of capital a right to its interest, as founded on the "original labour" to which the capital owes its existence (p. 111). Both branches of income, which, as income due to ownership, form a contrast to the income due to labour, he finally manages to commend as having precisely the same origin as the income of labour, except that their origin goes back to another point of time. The labourer earns yearly a new right to income by new labour, while the owner has acquired at an earlier period of time a perpetual right in virtue of an original labour which the yearly labour renders more profitable (p. 112).[1] "Every one," he concludes, "receives his share in the national income only according to the measure of what he himself or his representative has contributed, or contributes, towards its origin." How this statement can be said to agree with the former one, where interest appears as something taken from the fruits of the labour of other people, must remain a mystery.

The conclusions that Sismondi did not venture to draw from his own theory were soon very decidedly drawn by others. Sismondi forms the bridge between Adam Smith and Ricardo on the one side, and the Socialism and Communism that succeeded on the other. The two former had, by their theory of value, given occasion for the appearance of the Exploitation theory, but had in no way themselves developed it. Sismondi has, substantially, all but arrived at this theory, but has not given it any social or political application. After him comes the great mass of Socialism and Communism following the old theory of

[1] In these words one may find a very condensed statement of James Mill's labour theory (see above, p. 298).

value into all its theoretical and practical consequences, and coming to the conclusion that interest is plunder, and ought therefore to cease.

It would not be interesting from the point of theory were I to excerpt, from the mass of socialist literature produced in this century, all expressions in which the Exploitation theory is suggested or implied. I should only weary the reader with innumerable parallel passages, scarcely varying in words, and exhibiting in substance a dull monotony; passages, moreover, which for the most part only repeat the cardinal propositions of the Exploitation theory, without adding to its proof more than a few commonplaces and appeals to the authority of Ricardo. In fact the majority of socialists have exercised their intellectual powers, not so much in laying the foundations of their own theory, as in bitterly criticising the theories of their opponents.

Out of the mass of writers with socialist tendencies I content myself therefore with naming a few who have become specially important in the development and spread of this theory.

Among those the author of the *Contradictions Economiques*, P. J. Proudhon, is pre-eminent for honesty of intention and brilliant dialectic; qualities which rendered him the most efficient apostle of the theory in France. As we are more concerned with substance than with form, I shall not give any detailed example of his style, but content myself with condensing his doctrine into a few sentences. It will be seen at once that, with the exception of a few peculiarities of expression, it differs very little from the general scheme of the theory as given at the beginning of this chapter.

At the outset Proudhon takes it for granted that all value is produced by labour. Thus the labourer has a natural claim to the possession of his whole product. In the wage contract, however, he waives this claim in favour of the owner of capital, and gets in return a wage which is less than the product he gives up. Thereby he is defrauded, for he does not know his natural rights, nor the extent of what he gives up, nor yet the meaning of the contract which the owner concludes with him. And thus the capitalist avails himself of error and surprise, if not cunning and fraud (*erreur et surprise si même on ne doit dire dol et fraud*).

So it comes that at the present day the labourer cannot buy his own product. In the market his product costs more than he has received in wage; it costs more by the amount of many profits, which are made possible by the existence of the right of property; and these profits under the most various names, such as profit, interest, rent, hire, tithe, and so on, form just so many tolls (*aubaines*) laid upon labour. For example, what twenty million labourers have produced for a year's wage of twenty milliards of francs is sold for the price (including these profits, and on account of them) of twenty-five milliards. But this is equivalent to saying that the labourers who are compelled to purchase back these same products are forced to pay five for that which they have produced for four; or that in every five days they must go without food for one. Thus interest is an additional tax on labour, a something kept back (*rétenue*) from the wages of labour.[1]

Equal to Proudhon in the purity of his intentions, and far surpassing him in depth of thought and judgment, though certainly behind the impetuous Frenchman in power of statement, is the German Rodbertus.

As regards the history of theory Rodbertus is the weightiest personage we have to mention in this chapter. His scientific importance was long misunderstood, and that, strangely enough, precisely on account of the scientific character of his writings. Not addressing himself, like others, to the people, but restricting himself for the most part to the theoretical investigation of the social problem; moderate and reserved in those practical proposals which, with the great majority, are the chief objects of concern; his reputation for a while lagged behind that of less important writers who accepted his intellectual wares at second hand, and made them acceptable by appealing to popular interests. It is only in recent times that full justice has been done to this most amiable socialist, and that he has been recognised as what he is—the spiritual father of modern scientific Socialism. Instead of fiery attacks

[1] See Proudhon's numerous writings *passim*, particularly *Qu'est ce que la propriété?* (1840: in the Paris edition of 1849, p. 162), *Philosophie de la Misère* pp. 62, 287 of the German translation), *Defence before the Assizes at Besançon on 3d February* 1842 (collected edition, Paris, 1868, ii.)

and rhetorical antitheses, by which most socialists are fond of drawing a crowd, Rodbertus has left behind him a profound, honestly thought-out theory of the distribution of goods, which, erroneous as it may be in many points, contains enough that is really valuable to ensure its author an abiding rank among the theorists of political economy.

Reserving meanwhile his formulation of the Exploitation theory to return to it later on in detail, I turn to two of his successors, who differ from each other as widely as they differ from their predecessor Rodbertus. One of these is Ferdinand Lassalle, the most eloquent, but, as regards substance, the least original among the leaders of Socialism. I only mention him here because his brilliant eloquence exerted a great influence on the spread of the Exploitation theory; to its theoretical development he contributed almost nothing. His doctrine is substantially that of his predecessors, and I may therefore pass on without reproducing it in quotations or extracts, and merely refer to some of the most characteristic passages in a note.[1]

While Lassalle is an agitator and nothing else, Karl Marx is a theorist, and indeed, after Rodbertus, the most important theorist of Socialism. His doctrine is certainly founded in many respects on the pioneering work of Rodbertus, but it is built up with some originality and a considerable degree of acute logical power into an organic whole. This theory also we shall consider in detail later on.

If the perfecting of the Exploitation theory has been, *par excellence*, the work of socialist theorists, the ideas peculiar to it have nevertheless found admittance into other circles, though in different ways and in different degrees. Many adopted the

[1] Among his numerous writings, the one in which he expresses his opinions on the interest problem most fully, and which most brilliantly displays his agitator genius, is *Herr Bastiat-Schulze von Delitzsch, der ökonomische Julian, oder Kapital und Arbeit* (Berlin, 1864). The principal passages are these: Labour is "source and factor of all values" (pp. 83, 122, 147). The labourer does not receive the whole value, but only the market price of labour considered as a commodity, this price being equal to its costs of production, that is, to bare subsistence (p. 186, etc.) All surplus falls to capital (p. 194). Interest is therefore a deduction from the return of the labourer (p. 125, and very scathingly p. 97). Against the doctrine of the Productivity of capital (p. 21, etc.) Against the Abstinence theory (p. 82, etc., and particularly p. 110, etc.) See also Lassalle's other writings.

Exploitation theory in its entirety, and, at the most, only refused to acknowledge its last practical consequences. Guth, for example, takes this position.[1] He accepts all the essential propositions of the socialists, and accepts them in their entire extent. Labour is to him the sole source of value. Interest arises from the fact that, in virtue of the unfavourable circumstances of competition, the wages of labour are always less than the product of labour. Indeed Guth does not scruple to introduce the harsh expression *Ausbeutung* for this fact as *terminus technicus.* Finally, however, he draws back from the practical consequences of the doctrine by introducing some saving clauses. "Far be it from us to declare that the *Ausbeutung* of the labourer, which is the source of profit, is unjustifiable from a legal point of view. It rests rather on a free alliance between the employer and the labourer, which takes place under circumstances of the market that are, as a rule, unfavourable to the latter." The sacrifice which the exploited labourer suffers is rather an "advance against replacement." For the increase of capital is always increasing the productivity of labour; consequently the products of labour grow cheaper, the labourer is able to buy more of these products with his wages, and thus his real wages rise. At the same time the labourer's sphere of employment is enlarged "on account of greater demand, and his money wage also rises." Thus the *Ausbeutung* is equivalent to an investment of capital, which, in its indirect consequences, yields the labourer a rising percentage of interest.[2]

Dühring also in his theory of interest takes an entirely socialistic position. "The nature of profit is that of an appropriation of the principal part of the return to labour. The increase of the return and the saving of labour are results of the improved and enlarged means of production. But the circumstance that the hindrances and difficulties of production are lessened, and that bare labour, in furnishing itself with tools, renders itself more productive, does not give the *inanimate* tool any claim to absorb a fraction more than what is required to reproduce it. The idea of profit therefore is not one that could be evolved from the productivity of

[1] *Die Lehre vom Einkommen in dessen Gesammtzweigen*, 1869. I quote from the second edition of 1878.

[2] *Ibid.* pp. 109, etc., 122, etc. See also p. 271, etc.

labour, or in any system where the economical subject was looked on as an economically self-contained individual. It is a form of appropriation, and is a creation of the peculiar circumstances of distribution."[1]

A second group of eclectic writers add the ideas of the Exploitation theory to their other views on the interest problem; as, for example, John Stuart Mill and Schäffle.[2]

Finally, there are others who have allowed themselves to be swayed by the impression made on them by socialist writers, and while not acknowledging the entire system of these writers, have still accepted individual points of importance. The most noteworthy feature in this direction seems to me the acceptance, by a considerable number of the German Katheder Socialists, of the old proposition that labour is the sole source of all value, the sole value-producing power.

This proposition, the acceptance or rejection of which has such an enormous weight in determining our judgment of the most important economic phenomena, has had a peculiar fate. It was originally started by the political economy of England, and in the first twenty years or so after the appearance of the *Wealth of Nations* it had gained a wide circulation along with Adam Smith's system. Later on, under the influence of Say, who developed the theory of the three productive factors, nature, labour, and capital, and then under the influence of Hermann and Senior, it came into disrepute with the majority of political economists, even of the English school. For a time the tradition was maintained only by a few socialist writers. Then the Katheder Socialists accepted it from the writings of such men as Proudhon, Rodbertus, and Marx, and it once more gained a firm position in scientific political economy. At the present time it almost looks as if the authority enjoyed by the distinguished leaders of that school was on the eve of starting it for the second time on a triumphant march round the literature of all nations.

Whether this is to be desired or not will be shown by the

[1] *Kursus der National-und Sozialökonomie*, Berlin, 1873, p. 183. A little further on (p. 185), evidently borrowing from Proudhon's *Droit d'Aubaine*, he explains interest as a "toll" imposed in return for the giving over of economic power, the rate of interest representing the rate at which the toll is levied.

[2] See below, book vii.

critical examination of the Exploitation theory to which I now address myself.

In criticising this theory several courses were open to me. I might have criticised all its representatives individually. This would certainly have been the most accurate way, but the strong resemblance between individual statements would have led to superfluous and extremely wearisome repetitions. Or, without going into individual statements, I might have directed my criticism against the general scheme that these individual statements really have in common. In doing so, however, there would have been a double difficulty. On the one hand, I should have encountered the danger of making too little account of certain individual variations in the doctrine, and on the other hand, if this had been avoided, I should certainly not have escaped the reproach of making too light of the subject, and of directing my criticism against a wilful caricature, instead of against the real doctrine. I decided, therefore, to take a third course; to select those individual statements that appear to me the best and most complete, and to submit them to a separate criticism.

For this purpose I have chosen the statements of the Exploitation theory given by Rodbertus and Marx. They are the only ones that offer anything like a firm and coherent foundation. While that of Rodbertus is to my mind the best, that of Marx is the one which has won most general acceptance, and the one which may to a certain extent be regarded as the official system of the Socialism of to-day. In subjecting these two to a close examination I think I am taking the Exploitation theory on its strongest side, remembering that fine saying of Knies, "He that would be victorious on the field of scientific research must let his adversary advance fully armed and in all his strength."[1]

To avoid misunderstandings, one more remark before beginning. The purpose of the following pages is to criticise the Exploitation theory exclusively as a theory; that is to say, to investigate whether the causes of the economic phenomenon of interest really consist in those circumstances which the Exploitation theory asserts to be its originating causes. It is not

[1] *Der Kredit*, part ii. Berlin, 1879, p. 7.

my intention to offer an opinion in this place on the practical and social side of the interest problem, whether it is objectionable or unobjectionable, whether it should be retained or abolished. Of course no one would think of writing a book on interest and remaining silent on the most important question connected with it. But I can only speak to any purpose of the practical side of the matter when the theoretical side has first been made perfectly clear, and I must therefore reserve the examination of these questions for my second volume. I repeat, then, that in the present instance I shall merely examine whether interest, be it good or be it bad, comes into existence from the causes asserted by the Exploitation theory.

CHAPTER II

RODBERTUS

THE starting-point of Rodbertus's[1] theory of interest is the proposition, introduced into the science by Adam Smith and more firmly established by the Ricardian school, that goods, economically considered, are to be regarded as products of labour alone, and cost nothing but labour. This proposition, which is usually expressed in the words "Labour alone is productive," is amplified by Rodbertus as follows :—

1. Only those goods are economical goods which have cost labour; all other goods, be they ever so useful or necessary to mankind, are natural goods, and have no place in economical consideration.

2. All economic goods are the product of labour and labour only; for the economic conception they do not count as products of nature or of any other power, but solely as products of labour; any other conception of them may be physical, but it is not economic.

3. Goods, economically considered, are the product solely of

[1] A tolerably complete list of the writings of Dr. Karl Rodbertus-Jagetzow is to be found in Kozak's *Rodbertus' sozialökonomische Ansichten*, Jena, 1882, p. 7, etc. I have made use by preference of the second and third *Social Letters* to Von Kirchmann in the (somewhat altered) copy published by Rodbertus in 1875, under the name of *Zur Beleuchtung der sozialen Frage;* also of the tract *Zur Erklärung und Abhilfe der heutigen Kreditnoth des Grundbesitzes;* and of the fourth *Social Letter* to Von Kirchmann (Berlin, 1884), published under Rodbertus's bequest by Adolf Wagner and Kozak under the name *Das Kapital.* A few years ago Rodbertus's interest theory was subjected to an extremely close and conscientious criticism by Knies (*Der Kredit*, part ii. Berlin, 1879, p. 47, etc.), with which in its most important points I fully agree. I feel myself, however, bound to take up the task of criticism independently, my theoretic point of view being so different from that of Knies that I cannot help looking at many things in an essentially different light.

that labour which has performed the material operations necessary to their production. But to this category belongs not merely that labour which immediately produces the goods, but also that labour which first creates the instrument by which the goods are made. Thus grain is not merely the product of the man who held the plough, but also of him who made the plough, and so on.[1]

The fundamental proposition that all goods, economically considered, are the product of labour alone, has with Rodbertus very much the claim of an axiom. He considers it a proposition about which, "in the advanced state of political economy, there is no longer any dispute;" it is naturalised among English economists, has its representatives among those of France, and, "what is most important, in spite of all the sophisms of a retrograde and conservative doctrine, is indelibly imprinted upon the consciousness of the people."[2] Only once do I find any attempt in Rodbertus to put this proposition on a rational foundation. He says that "every product that comes to us through labour in the shape of a good ought to be put solely to the account of human labour, because labour is the only original power, and also the only original cost with which human economy is concerned."[3] This proposition also is put down as an axiom, and Rodbertus does not go any farther into the subject.

The actual labourers who produce the entire product in the shape of goods have, at least "according to the pure idea of justice," a natural and just claim to obtain possession of this entire product.[4] But this with two rather important limitations. First, the system of the division of labour, under which many co-operate in the production of one product, makes it technically impossible that each labourer should receive his product *in natura*. There must therefore be substituted, for the claim to the whole product, the claim to the whole *value* of the product.[5]

Further, all those who render society useful services without immediately co-operating in the material producing of the

[1] *Zur Beleuchtung der sozialen Frage*, pp. 68, 69.

[2] *Soziale Frage*, p. 71.

[3] *Erklärung und Abhilfe*, ii. p. 160 note.

[4] *Soziale Frage*, p. 56; *Erklärung*, p. 112.

[5] *Soziale Frage*, pp. 87 90; *Erklärung*, p. 111; *Kapital*, p. 116.

goods must have a share in the national product; such, for example, as the clergyman, the physician, the judge, the scientific investigator, and, in Rodbertus's opinion, even the undertakers, who "understand how to employ a number of labourers productively by means of a capital."[1] But such labour, being only "indirect economic labour," may not put in its claim of payment at the "original distribution of goods," in which the producers alone take part, but only at a "secondary distribution of goods." What then is the claim which the actual labourers have to put forward, according to the pure idea of justice? It is a claim to receive the entire value of the product of their labour in the original distribution, without prejudice to the secondary claims on salary of other useful members of society.

This natural claim Rodbertus does not find recognised in present social arrangements. The labourers of to-day receive as wages, in the original distribution, only a part of the value of their product, while the remainder falls as rent to the owners of land and capital.

Rent is defined by Rodbertus as "all income obtained without personal exertion solely in virtue of possession."[2] It includes two kinds of rent—land-rent and profit on capital.

Rodbertus then asks, As every income is the product of labour alone, what is the reason that certain persons in society draw incomes (and, moreover, original incomes) without stirring a finger in the work of production? In this question Rodbertus has stated the general theoretical problem of the theory of rent.[3] The answer he gives is the following:—

Rent owes its existence to the coincidence of two facts, one economical and one legal. The economic ground of rent lies in the fact that, since the introduction of the division of labour, the labourers produce more than they require to support themselves in life and to allow them to continue their labour, and thus others also are able to live upon the product. The legal ground lies in the existence of private property in land and capital. As, therefore, through the existence of private property the labourers have lost all control over the conditions that are indispensable to production, they cannot, as a rule, do otherwise than produce in the service of the proprietors, and

[1] *Soziale Frage*, p. 146; *Erklärung*, ii. p. 109, etc.

[2] *Soziale Frage*, p. 32.

[3] *Ibid.* p. 74, etc.

that according to an agreement previously made. These proprietors impose upon the labourers the obligation of surrendering a part of the product of their labour as rent, in return for the opportunity of using the conditions of production just mentioned. Indeed this surrender even takes an aggravated form, for the labourers have to give up to the owners the possession of their *entire* product, receiving back from the owners only a part of its value as wage, and a part that is no more than the labourers absolutely require to keep them in life and allow them to continue their labour. The power which forces the labourers to agree to this contract is Hunger. To let Rodbertus speak for himself:—

"As there can be no income unless it is produced by labour, rent rests on two indispensable conditions. First, there can be no rent if labour does not produce more than the amount which is just necessary to the labourers to secure the continuance of their labour, for it is impossible that without such a surplus any one, without himself labouring, can regularly receive an income. Secondly, there could be no rent if arrangements did not exist which deprive the labourers of this surplus, either wholly or in part, and give it to others who do not themselves labour, for in the nature of things the labourers themselves are always the first to come into possession of their product. That labour yields such a surplus rests on economic grounds that increase the productivity of labour. That this surplus is entirely or in part withdrawn from the labourers and given to others rests on grounds of positive law; and as law has always united itself with force it only effects this withdrawal by continual compulsion.

"The form which this compulsion originally took was slavery, the origin of which is contemporaneous with that of agriculture and landed property. The labourers who produced such a surplus in their labour-product were slaves, and the master to whom the labourers belonged, and to whom consequently the product itself also belonged, gave the slaves only so much as was necessary for the continuance of their labour, and kept the remainder or surplus to himself. If all the land, and at the same time all the capital of a country, have passed into private property, then landed property and property in capital exert a similar compulsion even over freed or free labourers. For, first, the result will be the same as in slavery, that the product will not belong to the labourers, but to the masters of land and capital; and secondly, the labourers who possess nothing, in face of the masters possessing land and capital, will be glad to receive a part only of the product of their own labour with which to support themselves in life; that is to say, again, to enable them to continue their labour. Thus, although the contract of labourer and employer has taken the place of slavery, the contract is only formally and not actually free, and Hunger makes a good substitute for the whip. What was formerly called food is now called wage."[1]

Thus, then, all rent is an exploitation,[2] or, as Rodbertus sometimes calls it still more forcibly, a robbery of the product of other people's labour.[3] This character applies to all kinds of rent equally; to land-rent as well as to profit on capital, and to the emoluments of hire and loan interest derived from them. Hire and interest are as legitimate in connection with the undertakers as they are illegitimate in connection with the labourers, at whose cost, in the last resort, they are paid.[4]

The amount of rent increases with the productivity of labour; for under the system of free competition the labourer receives, universally and constantly, only the amount necessary for his maintenance—that is, a definite quantum of the product. Thus the greater the productivity of labour the less will be the proportion of the total value of the product claimed by this quantum, and the greater will be the proportion of the product and of the value remaining over to the proprietor as his share, as rent.[5]

Although, according to what has been already said, all rent forms a homogeneous mass having one common origin in practical economic life, it is divided into two branches, land-rent and profit on capital. Rodbertus then explains the reason and the laws of this division in a most peculiar way. He starts from the theoretical assumption, which he carries through all his investigation, that the exchange value of all products is equal

[1] *Soziale Frage*, p. 33; similarly and more in detail, pp. 77-94.

[2] *Ibid.* p. 115, and other places.

[3] *Ibid.* p. 150; *Kapital*, p. 202.

[4] *Soziale Frage*, pp. 115, 148, etc. See also the criticism of Bastiat, pp. 115-119.

[5] *Ibid.* p. 123, etc.

to their labour-costs; in other words, that all products exchange with each other in proportion to the labour they have cost.[1] Rodbertus indeed is aware that this assumption does not exactly correspond with reality. Still he believes that the deviations amount to nothing more than that "the actual exchange value falls sometimes on the one side, sometimes on the other," in which cases there is at least always a point towards which they gravitate, "that point being the natural as well as the just exchange value."[2] He entirely rejects the idea that goods normally exchange with each other according to any other proportion than that of the labour incorporated in them; that deviations from this proportion may be the result, not merely of accidental and momentary fluctuations of the market, but of a fixed law drawing the value in another direction.[3] At this stage I merely draw attention to the circumstance, and will show its importance later on.

The total production of goods may, according to Rodbertus, be divided into two branches—raw production, which with the assistance of land obtains raw products, and manufacture which works up the raw products. Before division of labour was introduced the obtaining and working up of raw products were performed in immediate succession by one undertaker, who then received without division the whole resulting rent. In this stage of economic development there was no separation of rent into land-rent and profit on capital. But, since the introduction of the division of labour, the undertaker of the raw production and the undertaker of the manufacture which follows it are distinct persons. The preliminary question is, In what proportion will the rent that results from the total production now be divided among the producers of the raw material on the one hand and the manufacturers on the other?

The answer to this question follows from the character of rent. Rent is a proportion of and deduction from the value of the product. The amount of rent that can be obtained in any branch of production is regulated by the value of the product created in this branch of production. As, however, the amount of the value of the product is regulated here also by the amount

[1] *Soziale Frage*, p. 106.

[2] *Ibid.* p. 107; similarly pp. 113, 117. *Erklärung*, i. p. 123.

[3] *Soziale Frage*, p. 148.

of the labour spent on it, the total rent will be divided between raw production and manufacture, according to the expenditure of labour in each of these branches. To illustrate this by a concrete example.[1] Say that it requires 1000 days of labour to obtain a certain amount of raw product, and that its manufacture requires 2000 days more; then if rent takes 40 per cent of the value of the product as the share of the owners, the product of 400 days of labour will fall as rent to the producers of raw material, and the product of 800 days of labour as rent to the manufacturing undertakers. On the other hand, the amount of capital employed in each branch of production is a matter of no consequence as regards this division, for though the rent is estimated in relation to this capital, it is not determined by it, but by the amount of labour supplied.

Now the very fact that the amount of capital employed has no causal influence on the amount of rent obtainable in any branch of production becomes the cause of land-rent. Rodbertus proves this in the following manner.

Rent is the product of labour. But it is conditioned by the possession of wealth. Therefore rent is looked on as a return to that wealth. In manufacture this wealth takes the form of capital alone, and not of land. Thus the total rent obtained in manufacture is regarded as return on capital, or profit on capital. And thus by calculating, in the usual way, the proportion between the amount of return and the amount of the capital on which the return is obtained, we come to say that a definite percentage of profit is obtainable from capital engaged in manufacture. In virtue of well-known tendencies of competition this rate of profit will approximate to equality in all branches, and will also become the standard for calculating the profit of capital engaged in raw production; for a much greater portion of the national capital is engaged in manufacture than in agriculture, and obviously the return of the greater portion of capital must dictate to the smaller portion the rate at which its profit shall be calculated. Therefore the raw producers must calculate, as profit on their capital, so much of the total rent gained in the raw production

[1] This illustration is not given by Rodbertus; I only add it to put the difficult line of argument more clearly.

as corresponds with the amount of capital that has been employed and with the usual rate of profit. The remainder of the rent, on the other hand, must be considered as return from land, and forms the land-rent.

Now, according to Rodbertus, there must always be such a remainder in raw production, in virtue of the assumption that products exchange in proportion to the amount of labour incorporated in them. He proves this as follows. The amount of rent obtainable in manufacture depends, as we have seen, not on the amount of the capital laid out, but on the quantity of labour performed in the manufacture. This labour is made up of two constituent parts; on the one side, the immediate labour of manufacture, on the other side, that indirect labour "which must also be taken into calculation as representing the tools and machines used." Therefore of the different constituent portions of the capital laid out, only those portions will affect the amount of rent which consist of wages and expenditure for machines and tools. On the other hand, no such influence affects the capital laid out in raw materials, because this outlay does not express any labour performed in the manufacturing stage. Yet this part of the outlay increases the capital on which the rent obtainable as return is calculated. The existence of a portion of capital which increases the manufacturing capital on which the share of the rent that falls to it as profit is calculated, while it does not increase this profit itself, must evidently lower the proportion of the profit to the capital; in other words, it must lower the rate of profit on capital engaged in manufacture.

Now the profit on capital engaged in raw production also will be calculated at this reduced rate. But here (in raw production) the circumstances are generally more favourable. For as agriculture begins production *ab ovo*, and does not work up material derived from a previous production, its outlay of capital has no constituent "value of material." The analogue of material is simply land, and land in all theories is assumed to cost nothing. Hence no portion of capital has any share in the division of the profit which does not also have an influence upon its amount, and hence also the proportion between the rent gained and the capital employed must be more favourable in agriculture than in manufacture. As however, in agriculture also, the profit on capital is calculated at the reduced rate determined by manufacture, there must always remain a surplus of rent, which falls to the landowner as land-rent. This, according to Rodbertus, is the origin of land-rent, and its distinction from profit on capital.[1]

I may shortly supplement this by remarking that, notwithstanding the very severe theoretical judgment that he pronounces on profit in describing it as plunder, Rodbertus will not hear of abolishing either private property in capital or profit on capital. Nay, he ascribes to property in land and capital "an educating power" which we cannot spare; a "kind of patriarchal power that could only be replaced after a completely altered system of national instruction, for which at present we have not got even the conditions."[2] Property in land and capital appear to him in the meanwhile to have "a

[1] *Soziale Frage*, p. 94, etc.; particularly pp. 109-111. *Erklärung*, i. p. 123. It may be advisable, in the interest of the English reader, to put this theory of land-rent in a different way.

According to Rodbertus, all rent is a deduction from product, and an exploitation of the labour that produces the product. Both land-rent then and capital-rent (profit) must be accounted for by this deduction, and only by this deduction. Now rent cannot emerge at all unless the necessary resources are provided. The owners give these resources; the labourer works with them; the owner takes his rent from the product, and, naturally enough, calculates it as a percentage on the amount of the resources he provides. In reality, however, rent does not depend on the amount and duration of these resources, but on the amount of labour employed and exploited.

But resources are of two kinds, land and capital. In manufacturing the resources consist of capital alone. The profit exploited from the manufacturing labourers is calculated as a rate on the capital, and comes to be ascribed to the capital. Under the competitive system profits tend to an equality over the whole field, and accordingly we should expect the landowner to get simply the same rent for the resources he lends (land) as the capitalist gets for the resources he lends (capital). But as a fact the landowner gets more; in fact, sufficient to pay another rent, which is properly called land-rent. How is this?

The reason is that in manufacture there are two outlays of capital, one for wages and one for raw materials. But there is only one field of exploitation, wages. There is, then, in manufacturing a portion of capital employed which yields no profit, and the profit that is made in the total manufacture, being calculated on this portion plus the portion employed in paying wages, the rate of profit is lower than it would be otherwise.

Now in agriculture there is indeed only one source of rent or profit, labour, but there is no outlay for raw materials. The profit thus in agriculture is calculated on a smaller capital, and so must leave, over and above the ordinary manufacturing rate of profit, a surplus which is land-rent.—W. S.

[2] *Erklärung*, ii. p. 303.

kind of official position involving the national functions of managing the economic labour and the economic resources of the nation in correspondence with national need."

Thus from this, its most favourable point of view, rent may be regarded as a form of salary which certain "officers" receive for the execution of their functions.[1] I have already observed above how this remark, casually expressed in a mere note, formed the basis on which later writers, particularly Schäffle, have built up a peculiar form of the Labour theory.

To come now to criticism of Rodbertus's system. Without circumlocution I may say at once that I consider the theory which it contains to be an entire failure. I am convinced that it suffers from a series of grave theoretical defects which I shall endeavour to set forth in the following pages as clearly and as impartially as may be.

At the outset I am obliged to take exception to the very first stone that Rodbertus lays in the structure of his system—the proposition that all goods, economically considered, are products of labour and of labour alone.

First of all, what do the words "economically considered" mean? Rodbertus explains them by a contrast. He puts the economical standpoint in opposition to the physical standpoint. That goods, physically speaking, are the products not only of labour but of natural powers, he explicitly allows. If then it is said that, from the economic standpoint, goods are the product of labour only, the statement can surely have but one meaning, viz. that the co-operation of natural powers in production is a matter of utter indifference so far as human economy is concerned. On one occasion Rodbertus gives forcible expression to this conception when he says: "All other goods except those that have cost labour, however useful or necessary they may be to mankind, are natural goods, and have no place in economic consideration." "Man may be thankful for what nature has done beforehand in the case of economic goods, as it has spared him so much extra labour, but economy takes

[1] *Erklärung*, p. 273, etc. In the posthumous tract on "Capital" Rodbertus expresses himself more severely on the subject of private property in capital, and would have it redeemed, if not abolished (p. 116, etc.)

notice of them only in so far as labour has completed the work of nature."[1]

Now this is simply false. Even purely natural goods have a place in economic consideration, provided only they are scarce as compared with the need for them. If a lump of solid gold in the shape of a meteoric stone falls on a man's field, is it not to be economically considered? Or if a silver mine is discovered by chance on his estate, is the silver not to be economically considered? Will the owner of the field really pay no attention to the gold and silver given him by nature, or give them away, or waste them, simply because they were bestowed on him by nature without exertion on his part? Will he not preserve them just as carefully as he would gold and silver that he had earned by the labour of his hands; place them in security from the greed of others; cautiously convert them into money in the market—in short, treat them economically? And again, is it true that economy has regard to those goods which have cost labour only in so far as labour has completed the work of nature? If that were the case, men acting economically would have to put a cask of the most exquisite Rhine wine on the same level with a cask of well-made but naturally inferior country wine, for human labour has done pretty much the same for both. That, notwithstanding this, the Rhine wine is often valued economically at ten times the amount of the other, is a striking confutation of Rodbertus's theorem at the hands of everyday experience.

All this is so obvious that we might fairly expect Rodbertus to have taken every precaution to guard this, his first and most important fundamental proposition, against such objections. In this expectation, however, we are disappointed. With peculiar carelessness he is content on almost every occasion to assert this proposition in the tone of an axiom. Sometimes he appeals on its behalf to the authority of Adam Smith and Ricardo, and only on one single occasion does he say anything that might be construed as an attempt to give it any real foundation.

The critic will scarcely be satisfied with such poor support for a proposition so important. As regards the authorities appealed to, in a scientific discussion authorities in themselves

[1] *Soziale Frage*, p. 69.

prove nothing. Their strength is simply the strength of the arguments which they represent. But we shall shortly have an opportunity of convincing ourselves that Adam Smith and Ricardo merely assert the proposition as an axiom without giving any kind of argument for it. Moreover, as Knies has on a recent occasion very properly pointed out,[1] Adam Smith and Ricardo themselves have not held consistently to it.

In the one seriously argued passage Rodbertus says: "Every product that comes to us through labour in the shape of a good is, economically speaking, to be placed to the credit of human labour alone, because labour is the only original power, and also the only original cost with which human economy is concerned."[2] As regards this argument, however, one may seriously doubt, in the first place, whether the premiss made use of is itself correct, and Knies has shown that there is good reason for questioning it.[3] And in the second place, even if the premiss be correct, the conclusion is not necessarily so. Even if labour actually were the sole original power with which human economy has anything to do, I do not at all see why it should not be desirable to act economically in regard to some things besides "original powers." Why not in regard to certain results of these original powers, or to the results of other original powers? Why not, for instance, with the golden meteorite we spoke of? Why not with the precious stone we accidentally find? Why not with natural deposits of coal? Rodbertus has too narrow a conception both of the nature and of the motive of economy. We deal economically with the original power, labour, because, as Rodbertus quite correctly says, "Labour is limited by time and strength, because in being employed it is expended, and because in the end it robs us of our freedom." But all these are only secondary motives,

[1] *Kredit*, part second, p. 60, etc.

[2] *Erklärung und Abhilfe*, ii. p. 160; similarly *Soziale Frage*, p. 69.

[3] *Der Kredit*, part second, p. 69: "What Rodbertus brings forward as his sole reason, viz. that 'labour is the only original power, and also the only original cost with which human economy is concerned,' is simply, in point of fact, untrue. What surprising blindness it is not to see that in the case of a landlord the effectual power of the soil in our limited fields could not be allowed 'to lie dead' by uneconomic men, could not be wasted in growing weeds, etc. etc. So absurd an opinion would certainly in the long run justify any one in defending the proposition that the loss to a landlord of X acres, and the loss to a people's economy of Y square miles, represents no 'economical loss.'"

not the final motive for our economic conduct. In the last resort we deal economically with limited and toilsome labour because we should suffer loss of wellbeing by an uneconomic treatment. But exactly the same motive impels us to deal economically with every other useful thing which, as existing in a limited quantity, we could not want or lose without losing something of the enjoyment of life. It matters not whether it be an original power or not; whether the thing has cost the original power we call labour or not.

Finally, the position taken by Rodbertus becomes entirely untenable when he adds that goods are to be regarded as the products of material manual labour alone. This principle would forbid even direct intellectual guidance of labour from being recognised as having any productive function, and would lead to an amount of internal contradiction and false conclusion that leaves no doubt of its incorrectness. This, however, has been shown by Knies in such a striking way that it would be mere superfluous iteration to dwell further on the point.[1]

Thus in the very first proposition he has laid down Rodbertus comes into collision with fact. To be entirely just, however, I must here make one concession which Knies, as representing the Use theory, was unable to make. I admit that, in confuting this fundamental principle, the whole of Rodbertus's interest theory has not been confuted. The proposition is wrong; not, however, because it mistakes the part played by capital in the production of goods, but because it mistakes the part played by nature.

I believe with Rodbertus that, if we consider the result of all the stages of production as a whole, capital cannot maintain an independent place among the costs of production. It is not exclusively "previous labour," as Rodbertus thinks, but it

[1] See Knies, *Der Kredit*, part second, p. 64, etc.: "A man who wishes to 'produce' coal must not simply dig; he must dig in a particular place; in thousands of places he may perform the same material operation of digging without any result whatever. But if the difficult and necessary work of finding the proper place is undertaken by a separate person, say a geologist; if without some other and "intellectual power" no shaft is sunk, and so on, how can the 'economic' work be digging only? When the choice of materials, the decision on the proportions of the ingredients, and such like, are made by another person than by him who rolls the pills, are we to say that the economical value of this material body, this medicine, is a product of nothing but the hand labour employed in it?"

is partly, and indeed, as a rule, it is principally "previous labour": for the rest, it is valuable natural power stored up for human purposes. Where natural power is conspicuous—as in a production which, in all its stages, only makes use of free gifts of nature and of labour, or which makes use of such products as have themselves originated exclusively in free gifts of nature and in labour—in such cases we could, indeed, say with Rodbertus that the goods, economically considered, are products of labour only. Since then Rodbertus's fundamental error does not refer to the rôle of capital, but only to that of nature, the inferences regarding the nature of profit on capital which he deduces are not necessarily false. It is only if essential errors appear as well in the development of his theory that we may reject these inferences as false. Now such errors there undoubtedly are.

Not to make an unfair use of Rodbertus's first mistake, I shall, in the whole of the following examination, put all the hypotheses in such a way that the consequences of that mistake may be completely eliminated. I shall assume that all goods are produced only by the co-operation of labour and of free natural powers, and by the assistance exclusively of such objects of capital as have themselves originated only by the co-operation of labour and free natural powers, without the intervention of such natural gifts as possess exchange value. On this limited hypothesis it is possible for us to admit Rodbertus's fundamental proposition that goods, economically considered, cost labour alone. Let us now look farther.

The next proposition of Rodbertus runs thus: that, according to nature and the "pure idea of justice," the whole product, or the whole value of the product, ought to belong without deduction to the labourer who produced it. In this proposition also I fully concur. In my opinion no objection could be taken to its correctness and justice under the presupposition we have made. But I believe that Rodbertus, and all socialists with him, have a false idea of the actual results that flow from this true and just proposition, and are led by this mistake into desiring to establish a condition which does not really correspond with the principle, but contradicts it. It is remarkable that, in the many attempts at confutation that have been directed up till now against the Exploitation theory, this decisive point has been touched on only in the most superficial way, and never yet been placed in the proper light. It is on this account that I ask my readers to give some attention to the following argument; all the more so as it is by no means easy.

I shall first simply specify and then examine the blunder. The perfectly just proposition that the labourer should receive the entire value of his product may be understood to mean, either that the labourer should *now* receive the entire *present* value of his product, or should receive the entire *future* value of his product *in the future.* But Rodbertus and the socialists expound it as if it meant that the labourer should *now* receive the entire *future* value of his product, and they speak as if this were quite self-evident, and indeed the only possible explanation of the proposition.

Let us illustrate the matter by a concrete example. Suppose that the production of a steam-engine costs five years of labour, and that the price which the completed engine fetches is £550. Suppose further, putting aside meanwhile the fact that such work would actually be divided among several persons, that a worker by his own continuous labour during five years makes the engine. We ask, What is due to him as wages in the light of the principle that to the labourer should belong his entire product, or the entire value of his product? There cannot be a moment's doubt about the answer. The whole steam-engine belongs to him, or the whole of its price, £550. But at what time is this due to him? There cannot be the slightest doubt about that either. Clearly it is due on the expiry of five years. For of course he cannot get the steam-engine before it exists; he cannot take possession of a value of £550 created by himself before it is created. He will, in this case, have to get his compensation according to the formula, The whole future product, or its whole future value, at a future period of time.

But it very often happens that the labourer cannot or will not wait till his product be fully completed. Our labourer, for instance, at the expiry of a year, wishes to receive a part payment corresponding to the time he has worked. The question is, How is this to be measured in accordance with the above proposition? I do not think there can be a moment's doubt about the answer. The labourer has got his due if he now receives the whole of what he has made up till now. Thus, for example, if up till now he has produced a heap of brass, iron, or steel, in the raw state, then he will receive his due if he is handed over just this entire heap of brass, iron, or steel, or the entire value which this heap of materials has, and of course the value which it has *now*. I do not think that any socialist whatever could have anything to object to in this conclusion.

Now, how great will this value be in proportion to the value of the completed steam-engine? This is a point on which a superficial thinker may easily make a mistake. The point is, the labourer has up till now performed a fifth part of the technical work which the production of the whole engine requires. Consequently, on a superficial glance, one is tempted to infer that his present product will possess a fifth part of the value of the whole product—that is, a value of £110. On this view the labourer ought to receive a year's wage of £110.

This, however, is incorrect. £110 are a fifth part of the value of a steam-engine *when completed*. But what the labourer has produced up till now is not a fifth part of an engine that is already completed, but only a fifth part of an engine that will not be completed till four years more have elapsed. And these are two different things; not different in virtue of a sophistical quibble, but different in very fact. The one-fifth part has a different value from the other so surely as, in the valuation of to-day, an entire and finished engine has a different value from an engine that will only be ready for use in four years; so surely as, generally speaking, present goods have a different value in the present from future goods.

That present goods, in the estimation of the present time, in which our economical transactions take place, have a higher value than future goods of the same kind and quality, is one of the most widely known and most important economic facts. In the second volume of this work I shall have to make thorough examination into the causes to which this fact owes its origin, into the many and various ways in which it shows itself, and into the no less many and various consequences to which it leads in economic life; and that examination will be neither so easy nor so simple as the simplicity of the fundamental thought seems to promise. But in the meantime I think I may be allowed to appeal to the fact that present goods have a higher value than similar kinds of goods in the future, as one that is already put beyond dispute by the most ordinary experience of everyday life. If one were to give a thousand persons the choice whether they would rather take a gift of £100 to-day, or take it fifty years hence, surely all the thousand persons would prefer to take the £100 now. Or if one were to ask a thousand persons who wished a horse, and were disposed to give £100 for a good one, how much they would give *now* for a horse that they would only get possession of in ten or in fifty years, although as good an animal were guaranteed at that time, surely they would all name an infinitely smaller sum, if they named one at all; and thereby they would surely prove that everybody considers present goods to be more valuable than future goods of the same kind.

If this is so, that which has been made by our labourer in the first year, *i.e.* the fifth part of a steam-engine which is to be completed four years later, has not the entire value of a fifth part of an already completed engine, but has a smaller value.

How much smaller? That I cannot explain at present without anticipating my argument in a confusing way. Enough here to remark that it stands in a certain connection with the rate of interest usual in the country[1]—a rate which is a matter of experience—and with the remoteness of the period at which the whole product will be completed. If we assume the usual rate of interest to be 5 per cent, then the product of the first year's labour will, at the close of the year, be worth about £100.[2] Therefore, according to the proposition that the labourer ought to receive his whole product, or its whole value, the wages due him for the first year's labour will amount to the sum of £100.

If, notwithstanding the above deductions, any one should

[1] Of course I do not mean to put forward the rate of interest as the *cause* of the smaller valuation of future goods. I know quite well that interest and rate of interest can only be a result of this primary phenomenon. I am not here explaining but only depicting facts.

[2] The appropriateness of these figures, which seem strange at the first glance, will be seen immediately.

have the impression that this sum is too small, let me offer the following for his consideration. No one will doubt that the labourer gets his full rights if at the end of five years he receives the entire steam-engine, or the whole value of £550. Let us calculate then for comparison's sake what would be the value of the part-wage anticipated as above at the end of the fifth year? The £100 which the labourer has received at the end of the first year can be put out at interest for the next four years—that is, till the end of the fifth year; at the rate of 5 per cent (without calculating compound interest), the £100 may therefore increase by £20—this course being open even to the wage-paid labourer. Thus, it is clear, the £100 paid at the end of the first year are equivalent to £120 at the end of the fifth. If the labourer then, for the fifth part of the technical labour, receives £100 at the end of a year, clearly he is paid according to a scale which puts him in as favourable a position as if he had received £550 for the whole labour at the expiry of five years.

But what do Rodbertus and the socialists suppose to be the application of the principle that the labourer should receive the whole value of his product? They would have the whole value that the completed engine will have at the end of the process of production applied to the payment of wages, but they would have this payment not made at the conclusion of the whole production, but spread proportionally over the whole course of the labour. We should consider well what that means. It means that the labourer in our example, through this averaging of the part payments, is to receive in two and a half years the whole of the £550 which will be the value of the completed steam-engine at the end of five years.

I must confess that I consider it absolutely impossible to base this claim on these premises. How should it be according to nature, and founded on the pure idea of justice, that any one should receive at the end of two and a half years a whole that he will only have produced in five years? It is so little "according to nature," that, on the contrary, in the nature of things it could not be done. It could not be done even if the labourer were released from all the shackles of the much-abused wage-contract, and put in the most favourable position that can be conceived—that of undertaker in his own right. As labourer-undertaker he will certainly receive the whole of the £550, but not before they are produced; that is to say, not till the end of the five years. And how can that which the very nature of things denies to the undertaker himself be accomplished, in the name of the pure idea of justice, through the contract of wages?

To give the matter its proper expression, what the socialists would have is, that the labourers, by means of the wage-contract, should get *more* than they have made; more than they could get if they were undertakers on their own account; and more than they produce for the undertaker with whom they conclude the wage-contract. What they have created, and what they have just claim on, is the £550 at the end of the five years. But the £550 at the end of two and a half years which the socialists claim for them is more; if the interest stand at 5 per cent it is about as much as £620 at the end of five years. And this difference of value is not, as might be thought, a result of social institutions which have created interest and fixed it at 5 per cent—institutions that might be combated. It is a direct result of the fact that the life of all of us plays itself out in time; that to-day with its wants and cares comes before to-morrow; and that none of us is sure of the day after to-morrow. It is not only the capitalist greedy of profit, it is every labourer as well, nay, every human being that makes this distinction of value between present and future. How the labourer would cry out that he was defrauded if, instead of the 20s. which are due him for his week's wage to-day, one were to offer him 20s. a year hence! And that which is not a matter of indifference to the labourer is to be a matter of indifference to the undertaker! He is to give £550 at the end of two and a half years for the £550 which he is to receive, in the form of the completed product, only at the end of five years. That is neither just nor natural. What is just and natural is—I willingly acknowledge it again—that the labourer should receive the whole value, the £550, at the end of five years. If he cannot or will not wait five years, yet he should, all the same, have the value of his product; but of course the *present* value of his *present* product. This value, however, will require to be less than the corresponding proportion of the future value of the product of the technical labour, because in the economic world the law holds that the present value of future goods is less than that of present goods,—a law that owes its existence to no social or political institution, but directly to the nature of men and the nature of things.

If prolixity may ever be excused, it is in this instance, where we have to confute a doctrine with issues so extremely serious as the socialist Exploitation theory. Therefore at the risk of being wearisome to many of my readers I shall put a second concrete case, which, I hope, will afford me an opportunity of pointing out still more convincingly the blunders of the socialists.

In our first illustration we took no account of the division of labour. Let us now vary the hypothesis in such a way that at this point it will come nearer to the reality of economic life.

Suppose then that, in the making of the engine, five different workers take separate parts, each contributing one year's labour. One labourer obtains, say, by mining, the needful iron ore; the second smelts it; the third transforms the iron into steel; the fourth takes the steel and manufactures the separate constituent parts; and finally the fifth gives the parts their necessary connection, and in general puts the finishing touches to the work. As each succeeding labourer in this case, by the very nature of things, can only begin his work when his predecessors have finished theirs, the five years' work of our labourers cannot be performed simultaneously but only successively. Thus the making of the engine will take five years just as in the first illustration. The value of the completed engine remains, as before, £550. According to the proposition that the labourer is to receive the entire value of his product, how much will each of the five partners be able to claim for what he has done?

Let us try to answer this question first on the assumption that the claims of wages are to be adjusted, without the intervention of an outside undertaker, solely among the labourers themselves; the product obtained is to be divided simply among the five labourers. In this case two things are certain.

First, a division can only take place after five years, because before that date there is nothing suitable for division. For if one were now to give away in payment of wages to individuals, say the brass and iron which had been secured during the first two years, the raw material for the next stage of the work would be wanting. It is abundantly clear that the product acquired in the first years is necessarily withdrawn from any earlier division, and must remain bound up in the production till the close.

Second, it is certain that a total value of £550 will have to be divided among the five labourers.

In what proportion will it be divided?

Certainly not, as one might easily think at the first hasty glance, into equal parts. For this would be distinctly to favour those labourers whose labour comes at a later stage of the total production, in comparison with their colleagues who were employed in the earlier stages. The labourer who completed the engine would receive for his year's labour £110 immediately on the conclusion of his work; the labourer who turned out the separate constituent portions of the engine would receive the same sum, but must wait on his payment for a whole year after the completion of his year's labour; while that labourer who procured the ore would not receive the same amount of wages till four years after he had done his share of the work. As such a delay could not possibly be indifferent to the partners, every one would wish to undertake the final labour (which has not to suffer any postponement of wage), and nobody would be willing to take the preparatory stages. To find labourers to take the preparatory stages then, the labourers of the final stages would be compelled to grant to their colleagues who prepared the work a larger share in the final value of the product, as compensation for the postponement. The amount of this larger share would be regulated, partly by the period of the postponement, partly by the amount of difference that subsists between the valuation of present and the valuation of future goods,—a difference which would depend on the economic circumstances of our little society, and on its level of culture. If this difference, for instance, amounted to 5 per cent per annum, the shares of the five labourers would graduate in the following manner:—

The first labourer employed, who has to wait for his payment four years after the conclusion of his year's work, receives at the end of the fifth year .	£120
The second, who has to wait three years . . .	115
The third, who waits two years	110
The fourth, who waits one year	105
The last, who receives his wages immediately on the conclusion of his labour	100
Total	£550

That all the labourers should receive the same amount of £110 is only conceivable on the assumption that the difference of time is of no importance whatever to them, and that they find themselves quite as well paid with the £110, which they receive three or four years after, as if they had received the £110 immediately on the conclusion of their labour. But I need scarcely emphasise that such an assumption never corresponds with fact, and never can. That they should each receive £110 *immediately on the accomplishment of their labour* is, if a third party do not step in, altogether impossible.

It is well worth the trouble, in passing, to draw particular attention to one circumstance. I believe no one will find the above scheme of distribution unjust. Above all, as the labourers divide their own product among themselves alone, there cannot be any question of injustice on the part of a capitalist-undertaker. And yet that labourer who has performed the second last fifth part of the work does not receive the full fifth part of the final value of the product, but only £105; and the last labourer of all receives only £100.

Now assume, as is generally the case in actual fact, that the labourers cannot or will not wait for their wage till the very end of the production of the engine, and that they enter into a negotiation with an undertaker, with the view of obtaining a wage from him immediately on the performance of their labour, in return for which he is to become the owner of the final product. Assume, further, that this undertaker is a perfectly just and disinterested man, who is far from making use of the position into which the labourers are possibly forced, to usuriously depress their claim of wages; and let us ask, On what conditions will the wage-contract be concluded under such circumstances?

The question is tolerably easy to answer. Clearly the labourers will be perfectly justly treated if the undertaker offers them as wage the sums which they would have received as parts of the division, if they had been producing on their own account. This principle gives us first a firm standing ground for *one* labourer, namely, for the last. This labourer would in the former case have received £100 immediately after the accomplishment of his labour. This £100, therefore, to be perfectly just, the undertaker must now offer him. For the remaining labourers the above principle gives no immediate indication. The wages in this case are not paid at the same time as they would have been in the case of the division, and the sums paid in the former case cannot afford a direct standard. But we have another standing ground. As all five labourers have performed an equal amount towards the accomplishment of the work, in justice an equal wage is due to them; and where every labourer is to be paid immediately on the performance of his labour, this wage will be expressed by an equal amount. Therefore, in justice, all five labourers, at the end of their year's labour, will receive each £100.

If this seems too little, let me refer to the following simple calculation, which will demonstrate that the labourers receive quite the same value in this case as they would have received had they divided the whole product among themselves alone, in which case, as we have seen, the justice of the division would have been beyond question.

Labourer No. 5 receives, in the case of division, £100 immediately after the year's labour; in the case of the wage-contract he receives the same sum at the same time.

Labourer No. 4 receives, in the case of division, £105 a year after the termination of the year's labour; in the case of the wage-contract £100 immediately after the labour. If, in the latter case, he lets this sum lie at interest for a year he will be in exactly the same position as he would have been in the case of division; he will be in possession of £105 one year after the conclusion of his labour.

Worker No. 3 receives, in the case of division, £110 two years after the termination of his labour; in the wage-contract, £100 at once, which sum, placed at interest for two years, will increase to £110.

And in the same way, finally, the £100 which the first and second labourers receive are, with the addition of the respective interests, quite equivalent to the £120 and the £115 which, in the case of division, these two labourers would have received respectively four and three years after the conclusion of their labour.

But if each single wage under the contract is equal to the corresponding quota under the division, of course the sum of the wages must also be equal to the sum of the division quotas; the sum of £500 which the undertaker pays to the labourers immediately on the completion of their work is entirely equal in value to the £550 which, in the other case, would have been divided among the labourers at the end of the fifth year.

A higher wage payment, *e.g.* to pay the year's labour at £110 each labourer, is only conceivable in one of two cases; either if that which is not indifferent to the labourers, namely, the difference of time, were completely indifferent to the undertaker; or if the undertaker were willing to make a gift to the labourers of the difference in value between a present £110 and a future £110. Neither the one nor the other is to be expected of private undertakers, at least as a rule; nor do they deserve the slightest reproach on that account, and, least of all, the reproach of injustice, exploitation, or robbery.

There is only one personage from whom the labourers could expect such a treatment—the State. For on the one hand, the state, as a permanently existing entity, is not bound to pay as much regard to the difference of time in the outgoing and replacing of goods as the short-lived individual. And on the other hand, the state, whose end is the welfare of the whole, can, if it is a question of the welfare of a great number of the members, quit the strict standpoint of service and counter-service, and, instead of bargaining, may give. So then it certainly is conceivable that the state—but certainly only the state—assuming the function of a gigantic undertaker of production, might offer to the labourers as wage the full future value of their future product at once, that is, immediately after the accomplishment of their labour.

Whether the state *ought* to do this,—by which, in the view

of Socialism, the social question would be practically solved,—is a question of propriety which I have no intention of entering on at this moment. But this must be repeated with all emphasis: if the socialist state pays down at once, as wages to the labourer, the whole future value of his product, it is not a fulfilment of the fundamental law that the labourer should receive the value of his product as wages, but a *departure* from it on social and political grounds. And such a proceeding would not be the bringing back of a state of things that was in itself natural, or in accordance with the pure idea of justice,—a state of things only temporarily disturbed by the exploiting greed of the capitalists. It would be an artificial interference, with the intention of making something possible which, in the natural course of things, was not possible, and of making it possible by means of a disguised continuous gift from the magnanimous commonwealth state to its poorer members.

And now a brief practical application. It is easy to recognise that the method of payment which I have just now described in our illustration is that which actually does obtain in our economic world. In it the full final value of the product of labour is not divided as wages, but only a smaller sum; this smaller sum, however, being divided at an earlier period of time. Now, so long as the total sum of the wages spread over the course of the production is not less than the final value of the finished product by more than is necessary to make up the difference in the valuation of present as compared with future goods—in other words, so long as the sum of the wages does not differ from the final value of the product by more than the amount of the interest customary in the country—no curtailment is made on the claims that the workers have on the whole value of their product. They receive their whole product *according to its valuation at the point of time in which they receive their wages.* Only in so far as the total wages differ from the final value of the product by more than the amount of interest customary in the country, can there be, under the circumstances, any real exploitation of the labourers.[1]

[1] More exact criticism on this head I postpone till my second volume. To protect myself against misunderstandings, however, and particularly against the

To return to Rodbertus. The second, and most distinct blunder of which I have accused him in the foregoing, is that he interprets the proposition I have conceded (the labourer is to receive the whole value of his product) in an unwarrantable and illogical manner, as if it meant that the labourer is to receive now the whole value which his completed product will have at some future time.

If we inquire how it was that Rodbertus fell into this mistake, we shall find that the cause of it was another mistake, this being the third important error in the Exploitation theory. It is that he starts with the assumption that the value of goods is regulated solely by the amount of labour which their production has cost. If this were correct, then the first product, in which is embodied the labour of one year, must now possess a full fifth part of the value which the completed product, in which is embodied five years of labour, will possess. In this case the claim of the labourer to receive as wages a full fifth part of that completed value would be justified. But this assumption, as Rodbertus puts it, is undoubtedly false. To prove this I need not question in the least the theoretical validity of Ricardo's celebrated theory, that labour is the source and measure of all value. I need only point out the existence of a distinct exception to this law, noticed by Ricardo himself and discussed by him in detail in a separate chapter, but, strangely enough, passed

imputation of considering undertaking profit to be a "profit of plunder" when it exceeds the usual rate of interest, I may add a short note.

In the total difference, between value of product and wages expended, which falls to the undertaker, there may possibly be four constituents, essentially different from each other.

1. A premium for risk, to provide against the danger of the production turning out badly. Rightly measured, this will, on an average of years, be spent in covering actual losses, and this of course involves no curtailment of the labourer.

2. A payment for the undertaker's own labour. This of course is equally unobjectionable, and in certain circumstances, as in the using of a new invention of the undertaker, may be very highly assessed without any injustice being done to the labourer.

3. The compensation referred to in the text, viz. the compensation for difference of time between the wage payment and the realising of the final product, this being afforded by the customary interest.

4. The undertaker may possibly get an additional profit by taking advantage of the necessitous condition of the labourers to usuriously force down their wages.

Of these four constituents only the latter involves any violation of the principle that the labourer should receive the whole value of his product.

over without notice by Rodbertus. This exception is found in the fact that, of two goods which have cost an equal amount of labour to produce, that one obtains a higher exchange value the completion of which demands the greater advances of previous labour, or the longer period of time. Ricardo notices this fact in a characteristic manner. He declares (§ 4 of the first chapter of his *Principles*) that "the principle that the quantity of labour employed in the production of goods regulates their relative value, suffers a considerable modification by the employment of machinery and other fixed and durable capital," and further, in § 5, "on account of the unequal durability of capital, and of the unequal rapidity with which it is returned to its owner." That is to say, in a production where much fixed capital is used, or fixed capital of a greater durability, or where the time of turn-over on which the floating capital is paid back to the undertaker is longer, the goods made have a higher exchange value than goods which have cost an equal amount of labour, but into the production of which the elements just named do not enter, or enter in a lesser degree,—indeed an exchange value which is higher by the amount of the profit which the undertaker expects to obtain.

That this exception to the law of labour-value noticed by Ricardo really exists cannot be questioned, even by the most zealous advocates of that law. Just as little can it be questioned that, under certain circumstances, the consideration of the postponement may have even a greater influence on the value of goods than the consideration of the amount of labour-costs. I may remind the reader, for example, of the value of an old wine that has been stored up for scores of years, or of a hundred years old tree in the forest.

But on that exception hangs a tale. It does not require any great penetration to see that the principal feature of natural interest on capital is really involved in it. For when, on the division of the value, those goods that require for their production an advance of foregoing labour show a surplus of exchange value, it is just this surplus that remains in the hands of the capitalist-undertaker as profit. If this difference of value did not exist natural interest on capital would not exist either. This difference of value makes it possible, contains it, is identical with it.

Nothing is more easily demonstrated than this, if any proof is wanted of so obvious a fact. Supposing each of three goods requires for its making a year's labour, but a different length of time over which the labour is advanced. The first good requires only one year's advance of the year's labour; the second a ten years' advance; the third a twenty years' advance. Under these circumstances the exchange value of the first good will, and must be, sufficient to cover the wages of a year's labour, and, beyond that, one year's interest on the advanced labour. It is perfectly clear that the same exchange value cannot be sufficient to cover the wages of a year's labour, and a ten or twenty years' interest on the ten or twenty years' advance of labour as well. That interest can only be covered if and because the exchange value of the second and third good is correspondingly higher than that of the first good, although all three have cost an equal amount of labour. The difference of exchange value is clearly the source from which the ten and twenty years' interest flows, and the only source from which it can flow.

Thus this exception to the law of labour-value is nothing less than the chief feature in natural interest on capital. Any one who would explain natural interest must, in the first place, explain this; without an explanation of the exception here can be no explanation of the problem of interest. Now if, notwithstanding, in treatises on interest this exception is ignored, not to say denied, it is as gross a blunder as could well be conceived. When Rodbertus ignores the exception, it means nothing else than ignoring the chief part of what he ought to have explained.

Nor can one excuse Rodbertus's blunder by saying that he did not intend to lay down a rule which should hold in actual life, but only a hypothetical assumption by which he might carry through his abstract inquiries more easily and more correctly. It is true that Rodbertus, in some passages of his writings, does clothe the proposition, that the value of all goods is determined by their labour costs, in the form of a simple hypothesis.[1] But, firstly, there are many passages

[1] E.g. *Soziale Frage*, pp. 44, 107.

where Rodbertus expresses his conviction that his principle of value also holds in actual economic life.[1] And, secondly, a man may not assume anything that he likes, even as a simple hypothesis. That is to say, even in a purely hypothetical assumption, one may omit only such circumstances of actual fact as are irrelevant to the question under examination. But what is to be said for a theoretical inquiry into interest which at the critical point leaves out the existence of the most important feature; which gets rid of the principal part of what it had to explain with a "let us assume"?

On one point it may be admitted that Rodbertus is right: if we wish to discover a principle like that of land-rent or interest, we must "not let value dance up and down";[2] we must assume the validity of a fixed law of value. But is it not also a fixed law of value that goods which require a longer time between the expenditure of labour and their completion have, *ceteris paribus*, a higher value? And is not this law of value of fundamental importance in relation to the phenomenon of interest? And yet it is to be left out of account like an irregular accident of the circumstances of the market![3]

[1] *Soziale Frage*, pp. 113, 147. *Erklärung und Abhilfe*, i. p. 123. In the latter Rodbertus says: "If the value of agricultural and manufacturing product is regulated by the labour incorporated in it, as always happens on the whole, even where commerce is free," etc.

[2] *Ibid.* p. iii. n.

[3] The above was written before the publication of Rodbertus's posthumous work, *Capital*, in 1884. In it Rodbertus takes an exceedingly strange position towards our question,—a position which calls rather for a strengthening than a modification of the above criticism. He strongly emphasises the point that the law of labour value is not an exact law, but simply a law that determines the point towards which value will gravitate (p. 6, etc.) He even owns in as many words that, on account of the undertaker's claim on profit, a constant divergence takes place between the actual value of the goods and their value as measured by labour (p. 11, etc.) Only he makes the extent of this concession much too trifling when he assumes that the deviation obtains only in the relations of the different stages of production of one and the same good; and that the deviation does not obtain in the case of all the stages of production as a whole. That is, if the making of a good is divided into several sections of production, of which each section develops into a separate trade, according to Rodbertus the value of the separate product which is made in each individual section cannot remain in exact correspondence with the quantity of labour expended on it; because the undertakers of the later stages of production have to make a greater outlay for material, and therefore a greater expenditure of capital, and on that account have to calculate on a higher profit, which higher profit can only be provided by a relatively higher value of the product in question.

This singular omission is not without result. On the first result I have already touched. In overlooking the influence of time upon the value of products, Rodbertus could not avoid falling into the mistake of confounding the claim of the labourer to the whole present value of his product with the claim to its future value. Some other consequences we shall encounter shortly.

A fourth criticism which I have to make on Rodbertus is, that his doctrine contradicts itself in important points.

His entire theory of land-rent is based upon the repeatedly and emphatically expressed proposition that the absolute

However correct this is, it is clear that it does not go far enough. The divergence of the actual value of goods from the quantity of labour expended does not take place only between the fore-products of one good in relation to each other, in such a way that, in the course of the various stages of production, it cancels itself again through reciprocal compensation, and so the final result of all the stages of production, the goods ready for consumption, obeys the law of labour-value. On the contrary, the amount and the duration of the advance of capital definitively forces the value of *all* goods away from exact correspondence with their labour costs. To illustrate. Say that the production of a commodity requiring ninety days for its manufacture is divided into three stages of thirty days' labour in each. Rodbertus would say that the product of the first thirty days' labour might only attain the value of twenty-five days' labour, while the second thirty attained the value of thirty days', and the third thirty of thirty-five days' labour. But on the whole the final value of the product would be equal to ninety days' labour. But it is a matter of common experience that, in normal successive production, the value of such a commodity will increase during the three stages by a definite amount, say 30 + 31 + 32, and that the final product will be equal to, say, ninety-three days of labour; *i.e.* a value greater than the value of the labour incorporated in it by the amount of the customary interest.

Besides this, Rodbertus deserves the severest censure that, in spite of his own admission, he always persists in developing the law of the distribution of all goods in wages and rent under the theoretical hypothesis that all goods possess "normal value"; that is, a value that corresponds to their labour costs. He thinks he is justified in doing this because the "normal value, in regard to the derivation both of rent in general and of land-rent and capital-rent in particular, is the least captious; it alone does not quietly beg the question, and assume what was first to be explained by it, as every value does in which is included beforehand an element for rent."

Here Rodbertus is grievously mistaken. He begs the question quite as improperly as any of his opponents ever did; only in an opposite way. His opponents, by their assumptions, have begged the question of the existence of interest. Rodbertus has begged the question of its non-existence. In taking no notice of the constant divergence from "normal value" (which divergence gives natural interest its source and its nourishment), he himself altogether abstracts the chief feature in the phenomenon of interest.

amount of "rent" to be gained in a production does not depend upon the amount of the capital employed, but exclusively upon the amount of labour connected with the production.

Supposing that in a certain industrial production—for example, in a shoemaking business—ten labourers are employed. Each labourer produces per year a product of the value of £100. The necessary maintenance which he receives as wages claims £50 of this sum. Thus, whether the capital employed be large or small, the year's rent (as we shall call it with Rodbertus) drawn by the undertaker will amount to £500. If the capital employed amounts, say to £1000, namely, £500 for wages of labour and £500 for material, then the rent will make up 50 per cent of the capital. If in another production, say a jeweller's business, ten labourers likewise are employed, then, under the assumption that the value of products is regulated by the amount of labour incorporated in them, they also will produce another yearly product of £100 each, of which the half falls to them as wages, while the other half falls to the undertaker as rent. But as in this case the material, the gold, represents a considerably higher value than the leather of the shoemaking business, the total rent of £500 is distributed over a far larger business capital. Assume that the jeweller's capital amounts to £20,000, £500 for wages and £19,500 for material, then the rent of £500 will only show a 2½ per cent interest on the business capital.

Both examples are carried out entirely on the lines of Rodbertus's theory.

As in almost every "manufacture" the proportion between the number of the (directly and indirectly) employed labourers and the amount of business capital employed is different, it follows that, in almost every manufacture, business capital must bear interest at the most various possible rates. Now even Rodbertus does not venture to maintain that this is really the case in everyday life. On the contrary, in a remarkable passage in his theory of land-rent, he assumes that, in virtue of the competition of capitals over the whole field of manufacture, an equal rate of profit will become established. I will give the passage in his own words. After remarking that the rent derived from manufacture is considered wholly as profit on capital, since here it is exclusively wealth in the form of capital that is employed, he goes on to say:—

"This, further, will give a rate of profit which will tend to the equalisation of profits, and according to this rate, therefore, must be calculated that profit which, as one part of the rent falling to the raw product, accrues to the capital required for agriculture. For if, in consequence of the universal presence of value in exchange, there now exists a homonymous standard for indicating the ratio between return and resources, this standard, in the case of the portion of rent accruing to the capital employed in manufacture, also serves to indicate the ratio between profit and capital. In other words, it will be right to say that the profit in any trade amounts to ten per cent of the capital employed. This rate will then furnish a standard for the equalisation of profits. In whatever trade this rate indicates a higher profit, competition will cause increased investment of capital, and thereby cause a universal tendency towards the equalising of profits. Similarly no one will invest capital where he does not expect profit corresponding to this rate."

It will repay us to look more closely into this passage.

Rodbertus speaks of competition as that factor which will establish a uniform rate of profit over the field of manufacture. In what manner it will do so is only slightly indicated by him. He assumes that every rate of profit which is higher than the average level is reduced to the average by an increase of the supply of capital; and we may supplement this by saying that every lower rate of profit is raised to the average level by the flowing off of capital.

Let us continue a little farther the consideration of the process from the point at which Rodbertus breaks off. In what manner can an increased supply of capital level down the abnormally high rate of profit? Clearly in this way; that with the increased capital the production of the particular article is increased, and through the increase of supply the exchange value of the product is lowered till such time as after deducting the wages of labour, it only leaves the usual rate of profit as rent. In our above example of the shoemaking business we might evidently have pictured to ourselves the levelling down of the abnormal rate of profit of 50 per cent to the average rate of 5 per cent in the following manner. Attracted by the high rate of profit of 50 per cent, a great many persons will go into the shoemaking business. At the same time those who have been engaged in producing will extend their business. Thus the supply of shoes is increased, and their price and exchange value reduced. This process will continue till such time as the exchange value of the year's product of ten labourers in the shoemaking trade is reduced from £1000 to £550. Then the undertaker, after deducting £500 for necessary wages, has only £50 over as rent, which, distributed over a business capital of £1000, shows interest at the usual rate of 5 per cent. On reaching this point the exchange value of shoes will require to remain fixed if the profit in the shoemaking trade is not to become abnormal again, in which case a repetition of the process of levelling down would ensue.

On the same analogy, if the rate of profit in the jeweller's trade be under the average, say 2½ per cent, it will be raised to 5 per cent in this way. The profit in jewellery being so small, its manufacture will be curtailed, the supply of jewellery thereby reduced and its exchange value raised, till such time as the additional product of ten labourers in the jewellery trade reaches an exchange value of £1500. There now remain to the undertaker, after deducting £500 for necessary wages, £1000 as rent, this being interest on the business capital of £20,000 at the usual rate of 5 per cent. Thus is reached the resting-point at which the exchange value of jewellery, as in the former example the exchange value of shoes, may remain steady.

Before going farther I shall, by looking at the matter from another side, make entirely clear the important point that the levelling of abnormal profits cannot take place without a steady alteration in the exchange value of the products concerned.

If the exchange value of the products were to remain unaltered, then an insufficient rate of profit could only be raised to the normal level if the difference were made up at the cost of the labourers' necessary wages. For example, if the product of ten labourers in the jewellery manufacture retained without alteration the value of £1000, corresponding to the amount of labour expended, then evidently a levelling up of the rate of profit to 5 per cent—that is, an increase in the amount of profit from £500 to £1000—is only conceivable if the wages which the ten labourers have hitherto received were to be wholly withdrawn, and the entire product handed over to the capitalist as profit. To say nothing of the fact that such a supposition contains in itself a simple impossibility, I need merely point out that it is equally opposed to experience and to Rodbertus's own theory. It is contrary to experience; for experience shows that the usual effect of a restriction of supply in any branch of production is not a depression of the wages of labour, but a raising of the prices of product. And again, experience does not bear witness that the wages of labour, in such trades as require a large investment of capital, stand essentially lower than in other trades—which would necessarily be the case if the demand for a higher profit had to be met from wages instead of from prices of product. And it is also contrary to Rodbertus's own theory. For that theory assumes that the labourers in the long run always receive the amount of the necessary costs of their maintenance as wages,—a law which would be sensibly violated by this kind of equalisation.

It is just as easy to show conversely that, if the value of the products remained unaltered, a limitation of profits could only take place by raising the wages of the labourers in the trades concerned above the normal scale, which again, as we have said, is contrary to experience and to Rodbertus's own theory.

I may venture then to claim that I have described the process of the equalisation of profits in accordance with facts, and in accordance with Rodbertus's own hypothesis, when I assume that the return of profits to their normal level is brought about by means of a steady alteration in the exchange value of the products concerned. But if the year's product of ten labourers in the shoemaking trade has an exchange value of £550, and the year's product of ten labourers in the jewellery trade has an exchange value of £1500,—and it must be so if the equalisation of profits assumed by Rodbertus always takes place,—what becomes of his assumption that products exchange according to the labour incorporated in them? And if, from the employment of the same amount of labour, there result in the one trade

£50, in the other £1000 as rent, what becomes, further, of the doctrine that the amount of rent to be obtained in a production is not regulated by the amount of capital employed, but only by the amount of labour performed in it?

The contradiction in which Rodbertus has involved himself here is as obvious as it is insoluble. Either products do really exchange, in the long run, in proportion to the labour incorporated in them, and the amount of rent in a production is really regulated by the amount of labour employed in it,—in which case an equalisation of profits is impossible; or there is an equalisation of the profits of capital,—in which case it is impossible that products should continue to exchange in proportion to the labour incorporated in them, and that the amount of labour spent should be the only thing that determines the amount of rent obtainable. Rodbertus must have noticed this very evident contradiction if he had only devoted a little real reflection to the manner in which profits become equalised, instead of dismissing the subject in the most superficial way with his phrase about the equalising effect of competition.

But we are not done with criticism. The whole explanation of land-rent, which, with Rodbertus, is so intimately connected with the explanation of interest, is based upon an inconsistency so striking that the author's carelessness in not observing it is almost inconceivable.

There are only two possibilities here: either, as the effect of competition, an equalisation of profits does take place, or it does not. Assume first that it does take place. What justification has Rodbertus for supposing that the equalisation will certainly embrace the whole sphere of manufacture, but will come to a halt, as if spellbound, at the boundary of raw production? If agriculture promises an attractive profit why should not more capital flow to it? why should not more land be cultivated, or the land be more intensively cultivated, or cultivated by more improved methods, till the exchange value of raw products comes into correspondence with the increased capital now devoted to agriculture, and yields to it also no more than the common rate of profit? If the "law" that the amount of rent is not regulated by the outlay of capital, but only by the amount of labour expended, has not prevented equalisation in manufacture, how could it prevent it in raw production? But what in that case would become of the constant surplus over the usual rate of profit, the land-rent?

Or assume that an equalisation does not take place. In that case, there being no universal rate of profit, then in agriculture, as in everything else, there is no definite rule as to how much "rent" one may calculate as profit of capital. And, finally, there is no division line between capital and rent of land.

Therefore, in either case, whether an equalisation of profits does take place or does not, Rodbertus's theory of land-rent hangs in the air. There is contradiction upon contradiction, and that, moreover, not in trifles, but in the fundamental doctrines of the theory.

My criticism has hitherto been directed to the individual parts of Rodbertus's theory. I may conclude by putting the theory as a whole to the test. If correct, it must be competent to give a satisfactory explanation of the phenomenon of interest as presented in actual economic life, and, moreover, of all the essential forms in which it presents itself. If it cannot do so, it is self-condemned; it is not correct.

I now maintain, and shall attempt to prove, that although Rodbertus's Exploitation theory might possibly account for the interest borne by that part of capital which is invested in wages, it is absolutely impossible for it to explain the interest on that part of capital which is invested in the materials of manufacture. Let the reader judge.

A jeweller, whose chief business it is to make strings of pearls, employs annually five labourers to make strings to the value of £100,000, and sells them on an average in a year's time. He will accordingly have a capital of £100,000 constantly invested in pearls, which, at the usual rate of interest, must yield him a clear annual profit of £5000. We now ask, How is it to be explained that he gets this income?

Rodbertus answers, Interest on capital is a profit of plunder, got by curtailing the natural and just wages of labour. Wages of what labour? Of the five labourers who sorted and strung the pearls? That cannot well be; for if, by curtailing the just wages of the five labourers, one could gain £5000, then the just wages of these labourers must, in any case, have amounted to more than £5000. That is to say, these wages must have amounted, in any case, to more than £1000 per man,—a height of just wages that can hardly be taken seriously, especially as the business of sorting and stringing pearls is very little above the character of unskilled labour.

But let us look a little farther. Perhaps it is the labourers of an earlier stage of production from the product of whose labour the jeweller obtains his stolen profit; say the pearl-fishers. But the jeweller has not come into contact at all with these labourers, for he buys his pearls direct from an undertaker of pearl-fishing, or from a middleman; he has therefore had no opportunity whatever of deducting from the pearl-fishers a part of their product, or a part of the value of their product. But perhaps the undertaker of pearl-fishing has done so instead of him, so that the jeweller's profit originates in a deduction which the undertaker of the pearl-fishing has made from the wages of his labourers. That, however, is impossible; for clearly the jeweller would make his profit even if the undertaker of the pearl-fishing had made no deduction whatever from the wages of his labourers. Even if this latter undertaker were to divide among his labourers as wages the whole £100,000 that the pearls so obtained are worth—the whole £100,000 he receives from the jeweller as purchase money—then it only comes to this, that *he* makes no profit. It in no wise follows that the jeweller loses his profit. For to the jeweller it is a matter of complete indifference how this purchase money which he pays is distributed, so long as the price is not raised. Whatever then be the flights of our fancy, we shall seek in vain for the labourers from whose just wages the jeweller's profit of £5000 could possibly have been withheld.

Perhaps, however, even after this illustration there may be some readers still unconvinced. Perhaps they may think it certainly a little strange that the labour of the five pearl stringers should be the source from which the jeweller can exploit so considerable a profit as £5000, but yet not quite inconceivable. Let me therefore bring forward another and still more striking illustration,—a good old example by which many an interest theory has already been tested and found false.

The owner of a vineyard has harvested a cask of good young wine. Immediately after the vintage it has an exchange value of £10. He lets the wine lie undisturbed in the cellar, and after a dozen years the wine, now of course an old wine, has an exchange value of £20. This is a well-known fact. The difference of £10 falls to the owner of the wine as interest on the capital contained in the wine. Now who are the labourers that are exploited by this profit of capital?

During the storage there has been no further labour expended on the wine. The only conceivable thing is that the exploitation has been at the expense of those labourers who produced the new wine. The owner of the vineyard has paid them too small a wage. But I ask, How much ought he "in justice" to have paid them as wage? Even if he pays them the entire £10, which was the value of the new wine at the time of harvest, there stills remains to him the increment in value of £10, which Rodbertus brands as profit of plunder. Indeed even if he pays them £12 or £15 as wages, the accusation of plundering will still hang over him; he will only be free from it if he has paid the full £20. Now can any one seriously ask that £20 should be paid as "just wages of labour" for a product that is not worth more than £10? Does the owner know beforehand whether the product will ever be worth £20? Is it not possible that he might be forced, contrary to his original intention, to use or to sell the wine before the expiry of twelve years? And would he not then have paid £20 for a product that was never worth more than £10 or perhaps £12? And then, how is he to pay the labourers who produce that other new wine which he sells at once for £10? Is he to pay them also £20? Then he will be ruined. Or only £10? Then different labourers will receive different wages for precisely similar work, which again is unjust; not to mention the fact that a man cannot very well know beforehand whose product it is that will be sold at once, and whose stored up for a dozen years.

But still further. Even a £20 wage for a cask of new wine would not be enough to protect the vine-grower from the accusation of robbery; for he might let the wine lie in the cellar twenty-four years instead of twelve, and then it would be worth not £20 but £40. Is he then, justly speaking, bound to pay the labourers who, twenty-four years before that, have produced the wine, £40 instead of £10? The idea is too absurd. But if he pays them only £10 or £20, then he makes a profit on capital, and Rodbertus declares that he has curtailed the labourer's just wage by keeping back a part of the value of his product!

I scarcely think any one will venture to maintain that the cases of interest which have been brought forward, and the numerous cases analogous to them, are explained by Rodbertus's theory. But a theory which has failed to explain any important part of the phenomena to be explained cannot be the true one, and so this final examination brings us to the same result as the detailed criticism which preceded it might lead us to expect. Rodbertus's Exploitation theory is, in its foundation and in its conclusions, wrong; it is in contradiction with itself and with the circumstances of actual life.

The nature of my critical task is such that, in the foregoing pages, I could not choose but confine myself to one side—that of pointing out the errors into which Rodbertus had fallen. I consider it due to the memory of this distinguished man to acknowledge, in equally candid terms, his conspicuous merits as regards the development of the theory of political economy. Unfortunately, to dwell on these lies beyond the limits of my present task.

CHAPTER III

MARX

MARX[1] starts from the proposition that the exchange value[2] of all goods is regulated entirely by the amount of labour which their production costs. He lays much more emphasis on this proposition than does Rodbertus. While Rodbertus only mentions it incidentally, in the course of his argument as it were, and puts it very often in the shape of a hypothetical assumption without wasting any words in its proof, Marx makes it his fundamental principle, and goes thoroughly into statement and explication. To be just to the peculiar dialectical style of the author I must give the essential parts of the theory in his own words.

"The utility of a thing gives it a value in use. But this utility is not something in the air. It is limited by the properties of the commodity, and has no existence apart from that commodity. The commodity itself, the iron, corn, or diamond, is therefore a use value or good. . . . Use values constitute the matter of wealth, whatever be their social form. In the social form we are about to consider they constitute at the same time the material substratum of exchange value. Exchange value in the first instance presents itself as the quantitative

[1] *Zur Kritik der politischen-Oekonomie*, Berlin, 1859. *Das Kapital, Kritik der politischen-Oekonomie*, vol. i. first edition, Hamburg, 1867; second edition, 1872. English translation by Moore and Aveling, Sonnenschein, 1887. I quote from *Das Kapital* as the book in which Marx stated his views last and most in detail. On Marx also Knies has made some very valuable criticisms, of which I make frequent use in the sequel. Most of the other attempts to criticise and refute Marx's work are so far below that of Knies in value that I have not found it useful to refer to them.

[2] With Marx simply called Value.

relation, the proportion in which use values of one kind are exchanged for those of another kind, a relation constantly changing with time and place. Hence exchange value seems to be something accidental and purely relative, and an intrinsic value in exchange seems a contradiction in terms. Let us look at the matter more closely.

"A single commodity, *e.g.* a quarter of wheat, exchanges with other articles in the most varying proportions. Still its exchange value remains unaltered, whether expressed in X boot-blacking, Y silk, or Z money. It must therefore have a content distinct from those various forms of expression. Now let us take two commodities, wheat and iron. Whatever be the proportion in which they are exchangeable, it can always be represented by an equation, in which a given quantity of wheat appears as equal to a certain quantity of iron. For instance, 1 quarter wheat = 1 cwt. of iron. What does this equation tell us? It tells us that there is a common element of equal amount in two different things—in a quarter of wheat and in a cwt. of iron. The two things are therefore equal to a third, which in itself is neither the one nor the other. Each of the two, so far as it is an exchange value, must therefore be reducible to that third. . . . This common element cannot be a geometrical, physical, chemical, or other natural property of the commodities. Their physical properties only come into consideration so far as they make the commodities useful; that is, make them use values. But, on the other hand, the exchange relation of goods evidently involves our disregarding their use value. Within this relation one use value counts for just as much as any other, provided only it be present in due proportion. Or, as old Barbon says, "one sort of wares is as good as another if the value be equal." There is no difference or distinction in things of equal value. One hundred pounds' worth of lead or iron is of as great a value as one hundred pounds' worth of silver and gold." As use values, commodities are, first and foremost, of different qualities; as exchange values they can only be of different quantities, and contain therefore not an atom of use value.

"If then we disregard the use value of commodities, they have only one common property left, that of being products of labour. But even as the product of labour they have changed in our hand. For if we disregard the use value of a commodity, we disregard also the special material constituents and shapes which give it a use value. It is no longer a table, a house, yarn, or any other useful thing. All its sensible qualities have disappeared. Nor is it any longer the product of the labour of the joiner, the mason, the spinner, or of any other distinct kind of productive labour. With the useful character of the products of labour disappears the useful character of the labours embodied in them, and also the different concrete forms of these labours; they are no longer distinguished from each other, but are all reduced to equal human labour, abstract human labour.

"Consider now what is left. It is nothing but the same immaterial objectivity, a mere congelation of homogeneous human labour, *i.e.* of labour power expended without regard to the form of its expenditure. All that these things now tell us is that human labour was expended in their production, that human labour is stored up in them; as crystals of this common social substance they are—Values. . . . A use value or good, therefore, only has a value because abstract human labour is objectified or materialised in it."

As labour is the source of all value, so, Marx continues, the amount of the value of all goods is measured by the quantity of labour contained in them, or in labour time. But not by that particular labour time which the individual who made the good might find necessary, but by the "socially necessary labour time." This Marx explains as the "labour time required to produce a use value under the conditions of production that are socially normal at the time, and with the socially necessary degree of skill and intensity of labour." It is only the quantity of socially necessary labour, or the labour time socially necessary for the making of a use value, that determines the amount of the value. "The single commodity here is to be counted as the average sample of its class. Commodities, therefore, in which equally great amounts of labour are contained, or which could be made in the same labour time, have the same amount of value. The value of one commodity is to the value of every other commodity as the labour time necessary to the production of the one is to the labour time necessary to the production of the other. . . . As values all commodities are only definite amounts of congealed labour time."[1]

Later on I shall try to estimate the value of these fundamental principles which Marx puts forward on the subject of value. In the meantime I go on to his theory of interest.

Marx finds the problem of interest in the following phenomenon. The usual circulation of commodities carried on by the medium of exchange, money, proceeds in this way: one man sells the commodity which he possesses for money, in order to buy with the money another commodity which he requires for his own purposes. This course of circulation may be expressed by the formula, Commodity — Money — Commodity. The starting point and the finishing point of the circulation is a commodity, though the two commodities be of different kinds.

"But by the side of this form of exchange we find another and specifically different form, namely, Money—Commodity—Money; the transformation of money into a commodity and the transformation back again of the commodity into money—buying in order to sell. Money that in its movement describes this circulation becomes capital, and is already capital when it is dedicated to be used in this way. . . . In the simple circulation of commodities the two extremes have the same economic form. They are both commodities. They are also of the same value. But they are qualitatively different use values, as, for instance, wheat and clothes. The essence of the movement consists in the exchange of those products in which the labour of society is embodied. It is different with the circulation M—C—M. At the first glance it looks as if it were meaningless, because tautological. Both extremes have the same economic form. They are both money, and therefore not qualitatively different use values, for money is but the converted form of commodities in which their different use values are lost. First to exchange £100 for wool, and then to exchange the same wool again for £100—that is, in a roundabout way to exchange money for money, like for like—seems a transaction as purposeless as it is absurd. One sum of money can only be distinguished from another sum of money by its amount. The process M—C—M does not owe its character therefore to any qualitative difference

[1] *Das Kapital*, second edition, p. 10, etc.

between its extremes, since they are both money, but only to this quantitative difference. At the end of the process more money is withdrawn from the circulation than was thrown in at the beginning. The wool bought for £100 is sold again, that is to say, for £100 + £10, or £110. The complete form of this process therefore is M—C—M′, where $M' = M + \Delta M$; that is, the sum originally advanced plus an increment. This increment, or surplus over original value, I call Surplus Value (*Mehrwerth*). The value originally advanced, therefore, not only remains during the circulation, but changes in amount; adds to itself a surplus value, or makes itself value. And this movement changes it into capital" (p. 132).

"To buy in order to sell, or, to put it more fully, to buy in order to sell at a higher price, M—C—M′, seems indeed the peculiar form characteristic of one kind of capital only, merchant capital. But industrial capital also is money that changes itself into commodities, and by the sale of these commodities changes back into more money. Acts which take place outside the sphere of circulation, between the buying and the selling, do not make any alteration in the form of the movement. Finally, in interest bearing capital the circulation M—C—M′ presents itself in an abridged form, shows its result without any mediation, *en style lapidaire* so to speak, as M—M′; *i.e.* money which is equal to more money, value which is greater than itself" (p. 138).

Whence then comes the surplus value?

Marx works out the problem dialectically. First he declares that the surplus value can neither originate in the fact that the capitalist, as buyer, buys commodities regularly under their value, nor in the fact that the capitalist, as seller, sells them regularly over their value. It cannot therefore originate in the circulation. But neither can it originate outside the circulation. For "outside the circulation the owner of the commodity only stands related to his own commodity. As regards its value the relation is limited to this, that the commodity contains a quantity of the owner's own labour measured by definite social laws. This quantity of labour is expressed in the amount of the value of the commodity produced, and, since the amount of the value is expressed in money, the quantity of labour is expressed in a price, say £10. But the owner's labour does not represent itself in the value of the commodity and in a surplus over its own value—in a price of £10, which is at the same time a price of £11—in a value which is greater than itself! The owner of a commodity can by his labour produce value, but not value that evolves itself. He can raise the value of a commodity by adding new value to that which is there already, through new labour; as, *e.g.* in making boots out of leather. The same material has now more value, because it contains a greater amount of labour. The boot then has more value than the leather, but the value of the leather remains as it was. It has not evolved itself; it has not added a surplus value to itself during the making of the boot" (p. 150).

And now the problem stands as follows: "Our money owner, who is yet only a capitalist in the grub stage, must buy the commodities at their value, must sell them at their value, and yet at the end of the process must draw out more money than he put in. The bursting of the grub into the butterfly must take place in the sphere of circulation, and not in the sphere of circulation. These are the conditions of the problem. *Hic Rhodus, hic salta!*" (p. 150).

The solution Marx finds in this, that there is one commodity whose use value possesses the peculiar quality of being the source of exchange value. This commodity is the capacity of labour, or Labour Power. It is offered for sale on the market under the double condition that the labourer is personally free, for otherwise it would not be his labour power that would be on sale, but his entire person as a slave; and that the labourer is deprived of "all things necessary for the realising of his labour power," for otherwise he would prefer to produce on his own account, and to offer his *products* instead of his labour power for sale. It is by trading in this commodity that the capitalist receives the surplus value. In the following way.

The value of the commodity, labour power, like that of all other commodities, is regulated by the labour time necessary for its reproduction; that is, in this case, by the labour time that is necessary to produce as much means of subsistence as are required for the maintenance of the labourer. Say, for instance, that, to produce the necessary means of subsistence for one day, a social labour time of six hours is necessary, and assume that this same labour time is embodied in three shillings of money, then the labour power of one day is to be bought for three shillings. If the capitalist has completed this purchase, the use value of the labour power belongs to him, and he realises it by getting the labourer to work for him. If he were to get him to work only so many hours per day as are incorporated in the labour power itself, and as must have been paid in the buying of the same, no surplus value would emerge. For, according to the assumption, six hours of labour cannot put into the product in which they are incorporated any greater value than three shillings, and so much the capitalist has paid as wage. But this is not the way in which capitalists act. Even if they have bought the labour power for a price that only corresponds to six hours' labour time, they get the worker to labour the whole day for them. And now, in the product made during this day, there are more hours of labour incorporated than the capitalist was obliged to pay for; he has consequently a greater value than the wage he has paid, and the difference is the "surplus value" that falls to the capitalist.

To take an example. Suppose that a worker can in six hours spin 10 lbs. of wool into yarn. Suppose that this wool for its own production has required twenty hours of labour, and possesses, accordingly, a value of 10s. Suppose, further, that during the six hours of spinning the spinner uses up so much of his tools as corresponds to the labour of four hours, and represents consequently a value of 2s. The total value of the means of production consumed in the spinning will amount to 12s., corresponding to twenty-four hours' labour. In the spinning process the wool "absorbs" other six hours of labour; the yarn spun is therefore, on the whole, the product of thirty hours of labour, and will have in conformity a value of 15s. Under the assumption that the capitalist gets the hired labourer to work only six hours in the day, the making of the yarn has cost the capitalist quite 15s.—10s. for wool; 2s. for wear and tear of tools; 3s. for wage of labour. There is no surplus value here.

Quite otherwise is it if the capitalist gets the labourer to work twelve hours a day for him. In twelve hours the labourer works up 20 lbs. of wool, in which previously forty hours of labour have been incorporated, and which, consequently, are worth 20s.; further he uses up in tools the product of eight hours' labour, of the value of 4s.; but during a day he adds to the raw material twelve hours' labour,—that is, a new value of 6s. And now the balance-sheet stands as follows: The yarn produced during a day has cost in all sixty hours' labour; it has therefore a value of 30s. The outlays of the capitalist amounted to 20s. for wool, 4s. for wear and tear of tools, and 3s. for wage; in all, therefore, only 27s. There remains now a "surplus value" of 3s.

Surplus value therefore, according to Marx, is a consequence of the capitalist getting the labourer to work a part of the day for him without paying for it. In the labourer's work day two portions may be distinguished. In the first part, the "necessary labour time," the worker produces the means of his own maintenance, or the value of that maintenance; for this part of his labour he receives an equivalent in wage. During the second portion, the "surplus labour time," he is "exploited"; he produces "surplus value" without receiving any equivalent whatever for it.[1] "Capital is therefore not merely a command over labour, as Adam Smith calls it. It is essentially a command over unpaid labour. All surplus value, in whatever particular form it may afterwards crystallise itself, be it profit, interest, rent, or any other, is in substance only the material shape of unpaid labour. The secret of the power of capital to evolve value is found in its disposal over a definite quantity of the unpaid labour of others" (p. 554).

In this statement the careful reader will have recognised—if partly in a somewhat altered dress—all the essential propositions combined by Rodbertus in his theory of interest: the doctrine that the value of goods is measured by quantity of labour; that labour alone creates all value; that in the loan contract the worker receives less value than he creates, and that necessity compels him to acquiesce in this; that the capitalist appropriates the surplus to himself; and that consequently the profit so obtained has the character of plunder from the produce of the labour of others.

[1] *Das Kapital*, p. 205, etc.

On account of the substantial agreement of both theories, or, to speak more correctly, of both ways of formulating the same theory, almost everything that I have adduced against Rodbertus's doctrine has equal force against Marx. I may therefore limit myself now to some supplementary remarks that I consider necessary; partly for the purpose of adapting my criticism in particular places to Marx's peculiar statement of the theory, partly also for dealing with some new matter introduced by Marx.

Of this by far the most important is the attempt to prove the proposition that all value rests on labour, instead of merely asserting it. In criticising Rodbertus I laid as little emphasis on that proposition as he had done. I was content to point out some undoubted exceptions to it, but I did not go to the root of the matter. In the case of Marx I neither can nor will intermit this. It is true that in doing so I venture on a field already traversed many a time, and by distinguished writers. I can scarcely hope then to bring forward much that is new. But in a book which has for its subject the critical statement of theories of interest, it would ill become me to avoid the thorough criticism of a proposition which has been placed at the head of one of the most important of these theories, as its most important fundamental principle. And, unfortunately, the present position of our science is not such that it can be considered superfluous once more to undertake this task. Although this proposition is, in truth, nothing more than a fallacy once perpetrated by a great man, and repeated ever since by a credulous crowd, in our day it is like to be accepted in widening circles as a kind of gospel.

For the doctrine that the value of all goods depends upon labour, the proud names of Adam Smith and Ricardo have usually been claimed both as authors and authorities. This is correct; but it is not altogether correct. The doctrine is to be found in the writings of both; but Adam Smith now and then contradicts it,[1] and Ricardo so narrows the

[1] *e.g.* when in the fifth chapter of the second book he says of the farmer: "Not only his labouring servants, but his labouring cattle are productive labourers;" and further, "In agriculture too Nature labours along with man, and though her labour costs no expense, its produce has its value as well as that of the most expensive workmen." See also Knies, *Der Kredit*, part ii. p. 62.

sphere within which it is valid, and surrounds it with such important exceptions, that it is scarcely justifiable to assert that he has represented labour as the universal and the exclusive principle of value. He begins his *Principles* with the express assertion that the exchange value of goods has its origin in two sources—in their scarcity and in the quantity of labour that their production has cost. Certain goods, such as rare statues and paintings, get their value exclusively from the former source, and it is only the value of those goods that can be multiplied, without any assignable limit, by labour, which is determined by the amount of labour they cost. These latter, indeed, in Ricardo's opinion, constitute "by far the greatest part of those goods which are the objects of desire"; but even in regard to them Ricardo finds himself compelled to a further limitation. He has to admit that, even in their case, the exchange value is not determined exclusively by labour; that time also—the time elapsing between the advancing of the labour and the realising of the finished product—has a considerable influence on it.[1]

It appears then that neither Adam Smith nor Ricardo have stated the principle that stands in their name in such an unqualified way as they generally get credit for. Still, to a certain extent, they have stated it, and we have to inquire on what grounds they did so.

On seeking to answer this question we shall make a remarkable discovery. It is that neither Adam Smith nor Ricardo have given any reason for this principle, but simply asserted its validity as something self-explanatory. The celebrated passage in Adam Smith, which Ricardo afterwards verbally adopted in his own doctrine, runs thus: "The real price of everything, what everything really costs to the man who wants to acquire it, is the toil and trouble of acquiring it. What everything is really worth to the man who has acquired it, and who wants to dispose of it, or exchange it for something else, is the toil and trouble which it can save to himself, and which it can impose upon other people."[2]

Let us pause here a moment. The tone in which Adam

[1] See above, p. 354, and Knies as before, p. 60, etc.

[2] *Wealth of Nations*, book i. chap. v. (p. 13 of M'Culloch's edition); Ricardo, *Principles*, chap. i.

Smith speaks signifies that the truth of these words must be immediately obvious. But is it really obvious? Are value and trouble really so closely related that the very conception of them at once carries conviction that trouble is the ground of value? I do not think any unprejudiced person will maintain this. That I have given myself trouble about a thing is one fact; that the thing is worth the trouble is another and a different fact; and that the two facts do not always go hand in hand is too well confirmed by experience for any doubt about it to be possible. It is confirmed by every one of the innumerable cases in which, from want of technical skill, or from unsuccessful speculation, or simply from ill-luck, labour is every day being followed by a valueless result. But not less is it confirmed by every one of the numerous cases where little trouble is rewarded with high gains; such as the occupation of a piece of land, the finding of a precious stone, the discovery of a gold mine.

But not to mention cases that may be considered as exceptions from the regular course of things, it is a fact, as indubitable as it is perfectly normal, that the same amount of labour exerted by different persons has a quite different value. The result of one month's labour on the part of a famous artist is, quite regularly, a hundred times more valuable than the same period of labour on the part of a common carpenter. How could that be possible if trouble were really the principle of value? How could it be possible if, in virtue of some immediate psychological connection, we were forced to base our estimate of value on the consideration of toil and trouble, and only on that consideration? [1] Or perhaps it is that nature is so

[1] Adam Smith gets rid of the difficulty mentioned in the text as follows: "If the one species of labour requires an uncommon degree of dexterity and ingenuity, the esteem which men have for such talents will naturally give a value to their produce superior to what would be due to the time employed about it. Such talents can seldom be acquired, but in consequence of long application and the superior value of their produce may frequently be more than a reasonable compensation for the time and labour which must be spent in acquiring them" (book i. chap. vi.)

The insufficiency of this explanation is obvious. In the first place, it is clear that the higher value of the products of exceptionally skilled men rests on a quite different foundation from the "esteem which men have for such talents." How many poets and scholars does the public leave to starve in spite of the very high esteem which it pays to their talents, and how many unscrupulous speculators has it rewarded for their adroitness by hundreds of thousands, although it

aristocratic that its psychological laws force our spirit to reckon the trouble of a skilled artist a hundred times more valuable than the more modest trouble of a carpenter! I think that any one who reflects for a little, instead of blindly taking it on trust, will be convinced that there is no immediately obvious and essential connection between trouble and value, such as the passage in Adam Smith seems to assume.

But does the passage actually refer to exchange value, as has been tacitly assumed? I do not think that any one who reads it with unprejudiced eye can maintain that either. The passage applies neither to exchange value, nor to use value, nor to any other kind of value in the strict scientific sense. The fact is—as shown by the employment of the expression "worth" instead of value—that in this case Adam Smith has used the word in that very wide and vague sense which it has in everyday speech. And this is very significant. Feeling involuntarily that, at the bar of strictly scientific reflection, his proposition could not be admitted, he turns to the loose impressions of everyday life, and makes use of the ill-defined expressions of everyday life,—with a result, as experience has shown, very much to be deplored in the interests of the science.

Finally, how little the whole passage can lay claim to scientific exactitude is shown by the fact that, even in the few words that compose it, there is a contradiction. In one breath he claims for two things the distinctive property of being the principle of "real" value: first, for the trouble that a man can save himself through the possession of a good; second, for the trouble that a man can impose upon other people. But these are two quantities which, as every one knows, are not absolutely identical. Under the regime of the division of labour, the trouble which I personally would be obliged to undergo to obtain possession of a thing I desired is usually much greater than the trouble with which a labourer technically trained produces it. Which of these two troubles, the "saved"

has no esteem whatever for their "talents"! But suppose esteem were the foundation of value, in that case the law that value depends on trouble would evidently not be confirmed but violated. If, again, in the second of the above sentences, Adam Smith attempts to trace that higher value to the trouble expended in acquiring the dexterity, by his insertion of the word "frequently" he confesses that it will not hold in all cases. The contradiction therefore remains.

or the "imposed," are we to understand as determining the real value?

In short, the celebrated passage where our old master Adam Smith introduces the Labour Principle into the theory of value is as far as possible from being the great and well grounded scientific principle it has usually been considered. It does not of itself carry conviction. It is not supported by a particle of evidence. It has the slovenly dress and the slovenly character of a popular expression. Finally, it contradicts itself. That, notwithstanding this, it found general acceptance is due, in my opinion, to the coincidence of two circumstances; first, that an Adam Smith said it, and, second, that he said it without adducing any evidence for it. If Adam Smith had but addressed a single word in its proof to the intelligence of his readers, instead of simply appealing to their immediate impressions, they would have insisted upon putting the evidence before the bar of their intelligence, and then the absence of all real argument would infallibly have shown itself. It is only by taking people by surprise that such propositions can win acceptance.

Let us see what Adam Smith, and after him, Ricardo, says further. "Labour was the first price—the original purchase money that was paid for all things." This proposition is comparatively inoffensive, but it has no bearing on the principle of value.

"In that early and rude state of society which precedes both the accumulation of stock and the appropriation of land, the proportion between the quantities of labour necessary for acquiring different objects seems to be the only circumstance which can afford any rule for exchanging them for one another. If, among a nation of hunters, for example, it usually cost twice the labour to kill a beaver which it does to kill a deer, one beaver should naturally exchange for or be worth two deer. It is natural that what is usually the produce of two days' or two hours' labour should be worth double of what is usually the produce of one day's or one hour's labour."

In these words also we shall look in vain for any trace of a rational basis for the doctrine. Adam Smith simply says, "seems to be the only circumstance," "should naturally," "it is natural," and so on, but throughout he leaves it to the reader to convince himself of the "naturalness" of such judgments—a task, be it remarked in passing, that the critical reader will not find easy. For if it is "natural" that the exchange of products should be regulated exclusively by the proportion of labour time that their attainment costs, it must also be natural that, for instance, any uncommon species of butterfly, or any rare edible frog, should be worth, "among a nation of hunters" ten times more than a deer, inasmuch as a man might spend ten days in looking for the former, while he could capture the latter usually by one day's labour. But the "naturalness" of this proportion would scarcely be obvious to everybody!

The result of these considerations may, I think, be summed up as follows. Adam Smith and Ricardo have asserted that labour is the principle of the value of goods simply as an axiom, and without giving any evidence for it. Consequently any one who would maintain this principle must not look to Adam Smith and Ricardo as guaranteeing its truth, but must seek for some other and independent basis of proof.

Now it is a very remarkable fact that of later writers scarcely any one has done so. The men who in other respects sifted the old-fashioned doctrine inside and out with their destructive criticism, with whom no proposition, however venerable with age, was secure from being put once more in question and tested, these very men have not uttered a word in criticism of the weightiest principle that they borrowed from the old doctrine. From Ricardo to Rodbertus, from Sismondi to Lassalle, the name of Adam Smith is the only guarantee thought necessary for this doctrine. No writer adds anything of his own but repeated asseverations that the proposition is true, incontrovertible, indubitable; there is no real attempt to prove its truth, to meet objections, to remove doubts. The despisers of proof from authority content themselves with appealing to authority; the sworn foes of unproved assumptions and assertions content themselves with assuming and asserting. Only a very few representatives of the Labour Value theory form any exception to this rule; one of these few, however, is Marx.

An economist looking for a real confirmation of the principle in question might proceed in one of two directions; he might either attempt to develop the proof from grounds involved in its very statement, or he might deduce it from experience.

Marx has taken the former course, with a result on which the reader may presently form his own opinion.

I have already quoted in Marx's own words the passages relative to the subject. The line of argument divides itself clearly into three steps.

First step. Since in exchange two goods are made equal to one another, there must be a common element of similar quantity in the two, and in this common element must reside the principle of Exchange value.

Second step. This common element cannot be the Use value, for in the exchange of goods the use value is disregarded.

Third step. If the use value of commodities be disregarded there remains in them only one common property—that of being products of labour. Consequently, so runs the conclusion, Labour is the principle of value; or, as Marx says, the use value, or "good," only has a value because human labour is made objective in it, is materialised in it.

I have seldom read anything to equal this for bad reasoning and carelessness in drawing conclusions.

The first step may pass, but the second step can only be maintained by a logical fallacy of the grossest kind. The use value cannot be the common element because it is "obviously disregarded in the exchange relations of commodities, for"—I quote literally—"within the exchange relations one use value counts for just as much as any other, if only it is to be had in the proper proportion." What would Marx have said to the following argument?

In an opera company there are three celebrated singers—a tenor, a bass, and a baritone—and these have each a salary of £1000. The question is asked, What is the common circumstance on account of which their salaries are made equal? And I answer, In the question of salary one good voice counts for just as much as any other—a good tenor for as much as a good bass or a good baritone—provided only it is to be had in proper proportion; consequently in the question of salary the good voice is evidently disregarded, and the good voice cannot be the cause of the good salary.

The fallaciousness of this argument is clear. But it is just as clear that Marx's conclusion, from which this is exactly copied, is not a whit more correct. Both commit the same fallacy.

They confuse the disregarding of a genus with the disregarding of the specific forms in which this genus manifests itself. In our illustration the circumstance which is of no account as regards the question of salary is evidently only the special form which the good voice assumes, whether tenor, bass, or baritone. It is by no means the good voice in general. And just so is it with the exchange relations of commodities. The special forms under which use value may appear, whether the use be for food, clothing, shelter, or any other thing, is of course disregarded; but the use value of the commodity in general is never disregarded. Marx might have seen that we do not absolutely disregard use value from the fact that there can be no exchange value where there is not a use value—a fact which Marx himself is repeatedly forced to admit.[1]

But still worse fallacies are involved in the third step of the demonstration. If the use value of commodities is disregarded, says Marx, there remains in them only one common property—that of being products of labour. Is this true? Is there only one property? In goods that have exchange value, for instance, is there not also the property of being *scarce* in proportion to the demand? Or that they are objects of demand and supply? Or that they are appropriated? Or that they are natural products? For that they are products of nature just as they are products of labour no one declares more plainly than Marx himself, when in one place he says, "Commodities are combinations of two elements, natural material and labour;" or when he incidentally quotes Petty's expression about material wealth, "Labour is its father and the earth its mother."[2]

Now why, I ask, may not the principle of value reside in any one of these common properties, as well as in the property of being the product of labour? For in support of this latter proposition Marx has not adduced the smallest positive argument. His sole argument is the negative one, that the use value, thus happily disregarded and out of the way, is *not* the principle of exchange value. But does not this negative argument apply

[1] For instance, in p. 15 at the end: "Finally, nothing can be valuable without being an object of use. If it is useless the labour contained in it is also useless; it does not count as labour (*sic*), and therefore confers no value." Knies has already drawn attention to the logical blunder here criticised (*Das Geld*, Berlin, 1873, p. 123, etc.)

[2] *Das Kapital*, p. 17 etc.

with equal force to all the other common properties overlooked by Marx? Wantonness in assertion and carelessness in reasoning cannot go much farther.

But this is not all. Is it even true that in all goods possessing exchange value there is this common property of being the product of labour? Is virgin soil a product of labour? Or a gold mine? Or a natural seam of coal? And yet, as every one knows, these often have a very high exchange value. But how can an element that does not enter at all into one class of goods possessing exchange value be put forward as the common universal principle of exchange value? How Marx would have lashed any of his opponents who had been guilty of such logic![1]

Without doing Marx any wrong then we shall here take the liberty of saying that his attempt to prove the truth of his principle deductively has completely fallen through.

If the proposition that the value of all goods rests on labour is neither an axiom nor capable of proof by deduction, there still remains at least one possibility in its favour; it may be capable of demonstration by experience. To give Marx every chance we shall look at this possibility also. What is the testimony of experience?

Experience shows that the exchange value of goods stands in proportion to that amount of labour which their production costs only in the case of one class of goods, and even then only approximately. Well known as this should be, considering that the facts on which it rests are so familiar, it is very seldom estimated at its proper value. Of course everybody, including the socialist writers, agrees that experience does not entirely confirm the Labour Principle. It is commonly imagined, however, that the cases in which actual facts confirm the labour principle form the rule, and that the cases which contradict the principle form a relatively insignificant exception. This view is very erroneous, and to correct it once and for all I shall put together in groups the exceptions by which experience proves the labour principle to be limited in economic life. We shall see that the exceptions so much preponderate that they scarcely leave any room for the rule.

1. From the scope of the Labour Principle are excepted

[1] See also on the subject Knies, *Das Geld*, p. 121.

all "scarce" goods that, from actual or legal hindrances, cannot be reproduced at all, or can be reproduced only in limited amount. Ricardo names, by way of example, rare statues and pictures, scarce books and coins, wines of a peculiar quality, and adds the remark that such goods form only a very small proportion of the goods daily exchanged in the market. If, however, we consider that to this category belongs the whole of the land, and, further, those numerous goods in the production of which patents, copyright, and trade secrets come into play, it will be found that the extent of these "exceptions" is by no means inconsiderable.[1]

2. All goods that are produced not by common, but by skilled labour, form an exception. Although in the day's product of a sculptor, a skilled joiner, a violin-maker, an engineer, and so on, no more labour be incorporated than in the day's product of a common labourer or a factory operative, the former has a greater exchange value, and often a many times greater exchange value. The adherents of the labour value theory have of course not been able to overlook this exception. Sometimes they mention it, but in such a way as to suggest that it does not form a real exception, but only a little variation that yet comes under the rule. Marx, for instance, adopts the expedient of reckoning skilled labour as a multiplex of common labour. "Complicated labour," he says (p. 19), "counts only as strengthened, or rather multiplied, simple labour, so that a smaller quantity of complicated labour is equal to a greater quantity of simple labour. Experience shows that this reduction is constantly made. A commodity may be the product of the most complicated labour; its value makes it equal to the product of simple labour, and represents therefore only a definite quantity of simple labour."

The naïvety of this theoretical juggle is almost stupefying. That a day's labour of a sculptor may be considered equal to five days' labour of a miner in many respects—for instance, in money valuation—there can be no doubt. But that twelve hours' labour of a sculptor actually *are* sixty hours' common labour no one will maintain. Now in questions of theory—for instance, in the question of the principle of value—it is not a matter of what fictions men may set up, but of what actually is.

[1] See also Knies, *Kredit*, part ii. p. 61.

For theory the day's production of the sculptor is, and remains, the product of one day's labour, and if a good which is the product of one day's labour is worth as much as another which is the product of five days' labour, men may invent what fictions they please; there is here an exception from the rule asserted, that the exchange value of goods is regulated by the amount of human labour incorporated in them. Suppose that a railway generally graduates its tariff according to the distances travelled by persons and goods, but, as regards one part of the line in which the working expenses are peculiarly heavy, arranges that each mile shall count as two, can it be maintained that the length of the distances is really the exclusive principle in fixing the railway tariff? Certainly not; by a fiction it is assumed to be so, but in truth the application of that principle is limited by another consideration, the *character* of the distances. Similarly we cannot preserve the theoretical unity of the labour principle by any such fiction.

Not to carry the matter further, I may say that this second exception embraces a considerable proportion of all bought and sold goods. In one respect, strictly speaking, we might say that almost all goods belong to it. For into the production of almost every good there enters some skilled labour—labour of an inventor, of a manager, of a pioneer, or some such labour—and this raises the value of the good a little above the level which would have been determined if the quantity of labour had been the only consideration.

3. The number of exceptions is increased by those goods—not, it is true, a very important class—that are produced by abnormally badly paid labour. For reasons that need not be discussed here, wages remain constantly under the minimum of subsistence in certain branches of production; for instance, in certain women's industries, such as sewing, embroidering, and knitting. The products of these employments have thus an abnormally low value. There is, for instance, nothing unusual in the product of three days' labour on the part of a white seam worker only fetching as much as the product of two days' labour on the part of a factory worker.

All the exceptions mentioned hitherto take the form of exempting certain groups of goods altogether from the law of labour value, and therefore tend to narrow the sphere of that law's validity. The only goods then left to the action of the law are those goods which can be produced at will, without any limitations, and which at the same time require nothing but unskilled labour for their production. But even in this contracted sphere the law of labour value does not rule absolutely. There are some further exceptions that go a great way to break down its strictness.

4. A fourth exception to the Labour Principle may be found in the familiar and universally admitted phenomenon that even those goods, in which exchange value entirely corresponds with the labour costs, do not show this correspondence at every moment. By the fluctuations of supply and demand their exchange value is put sometimes above, sometimes below the level corresponding to the amount of labour incorporated in them. The amount of labour only indicates the point towards which exchange value gravitates,—not any fixed point of value. This exception, too, the socialist adherents of the labour principle seem to me to make too light of. They mention it indeed, but they treat it as a little transitory irregularity, the existence of which does not interfere with the great "law" of exchange value. But it is undeniable that these irregularities are just so many cases where exchange value is regulated by other determinants than the amount of labour costs. They might at all events have suggested the inquiry whether there is not perhaps a more universal principle of exchange value, to which might be traceable, not only the regular formations of value, but also those formations which, from the standpoint of the labour theory, appear to be "irregular." But we should look in vain for any such inquiry among the theorists of this school.

5. Apart from these momentary fluctuations, it is clear that in the following case the exchange value of goods constantly diverges, and that not inconsiderably, from the level indicated by the quantity of labour incorporated in them. Of two goods which cost exactly the same amount of social average labour to produce, that one maintains a higher exchange value the production of which requires the greater advance of "previous" labour. Ricardo, as we saw, in two sections of the first chapter of his *Principles*, has spoken in detail of this exception from the labour principle. Rodbertus and Marx ignore, without expressly denying it; indeed they could not very

well do so; for that an oak-tree of a hundred years possesses a higher value than corresponds to the half minute's labour required in planting the seed is too well known to be successfully disputed.

To sum up. The asserted "law" that the value of goods is regulated by the amount of the labour incorporated in them, does not hold at all in the case of a very considerable proportion of goods; in the case of the others, does not hold always, and never holds exactly. These are the facts of experience with which the value theorists have to reckon.

What conclusions can an unprejudiced theorist draw from such facts? Certainly not the conclusion that the origin and measure of all value is to be ascribed exclusively to labour. Such a conclusion would be very like deducing the law. All electricity is caused by friction, from the experience that electricity is produced in many ways, and is very often produced by friction.

On the other hand, the conclusion might very well be drawn that expenditure of labour is one circumstance which exerts a powerful influence on the value of many goods; always remembering that labour is not an ultimate cause—for an ultimate cause must be common to all the phenomena of value—but a particular and intermediate cause. It would not be difficult to find a deductive proof of such an influence, though no deductive proof could be given of the more thoroughgoing principle. And, further, it may be very interesting and very important accurately to trace the influence of labour on the value of goods, and to express the results in the form of laws. Only in doing so we must keep before us the fact that these will be only particular laws of value not affecting the universal nature of value. To use a comparison. The law that formulates the influence of labour on the exchange value of goods will stand to the universal law of value in the same relation as the law, The west wind brings rain, stands to a universal theory of rain. West wind is a very general intermediate cause of rain, just as expenditure of labour is a very general intermediate cause of value; but the ultimate cause of rain is as little the west wind as that of value is the expended labour.

Ricardo himself only went a very little way over the

proper limits. As I have shown, he knew right well that his law of value was only a particular law; he knew, for instance, that the value of scarce goods rests on quite another principle. He only erred in so far as he very much over-estimated the extent to which his law is valid, and practically ascribed to it a validity almost universal. The consequence is that, later on, he forgot almost entirely the little exceptions he had rightly made but too little considered at the beginning of his work, and often spoke of his law as if it were really a universal law of value.

It was his shortsighted followers who first fell into the scarcely conceivable blunder of deliberately and absolutely representing labour as the universal principle of value. I say, the scarcely conceivable blunder, for really it is not easy to understand how men trained in theoretical research could, after mature consideration, maintain a principle for which they could find such slight support. They could find no argument for it in the nature of things, for that shows no necessary connection whatever between value and labour; nor in experience, for experience shows, on the contrary, that value for the most part does not correspond with labour expended; nor, finally, even in authority, for the authorities appealed to had never maintained the principle with that pretentious universality now given it.

And this principle, entirely unfounded as it is, the socialist adherents of the Exploitation theory do not maintain as something unessential, as some innocent bit of system building; they put it in the forefront of practical claims of the most aggressive description. They maintain the law that the value of all commodities rests on the labour time incorporated in them, in order that the next moment they may attack, as "opposed to law," "unnatural," and "unjust," all formations of value that do not harmonise with this "law,"—such as the difference in value that falls as surplus to the capitalist—and demand their abolition. Thus they first ignore the exceptions in order to proclaim their law of value as universal. And, after thus assuming its universality, they again draw attention to the exceptions in order to brand them as offences against the law. This kind of arguing is very much as if one were to assume that there are many foolish people in the world, and to ignore that there are also many wise ones; and thus coming to the "universally valid law" that "all men are foolish," should demand the extirpation of the wise on the ground that their existence is obviously "contrary to law"!

I have criticised the law of Labour Value with all the severity that a doctrine so utterly false seemed to me to deserve. It may be that my criticism also is open to many objections. But one thing at any rate seems to me certain: earnest writers concerned to find out the truth will not in future venture to content themselves with asserting the law of labour value as has been hitherto done.

In future any one who thinks that he can maintain this law will first of all be obliged to supply what his predecessors have omitted—a proof that can be taken seriously. Not quotations from authorities; not protesting and dogmatising phrases; but a proof that earnestly and conscientiously goes into the essence of the matter. On such a basis no one will be more ready and willing to continue the discussion than myself.

To return to Marx. Sharing in Rodbertus's mistaken idea that the value of all goods rests on labour, he falls later on into almost all the mistakes of which I have accused Rodbertus. Shut up in his labour theory Marx, too, fails to grasp the idea that Time also has an influence on value. On one occasion he says expressly that, as regards the value of a commodity, it is all the same whether a part of the labour of making it be expended at a much earlier point of time or not.[1] Consequently he does not observe that there is all the difference in the world whether the labourer receives the final value of the product at the end of the whole process of production, or receives it a couple of months or years earlier; and he repeats Rodbertus's mistake of claiming *now*, in the name of justice, the value of the finished product as it will be *then*.

Another point to be noted is that, in business capital, Marx distinguishes two portions; of which one, in his peculiar terminology called Variable capital, is advanced for the wages of labour; the other, which he calls Constant capital, is advanced for the means of production. And Marx

[1] P. 175.

maintains that only the amount of the variable capital has any influence on the quantity of surplus value obtainable,[1] the amount of the constant capital being in this respect of no account.[2] But in this Marx, like Rodbertus before him, falls into contradiction with facts; for facts show, on the contrary, that, under the working of the law of assimilation of profits, the amount of surplus value obtained stands, over the whole field, in direct proportion to the amount of the total capital—variable and constant together—that has been expended. It is singular that Marx himself became aware of the fact that there was a contradiction here,[3] and found it necessary for the sake of his solution to promise to deal with it later on.[4] But the promise was never kept, and indeed could not be kept.

Finally, Marx's theory, taken as a whole, was as powerless as Rodbertus's to give an answer even approximately satisfactory to one important part of the interest phenomena. At what hour of the labour day does the labourer begin to create the surplus value that the wine obtains, say between the fifth and the tenth year of its lying in the cellar? Or is it, seriously speaking, nothing but robbery—nothing but the exploitation of unpaid labour—when the worker who sticks the acorn in the ground is not paid the full £20 that the oak will be worth some day when, without further labour of man, it has grown into a tree?

Perhaps I need not go farther. If what I have said is true, the socialist Exploitation theory, as represented by its two most distinguished adherents, is not only incorrect, but, in theoretical value, even takes one of the lowest places among interest theories. However serious the fallacies we may meet among the representatives of some of the other theories, I scarcely think that anywhere else are to be found

[1] "The rate of surplus value and the value of labour power being given, the amounts of surplus value produced are in direct ratio with the amounts of variable capital advanced. . . . The value and the degree of exploitation of labour power being equal, the amounts of value and surplus value produced by various capitals stand in direct ratio with the amounts of the variable constituent of these capitals; that is, of those constituents which are converted into living labour power" (p. 311, etc.)

[2] "The value of these contributory means of production may rise, fall, remain unchanged, be little or much, it remains without any influence whatever in producing surplus value" (p. 312).

[3] Pp. 204, 312.

[4] Pp. 312, 542 at end.

together so great a number of the worst fallacies—wanton, unproved assumption, self-contradiction, and blindness to facts. The socialists are able critics, but exceedingly weak theorists. The world would long ago have come to this conclusion if the opposite party had chanced to have had in its service a pen as keen and cutting as that of Lassalle and as slashing as that of Marx.

That in spite of its inherent weakness the Exploitation theory found, and still finds, so much credence, is due, in my opinion, to the coincidence of two circumstances. The first is that it has shifted the struggle to a sphere where appeal is usually made to the heart as well as to the head. What we wish to believe we readily believe. The condition of the labouring classes is indeed most pitiful; every philanthropist must wish that it were bettered. Many profits do in fact flow from an impure spring; every philanthropist must wish that such springs were dried up. In considering a theory whose conclusions incline to raise the claims of the poor, and to depress the claims of the rich,—a theory which agrees partly, or it may be entirely, with the wishes of his heart,—many a one will be prejudiced in its favour from the first, and will relax a great deal of the critical severity that, in other circumstances, he would have shown in examining its scientific basis. And it need scarcely be said that theories such as these have a strong attraction for the masses. Their concern is not with criticism; they simply follow the line of their own wishes. They believe in the Exploitation theory because it is agreeable to them, and although it is false; and they would believe in it even if its theoretical argument were much worse than it is.

A second circumstance that helped to spread the theory was the weakness of its opponents. So long as the scientific opposition to it was led chiefly by men who adhered to the Abstinence theory, the Productivity theory, or the Labour theory of a Bastiat or M'Culloch, a Roscher or Strasburger, the battle could not go badly for the socialists. From positions so faultily chosen these men could not strike at the real weaknesses of Socialism; it was not too difficult to repel their lame attacks, and to follow the fighters triumphantly into their own camp. This the socialists were strong enough to do, with as much success as skill. If many socialistic writers have won an abiding place in the history of economic science, it is due to the strength and cleverness with which they managed to destroy so many flourishing and deeply-rooted erroneous doctrines. This is the service, and almost the only service, which Socialism has rendered to our science. To put truth in the place of error was beyond the power of the Exploitation theorists—even more than it was beyond the power of their much abused opponents.

BOOK VII

MINOR SYSTEMS

CHAPTER I

THE ECLECTICS

THE difficulties which the interest problem presented to the science of political economy are reflected, perhaps, nowhere more significantly than in the fact, that most economic writers of our century did not form any definite opinion on the subject.

This indefiniteness took a different shape somewhere about the year 1830. Before that date those who were undecided—and at that time there were many such—simply avoided entering on the interest problem. They come under that category which I have called the Colourless school. Later on, when the problem had become a common subject of scientific discussion, this was no longer possible. Economists were obliged to own to an opinion, and those who could not come to a decision of their own became eclectics. Interest theories were put forward in abundance. Writers who neither could nor would make one for themselves, nor decide exclusively on one of those already made, would choose from two or three or more heterogeneous theories the parts that suited them, and weave them into what generally proved a rather badly connected whole. Or, without even trying to obtain the appearance of a whole, they would in the course of their writings employ sometimes one, sometimes another theory, as suited best for the purposes they might happen to have in view.

It need not be said that an eclecticism on which the cardinal duty of the theorist, logical consistency, sat so lightly, does not indicate any very high degree of theoretical excellence. Still, here also, as with the Colourless theorists, among many men of secondary importance we meet with a few writers of the first rank. Nor is this to be wondered at. The development of the theory had been so peculiar that, for capable writers especially, the temptation to become eclectic must have been almost overpowering. There were so many heterogeneous theories in existence that one might be pardoned for thinking it impossible that there should be any more. A critical mind, indeed, could not find any one of them entirely satisfactory. But neither could the fact be ignored that in many of them there was at least a kernel of truth. The Productivity theory as a whole, for instance, was certainly unsatisfactory, but no unprejudiced person could help feeling that the existence of interest must have something to do with the greater return obtained by capitalist production, or, as it was generally called, the productivity of capital. Or, granted that a complete explanation of interest was not to be found in the "abstinence of the capitalist," it could scarcely be denied that the privation which saving usually costs is not a thing altogether without influence on the fact and on the amount of interest. In such circumstances nothing was more natural than that economists should try to piece together the fragments of truth from different theories. This tendency was strengthened by the fact that the social and political question of interest, as well as the theoretical, was now before the public; and many a writer, in his eagerness to justify the existence of interest, preferred to give up the unity of his theory rather than cease heaping together arguments in its favour. As might be expected, the fragments of truth thus collected remained, at the hands of the eclectics, nothing but fragments, their rough edges grating against each other and stubbornly resisting all attempts to work them into a homogeneous whole.

There are many ways in which eclecticism has combined the various interest theories. The greatest preference has been shown towards a combination of those two theories that came nearest the truth, the Productivity and the Abstinence theory. Among the numerous writers who follow this direction Rossi deserves to be mentioned at some length; partly because his rendering of the Productivity theory is not without a certain originality; partly because he may serve as a type of the illogical method usual among the eclectics.

In his *Cours d'Economic Politique*,[1] Rossi makes use of the Productivity and the Abstinence theories alternately, without making any attempt to weld the two into one organic theory. On the whole, on those occasions when he makes general mention of the phenomenon of interest and its origin, he follows the Abstinence theory; while in details, particularly in the inquiry as to the rate of interest, he prefers to follow the Productivity theory. To prove this I may put down in the order of their statement the most important passages, without taking more pains than the author has done to make them consistent with each other.

In the traditionary way Rossi recognises capital as a factor in production by the side of labour and land. In return for its co-operation it requires a compensation—profit. To the question why this is so, the answer is given provisionally in the mystic words, which seem to point rather to the Productivity theory, "on the same grounds and by the same title as labour" (p. 93). More definitely, and here distinctly according to the Abstinence theory, Rossi expresses himself in the summary to the third lecture of the third volume: "The capitalist demands the compensation due to the privation which he imposes on himself" (iii. p. 32). In the course of the following lecture he develops this idea more carefully. First of all, he blames Malthus for putting profit, which certainly is not an expense but an income of the capitalist, among the costs of production,—a criticism, however, which he might have first taken to himself, since in the sixth lecture of the first volume he has formally, and in the most explicit manner, enumerated the profit of capital among the costs of production.[2] The true constituent of cost which he puts in the place of profit is, "capitalised saving" (*l'épargne capitalisée*), the non-consumption and the productive employment of goods over which the capitalist has command. Later too we find repeated allusions (*e.g.* iii. pp. 261, 291) to the capitalist's renunciation of enjoyment as a factor in the origination of profit.

If up to this point Rossi has shown himself for the most part an Abstinence theorist, from the second half of the third

[1] Fourth edition, Paris, 1865.

[2] "The costs of production are made up of (1) the recompense to the workers; (2) the profits of the capitalist," etc. (p. 93)

volume onwards we come upon expressions, at first occasionally and then frequently, which show that Rossi had also come under the influence of the popular Productivity theory. He begins in somewhat vague terms by bringing profit into connection with the circumstance that "capitals contribute to production" (iii. p. 258). A little later (p. 340) he says quite distinctly, "Profit is the compensation due to productive power"—no longer, be it observed, to privation. Finally, the rate of interest is explained at great length by the productivity of capital. He regards it as "natural" that the capitalist should receive for his share in the product as much as his capital has produced in it, and that will be much if the productive power of capital is great, little if the productive power of capital is little. Thus Rossi arrives at the law that the natural height of profit is in proportion to the productive power of capital. He develops this law first in the case where production requires capital alone in its operations, the factor labour being left out of account as vanishingly small and only the use value of the product being taken into consideration. Under these assumptions he finds it evident that if, for instance, the employment of a spade on a definite piece of ground, after replacing the capital laid out, procures twenty bushels of grain as profit, the employment of a more efficient capital, say a plough, on the same piece of land, after fully replacing the capital, will bring in more profit, say sixty bushels, "because a capital of greater productive power has been employed." But the same natural principle obtains in the complicated relations of our actual economic life. There also it is "natural" that the capitalist should share the product with the labourers in the ratio of the productive power of his capital to the productive power of the labourers. If, in a production that has hitherto employed a hundred workers, a machine is introduced which replaces the power of fifty workers, the capitalist has a natural claim to one-half the total product, or the wage of fifty labourers.

This natural relation is only disturbed by one thing; that the capitalist plays a double rôle. Not only does he contribute his capital to the common co-operation, but he connects with that a second business, the buying of labour. In virtue of the former, he would always receive the natural profit that corresponds to the productive power of capital, and that alone. But in buying labour sometimes cheap, sometimes dear, he may either increase his natural profit at the expense of the natural wage of labour, or may give up a portion of his profit to the advantage of the labourers. Thus if the fifty workers displaced by the machine compete with those left in employment and depress the wages of labour, it may be that the capitalist buys the labour of the fifty still employed for a less share of the total return than would naturally fall to them according to the ratio of their productive power to the productive power of capital. Say that he buys their labour for 40 per cent instead of 50 per cent of the total product, a profit of 10 per cent is added to the natural profit on capital. But this, although usually classed with profit on capital, is in its nature entirely foreign to it, and should be looked on as a profit made by the buying of labour. It is not the natural profit on capital, but this foreign addition that causes an antagonism between capital and labour, and it is only in the case of this addition that the principle of wages falling as profits increase and *vice versâ* has any validity. The natural and true profit on capital leaves wages untouched, and depends altogether on the productive power of capital (lecture iii. pp. 21, 22).

After all that has been said in former chapters on the Productivity theories, we may well dispense with any thorough and detailed criticism of such views. I shall merely point out one monstrous conclusion that follows logically from Rossi's theory. According to him all the surplus returns obtained by the introduction and improvement of machinery, or from the development of capital in general, must to all eternity wholly and entirely flow into the pockets of the capitalists, without the labourer getting any share whatever in the advantages of these improvements; for those surplus returns are due to the increased productive power of capital, and their result forms the "natural" share of the capitalist![1]

On the same lines as Rossi, and contributing nothing new, we meet among French writers Molinari[2] and Leroy-

[1] See also the sharp but most pertinent criticism of Pierstorff, *Lehre vom Unternehmergewinn*, p. 93, etc.

[2] *Cours d'Economie Politique*, second edition, Paris, 1863. His Productivity theory is similar to that of Say (*e.g.* "interest is a compensation for the productive

Beaulieu,[1] and among Germans Roscher, with his followers Schüz and Max Wirth.[2]

Among Italian economists who follow the same eclectic lines may be mentioned Cossa. Unfortunately this admirable writer, in his monograph on the conception of capital,[3] has not extended his researches to the question of interest, and we have to go by the very scanty hints that occur in his well-known *Elementi di Economia Politica.*[4] From it one would judge Cossa to be an eclectic; yet his way of speaking, as if interpreting the ordinary doctrines, appears to me evidently to betray that he has some critical scruples about them. Thus while looking on interest as compensation for the "productive service" of capital (p. 119), he refuses to recognise this service as a primary factor in production, and only allows it the place of a secondary or derivative instrument.[5] Again, like the Abstinence theorists, he puts "privations" among the costs of production (p. 65), but in the theory of interest he adopts a tone which seems to imply that this did not express his own conviction, but only that of other people.[6]

The most interesting of those eclectic systems that combine the Abstinence and the Productivity conceptions I consider to be that of Jevons, with which I shall finish consideration of this group.[7]

service of capital," i. p. 302). His Abstinence theory (1,289,293,300) is particularly unsatisfactory on account of the peculiar meaning he gives to the conception of "privation." He means by it what the capitalist may suffer on account of the capital sunk in production not being available for the satisfaction of pressing wants which may possibly arise in the meantime. Surely a very unsuitable foundation for a universal theory of interest!

[1] *Essai sur la Répartition des Richesses*, second edition, Paris, 1885. See particularly pp. 236 (Abstinence theory), 233, 238 (Productivity theory); see also above, p. 131.

[2] On Roscher, see above, p. 129, Schüz, *Grundsätze der National-Oekonomie*, Tübingen, 1843; particularly pp. 70, 285, 296, etc. Max Wirth, *Grundzüge der National-Oekonomie*, third edition, i. p. 324; fifth edition, i. 327. See further Huhn, *Allgemeine Volkswirthschaftslehre*, Leipzig, 1862, p. 204; H. Bischof, *Grundzüge eines Systems der National-Oekonomik*, Graz, 1876, p. 459, and particularly note on p. 465; Schülze-Delitzsch, *Kapitel zu einem deutschen Arbeiterkatechismus*, pp. 23, 27, 28, etc.

[3] *La Nozione del Capitale*, in the *Saggi di Economia Politica*, Mailand, 1878, p. 155.

[4] Sixth edition, 1883.

[5] P. 34, and more at length in the *Saggi*.

[6] "The elements of interest are two: first, compensation for the non-use of capital, or, as some say, for its formation, and for its productive service" (p. 119).

[7] *Theory of Political Economy*, second edition, London, 1879.

Jevons begins by giving a very clear statement of the economic function of capital, in which he steers clear of the mysticism of any particular "productive power." The function of capital he finds simply in this, that it enables us to expend labour in advance. It assists men to surmount the difficulty caused by the time that elapses between the beginning and the end of a work. It makes possible an infinite number of improvements in the production of those goods the manufacture of which necessarily depends upon the lengthening of the interval between the moment when labour is exerted and the moment when the work is finished. All such improvements are limited by the use of capital, and in making these improvements possible lies the great and almost the only use of capital.[1]

This being the foundation, Jevons explains interest as follows. He assumes that every extension of time between employment of labour and enjoyment of result makes it possible to obtain a greater product with the same amount of labour. The difference between the product that would have been obtained in the shorter period, and the greater product that may be obtained when the time is extended, forms the profit of that capital by the investing of which the lengthening of the interval has been made possible. If we call the shorter interval t, and the longer interval made possible by an additional investment of capital $t + \Delta t$, and further, the product obtainable by a definite quantity of labour in the shorter interval Ft, then by hypothesis the product obtainable in the longer interval will be correspondingly greater; that is $F(t + \Delta t)$. The difference of these two quantities $F(t + \Delta t) - Ft$ is profit.

To ascertain the rate of interest represented by this amount of profit we must calculate the profit on that amount of capital by which the extension of the time was made possible. If Ft is the invested capital, then this is the amount of produce that could have been obtained on the expiry of t, without any additional investment. The duration of the additional investment is Δt. The whole amount of the additional investment is therefore represented in the product $= (Ft . \Delta t)$. Dividing the above increment of produce by the latter amount, the rate of interest appears thus—

[1] P. 243.

$$\frac{F(t + \Delta t) - Ft}{\Delta t} \times \frac{1}{Ft}.^{1}$$

The more abundantly a country is supplied with capital, the greater is the product Ft obtainable without any new investment of capital; the greater also is the capital on which the profit made by additional extension of time is calculated, and the less is the rate of interest corresponding to that profit. Hence the tendency of interest to fall with advancing prosperity. Since, further, all capitals tend to receive a similar rate of interest, they must all be content to take that lowest rate obtained by the additional capital last invested. Thus the advantage conferred on production by the last addition of capital determines the height of the usual rate of interest in the country.

The resemblance of this line of thought to that of the German Thünen is obvious. It presents the same weak points to criticism. Like Thünen, Jevons too lightly identifies the "surplus in products" with the "surplus in value." What his statement seems actually to point to is an "increment of produce" due to the assistance of the last increment of capital. But that this surplus in produce indicates at the same time a surplus in value over the capital consumed in the investment, Jevons has nowhere proved. To illustrate by a concrete case. It is easy to understand that a man employing imperfect, but quickly made machinery, may produce in a year's time 1000 pieces of a particular class of goods, and by employing machinery which is more perfect, but takes longer to make, may produce in the same time 1200 pieces of the goods. But there is nothing here to show that the difference of 200 pieces must be a net surplus in value. Two things might prevent its being so. (1) It might be that the more perfect machinery to which the increment of 200 pieces is due should obtain so high a value on account of this capability that the increment of 200 pieces is absorbed by the amount set aside for depreciation. (2) It is conceivable that the new method of production, which gives these good results, might be employed so extensively that the increased supply of pro-

[1] P. 266. Jevons puts the same formula in other ways that need not be specified here.

ducts would press down the value of the present 1200 pieces to the same level as the former 1000 pieces. In neither case would there be any surplus value. Jevons, therefore, has here fallen into the old error of the Productivity theorists, and mechanically translated the surplus in products, which everybody would grant, into a surplus in value.

Of course in his system there are attempts at explanation of this difference of value. But he has not brought these attempts into connection with his Productivity theory; they do not complete that theory, but traverse it.

One of these attempts is where he accepts parts of the Abstinence theory. Jevons quotes Senior with approval; he explains what Senior called "abstinence" as that "temporary sacrifice of enjoyment that is essential to the existence of capital," or as the capitalist's "endurance of want"; and he gives formulæ for calculating the amount of the sacrifice of abstinence (p. 253, etc.) He reckons this abstinence—sometimes indeed, writing loosely, he reckons even interest—among the costs of production; and in one place he expressly speaks of the capitalist's income as "compensation for abstinence and risk" (p. 295).

Jevons has some very interesting remarks on the effect of time on the valuation of needs and satisfactions. He points out that we anticipate future pleasures and pains, the prospect of future pleasure being already felt as anticipated pleasure. But the intensity of the anticipated pleasure is always less than that of the future pleasure itself, and depends on two factors—the intensity of the pleasure anticipated, and the time that intervenes before the emergence of the pleasure (p. 36, etc.) Somewhat strangely Jevons holds that the distinction we thus make in immediate valuation between a present and a future enjoyment is, rightly considered, unjustifiable. It rests only, he says, on an intellectual error, or an error of natural disposition; and, properly speaking, time should have no such influence. All the same, on account of the imperfection of human nature, it is a fact that "a future feeling is always less influential than a present one" (p. 78).

Now Jevons is quite correct in saying that this power of anticipation must exert a far-reaching influence in economics, for, among other things, all accumulation of capital depends upon it (p. 37). But, unfortunately, he is satisfied with throwing out suggestions of the most general description, and applying them quite fragmentarily.[1] He fails to develop the idea, or to give it any fruitful application to the theory of income and value. This omission is the more surprising that there are some features in his interest theory which strongly suggested the possibility of making a very good use of the element of time in the explanation of interest. With more emphasis than any one before him, he had asserted the rôle played by time in the function of capital. The next step evidently would have been to inquire whether the difference of time might not also exert an immediate influence on the valuation of the product of capital, of such a kind that the difference of value, on which interest is founded, might be explained by it. Instead of this Jevons, as we have seen, persists in the old method of explaining interest simply by the difference in the quantity of the product.

Still more obvious, probably, would it have been to connect his other conception of "abstinence" with the difference that we make in the estimation of present and future enjoyments, and to account for the sacrifice that lies in the postponement of enjoyment by that lesser valuation of the future utility. But Jevons gives no positive expression to this. Indeed, indirectly, he even excludes it; for, as we have seen, on the one hand he pronounces the lesser valuation to be a simple error caused by the imperfection of our nature, and, on the other hand, he pronounces the abstinence to be a real and true sacrifice, viz. the continuance in the (painful) state of need.

Thus there is no reciprocal fructification between the many interesting and acute ideas that Jevons throws out regarding our subject; and Jevons himself remains an eclectic of genius perhaps, but still an eclectic.

A second group of eclectics add on ideas taken from the Labour theory in one or other of its varieties. First may be

[1] Thus, on one occasion, he says that, under the influence of this element of time, in the case of the distribution of a stock of goods in the present and in the future, "less commodity will be consigned to future days in some proportion to the intervening time" (p. 79).

mentioned Read,[1] whose work, appearing as it did at the period when English economic literature on the subject of interest was most confused, shows a peculiarly inconsistent heaping together of opinions. He begins by laying the greatest emphasis on the independent productive power of capital, regarding the existence of which power he has no doubt. "How absurd," he exclaims on one occasion (p. 83), "must it appear to contend that labour produces all, and is the only source of wealth, as if capital produced nothing, and was not a real and distinct source of wealth also!" And a little farther on he finishes an exposition of what capital does in certain branches of production by saying, quite in the spirit of the Productivity theory, that everything remaining over, after payment of the workers who co-operate in the work, "may fairly be claimed as the produce and reward of capital."

Later still, however, he sees the matter in an essentially different light. He now puts in the foreground the fact that capital itself comes into existence through labour and saving, and builds on that an explanation of interest, half in the spirit of James Mill's Labour theory, and half in that of Senior's Abstinence theory. "The person who has laboured before, and not consumed but saved the produce of his labour, and which produce is now applied to assist another labourer in the work of production, is entitled to his profit or interest (which is the reward for labour that is past, and for saving and preserving the fruits of that labour) as much as the present labourer is entitled to his wages, which is the reward for his more recent labour" (p. 310). That eclectic hesitation of this kind must result in all sorts of contradictions goes without saying. Thus in this latter passage Read himself resolves capital into previous labour, although earlier he had protested against this in the most stubborn way.[2] Thus too he explains profit to be wage for previous labour, while in a previous passage [3] he had blamed M'Culloch most severely for effacing the distinction between the conception of profit and that of wage.

With Read may be appropriately classed the German econo-

[1] *An Inquiry into the Natural Grounds of Right to Vendible Property or Wealth.* Edinburgh, 1829.

[2] P. 131, and generally all through the argument against Godwin, and the anonymous tract "Labour Defended."

[3] Note to p. 247.

mist Gerstner. The "familiar question" whether capital by itself, and independently of the other two sources of goods, is productive, he answers in the affirmative. He believes that the part played in the production of the total product by the instrument of production we call capital, can be determined with mathematical exactitude, and without more ado looks upon this share as the "rent in the total profit that is due to capital."[1] With this frank and concise Productivity theory, however, Gerstner combines certain points of agreement with James Mill's Labour theory; as when (p. 20) he defines the instruments of production as "a kind of anticipation of labour," and on that basis calls "the rent of capital that falls to the instruments of production the supplementary wage for previously performed labour" (p. 23). But, like Read, he gives no thought to the question that naturally suggests itself, whether in that case the previously performed labour has not previously received its wages from the capital value of the capital, and why, over and above that, it still gets an eternal contribution in the shape of interest.

To the same division of the eclectics belong the French economists Cauwes[2] and Joseph Garnier.

I have already pointed out[3] how Cauwes, with some reservation, shows himself an adherent of Courcelle Seneuil's Labour theory. But at the same time he puts forward a number of views that have their origin in the Productivity theory. Arguing against the socialists he ascribes to capital an independent "active rôle" in production by the side of labour (i. p. 235). In the "productivity of capital" he finds what determines the current rate of loan interest.[4] Finally, he derives the existence of "surplus value" from the productivity of capital in a passage, where he bases the explanation of interest on the fact that we are indebted to the productive employment of capital for a "certain surplus value."[5]

[1] *Beitrag zur Lehre vom Kapital*, Erlangen, 1857, pp. 16, 22, etc.

[2] *Précis d'Economie Politique*, second edition, Paris, 1881.

[3] See above, p. 304.

[4] "The principle then is that the rate of interest is a direct consequence of the productivity of capital" (ii. p. 110).

[5] "We saw that the real value of interest depended on the productive employment given to capital; since a certain surplus value is due to capital, interest is one part of that surplus value presumably *fixée à forfait* (without consideration

In Joseph Garnier[1] we find the elements of no less than three different theories eclectically combined. The basis of his views is Say's Productivity theory, from which he even revived and adopted the feature long ago rejected by criticism; that of reckoning interest among the costs of production.[2] Then, in imitation of Bastiat, he calls the "privation" which the lender of the capital suffers through the alienation of it, the justification of interest. Finally, he declares that interest invites and compensates the "labour of saving."[3]

All the eclectics hitherto mentioned combine a number of theories which, if they do not agree in the character of their arguments, at least agree in the practical results at which these arguments arrive. That is to say, they combine theories which are favourable to interest. But, strangely enough, there are some writers who, with one or more theories favourable to interest, combine elements of the theory hostile to it, the Exploitation theory.

Thus J. G. Hoffmann lays down a peculiar theory that, on one side, is favourable to interest, and explains it as the remuneration of certain labours in the public service performed by the capitalists.[4] But, on the other side, he distinctly rejects the Productivity theory, which was then fashionable, speaking of it as a delusion to think "that in the dead mass of capital or land there dwell forces of acquisition" (p. 588); and in blunt terms declares that in taking interest the capitalist takes to himself the fruit of other people's labour. "Capital," he says, "can be employed for the promotion of one's own labour, or for the promotion of other people's. In the latter case a hire is due the owner for it, and this hire can only be paid from the fruit of labour. This hire, this interest, has so far the nature of land-rent that, like it, it comes to the receiver from the fruit of other people's labour" (p. 576).

Still more striking is the combination of opposed opinions in J. S. Mill. It has often been remarked that Mill takes a

of gain or loss) which the lender receives for the service rendered by him" (ii. p. 189).

[1] *Traité d'Economie Politique*, eighth edition, Paris, 1880.

[2] P. 47.

[3] P. 522.

[4] *Kleine Schriften staatswirthschaftlichen Inhalts*, Berlin, 1843, p. 566. See above, p. 312.

middle position between two very strongly diverging tendencies of political economy—the so-called Manchester school on the one side, and Socialism on the other. It is easy to understand that such a compromise cannot, as a rule, be favourable to the construction of a complete and organic system—least of all in that sphere where the chief struggle of socialism and capitalism is being fought out, the theory of interest. The fact is that Mill's theory of interest has got into such a tangle that it would be a serious wrong to this distinguished thinker were we to determine his scientific position in political economy by this very unsuccessful part of his work.

As Mill constructed his system in the main on the economical views of Ricardo, he adopted, among others, the principle that labour is the chief source of all value. But this principle is traversed by the actual existence of interest. Mill consequently modified it in the way of making the value of goods determined by their costs of production, instead of by labour in general. Among these costs of production, besides labour which constitutes "so much the principal element as to be very nearly the whole," he finds room for profit, and gives it an independent position. Profit with him is the second constant element in costs.[1]

That Mill should have fallen into the old mistake of Malthus, and described a surplus as a sacrifice, is all the more wonderful that in English political economy it had already been criticised, severely and forcibly, both by Torrens and Senior.

But whence comes profit? Instead of one, Mill gives three inconsistent answers to this question.

In these the Productivity theory has the smallest share, and it is only in isolated passages, and with all manner of reservations, that Mill tends in this direction. First, he explains with a certain hesitation that capital is the third independent factor in production. Of course capital itself is the product of labour; its efficiency in production is therefore that of labour in an indirect shape. Nevertheless he finds that it "requires to be specified separately."[2] In no less involved terms does he express himself on the kindred question whether capital

[1] *Principles*, book iii. chap. iv. §§ 1, 4, 6; chap. vi. § 1, No. 8, etc.

[2] Book i. chap. vii. § 1.

possesses independent productivity. "We often speak of the 'productive powers of capital.' This expression is not literally correct. The only productive powers are those of labour and natural agents; or if any portion of capital can by a stretch of language be said to have a productive power of its own, it is only tools and machinery which, like wind and water, may be said to co-operate with labour. The food of labourers and the materials of production have no productive power."[1] Thus tools are really productive, while raw materials are not—a distinction as startling as it is untenable.

Much more decisive is his profession of Senior's Abstinence theory. It forms, as it were, Mill's official theory on interest. It appears explicitly and completely in the chapter devoted to profit, and is often appealed to afterwards in the course of the work. "As the wages of the labourer are the remuneration of labour," says Mill in the fifteenth chapter of the second book of his *Principles*, "so the profits of the capitalist are properly, according to Mr. Senior's well-chosen expression, the remuneration of abstinence. They are what he gains by forbearing to consume his capital for his own uses, and allowing it to be consumed by productive labourers for their uses. For this forbearance he requires a recompense." And as distinctly in another place: "In our analysis of the requisites of production we found that there is another necessary element in it besides labour. There is also capital; and this being the result of abstinence, the produce or its value must be sufficient to remunerate not only all the labour required, but the abstinence of all the persons by whom the remuneration of the different classes of labourers was advanced. The return for abstinence is profit."[2]

But besides this, in the same chapter, under the heading of profit, Mill brings forward yet a third theory: "The cause of profit," he says in the fifth paragraph, "is that labour produces more than is required for its support. The reason why agricultural capital yields a profit is because human beings can grow more food than is necessary to feed them while it is being grown, including the time occupied in constructing the tools, and making all other needful preparations; from which it is a consequence that if a capitalist undertakes to feed the

[1] Book v. § 1. [2] Book iii. chap. iv. § 4.

labourers on condition of receiving the produce, he has some of it remaining for himself after replacing his advances. To vary the form of the theorem: the reason why capital yields a profit is because food, clothing, materials, and tools last longer than the time which was required to produce them; so that if a capitalist supplies a party of labourers with these things, on condition of receiving all they produce, they will, in addition to reproducing their own necessaries and instruments, have a portion of their time remaining to work for the capitalist." Here the cause of profit is found, not in a productive power of capital, nor in the necessity of compensating the capitalist's abstinence as a special sacrifice, but simply in this, that "labour produces more than is required for its support"; that "the workers have a portion of their time remaining to work for the capitalist": in a word, profit is explained according to the Exploitation theory, as an appropriation by the capitalist of the surplus value created by labour.

A similar middle course, on the boundary line between Capitalism and Socialism, is taken by the German Katheder Socialists. The result in this case also is not seldom an eclecticism, but it is an eclecticism which ends more in agreement with the Exploitation theory than was the case with Mill. I shall only mention here the Katheder Socialist whom we have already met repeatedly in the course of this work, Schäffle.

In those writings of Schäffle where he treats of our subject three clear and distinct currents of thought may be traced. In the first Schäffle follows Hermann's Use theory, which he weakens as a theory by the subjective colouring he gives to the conception of Use—so bringing it nearer to the second of his theories. The first current predominates in the *Gesellschaftliche System der menschlichen Wirthschaft*, and has left evident traces even in the *Bau und Leben*.[1] The second current takes the direction of making interest a kind of professional income, an income which is drawn by the capitalist for certain services he renders. This conception, which had already appeared in the *Gesellschaftliche System*, is explicitly confirmed in the *Bau und Leben*.[2] But, finally, by the side of

[1] See above, p. 206. [2] See above, p. 306.

this in the *Bau und Leben* there appear numerous approximations to the socialist Exploitation theory. The chief of these is the resolution of all the costs of production into labour. While in the *Gesellschaftliche System* [1] Schäffle had still recognised the uses of wealth as an independent and elementary factor in cost besides labour, he now says: "Costs have two constituents: expenditure of personal goods through the putting forth of labour, and expenditure of capital. But the latter costs also can be traced back to labour costs, for the productive expenditure of real goods may be reduced to a sum of labours expended at earlier periods; all costs, therefore, may be considered as costs of labour." [2]

If thus the labour which the production of goods costs is the only economic sacrifice that requires to be considered, it is but a step farther to claim the whole result of production for those who have made this sacrifice. Thus Schäffle repeatedly gives us to understand (*e.g.* iii. p. 313, etc.) that he considers the ideal economic distribution of goods to be the division to the members of the community according to work done. In the present day of course the realisation of this ideal is still prevented by all kinds of hindrances; among others, by the fact that wealth as capital serves as an instrument of appropriation—partly an illegal and immoral appropriation, partly a legal and moral appropriation of the product of labour.[3] This appropriation of surplus value by the capitalists Schäffle does not condemn unconditionally; he would let it continue as a temporary and artificial arrangement so long as we are not able to replace the "economic service of private capital by a more perfect public organisation, established by law, and less 'greedy of surplus value.'" [4]

But notwithstanding this opportunist toleration, Schäffle often brings forward in blunt terms the dogma of the Exploitation theory, that interest is a robbery of the product of other people's labour. Thus, in immediate continuation of these words, he says: "All the same the speculative, individualistic organisation of business is not the *non plus ultra*

[1] i. pp. 258, 268, 271, etc.

[2] *Bau und Leben*, iii. p. 273, etc.

[3] iii. p. 266, etc.

[4] iii. p. 423. See also iii. pp. 330, 386, 428, etc.

of the history of economics. It serves a social purpose only indirectly. It is immediately directed, not to the highest net utility of the whole, but to the greatest acquisition of the means of production by private owners, and towards procuring for the families of the capitalists the highest life of enjoyment. The possession of the means of production, movable and immovable, is made use of to appropriate from the produce of the national labour as much as possible. Proudhon has already put it in full critical evidence that capital forestalls labour in a hundred different forms. The only share of which the wage labourer is assured is the share that an upright beast of burden, endowed with reason, and therefore incapable of being reduced to simple animal wants, finds necessary to sustain him in the condition of life in which he has been placed by circumstances that are historical—this condition itself being necessary to allow of the capitalist's competition."

CHAPTER II

THE LATER FRUCTIFICATION THEORY

I HAVE pointed to the wide spread of eclecticism as a symptom of the unsatisfactory position of the economical doctrine of interest. Our economists select elements out of many theories, when and because no one of the existing theories is found sufficient.

A second symptom that points in the same direction is the fact that, in spite of the great number of existing theories, there is no check to the literature of the subject. Ever since scientific Socialism brought scepticism to bear on the old school of opinions there has been no lustrum, and in the latter lustrum no year, in which some new interest theory has not seen the light of day. So far as these have retained at least some principles of the older explanations, and have varied them only in the way of carrying out the original principles more strictly, I have tried to classify them according to the prevailing tendencies they show, and have included them in the statement of preceding chapters.

But some recent attempts strike out a way of their own,[1] and one of them seems remarkable enough to call for fuller notice,—that of the American writer, Henry George. From its likeness in fundamental ideas to Turgot's Fructification theory, it may be appropriately called the Later Fructification theory.

George's [2] interest theory occurs in the course of a polemic against Bastiat and his well-known illustration of the lending

[1] By desire of the author I here omit, as of little interest to English readers, a statement and criticism of Schellwien's theory (*Die Arbeit und ihr Recht*, Berlin, 1882, p. 195, etc.), which occupies pp. 477-486 of the German edition.—W. S.

[2] *Progress and Poverty*. Kegan Paul, 1885.

of the plane. A carpenter James has made a plane for his own use, but lends it for a year to another carpenter William. At the end of the year he is not content with getting back an equally good plane, because this would not compensate him for the loss of the advantage he might have had from the use of the plane during the year, and on that account he asks in addition a new plank as interest. Bastiat had explained and justified the payment of the plank by showing that William obtains "the power which exists in the tool to increase the productiveness of labour."[1] This explanation of interest from the productivity of capital George does not consider valid, for various reasons which do not concern us here, and then proceeds as follows: "And I am inclined to think that if all wealth consisted of such things as planes, and all production was such as that of carpenters—that is to say, if wealth consisted but of the inert matter of the universe, and production of working up this inert matter into different shapes—that interest would be but the robbery of industry, and could not long exist. . . . But all wealth is not of the nature of planes or planks, or money, nor is all production merely the turning into other things of the inert matter of the universe. It is true that if I put away money it will not increase. But suppose instead I put away wine. At the end of a year I will have an increased value, for the wine will have improved in quality. Or suppose that in a country adapted to them I set out bees; at the end of a year I will have more swarms of bees, and the honey which they have made. Or supposing, where there is a range, I turn out sheep, or hogs, or cattle; at the end of the year I will, upon the average, also have an increase. Now what gives the increase in these cases is something which, though it generally requires labour to utilise it, is yet distinct and separable from labour — the active power of nature; the principle of growth, of reproduction, which everywhere characterises all the forms of that mysterious thing or condition which we call life. And it seems to me that it is this that is the cause of interest, or the increase of capital over and above that due to labour."

The fact that, for the utilisation of the productive forces of nature, labour also is necessary, and that, consequently, the

[1] *Capital et Rente.* See above, p. 289.

produce of agriculture, for instance, is in a certain sense a produce of labour, is not sufficient to obliterate the essential difference that exists, according to George, between the different modes of production. In such modes of production as consist "merely of changing the form or place of matter, as planing boards or mining coal, labour alone is the efficient cause. . . . When labour stops production stops. When the carpenter drops his plane as the sun sets, the increase of value which he with his plane is producing ceases until he begins his labour again the following morning. When the factory bell rings for closing, when the mine is shut down, production ends until work is resumed. The intervening time, so far as regards production, might as well be blotted out. The lapse of days, the change of seasons, is no element in the production that depends solely on the amount of labour expended." But in the other modes of production "which avail themselves of the reproductive forces of nature time *is* an element. The seed in the ground germinates and grows while the farmer sleeps or ploughs the fields." [1]

So far George has shown how certain naturally fruitful kinds of capital bear interest. But, as every one knows, all kinds of capital, even those that are naturally unfruitful, produce interest. George explains this simply from the efficiency of the law of equalisation of profits. "No one would keep capital in one form when it could be changed into a more advantageous form. . . . And so in any circle of exchange the power of increase which the reproductive or vital force of nature gives to some species of capital must average with all; and he who lends or uses in exchange money or planes or bricks or clothing, is not deprived of the power to obtain an increase any more than if he had lent, or put to a reproductive use, so much capital in a form capable of increase."

To return to Bastiat's illustration: the reason why William at the end of the year should return to James more than an equally good plane, does not rest in the increased power "which the tool gives to labour," for "that is not an element . . . but it

[1] Parallel with the "vital forces of nature," according to George, works also "the utilisation of the variations in the forces of nature and of man by exchange." This too leads to "an increase which somewhat resembles that produced by the vital forces of nature" (p. 129). But I need not here enter into a more exact exposition of this somewhat obscure element, since George himself ascribes to it only a secondary rôle in the origination of interest.

springs from the element of time—the difference of a year between the lending and return of the plane. Now if the view is confined to the illustration, there is nothing to suggest how this element should operate, for a plane at the end of the year has no greater value than at the beginning. But if we substitute for the plane a calf, it is clearly to be seen that to put James in as good a position as if he had not lent, William at the end of the year must return not a calf, but a cow. Or if we suppose that the ten days' labour had been devoted to planting corn, it is evident that James would not have been fully recompensed if at the end of the year he had received simply so much planted corn, for during the year the planted corn would have germinated and grown and multiplied; so, if the plane had been devoted to exchange, it might during the year have been turned over several times, each increase yielding an increase to James. . . . In the last analysis the advantage which is given by the lapse of time springs from the generative force of nature and the varying powers of nature and of man."

The resemblance of all this to Turgot's Fructification theory is obvious. Both start with the idea that in certain kinds of goods there resides, as a natural endowment, the ability to bring forth an increment of value; and both demonstrate that, under the influence of exchange transactions and the efforts of economic men to get possession of this most remunerative fructification, the endowment must artificially become the general property of all kinds of goods. They differ only in that Turgot places the source of the increment of value quite outside of capital, in rent-bearing land, while George seeks it inside the sphere of capital, in certain naturally fruitful kinds of goods.

This difference avoids the weightiest objection that we had to urge against Turgot. Turgot had left unexplained how it is possible to purchase, for a relatively small sum of capital, land which yields successively an infinite sum of rent, and to secure the advantage of an enduring fructification for unfruitful capital. With George, on the other hand, it seems to need no proof that unfruitful wealth is exchanged in equal ratio with fruitful. For since the latter can be produced in any quantity at will, the possibility of increasing the supply of such goods will not permit of their enjoying a higher level of price than the unfruitful goods that cost as much to produce.

On the other hand, George's theory is open to two other criticisms, which are, I think, decisive.

First, the separation of production into two groups, in one of which the vital forces of nature form a distinct element in addition to labour, while in the other they do not, is entirely untenable. George here repeats in a somewhat altered form the old mistake of the physiocrats, who would not allow that nature co-operates in the work of production except in one single branch of it, agriculture. The natural sciences have long ago told us that the co-operation of nature is universal. All our production rests on the fact that, by the application of natural forces, we put imperishable matter into useful forms. Whether the natural power of which we avail ourselves in this be vegetative or inorganic, mechanical or chemical, makes no difference whatever in the relation in which natural power stands to our labour. It is quite unscientific to say that, in production by means of a plane, "labour alone is the efficient cause." The muscular movement of the man who planes would be of very little use if the natural powers and properties of the steel edge of the plane did not come to his assistance. Is it even true that, on account of the character of plank planing as a "simple change of form or place of the material," nature in this case can do nothing without labour? Can we not fasten the plane into an automatic machine, and get it driven by the force of a stream; and will not the plane, untiring, continue the production even when the carpenter sleeps? What more does nature do in the growing of grain?

Second, George has not explained that prior phenomenon of interest by which he seeks to explain all the other phenomena. He says all kinds of goods must bear interest because they can be exchanged for seed-corn, cattle, or wine, and these bear an interest. But why do these bear an interest?

Many a reader will perhaps think, at the first glance, as George himself evidently thinks, that it is self-evident. It is evident that the ten grains of wheat, into which the one grain has multiplied itself, are worth more than the one grain of wheat that was sown; that the grown-up cow is worth more than the calf out of which it grew. Only it would be well to consider that it is not a matter of ten grains simply growing out of one grain. The action of cultivated land, and a certain expenditure of labour, have had a share in it. And that ten grains are worth more than one grain + the action of the ground and + the labour expended, is obviously not self-evident. Just as little is it simply self-evident that the cow is worth more than the calf + the fodder which it has consumed during its growth + the labour which its rearing demanded. And yet it is only under these conditions that interest can fall to the share of the grain of wheat, or to the calf.

Indeed, even in the case of wine which improves in lying, it is not by any means self-evident that the wine which has grown better is of more value than the inferior and unripe wine. For in our method of valuing the goods which we possess we follow unhesitatingly the principle of anticipating future use.[1] We do not estimate the value of our goods according to the use—at least we do not value them *only* according to the use—which they bring us at the moment, but also according to that use which they will bring us in the future. We ascribe to the field, which for the moment lies useless in fallow, a value with regard to the crop which it will bring us by and by. We give a value even now to the scattered bricks, beams, nails, clamps, etc., which bring us no use when in that condition, in consideration of the use they will afford us when put together at some future time in the shape of a house. We value the fermenting must, which, as such, we cannot make any use of, because we know that by and by it will be serviceable wine. And so might we also value the unripe wine, which we know will become excellent wine after lying, by the amount of use which it will give us as matured wine. But if we ascribe to it here and now a value corresponding to that future use, there remains no room for an increase of value, and for interest. And why should we not?

And if we do not ascribe such a value, or not quite such a value, the cause is certainly not to be found, as George imagines, in the productive powers of nature which the wine possesses. For that there are vital forces of nature in the fermenting must, which in itself is even hurtful, or in the unripe wine, which of itself is of little use; and that these vital forces

[1] See my remarks on "Computation of Wealth" in *Rechte und Verhältnisse*, p. 80, etc.

tend to the furnishing of a costly product, can, in the nature of things, only afford a ground for valuing the goods which contain these precious forces at a high figure, not at a low one. If, nevertheless, we value them at a relatively low figure, we do it not because of their containing useful natural forces, but in spite of it. The surplus value of the products of nature, which George appeals to, is therefore not self-evident.

George makes one attempt to explain this surplus value, though it must be called a very lame one. He says that time, as well as labour, constitutes an independent element in its production. But is this really an explanation, or is it an evasion of the explanation? How comes the person who throws a seed of corn into the earth to get compensation, out of the value of the product, not only for his labour but also for the time that the seed has lain in the ground and grown? Is time then the object of a monopoly? Such an argument almost tempts one to recall the naïve words of the old canonist, that time is a good common to all, to the debtor as to the creditor, to the producer as to the consumer.

Of course George did not mean time, but the vegetative powers of nature actually working during time. But how should the producer manage to get himself paid for these vegetative forces of nature by a special surplus value in the product? Are, then, these natural powers objects of a monopoly? Are they not rather accessible to every man who owns a seed of corn? And cannot every one put himself in possession of a seed of corn? Since the production of seed-corn can be indefinitely augmented by labour, would the amount of corn not be steadily increased so long as a monopoly of the natural forces immanent in the grain made its possession appear peculiarly advantageous? And would not, on that account, the supply inevitably increase till the extra profit due to that monopoly was absorbed, and the production of corn became no more remunerative than any other kind of production?

The careful reader will note that in this discussion we have come back into the same groove of ideas into which we were brought by our criticism of Strasburger's Productivity theory.[1] In this part of his work George has under-estimated the interest problem in the same way as Strasburger did, only

[1] See above, p. 178.

to a greater extent and with still greater naïvety. Both hastily conclude that the powers of nature are the cause of interest. But Strasburger at least made an attempt to investigate exactly the alleged causal connection between the two, and to follow it out in detail. George, on the contrary, gives us nothing but assertions which take for granted that, in certain productions, time is an "element." It is certainly not in this superficial way that the great problem is to be solved.

CONCLUSION

Our attention has been too long fixed on individual theories. Let us, in conclusion, consider the subject as a whole. We have seen the rise of a motley array of interest theories. We have considered them all carefully and tested them thoroughly. No one of them contains the whole truth. Are they on that account quite fruitless? Taken all together, do they form nothing but a chaos of contradiction and error, that leaves us no nearer the truth than when we started? Is it not rather the case that, through the tangle of contradictory theories, there runs a line of development which, if it has not itself led to the truth, has at least pointed the way in which truth is to be found? And how runs the line of this development?

I cannot better introduce the answer to this last question than by asking my readers once more to put clearly before their minds the substance of our problem. What really is the problem of interest?

The problem is to discover and state the causes which guide into the hands of the capitalists a portion of the stream of goods annually flowing out of the national production. There can be no question then that the interest problem is a problem of *distribution*.

But in what part of the stream is it that the current branches off into different arms? On this point the historical development of theory has brought to light three essentially distinct views, and these views have led to three as distinct fundamental conceptions of the whole problem.

Let us keep for a moment to the figure of the stream: it will serve very well to illustrate the subject. The source represents the production of goods; the mouth the ultimate division into incomes whereby human needs are satisfied; the course of the stream represents that stage between source and ultimate division where goods pass from hand to hand in economic transactions, and receive their value by human estimation.

Now the three views are the following. One view has it that the capitalist's share is already separated out from the first. Three distinct sources—nature, labour, and capital—each in virtue of its inherent productive power, bring forth a definite quantity of goods, with a definite quantity of value, and just the same amount of value as has flowed from each source is discharged into the income of those persons who *own* the source. It is not so much one stream as three streams, that flow together for a long time in the same bed. But their waters do not mingle, and at the mouth they divide again in the same proportion as when they came out of the separate sources. This view transfers the whole explanation to the *source* of wealth; it treats the problem of interest as a problem of *production*. It is the view of the Naïve Productivity theories.

The second view is directly opposed to the first. It finds the division first and exclusively in the discharge. There is only one source, labour. Out of it pours the whole stream of wealth, one and undivided. Even the course of the stream is undivided; in the value of goods there is nothing to prepare the way for a division of them among different participants, for all value is measured simply by labour. It is just at the mouth, just where the stream of wealth is about to pour out, and should pour out into the income of the workers who produce it, that, from each side, the owners of land and the owners of capital thrust out a dam into the stream, and forcibly divert a part of the current into their own property. This is the view of the socialist Exploitation theory. It denies interest any previous history in the earlier stages of the career of wealth. It sees in it simply the result of an inorganic, accidental, and violent *taking*. It treats the problem as purely one of distribution or division in the most offensive sense of the word.

The third view lies midway between the two. According to it there are two, perhaps even three springs in the source out of which flows the undivided stream of wealth. But in its course this stream comes under the influences that create value, and under these influences it immediately begins to branch asunder again. That is to say, in their calculation of use values (and of exchange values based on these) men put a value on the importance they attach to various goods and classes of goods, taking into consideration the amount and intensity of their needs on the one hand, and the quantity of means available to satisfy them on the other, and thus come to make division between goods and goods; they raise one kind and lower another. Thus emerge complicated differences of level, complicated tensions and attractions, under the influence of which the stream of goods is gradually forced asunder into three branches, of which each has its particular mouth. The one mouth discharges into the income of the owners of the land; the second into that of the workers; the third into that of the capitalists. But these three branches are neither identical with the two or three springs, nor do they even correspond with them in force. What decides the force of each branch at its mouth is not the strength of each spring at its source, but the amount which the formation of values has forced from the united stream into each of the three branches.

This then is the view in which all the remaining theories of interest agree. They find the final division already suggested in the stage of the formation of values, and therefore they consider it their duty to carry back their theory into this sphere. They supplement and widen out the distribution problem of interest into a problem of *value*.

Which of these three fundamental conceptions is the right one? To any moderate and candid observer the answer cannot remain doubtful.

It certainly is not the first view. Not only is capital not an original source of wealth,—since it is at all times the fruit of nature and labour,—but, as we have sufficiently proved, there is no power whatever in a factor of production to turn out its physical products with a definite value attached to them. In the production of goods neither value in general, nor surplus value in particular, nor interest on capital comes ready-made into the world. The problem of interest is not a simple problem of production.

But neither can the second conception be the correct one. The facts are against it. It is not for the first time in the distribution of goods, but before that, in the formation of value, that a foreign element intrudes itself by the side of labour. An oak tree a hundred years old, which during its long growth has only required the attention of a single day's labour, has a hundred times higher value than the chair which another day's labour has made out of a pair of boards. In this case the oak trunk, the product of one day's labour, does not at once become a hundred times more valuable than the chair which costs one day's labour. But day by day, year by year, the growing value of the oak diverges from the value of the chair. And as it is with the value of the oak, so is it with the value of all those products the production of which costs, not only labour, but time.

Now it is the same quiet and stubborn working forces as, step by step, separated the value of the oak from that of the chair, that have at the same time produced interest on capital. These forces, effective long before goods come to division, have marked out the future limiting line between wage of labour and interest on capital. For labour can be paid on no other principle than "like wages for like work." But if the value of goods produced by similar labour becomes dissimilar through the action of these forces, the similar level of wages cannot everywhere be maintained and coincide with the dissimilar rise in the value of goods. It is only the value of goods *not* thus favoured that falls in level, and is appropriated by the general rate of wages which it determines. All goods that are favoured rise above this level in proportion as they have been favoured by the formation of value, and could not be appropriated by the general rate of wages. When then the final division comes, after all the workers have received like wages for like work, these favoured goods must of themselves leave something over which the capitalist can and may appropriate. They leave this something over, not because at the last moment the capitalist, by his sudden snatch at the spoil, artificially forces down the level of wages under the level of the value of goods, but because, long previously, the tendencies of the formation of value had raised the value of those goods which cost labour and time above the value of those other goods which cost only labour producing its result at once;—the value of which latter labour, as it must be sufficient to satisfy the labour of *its* production, forms at the same time the standard for the general rate of wages.

So speak the facts. The conclusions which they force us to draw are clear. The problem of interest is a problem of distribution. But the distribution has a previous history, and must be explained by that previous history. The sums of wealth do not start away from each other on a sudden; the diverging lines which they follow were quietly and gradually cut out in previous stages of their career. Whoever wishes really to understand the distribution, and truly to explain it, must go back to the origin of the quiet but distinct grooving of these lines of division, and this will lead him to the sphere of value. This is where the principal work is to be done in the explanation of interest. Whoever treats the problem as a simple problem of *production* breaks off his explanation before he has come to the principal point. Whoever treats it as a problem of *distribution*, and distribution only, begins it after the principal point is passed. It is only the economist who undertakes to clear up those remarkable rises and falls of value, where the rises are surplus value, who can hope, in explaining them, to explain interest in a really scientific way. The interest problem in its last resort is a problem of *value*.

If we keep this in view we shall easily find the order of merit into which these various groups of theories fall, and we shall ascertain where runs the upward line of the development.

Two theories have entirely mistaken the character of the interest problem; together—the one forming the counterpart of the other—they constitute the lowest step in the development. These are the Naïve Productivity theory and the socialist Exploitation theory. It may seem strange to mention these two in the same breath. How widely the two diverge in the results at which they arrive! How much superior the adherents of the Exploitation theory consider their arguments to the naïve assumptions of the Productivity theorists! How proudly they proclaim their own advanced critical attitude! The association, however, is justified. First, the two theories agree in what they do not do. Neither of them touches on the distinctive problem. Neither of them wastes words in explaining those peculiar waves which are thrown up by the value of goods, and out of which surplus value comes. The Productivity theory contents itself with saying, in regard to these waves of value, that they have been produced. The Exploitation theory, almost more culpably, does not even notice them; for it they do not exist; for it, however the facts of the economical world may run contrary, the level of the value of goods agrees simply with the level of the labour expended on them.

But not only negations, but positive ideas bind these two theories more closely together than could well be believed. They are in truth fruit of one and the same bough; children of one and the same naïve assumption that value grows out of production like the blade out of the field.

This assumption has an important history of its own in economic literature. In constantly changing shapes it has, for a hundred and thirty years, ruled our science, and by forcing the explanation of the fundamental phenomenon in a wrong direction has hindered its progress. First it appears in the physiocrat doctrine that land creates all surplus of value by its own fruitfulness. Adam Smith took the strength away from the assumption. Ricardo entirely uprooted it. But, before the first phenomenal form of it had quite disappeared, Say introduced it for a second time into the science in a new and extended form. Instead of the one productive power of the physiocrats appear three productive powers, which produce values and surplus values exactly in the same way as formerly the physiocrats had produced the *produit net*. Under this form the assumption held the science under its ban for ten long decades. At length the spell was broken, for the most part through the passionate but praiseworthy criticism of the socialist theorists. But still its tough vitality asserted itself. Giving up the form, not the substance, it managed to save itself under a new disguise, and by a strange freak of fortune found its new home in the writings of those who had most bitterly opposed it, the Socialists. The value-creating powers were gone; the value-creating power of labour remained, and with it the old fatal weakness that, instead of the subtle syntheses of the formation of value which should be the work and the pride of our science to unravel, there was nothing left but a stout assumption, or, so far as an assumption would not pass, a still more stout denial.

Thus the naïve theory of the Productivity of capital and the emancipated theory of the socialists are twin systems. So far as the latter aspires to be a critical theory, well and good; it is really so; but it is also obviously a naïve doctrine. It criticises one naïve extreme only to fall into an opposite extreme that is no less naïve. It is nothing else than the long-delayed counterpart of the Naïve Productivity theory.

In comparison with it the remaining theories of interest may take credit to themselves for standing a step higher. They seek for the solution of the interest problem on the ground where the solution is really to be found, the ground of value. The respective merits of these theories, however, are different.

Those which seek to explain interest by the external machinery of the theory of costs have to carry a heavy handicap in the assumption that value grows out of production. Their explanation always leaves something over to explain. Just as certain as is the fact that the fundamental forces which set in motion all economical efforts of men are their interests, egoistic or altruistic, so certain is it that no explanation of the economical phenomena can be satisfactory where the threads of explanation do not reach back unbroken to these fundamental and undoubted forces. This is why the cost theories fail. In thinking that they find the principle of value,—of that guide and universal intermediate motive of human economical affairs,—not in a relation to human welfare, but in a dry fact of the external history of the manufacture of goods, in the technical conditions of their production, they follow the thread of explanation into a *cul-de-sac*, from which it is impossible to find a way to the psychological interest-motive to which every satisfactory explanation must go back. This condemnation applies to the majority of the interest theories we have been considering, however different the individual theories may have been.

Lastly, one step higher in rank stand those theories which have quite cut themselves adrift from the old superstition that the value of goods comes from their past instead of from their future. These theories know what they wish to explain, and in what direction the explanation is to be sought. If they have, notwithstanding, not discovered the entire truth, it is rather the result of accident; while their predecessors, cut off from the right way of its seeking by a wall of assumption, sought it in a wrong direction, and so sought it in vain. The higher step of the development is indicated in certain individual formulations of the Abstinence theory, but principally in the later Use theories; and here it is the theory of Menger which, to my mind, appears the highest point of the development up till now. And that not because his positive solution is the most complete, but because his statement of the problem is the most complete—two things, of which, as is often the case, the second may perhaps be more important and more difficult than the first.

On the foundation thus laid I shall try to find for the vexed problem a solution which invents nothing and assumes nothing, but simply and truly attempts to deduce the phenomena of the formation of interest from the simplest natural and psychological principles of our science.

I may just mention the element which seems to me to involve the whole truth. It is the influence of Time on human valuation of goods. To expand this proposition must be the task of the second and positive part of my work.

INDEX OF AUTHORS MENTIONED

Where reference is given to several passages the principal ones are indicated by black figures.

THE END

Printed by R. & R. Clark, *Edinburgh*

www.ingramcontent.com/pod-product-compliance
Lightning Source LLC
Chambersburg PA
CBHW031816270326
41932CB00008B/443

* 9 7 8 3 3 3 7 2 3 8 6 5 0 *